THE WTO CASE LAW OF 2003
THE AMERICAN LAW INSTITUTE
REPORTERS' STUDIES

This book is the third in a series of annual volumes that will be utilized in the development of an American Law Institute (ALI) project on World Trade Organization (WTO) Law. The volumes undertake a yearly analysis of the case law from the adjudicating bodies of the WTO. The Reporters' Studies for 2003 cover a wide range of WTO law from trade in goods to trade in services. Each case is jointly evaluated by an economist and a lawyer, both well-known experts in the fields of trade law and international economics. The Reporters critically review the jurisprudence of WTO adjudicating bodies and evaluate whether the ruling "makes sense" from an economic as well as legal point of view, and if not, whether the problem lies in the interpretation of the law or the law itself. The Studies do not always cover all issues discussed in a case, but they seek to discuss both the procedural and the substantive issues that form, in the Reporters' view, the "core" of the dispute.

HENRIK HORN is Professor of International Economics at the Institute for International Economic Studies, Stockholm University. He is a member of the Editorial Board of the *World Trade Review* and is a member of the Centre of Economic Policy Research. He has previously worked for the Economic Research and Analysis Division of the World Trade Organization, and has been a judge in the Swedish Market Court (supreme court for competition law).

PETROS C. MAVROIDIS is Edwin B. Parker Professor of Law at Columbia Law School, Professor at the University of Neuchâtel, and a member of the Centre for Economic Policy Research. He was previously Chair of Competition Law, EUI, Florence, and a member of the Legal Affairs Division of the World Trade Organization.

THE WTO CASE LAW OF 2003

The American Law Institute
Reporters' Studies

Edited by

HENRIK HORN

AND

PETROS C. MAVROIDIS

CAMBRIDGE
UNIVERSITY PRESS

CAMBRIDGE UNIVERSITY PRESS
Cambridge, New York, Melbourne, Madrid, Cape Town, Singapore, São Paulo
Cambridge University Press
The Edinburgh Building, Cambridge CB2 2RU, UK
PUBLISHED IN THE UNITED STATES OF AMERICA BY CAMBRIDGE UNIVERSITY PRESS, NEW YORK

www.cambridge.org
Information on this title: www.Cambridge.org/9780521834230

First Published 2006

Printed in the United Kingdom at the University Press, Cambridge

A catalogue record for this publication is available from the British Library

Library of Congress Cataloguing in Publication data

ISBN-13 978-0-521-83423-0 hardback
ISBN-10 0-521-83423-6 hardback

CONTENTS

FOREWORD

This is the third volume in the American Law Institute's effort to analyze decisions rendered in disputes before the World Trade Organization.

Trade Law is in its infancy as a body of legal doctrine. In two prior volumes, the ALI sponsored analyses of decisions issued in 2001 and 2002. This book presents an examination of decisions rendered in 2003. As before, the work has been accomplished by teams consisting of a lawyer and an economist, each a distinguished expert on the world trading system. Early drafts were criticized by the various participants, and then redrafts were presented to an international group of experts at a meeting in April 2005 at the WTO headquarters in Geneva.

Having studied three years of WTO decisions in this "bottom-up" manner, we will now begin to draft the general principles of trade law. We also hope to continue with the analysis of individual decisions.

We are immensely grateful to the two leaders of this project, Henrik Horn of Stockholm University and Petros Mavroidis of the University of Neuchâtel and Columbia University. We also appreciate the work of the economists and lawyers who wrote the studies in this volume. And we appreciate the generous financial support for our project from Jan Wallander's and Tom Hedelius' Research Foundation, Svenska Handelsbanken, Stockholm, and the Milton and Miriam Handler Foundation.

Lance Liebman
Director
The American Law Institute

A Note on the American Law Institute

The American Law Institute was founded in 1923 and is based in Philadelphia. The Institute, through a careful and deliberative process, drafts and then publishes various restatements of the law, model codes, and other proposals for legal reform "to promote the clarification and simplification of the law and its better adaptation to social needs, to secure the better administration of justice, and to encourage and carry on scholarly and scientific legal work." Its membership consists of judges, practicing lawyers, and legal scholars from all areas of the United States as well as some foreign countries, selected on the basis of professional achievement and demonstrated interest in the improvement of the law. The Institute's incorporators included Chief Justice and former President William Howard Taft, future Chief Justice Charles Evans Hughes, and former Secretary of State Elihu Root. Judges Benjamin N. Cardozo and Learned Hand were among its early leaders.

The Institutes's restatements, model codes, and legal studies are used as references by the entire legal profession.

The American Law Institute's website is http://www.ali.org

AMERICAN LAW INSTITUTE REPORTERS

KYLE BAGWELL is Professor of Economics, Columbia University.

GENE M. GROSSMAN is Jacob Viner Professor of International Economics, Princeton University.

HENRIK HORN is Professor of International Economics, Institute for International Economic Studies, Stockholm University.

ROBERT L. HOWSE is Professor of Law, University of Michigan Law School.

PETROS C. MAVROIDIS is Edwin B. Parker Professor of Foreign and Comparative Law, Columbia Law School, and Professor of Law, University of Neuchâtel.

DAMIEN J. NEVEN is Professor of Economics, Graduate Institute for International Studies, University of Geneva.

ROBERT W. STAIGER is Professor of Economics, University of Wisconsin.

ALAN O. SYKES is Frank and Bernice Greenberg Professor of Law, University of Chicago Law School.

JOSEPH H. H. WEILER is Joseph Straus Professor of Law and Jean Monnet Chair, New York University School of Law.

1

Introduction

HENRIK HORN

PETROS C. MAVROIDIS

1 The project

This is the third volume of the Reporters' Studies undertaken in the context of the American Law Institute (ALI) project *Principles of World Trade Law: The World Trade Organization* (WTO). The aim of the project is to provide a systematic analysis of WTO law based in both Economics and Law. This year's focus has mainly been on disputes that came to an administrative end during the year 2003, either because they were not appealed or because the appeal process concluded. Each dispute has been evaluated jointly by an economist and a lawyer. The general task of this two-person team is to evaluate whether the ruling "makes sense" from an economic as well as a legal point of view and, if it does not, whether the problem lies in the legal text or in the interpretation thereof. The authors do not always cover all issues discussed in a case, but they seek to discuss both the procedural and the substantive issues that form the "core" of the dispute, as they see it.

The Reporters' Studies have, this year, been drafted by the following persons, who have been appointed Reporters for the project by the ALI:

Gene M. Grossman, Jacob Viner Professor of International Economics, Princeton University, USA.

Henrik Horn, Professor of International Economics, Institute for International Economic Studies, Stockholm University, Sweden.

Robert L. Howse, Alene and Allan F. Smith Professor of Law, University of Michigan Law School, USA.

Petros C. Mavroidis, Professor of Law, University of Neuchâtel, Switzerland, and Edwin B. Parker Professor of Law at Columbia Law School, USA.
Damien J. Neven, Professor of Economics, Graduate Institute for International Studies, University of Geneva, Switzerland.
Robert W. Staiger, Professor of Economics, University of Wisconsin, USA.
Alan O. Sykes, Frank and Bernice Greenberg Professor of Law, University of Chicago Law School, USA.
Joseph H.H. Weiler, Joseph Straus Professor of Law and Jean Monnet Chair, New York University School of Law, USA.

The Reporters' Studies were initially scrutinized in an October 2004 meeting of all of the Reporters in Princeton. After revisions, the Studies were presented and discussed in a meeting held in Geneva on April 12, 2005, with the following group of lawyers and economists:

Richard Baldwin, Graduate Institute of International Studies, Geneva, Switzerland.
Armin von Bogdandy, Max Planck Institut, Heidelberg, Germany.
Claus-Dieter Ehlermann, Wilmer Cutler, Brussels, Belgium.
Wilfred J. Ethier, Department of Economics, University of Pennsylvania, Philadelphia, USA.
Gary Horlick, Wilmer Cutler, Washington DC, USA.
Gabrielle Marceau, World Trade Organization, Geneva, Switzerland.
Mitsuo Matshushita, Seikei University School of Law, Tokyo, Japan.
Niall Meagher, Advisory Centre for WTO law, Geneva, Switzerland.
Håkan Nordström, National Board of Trade, Stockholm, Sweden.
Donald Regan, University of Michigan School of Law, Ann Arbor, USA.
Delissa Ridgway, US Court of International Trade, New York, USA.
Frieder Roessler, Advisory Centre for WTO law, Geneva, Switzerland.
André Sapir, Université Libre de Bruxelles, Brussels, Belgium.
Arun Venkataraman, World Trade Organization, Geneva, Switzerland.
Jasper Wauters, World Trade Organization, Geneva, Switzerland.
Eric White, EC Commission, Brussels, Belgium.
Claire Wright, Thomas Jefferson School of Law, San Diego, USA.
Werner Zdouc, World Trade Organization, Geneva, Switzerland.

The final versions, as published in this volume, have been subjected to yet another round of revisions derived from the advisory meeting. Despite these collective efforts, each pair of authors remains solely responsible for the Studies it has authored.

This project would not have existed had it not been for the efforts and commitment of Professor Lance Liebman, Director of the ALI. We have also benefited greatly from the support of the President of the ALI, Michael Traynor, the ALI Deputy Director, Elena Cappella, and the former ALI Deputy Director, Michael Greenwald. The ALI has also provided excellent assistance with the administration of our meetings. We are extremely grateful for the generous financial support the project has received from Jan Wallander's and Tom Hedelius' Research Foundation, Svenska Handelsbanken, Stockholm, and the Milton and Miriam Handel Foundation. Without their support, this project would not have materialized.

2 The Reporters' Studies on the WTO Case Law of 2003

We here provide a brief summary of this year's Studies in the order of their appearance in this volume.

A main theme in this year's Studies has been contingent protection. Grossman and Sykes discuss the compliance dispute between India and the European Community (EC) in which India alleged lack of compliance by the EC with an earlier WTO ruling on antidumping duties for cotton-type bed linen. India raised issues relating to the EC treatment of "other factors," that is, issues regarding the manner in which an investigating authority should treat factors, other than those mentioned in the body of the Agreement, that cause injury. India had briefly noted such factors in the original proceedings but had not argued them fully. Although, in their view, Grossman and Sykes can imagine cases where the failure by a panel to investigate factual aspects of a case might in and of itself warrant a reversal of its eventual finding, they decline to pronounce on the existence of such grounds in this dispute, lacking an effective demonstration by India that the Panel's omission led to abuse or a biased outcome. The authors go one step further, however, and suggest that this issue raises interesting questions regarding the proper scope of *res judicata*, issue preclusion, and waiver in WTO jurisprudence. To highlight these questions, they develop an analytical model to compare expected litigation costs in a judicial system with a rule of waiver to those in a system in which litigants can bring multiple claims. They show that a rule of waiver need not minimize litigation costs, because some disputes can be resolved at lower costs if a claimant is not forced to bring all of its arguments at once. India also claimed that the EC violated WTO rules when conducting its revised injury analysis, by treating all imports from firms not individually investigated as if they had been dumping, despite the fact that some of the firms individually investigated were found not to be dumping. On this score, the authors conclude that the Appellate Body's (AB) decision has some economic appeal, but rests on shaky legal foundations.

In their paper on *Corrosion Steel*, Howse and Staiger deal with the legal benchmark to be applied by an investigating authority when evaluating whether to retain antidumping duties beyond the original five-year period (the sunset review). The current law is quite open-ended and requires WTO Members to demonstrate the likelihood of continued or renewed dumping before agreeing on the extension of duties in place. In the authors' view, a meaningful assessment of the likelihood of continued or renewed dumping requires an understanding of the conditions that led to dumping in the first place, and a determination of whether these conditions have changed in a way that removes the original reason for dumping. In their opinion, neither of these two elements appears to have played any real role in the US investigating authority's methodology for determining likelihood, or in the AB's assessment of the legitimacy of this methodology. The authors note that Art. 9.1 of the Antidumping Agreement (AD) does not require an assessment of the conditions that have led the companies named in an antidumping order to dump; the authors maintain, however, that a different criterion should be applied in Art. 9.1 AD compared to that applied in Art. 11.3 AD. They see no necessary inconsistency in this: while a requirement *could* have been included in the AD that the particular reasons for dumping must be articulated as a condition for imposing antidumping duties under Art. 9.1 AD, there is no logical necessity that such a requirement must be included. By contrast, Howse and Staiger argue that an understanding and articulation of the conditions that led to dumping is logically necessary to assess the likelihood of continued or renewed dumping, and therefore, is an implied condition for extending definitive antidumping duties beyond the five-year termination date that Art. 11.3 AD otherwise dictates. In light of their preferred benchmark for the adjudicating of such cases, the authors conclude that the AB erred by not requiring the United States to provide such an assessment as part of its sunset review.

The "*Byrd*" litigation between the United States and a number of WTO Members over the *US Continued Dumping and Subsidy Offset Act of 2000* (CDSOA) is discussed by Horn and Mavroidis. This United States law reserves disbursement of collected antidumping and countervailing duties exclusively to those economic operators that have backed a petition to open a dumping (or countervailing) investigation. The AB, in part modifying the Panel's findings, concluded that the law was WTO-inconsistent in that it constituted an impermissible action against dumping (and subsidization). In the authors' view, the AB erred both in terms of its reasoning and in terms of its findings: the AB's treatment of the reasons advanced by the Panel to support its finding that the *Byrd* legislation violated Art. 18.1 AD and Art 32.1 of the Agreement on Subsidies and Countervailing Measures (SCM) was inconsistent; the AB, in striking down the legislation, used an economic theory that was inadequately motivated and of doubtful validity, if meant to describe the legislation's typical impact on various industries, and it failed to explain how general it believed the theory to be; the AB struck down the legislation on much weaker grounds than those it had previously established as a requirement in its case law; and finally, the AB should have undertaken a more comprehensive discussion of the claims under Art. 5.4 AD and 11.4 SCM, since an illegality could more naturally have been established under these provisions.

Horn and Mavroidis also discuss the *Pipe Fittings* litigation between Brazil and the EC. In this dispute, Brazil raised a series of issues concerning the lawfulness of the EC imposition of antidumping duties against imports of pipe fittings originating in Brazil. Chief among the issues raised were questions relating to the treatment of a devalued currency, the conditions under which low-volume imports should be considered imports in the ordinary course of trade, and the scope of information that should go into a final notice advising interested parties as to the extent of an antidumping imposition. In the authors' view, the AB's conclusions with respect to the first two issues are hardly supported by a contextual understanding of the various obligations laid down in the AD. Disregarding the implication of a devaluation (and its effect on pricing decisions) would lead the investigating authorities to practice antidumping against its very purpose: antidumping measures are not available to provide injured parties with a lump-sum payment, but, instead, to offset dumping occurring in future transactions (i.e. after the conclusion of the investigation). Additionally, the AB's understanding of the discretion conferred upon the investigating authorities when constructing the normal value would lead, as it did in the present case, to logically incoherent outcomes. Finally, the authors argue that the transparency obligations should be read in light of their purpose, which is to inform uninformed parties the basis of decisions made during the investigation and thus to ensure that due process has been adhered to throughout the whole administrative procedure, otherwise these obligations will be reduced to mere procedural requirements that do not perform their assigned function.

The *Softwood Lumber IV* litigation between Canada and the United States is also examined by Horn and Mavroidis. This dispute is part of the long-standing conflict between Canada and the United States concerning the forestry sector. A main issue in the present dispute concerns the benchmark that a WTO Member can use in order to calculate the amount of subsidization. In this dispute, the Panel concluded that there was a problem with the current text of the SCM Agreement in that it does not include sufficient flexibility to allow WTO Members to use alternative benchmarks when confronting a factual situation not envisaged by the law itself; accordingly, the Panel indirectly argued for some form of legislative amendment. The AB did not agree with the Panel's reading, however, concluding that the existing text reflects sufficient flexibility to allow WTO Members to deal with situations such as the one in the present dispute. The authors, however, find it hard to interpret Art. 14(d) SCM so as to allow for alternative benchmarks, such as the benchmark proposed by the United States. In their view, the AB here effectively took on the role of legislator, thus contravening the discipline laid down in Art. 3.2 of the Understanding on Dispute Settlement.

Grossman and Sykes discuss the steel disputes between the United States and a host of complainants that challenged the consistency of safeguards in the steel sector imposed by the United States against imports from a variety of sources. The authors take the position that the AB's decision in this dispute is one more link in a line of unsatisfactory decisions in the safeguards area. In their view, the underlying problem stems from the fact that the treaty text regarding the preconditions for the use of safeguard measures is seriously deficient. The AB, with its usual emphasis on textual interpretation, has done little to resolve the puzzles that the text creates. As a result, WTO members are still left with little guidance concerning the proper use of safeguards beyond some confusing and sometimes incoherent standards, notwithstanding the sizeable amount of jurisprudence in this field. The authors review these issues as they have arisen, not only in the instant decision, but in prior decisions as well, and then discuss the details of the steel dispute. They place more emphasis on the Panel report than the AB report, as the latter breaks little new ground. In the authors' opinion, although it is probably difficult to quarrel with the outcome in this particular case (in light of the procedural deficiencies they observe), it is high time to reverse the tide in the safeguards area by breaking with the current line of jurisprudence.

Some of the reports discussed in this year's volume deal with issues other than contingent protection. Neven and Mavroidis discuss the first "genuine" services litigation in the WTO context, the dispute between the United States and Mexico concerning the rates charged by the Mexican monopolist, Telmex, for terminating calls originating in the United States (*Mexico – Telecoms*). The Panel, whose findings were never appealed, found that Telmex was charging rates unrelated to its cost structure, thus violating its obligations under the *General Agreement of Trade in Services* (GATS). The authors critically distance themselves from both the Panel's reasoning and its findings: in the authors' opinion, the Panel mischaracterized the facts before it, and, moreover, applied the wrong law. In their view, Mexico had made no commitment regarding the factual situation as presented by the complaining party (and was hence not bound by the relevant legal framework). Furthermore, even if it had made such commitments, the relevant framework did not address the situation before the Panel (cross-border supply of termination services), but rather addressed only the mode-3 supply of telecoms services (commercial presence of the supplier in the market of the country terminating incoming calls). The authors conclude that the Panel's findings constitute an impermissible extension of the existing legal framework to transactions that the founding fathers did not intend to cover. They also take a critical stance with respect to the pure competition-law component of the dispute, where they argue that it was an overly bold move for the Panel to pronounce on whether the rates charged were cost-oriented, in light of the information presented before it. The Panel's approach is, from the authors' perspective, at odds with the approaches of numerous competition authorities on the same score.

Grossman and Sykes deal with the *Generalized System of Preferences* (GSP) dispute between India and the EC, where, for the first time, the legality of practices by donor countries under the terms of the Enabling Clause was being discussed. In this case, India complained against the EC practice of making distinctions among developing countries, and, based on such distinctions, granting additional preferences to some developing countries (those that had engaged in combating drug production and trafficking). The AB, overturning in part the Panel findings in this respect, condemned the specific EC practice (because the list of beneficiaries was closed), but accepted the principle that the making of distinctions among developing countries was perfectly compatible with the WTO legal order, to the extent that objective criteria had been established *ex ante*. The authors disagree with both the reasoning and the outcome of this litigation. In their view, the EC scheme could, at least theoretically, lead to trade diversion, with less efficient developing countries increasing their exports at the expense of the exports of more efficient developing countries. Moreover, in the authors' opinion, beyond the original distinction between developing and least developed countries that is enshrined in the WTO legal framework, and the graduation from developing to developed country status, there is no justification for schemes such as the one contested in this case. Finally, from a policy perspective, there is no reason to believe that such schemes are to the benefit of the countries receiving preferences.

Howse and Staiger discuss the arbitration on the *1916 Antidumping Act*, which addresses the meaning of equivalence between a violation of international law and the countermeasures applied to respond to the violation. In this case, the EC proposed countermeasures that "mirrored" the US WTO-inconsistent behavior (the availability of a private right of action for treble damages against a foreign firm engaging in certain kinds of dumping). Based largely on previous rulings, the Arbitrator held that, while the central purpose of countermeasures under DSU Art. 22 was to induce compliance and exclude punitive purposes, it could not endorse the proposed countermeasures of the EC, unless it had evidence that the trade or economic effect of the EC mirror-reaction on the United States would not exceed the trade or economic effect of the United States' original action on the EC. The authors reject the Arbitrator's approach for several reasons: *first*, in their view, the Arbitrator focused on the word "level" without also considering its immediate context—the notion of "equivalence." The word "equivalence" implies proportionality between two things that are not entirely commensurate or reducible in value to a common metric. *Second*, "normative countermeasures," where equivalence or proportionality is achieved by suspending a symmetrical obligation, have often been recognized as consistent with the principles of state responsibility. *Third*, the Arbitrator confused the issue of the limits on countermeasures with the issue of whether the purpose of countermeasures was to re-establish the pre-breach equilibrium between the parties, to achieve compliance, or to punish. The authors also advance in their paper some normative thoughts on the placement of efficient breach of contract inside the current WTO legal regime. They argue that the Arbitrator's focus on trade effects has some merit from an economic point of view, and they also propose how the trade foregone should be measured.

Neven and Weiler review the decision by the AB in the *Japan – Apples* dispute, which concerns measures affecting the importation of apples in Japan. The authors emphasize that a crucial aspect of the Sanitary and Phytosanitary (SPS) agreement is that it imposes a discipline on risk-reducing measures even in the absence of discrimination in favor of domestic products. Their discussion on the evaluation of risk-reducing measures focuses on two issues, namely the scope of the mandate given to the adjudicators and the standard of review that they should apply. Neven and Weiler emphasize the difficulty that adjudicators face in distinguishing between the level of risk that a country will find it optimal to support (which cannot be challenged), and the question of whether the risk-reducing measures are necessary to achieve the chosen level of risk. They further observe that the common methodology used by panels, evaluating the existence of risk in the absence of risk-reducing measures, has limited applicability. The authors also discuss how the Panel's approach can be abused, leading the adjudicators to slip from the evaluation of whether a measure is necessary to achieve a given level of risk to an implicit challenge of the level of risk itself (which should remain the preserve of the Members). Regarding the standard of review, they argue that a lower standard should be applied to measures that do not threaten fundamental principles like nondiscrimination. Finally, the authors also consider the Precautionary Principle in the context of the SPS Agreement. In their view, the provisions of the SPS Agreement reflect the distinction between risk and ambiguity: whereas the former would cover the provisions that concern science-based SPS measures, the latter would extend to cover precautionary measures. The authors consequently call into question the Panel's and the AB's unwillingness to apply the Precautionary Principle in the context of this dispute.

This year, we will not attempt to classify the papers according to whether the authors see the rationale provided by the adjudicating bodies, or the outcome, as correct. Nevertheless, we observe that, in basically all the disputes discussed, the authors raise serious concerns about the adjudicators' reasoning in support of the final outcome. Whether the outcomes of the disputes make sense from an economic point of view is more difficult to judge this year, since the Studies to a large extent address antidumping issues, and, as is well known, it is difficult to reconcile antidumping measures with standard economic reasoning.

2

European Communities – Anti-Dumping Duties on Imports of Cotton-Type Bed Linen from India (AB-2000-13, WT/DS141/AB/R:DSR 2003: III, 965): Recourse to Article 21.5 of the DSU by India

GENE M. GROSSMAN*

Princeton University

ALAN O. SYKES*

University of Chicago

1 Introduction

This chapter addresses the dispute brought to the World Trade Organization (WTO) by India concerning anti-dumping duties imposed by the European Communities (EC) on cotton-type bed linen. An earlier complaint brought by India challenged the anti-dumping duties on a number of points, including the EC practice of "zeroing" for the computation of dumping margins (which had the effect of assigning a negative dumping margin a weight of zero when computing a weighted average dumping margin).[1] India prevailed in that dispute,[2] and the EC responded with Council Regulation (EC) No. 1644/2001, amending the original anti-dumping measure on bed linen from India. India was of the view that the amended measure did not comply with EC obligations under the WTO Anti-dumping Agreement, and brought

* This chapter was prepared for the American Law Institute project on "The Principles of WTO Law." We thank Kathy Spier for thoughtful assistance.

[1] The decision in the earlier proceeding is the subject of an earlier chapter in this series. See Janow and Staiger (2003).

[2] See European Communities – Anti-Dumping Duties on Imports of Cotton-Type Bed Linen from India, WT/DS141/AB/R, adopted March 12, 2001.

the proceeding under Art. 21.5 of the DSU that is the subject of this chapter.

Several issues were raised before the Art. 21.5 Panel, but only three issues reached the Appellate Body. First, India argued that although the EC had corrected the "zeroing" problem, it had failed to ensure that injury attributable to "other factors" had not wrongly been attributed to dumped imports, in violation of Art. 3 of the Anti-dumping Agreement. Second, India argued that in conducting its revised injury analysis, the EC violated Art. 3 when it presumed that all imports from exporters not individually investigated were "dumped," even though 53% of the imports from exporters that were individually investigated were found not to have been dumped once the "zeroing" method of calculation was abandoned. Finally, India argued that the EC had not properly considered certain factors bearing on injury that it was required to consider under Art. 3.

The Appellate Body ruled in favor of the EC on the first issue, holding that it had been resolved definitively in the original proceeding. It ruled in favor of India on the second issue, however, concluding that imports from producers not individually investigated could not be presumed to be dumped for purposes of injury analysis when some of the individually investigated exporters were not dumping. On the third issue, the Appellate Body upheld the finding against India by the Panel, deferring to its resolution of what the Appellate Body considered an essentially factual issue.

From a legal perspective, the Appellate Body's decision on the first issue raises some interesting questions about the proper scope of *res judicata*, issue preclusion, and waiver in WTO jurisprudence, but provides few answers. The case breaks new ground with respect to the second issue noted above as well, and we quibble somewhat with the Appellate Body's legal and logical reasoning there. Finally, the Appellate Body's deference to the Panel on the third issue seems appropriate, as best we can determine.

From an economic perspective, we find the procedural issue to be an interesting one. Little analytical work has been done by economists on the proper scope of *res judicata* and the related notions of issue preclusion and waiver. We develop some simple points about these issues below, which provide some basis for questioning the refusal of the compliance Panel to entertain India's arguments on "non-attribution." Regarding the second issue, the Anti-dumping laws make so little economic sense in general that it is difficult to offer any guidance as to their "proper" administration. The ruling in favor of India on the presumption of dumping issue seems reasonable from a statistical standpoint, however, although it is less clear that it is right as a legal matter. Finally, the Appellate Body's deference to the factual conclusion of the Panel on the third issue raises no economic issues of note.

We lay out the legal issues and their resolution by the Panel and the Appellate Body in Section 2. Section 3 offers a critical analysis of the case from a law and economics perspective.

2 Factual and legal issues and their disposition

2.1 Non-attribution of injury caused by "other factors"

Article 3.5 of the Anti-dumping Agreement provides that investigating authorities must "examine any known factors other than the dumped imports which at the same time are injuring the domestic industry, and the injuries caused by these other factors must not be attributed to the dumped imports." In the original proceeding, India challenged the EC's duties, *inter alia,* on the grounds that the EC had failed to ensure that injury attributable to "other factors" was not attributed to dumped imports from India, although it did not pursue the issue very actively. The original Panel dismissed the one substantive point raised by India under this rubric, and otherwise said that India had failed to make out a *prima facie* case on the issue. That finding was not appealed.

The EC did not conduct a new analysis of "other factors" as part of its revised injury analysis when it promulgated Regulation No. 1644/2001, and had simply relied on its previous discussion of the matter. India then argued again that the EC had failed to ensure that injury caused by "other factors" was not attributed to dumped imports. In particular, it pointed to various "other factors" that had not been a subject of discussion before the original Panel, including rising input costs for European firms and the failure of output prices in the EC to keep up with inflation.

The EC requested a preliminary ruling from the Panel to the effect that such matters could not be raised in an Art. 21.5 proceeding, and the Panel agreed: "To rule on this aspect of India's claim under Article 3.5 in this proceeding would be to allow India a second chance to prevail on a claim which it raised, but did not pursue, in the original proceeding. We cannot conclude that such a result is required by

Article 21.5 of the DSU, or any other provision. The possibility for manipulative or abusive litigation tactics that would be opened by allowing Members an opportunity to obtain a ruling in an Article 21.5 proceeding that they could have sought and obtained in the original dispute would, in our view, be inestimably harmful to the effective operation of the dispute settlement system."[3] Although the Panel did not use these terms, its reasoning invokes notions of *res judicata*, issue preclusion, and waiver.

The Appellate Body affirmed the Panel's ruling on this issue. In doing so, it emphasized that new claims *can* at times be raised before an Art. 21.5 Panel. It noted that the purpose of such Panels is to review the WTO consistency of measures taken to comply with prior rulings, and that many such measures will differ significantly from the measures originally challenged, and may be inconsistent with WTO obligations in ways that the original measures were not. Although the Appellate Body made clear that new inconsistencies of this sort were the proper subject of discussion before an Art. 21.5 Panel, it stated: "[h]ere, India did not raise a *new* claim before the Art. 21.5 panel; rather, India reasserted in the Art. 21.5 proceedings the *same* claim that it had raised before the *original* panel in respect of a component of the implementation measure which was the same as the original measure. The *same* claim was dismissed by the original Panel, and India did not appeal that finding."[4] The Appellate Body went on to hold that when the original Panel report was adopted by the Dispute Settlement Body (DSB), it became a final resolution of the dispute on the "other factors" issue.[5]

Like the Panel, the Appellate Body relied for its ruling not so much on any treaty text that addressed the issue, but on policy considerations and on its earlier decision reviewing a similar issue that had arisen before the *Shrimp–Turtle* compliance Panel. The Appellate Body emphasized that India had raised the "same" claim earlier and lost, and put less emphasis than the Panel had on the notion that the particular issues raised by India could have been raised before but were not.

2.2 *Injury due to exporters not individually investigated*

In the second investigation, as in the first, the EC did not investigate every Indian exporter of cotton-type bed linen. Article 6.10 of the Anti-dumping Agreement allows importing nations to investigate only

[3] Panel Rep. ¶6.43. [4] AB Rep. ¶80. [5] AB Rep. ¶99.

a sample of all exporters in cases where an individual investigation of all of them would be "impracticable." Accordingly, the EC conducted individual investigations of five of the larger Indian exporters, and applied a weighted average anti-dumping duty to exports from other exporters as is allowed by Art. 9.4 of the Anti-dumping Agreement.

The most important change between the original investigation and the second was to eliminate the practice of "zeroing" in the computation of weighted average dumping margins. When zeroing was eliminated, two of the five exporters subject to individual investigation, accounting for 53% of the imports from the five individually investigated importers, were found not to be dumping at all. The issue before the compliance Panel was how this new finding should affect injury analysis by the EC.

Article 3.5 requires that the importing nation establish a causal link between the dumped imports and injury. In purporting to establish this link when promulgating Regulation No. 1644/2001, the EC assumed that all imports from Indian exporters not individually investigated had been dumped, even though 53% of the imports from the exporters individually investigated had not been dumped. India argued that the EC thereby violated Art. 3.1, which requires that the determination of injury be based on "positive evidence," including an "objective examination" of the "volume of dumped imports." India argued that the EC should presume that dumping was occurring by exporters not individually investigated in the same proportion as imports from exporters who were individually investigated (47%). This would suggest a smaller volume of dumped imports than the EC had presumed were present, and might reverse the conclusion that dumped imports were causing material injury.

The EC argued that the presumption of dumping by exporters not investigated individually is permissible under the Anti-dumping Agreement. Its principal argument was based on Art. 9.4 of the Anti-dumping Agreement, which permits an anti-dumping duty to be imposed on exporters not individually investigated as long as it does not exceed "the weighted average margin of dumping established with respect to the selected exporters." The EC contended that because it was allowed to impose an anti-dumping duty on those exports, it had to also be allowed to consider them "dumped" for purposes of injury analysis. Next, it argued that the group of exporters that it had chosen to investigate individually were not selected to be a statistically valid sample, but rather represented the "largest percentage of the volume of the exports . . . which can reasonably be investigated," one of the options under Art. 6.10. Thus, the percentage of exports found to be dumped by the individually investigated exporters could not be assumed to reflect the amount of dumping by exporters not individually investigated.

The Panel agreed with the EC. "We can find no textual obligation in the AD Agreement to separate out the unexamined producers' imports into dumped and not-dumped for purposes of the injury analysis . . ."[6] It also found India's position to be logically flawed, given the fact that all non-investigated imports could be subjected to a positive anti-dumping duty under Art. 9.4: "Under India's approach, only a portion of imports from producers subject to that anti-dumping duty could be considered as 'dumped' for injury purposes. This effectively treats the imports from the same producers as dumped for purposes of duty assessment, and not dumped for purposes of injury analysis. In our view, this is an unacceptable outcome, suggesting that the analysis which leads to it is untenable."

The Appellate Body reversed. It emphasized the requirement for an "objective examination" of the volume of dumped imports, and noted that imports not sold at dumped prices were specifically enumerated in Art. 3.5 as one of the "other factors" which may cause injury and should not be attributed to dumped imports. It was also unpersuaded that imports from exporters not individually investigated could be presumed to be dumped simply because Art. 9.4 permits them to be subjected to an anti-dumping duty – "[w]e do not see why the volume of imports that have been found to be dumped by non-examined producers, for purposes of determining *injury* under paragraphs 1 and 2 of Article 3, must be *congruent* with the volume of imports from those non-examined producers that is subject to the *imposition of anti-dumping duties* under Article 9.4."[7] The Appellate Body stopped short of endorsing India's proposed method for calculating the volume of dumped imports from exporters not individually investigated, however, allowing for the possibility that "positive evidence" of that volume might be based on something other than the percentage of exports dumped by the individually investigated exporters.[8]

Along the way, the Appellate Body was mindful of the standard of review under the Anti-dumping Agreement. Article 17.6(ii) of the

[6] Panel Rep. ¶6.139. [7] AB Rep. ¶126. [8] Id. ¶146.

Agreement provides that "[w]here the panel finds that a relevant provision of the Agreement admits of more than one permissible interpretation, the panel shall find the authorities' measure to be in conformity with the Agreement if it rests on one of those permissible interpretations." The EC argued that its interpretation of the injury provisions was at least a "permissible" interpretation that was entitled to deference, but the Appellate Body disagreed: "[W]hatever methodology investigating authorities choose for calculating the volume of 'dumped imports,' that calculation and, ultimately, the determination of injury under Article 3, clearly must be made on the basis of 'positive evidence' and an 'objective examination.' These requirements are not ambiguous, and they do not 'admit of more than one permissible interpretation' within the meaning of the second sentence of Article 17.6(ii)."[9]

2.3 Consideration of all "relevant factors" bearing on injury

Article 3.4 of the Anti-dumping Agreement requires importing nations to base their injury analysis on an examination of "all relevant economic factors . . . having a bearing on the state of the (domestic) industry." It then provides a non-exhaustive list of such factors. India asserted that the EC failed to gather data on and to evaluate two "relevant factors" – stocks and capacity utilization – when it promulgated Regulation No. 1644/2001. The EC asserted that such data had been presented before the investigative authorities, and had been properly considered. The Panel ruled for the EC on this point, and India argued that the Panel abused its discretion in doing so by, in effect, accepting the EC's unsupported assertions on the matter rather than conducting a more thorough investigation.

The Appellate Body upheld the Panel, which had "concluded that it was clear that the European Communities had 'in its record' information on stocks and capacity utilization – the two factors India had focused on – and that 'unlike the original determination, the EC's consideration of these factors [was] clearly set out on the face of the redetermination.'"[10] While India wished to characterize the Panel's conclusion as an abuse of its discretion, the Appellate Body saw it as a factual conclusion by the Panel that was within its proper discretion and should not be disturbed on appeal.

[9] AB Rep. ¶118. [10] AB Rep. ¶154.

3 Critical analysis

3.1 Non-attribution and the procedural issue

One can quibble with the willingness of the Appellate Body to permit the EC to rely on its original "other factors" analysis. In light of its resolution of the second issue in the case, discussed below, the EC is required to restate its assessment of the quantity of dumped imports, revising the estimate downward. The quantity of fairly traded imports, an "other factor" that might cause injury, must be revised upward. One might thus argue that the EC should redo both its analysis of harm attributable to "dumped imports" *and* its analysis of harm due to "other factors." The Appellate Body does not reach this conclusion, however, perhaps because India's arguments focused on EC input and output prices as the "other factors" to be considered.

The much more interesting aspect of the ruling on this issue, however, is its procedural implications. The WTO treaty text does not specifically address *res judicata* and related issues, leaving to Panels and to the Appellate Body the task of evolving sensible principles in the area. In this case, the Appellate Body insisted that "India did not raise a *new* claim before the Article 21.5 panel; rather, India reasserted in the Article 21.5 proceedings the *same* claim." At some level, it is difficult to quarrel with the proposition that parties to WTO disputes should not be permitted to relitigate the *same* claim over and over again. What the Appellate Body masks with this language, however, is that the concept of "sameness" can be interpreted broadly or narrowly.

Recall the facts: India had raised the "non-attribution" issue in its original complaint, but did not advance factual arguments in relation to that issue sufficient to make out a *prima facie* case. Then, before the compliance Panel, it sought to make those arguments seriously for the first time, pointing to "other factors" such as high EC input prices and low EC output prices. Here, to say that India had lost the *same* claim earlier is to imply that all arguments relating to a particular legal issue are part of the "same" claim, and are waived if they are omitted from the first round of litigation in which that issue appears. The Panel opinion hinted at an even broader principle when it stated that it would not afford India "an opportunity to obtain a ruling in an Article 21.5 proceeding that they could have sought and obtained in the original dispute." This language suggests that all legal issues that could have been raised in an earlier proceeding, but were not, are waived. For terminological simplicity, we refer to these principles as rules of waiver, although the reader should be aware that civil procedure treatises often attach the labels *res judicata*, issue preclusion, or claim preclusion to these types of rules.

Rules of waiver have the obvious consequence of encouraging litigants to raise issues sooner rather than later, and can hasten the final resolution of a dispute. Many legal systems have them.[11] It is possible that such rules are economically desirable when all the costs and benefits of the legal system are taken into account, but that is not obvious. We have found no treatment of the issue in the existing law and economics literature on procedure, perhaps because a complete accounting of all the relevant considerations in any particular context is exceedingly difficult to provide. An exhaustive treatment is beyond the scope of this comment as well, but we will sketch some of the pertinent considerations that bear on the design of optimal waiver principles. Before addressing waiver, however, we set forth our understanding of the justification for *res judicata* in its narrower sense.

3.1.1 Res judicata

Compliance with the law generally has a social value, and the prompt resolution of legal proceedings can hasten valuable compliance. This observation seemingly applies as much to the WTO as to other legal contexts. But legal decision makers are imperfect, and may make errors in their findings of law or fact. When litigants are required to comply with erroneous decisions, error costs arise, often of the same nature as the gains from compliance with correct decisions. A desire to avoid errors motivates principles of "due process" in many legal systems. Process itself is costly, however, and so it is unrealistic for most legal systems to avoid error altogether. The task of designing an optimal procedure thus balances competing considerations: the value of resolving legal issues sooner and of reducing process costs on the one hand, against the costs of errors on the other.

Because of concerns about error, it is not uncommon for litigants to be permitted to raise issues more than once. The usual setting for revisiting issues is the "appeal," a common feature in many legal systems, including now the WTO. But there will generally be diminishing returns to reopening issues that have been previously

[11] On the American rules in this area, see generally, Friedenthal, Kane and Miller (1999); James, Hazard and Leubsdorf (2001).

decided – at some point, the likelihood of error becomes sufficiently small that the benefits of ending the dispute and the associated process costs predominate over any concerns about error. Thus, rights of appeal are always limited (and some matters may not be appealable at all).

Res judicata in its narrowest sense simply precludes a litigant raising an *identical* claim in a new proceeding when the claim was previously adjudicated. It can be understood as a presumption that the legal system in question already provides an appropriate error-correction mechanism through its appellate process. Once a litigant has raised an argument, lost, and exhausted all available appeals, no further delays and litigation costs are likely to be justified.

To be sure, scenarios may arise in which concern for error is particularly acute, and the limits on the process available in typical cases may appear too stringent. The usual solution to such problems, however, is for the legal system to add a more extensive appellate process for particular categories of cases rather than to permit tribunals to retreat from *res judicata* in its narrow form. Criminal defendants in the United States, for example, receive additional layers of appellate review not made available to civil litigants and capital defendants – because the costs of error are great and irreversible – are afforded procedural protections not made available to other criminal defendants.

3.1.2 Waiver

The rationale for rules of waiver must be somewhat different. By definition, waiver applies to arguments and issues that were *not* adjudicated previously but that could have been. There can be no presumption that their prior disposition was correct if there was no prior disposition.

But rules of waiver might be based on a related presumption – if a litigant did not bother to raise an argument previously, perhaps the litigant has revealed it to be weak, so that the likely error cost of ignoring it is small. Rules of waiver encourage litigants to bring all potentially meritorious arguments before the court at once so that the dispute can be resolved with dispatch and the gains from compliance with the law can be realized more quickly; any claims "waived" are presumed to be so weak that they need not be addressed.

This simple intuition may have much to do with the justification for doctrines of waiver, but it is incomplete for two reasons. *First*, to the degree that complainants internalize the costs of delay in bringing other parties' behavior into conformity with the law, the legal system seemingly has no interest in encouraging complainants to pursue compliance at a faster clip. *Second*, litigation becomes more expensive as more claims are brought. Each claim must be researched, briefed, and argued. Factual support must be amassed. Even if the adjudicative body can exercise "judicial economy" to avoid issues that need not be reached to resolve the case, the parties to the proceeding must still bear additional costs as the number of issues and arguments grows. Hence, if a complainant prefers to start with what it believes to be its strongest claims, and to leave others in abeyance should the initial claims fail, some of the costs of litigation (including some that are externalized) will be avoided if the initial claims succeed and resolve the dispute. This consideration, too, seems to argue for allowing the complainant to bring claims at its own pace, in preference to rules of waiver that penalize claimants for failing to bring issues before the dispute process at the outset.

An important countervailing consideration arises, however, if litigation exhibits economies of scale in relation to the number of claims in each proceeding. It seems quite likely that dispute proceedings have considerable fixed costs. For the WTO in particular, panelists must be selected and assembled for hearings. Each panelist will invest considerable time in learning the (often complex) background facts of the dispute. Many of these costs will be the same whether the dispute involves a single legal claim or many. And like other costs of litigation, a complaining nation does not bear all of these fixed costs.

The presence of considerable fixed costs to litigation can supply a positive externality to the consolidation of claims in an initial proceeding. Plausibly, a complainant might prefer to proceed more or less *seriatim* with its claims to save itself the variable costs of litigating matters that may prove unnecessary. But if considerable economies of scale are lost when the complainant proceeds in this fashion and those costs are borne by others, the system may gain by foreclosing such a strategy.

Of course, the mere existence of fixed costs is not sufficient to justify rules of waiver. Their magnitude must be considered in relation to the added variable costs of litigating more claims at once, claims that may prove unnecessary to litigate *ex post*. Roughly speaking, the greater the fixed costs of a proceeding in relation to the variable costs per claim, the stronger the case for insisting that more issues be raised at once.

These points also suggest the possibility of more refined waiver rules. Some types of claims may have very low marginal litigation costs, perhaps because they resolve themselves readily with reference to facts already in evidence. Others may require much additional fact-finding or investigation. Similarly, some claims may be legally straightforward, and others may be highly debatable and complex. The case for a rule of waiver is stronger with respect to the relatively cheaper factual and legal claims.

Likewise, the fixed costs of each proceeding may vary with the nature of the proceeding. With particular reference to Art. 21.5 compliance Panels, we note that these Panels are comprised of the same members as the original dispute Panel. Each panelist is presumably familiar with the facts and basic legal issues of the case already. Under these circumstances, it may make sense to have somewhat more lenient rules of waiver because the fixed costs of the second proceeding will tend to be smaller in relation to the variable costs of litigating more issues initially.

We note one further consideration that may have some bearing on rules of waiver. The compliance Panel in the Bed Linen case noted its concern for "manipulative and abusive" litigation tactics. It did not detail its fears in this regard, but its phrasing hints at concern for vexatious proceedings, brought not because of their potential legal merits but because of their capacity to harass the respondent. There is a considerable economic literature on the use of frivolous litigation to extract settlements, and it is possible that complainants in the WTO might hope to extract trade concessions in meritless cases from respondents anxious to avoid litigation costs. For such a strategy to justify rules of waiver, of course, it must be the case that litigation is more expensive *seriatim* than in a consolidated proceeding, presumably because of the fixed costs noted above – otherwise, vexatious claims brought all at once would be just as effective "harassment."

Although waiver rules may make vexatious litigation less troublesome in the presence of fixed costs, other procedural devices are better tailored to address the problem of vexatious claims. Parties who bring claims that are adjudged to be frivolous can be sanctioned in a variety of ways ("Rule 11 sanctions" in the parlance of American civil procedure). A potentially effective sanction is fee shifting, where the complainant must pay the litigation costs of the respondent. Such measures target frivolous litigation directly without affecting the timing of potentially meritorious claims. Hence, waiver rules are at most a "second-best" response to vexatious litigation.

3.1.3 Modeling the effect of waiver rules in the WTO

Following the literature on efficient legal procedure, we would ideally like to model the problem of designing optimal rules of waiver. One would ask the question whether, in the absence of waiver rules, WTO complainants would bring too few claims at a time from a social standpoint. If so, one would then inquire whether waiver rules could correct the problem.

Such an analysis would be extremely complex, however, requiring attention to the social gains from litigation, the timing of those gains, and the magnitude and timing of litigation costs. The matter becomes all the more complicated in cases with multiple legal claims, in that the social returns to the proper adjudication of each claim may vary. Yet another complication is the fact that WTO litigants are governments. It is a commonplace in the procedure literature to treat litigants as expected profit maximizers, but governments cannot be presumed to behave in this fashion. Indeed, in WTO litigation, money rarely changes hands.

We thus limit ourselves to a very simple treatment of one piece of the puzzle that abstracts from these difficult issues. Our focus is on the question of how a rule of waiver affects the number of claims brought before the dispute resolution process, and thus the total variable costs of litigation.

Consider a two-period model. If the claimant wins at least one claim in period 1, it wins an award that it values at B_1. If it fails to win one claim in period 1 but wins at least one claim in period 2, it wins an award that it values at B_2, $B_2 < B_1$. The difference between B_1 and B_2 reflects the cost to the claimant of delay in receiving the remedy. Assume that there are many potential arguments available to the claimant, and approximate these by a continuum of claims with measure M. The (small) claim i has the (small) probability $p(i)\mathrm{d}i$ of success. It is brought at marginal cost $c(i)\mathrm{d}i$. It is optimal for the claimant to bring its "best" claims first; i.e. those with the highest $p(i)/c(i)$. Thus, we order the claims so that $p(i)/c(i)$ is a non-increasing function. Let $C(x)$ be the total cost of bringing the set of claims $[0, x]$.[12]

In a judicial system with waiver, the claimant must raise all arguments in a single "case." The case comprises the claims $[0, x]$, where x is a decision variable for the claimant. In a judicial system without waiver, the claimant may return to the adjudicating body with additional claims

[12] That is, $C(x) = \int_0^x c(i)\mathrm{d}i$.

in period 2, if it fails to win at least one of its claims in period 1. In this setting, the claimant brings claims $[0, x_1]$ in period 1 and claims $[x_1, x_1+x_2]$ in period 2 (if there has been no success in period 1).

Let $F(x)$ be the probability that there is at least one successful claim from among those in $[0, x]$; $F(0)=0$, $F(M) \leq 1$. The density, $f(x)$, is the probability that the first success comes on claim x. The hazard rate, $f(x)/[1-F(x)]$ is the probability that a success comes on x, given that there has been no success on any claims before x. Since the claims are independent, this is just $p(x)$. Bayes Rule tells us that the probability of at least one success before x_1+x_2, $F(x_1+x_2)$, is equal to the probability of at least one success before x_1 plus the probability of no successes before x_1 times the probability of at least one success between x_1 and x_2, or

$$F(x_1+x_2) = F(x_1) + [1-F(x_1)]\times \\ [\Pr\{\text{at least one success between } x_1 \text{ and } x_2\}]$$

or

$$\Pr\{\text{at least one success between } x_1 \text{ and } x_2\} \\ = \frac{F(x_1+x_2)-F(x_1)}{1-F(x_1)}$$

3.1.3.1 Judicial system with rule of waiver Here, the claimant must make any claims that it wishes to advance in the first period. The claimant chooses $x \geq 0$ to maximize

$$F(x)B_1 - C(x)$$

The first order condition is

$$f(x)B_1 = c(x);$$

that is, the claimant chooses the marginal claim x to equate the probability that the first success will come on that claim times the award from winning the case to the marginal cost.

3.1.3.2 Judicial system without rule of waiver Here the claimant can spread claims over the two periods, coming back in period 2 if the claims brought in period 1 do not succeed. The claimant chooses

$x_1 \geq 0$ and $x_2 \geq 0$ to maximize

$$F(x_1)B_1 + [1 - F(x_1)]\left\{\frac{F(x_1 + x_2) - F(x_1)}{1 - F(x_1)}\right\}B_2 \\ - C(x_1) - [1 - F(x_1)][C(x_1 + x_2) - C(x_1)]$$

Here, the first term is the probability of success in the first case times the first period award. The second term is the probability of no success in the first case times the probability of at least one success from among claims $[x_1, x_1+x_2]$ (see above) times the reward from a victory in case 2. The third term is the total cost of the first case. The last term is the incremental cost of the second case multiplied by the probability of a second case.

The first order conditions are:

$$f(x_1)(B_1 - B_2) + f(x_1 + x_2)B_2 - f(x_1)C(x_1) - F(x_1)c(x_1) \\ - [1 - F(x_1)]c(x_1 + x_2) + f(x_1)C(x_1 + x_2) = 0 \tag{1}$$

and

$$f(x_1 + x_2)B_2 - [1 - F(x_1)]c(x_1 + x_2) \leq 0, \tag{2}$$

where expression (2) holds with equality if and only if $x_2 > 0$. Assume that it is profitable to bring a second case, which requires a sufficiently large B_2 (if a second case is not profitable, a rule of waiver has no effect). Then $f(x_1 + x_2)B_2 - [1 - F(x_1)]c(x_1 + x_2) = 0$, which we can substitute into expression (1) to obtain

$$f(x_1)(B_1 - B_2) - f(x_1)C(x_1) - F(x_1)c(x_1) + f(x_1)C(x_1 + x_2) = 0. \tag{3}$$

3.1.3.3 An example Consider the case of a constant hazard rate, which arises when the probability of success in each claim is the same. Then $F(x) = 1 - e^{-\lambda x}$ for some $\lambda > 0$. Suppose also that every claim has the same cost, so that $c(x) = c$ and $C(x) = cx$. All claims are symmetric under these assumptions, but there are still diminishing returns to filing more and more claims, and the claimant generally will not file all of them.

3.1.3.4 The example with waiver The first order condition becomes

$$\lambda e^{-\lambda x} B_1 = c$$

or

$$e^{\lambda x} = \frac{\lambda B_1}{c}.$$

For convenience, define $\theta_i = \lambda B_i / c$, so the last expression can be written as

$$e^{\lambda x} = \theta_1 \quad \text{or} \quad x = \log \theta_1 / \lambda.$$

3.1.3.5 The example with no rule of waiver If $x_2 > 0$, then expression (2) implies

$$\lambda e^{-\lambda(x_1 + x_2)} B_2 = e^{-\lambda x_1} c$$

or

$$e^{\lambda x_2} = \frac{\lambda B_2}{c} = \theta_2.$$

Taking logs, $x_2 = \log \theta_2 / \lambda$.
Now, for the choice of x_1, expression (3) becomes

$$\lambda e^{-\lambda x_1}(B_1 - B_2) - \lambda e^{-\lambda x_1} c x_1 - (1 - \lambda e^{-\lambda x_1})c + \lambda e^{-\lambda x_1} c(x_1 + x_2) = 0$$

or

$$c e^{\lambda x_1} = \lambda B_1 - \lambda B_2 + c(1 + \log \theta_2),$$

where this last expression uses $\lambda x_2 = \log \theta_2$ from the solution for x_2. We can now write

$$e^{\lambda x_1} = \theta_1 - (\theta_2 - 1 - \log \theta_2).$$

The term in parentheses is positive for all $\theta_2 > 1$ (and unless $\theta_2 > 1$, $x_2 = 0$). Thus, comparing the solution for the case with a rule of waiver, the claimant files more claims in the first round under a rule of waiver than without waiver, as one might expect.
Note further that

$$e^{\lambda(x_1 + x_2)} = e^{\lambda x_1} \cdot e^{\lambda x_2} = \theta_2(\theta_1 - \theta_2 + 1 + \log \theta_2),$$

thus

$$e^{\lambda(x_1+x_2)} - \theta_1 = (\theta_1 - \theta_2)(\theta_2 - 1) + \theta_2 \log \theta_2 > 0,$$

which implies that the total number of claims filed in the two cases without a rule of waiver (if the second case is necessary) exceeds the number of claims that will be filed in a single case under a rule of waiver.

Finally, consider the expected number of claims brought under each regime. With no rule of waiver, expected claims are $x_1 + [1 - F(x_1)]x_2 = x_1 + e^{-\lambda x_1}x_2$. Using the results above, this expression becomes

$$\frac{\log \theta_2}{\lambda(\theta_1 - \theta_2 + 1 + \log \theta_2)} + \frac{\log(\theta_1 - \theta_2 + 1 + \log \theta_2)}{\lambda}.$$

This expression can be greater or smaller than the solution for x (the expected and actual number of claims) under a rule of waiver, $\log \theta_1/\lambda$. We have evaluated the difference numerically, and find that its sign depends on the sizes of the two parameters, θ_1 and θ_2.

For example, setting $\theta_1 = 3$ and allowing θ_2 to vary over its full possible range (from 1 at the lowest, given that x_2 positive requires $\theta_2 > 1$, to 3 at the highest, since $\theta_1 > \theta_2$), we find that the difference rises steadily from zero. In this case, the expected number of claims without a rule of waiver is higher for all $\theta_2 \in (1,3]$, and the difference is larger the greater θ_2 is. This suggests that a rule of waiver will reduce the variable costs of litigation.

But when $\theta_1 = 5$, a somewhat different picture emerges. The difference between the expected number of claims without and with a rule of waiver rises above zero as θ_2 rises initially, but it reaches a maximum and turns negative as θ_2 approaches θ_1. And when $\theta_1 = 10$, the difference is negative for all θ_2 above approximately 4.0, so that the expected number of claims with a rule of waiver can clearly exceed the number without a rule of waiver for some parameter values. In particular, when θ_1 is "high" and the cost of delay is not too great ($\theta_1 - \theta_2$ is not too big), a rule of waiver actually increases the expected number of claims filed.

The explanation for these findings is rather subtle. Fix θ_1 and consider an increase in B_2, which increases θ_2. Clearly, this has no effect on the number of claims brought in a regime with a rule of waiver. When there is no rule of waiver, an increase in θ_2 reduces the number of claims brought in a first case, but it increases both the probability that there will be a second case and the number of claims brought in such an event. The net effect on the expected number of claims can be positive or negative. We calculate that an increase in θ_2 actually decreases the expected number of claims in a regime without a rule of waiver if and only if $1+(\theta_1-\theta_2)(2-\theta_2)-(\theta_2-1-\log\theta_2)<0$. If $\theta_1-\theta_2$ is small (little cost of delay), this inequality is satisfied for $\theta_2>2+\log\ \theta_2$; i.e. θ_2 greater than approximately 3.15. Thus, when θ_1 and θ_2 are both large and the difference is small, the expected number of claims in a system without a rule of waiver is relatively small compared to the large number of arguments that the claimant brings with a rule of waiver.

Our results are only the beginning of a full treatment of the issues for reasons noted earlier – we have not modeled the social returns to litigation or any litigation cost externalities. But even the modest piece of the problem that we explore is quite complex, as the reader will no doubt have noticed. We can offer little definitive advice other than to urge caution in the evolution of rules of waiver in the WTO (and more generally). It is not at all obvious that social welfare will improve if tribunals insist that claimants bring all claims to an initial proceeding lest they be waived. Particularly when the fixed costs of additional proceedings are modest, it may be better to proceed on the strongest claims first and then to litigate others later only if necessary. And because the fixed cost aspects of Art. 21.5 compliance Panels may tend to be relatively modest, special caution is appropriate there. Compliance Panels should perhaps employ a rather narrow conception of what constitutes the "same" claim when following the Appellate Body's directive to deny claimants a second bite of the apple.

Returning to the facts of the Bed Linen case, it is not obvious to us that India's failure to develop its case fully on the non-attribution issue during the first proceeding should have precluded it from raising the issue again in the compliance proceeding. Its arguments regarding "other factors" such as EC input and output prices had not been vetted earlier, nor is it clear that the EC would have suffered any serious prejudice if forced to address them before the Art. 21.5 Panel. The decision by the Panel and the Appellate Body to foreclose those arguments may encourage WTO litigants to throw the "kitchen sink" into their initial complaints and arguments, so that initial Panel proceedings become even more (and perhaps unduly) cumbersome. This is particularly true if, as we imagine being the case, the rules of *res judicata* and waiver that apply before compliance Panels will apply more generally within the system, and bar the filing of new claims relating to the same facts when an initial set of claims proves unsuccessful.

3.2 Injury caused by exporters not individually investigated

From an economic perspective, we agree with the Appellate Body that if only 47% of the goods from the Indian exporters actually investigated were dumped, it is most unlikely that 100% of the goods from exporters not investigated were dumped. It is also clear from the Anti-dumping Agreement that fairly traded imports constitute one of the "other factors" that may cause injury to an industry, and that such injury should not be attributed to dumped imports. To allow the EC to presume that all exporters not investigated were dumping under these circumstances would almost certainly inflate the quantity of "dumped imports" above its true value, and might in theory produce an erroneous finding that material injury resulted from dumping.

We nevertheless have one reservation about the ruling in India's favor on this issue. The Panel was persuaded by the argument that India's position implies an odd lack of parallelism in the Anti-dumping Agreement between the imports that are considered dumped for purposes of injury analysis, and the imports that are considered dumped for purposes of duty collection. The Appellate Body found this disjunction less jarring, and we might agree if the issue was simply one of construction in the face of textual ambiguity. But, as noted earlier, the Anti-dumping Agreement contains a special standard of review Art. 17.6(ii), which requires deference to national implementation of WTO law that rests on a "permissible" interpretation. The Appellate Body's suggestion that the terms "positive evidence" and "objective examination" are not ambiguous, and do not "admit of more than one permissible interpretation," is a bit facile. The EC position is essentially that, in defining the quantity of "dumped imports," it can rely on the "objective evidence" provided by the set of imports to which anti-dumping duties may apply. We are hard pressed to conclude that such an interpretation of the Agreement is not "permissible."

3.3 Deference to the panel on the "relevant factors" issue

The Appellate Body's deference to the Panel on the question of whether the EC considered all "relevant factors" in its injury analysis raises no issues of note. Deference to the "trier of fact" on factual issues is routine in many legal systems, and is certainly a central tenet of appellate review in the WTO. Absent a showing of bias or abuse by India, the Appellate Body presumed that the Panel had satisfied itself on this essentially factual question, and would not allow the issue to be revisited under the guise of an argument that the Panel failed to make an adequate investigation as a "procedural" matter. We can imagine cases where a Panel might so clearly fail in its duties to investigate factual issues that a reversal of its findings might be warranted, but here, India did not make enough of a showing to convince the Appellate Body, and we would have no basis for second guessing that judgment.

References

Friedenthal, J. H., Kane, M. K. and Miller, A. R. (1999). *Civil Procedure 3rd Edn.* (Minneapolis: West).

James, F., Hazard, G. C. and Leubsdorf, J. (2001). *Civil Procedure 5th Edn.* (New York: Foundation).

Janow, M. E. and Staiger, R. W. (2003). European Communities – Anti-Dumping Duties on Imports of Cotton-Type Bed Linen from India. In H. Horn and P. C. Mavroidis, eds., *The WTO Case Law of 2001*, pp. 115–139 (Cambridge: Cambridge University Press).

3

United States – Sunset Review of Anti-Dumping Duties on Corrosion-Resistant Carbon Steel Flat Products From Japan (AB-2003-5, WT/DS244/AB/R): A Legal and Economic Analysis of the Appellate Body Ruling

ROBERT HOWSE*
University of Michigan Law School
ROBERT W. STAIGER*
University of Wisconsin

1 Introduction

The WTO Anti-Dumping (AD) Agreement requires that anti-dumping duties be reviewed at least every five years (Art. 11.3); pursuant to this requirement, domestic trade authorities in the United States are charged with the task of making a determination as to whether, after five years, revoking the duties would be likely to lead to continuation or recurrence of dumping (Commerce) and of material injury (US International Trade Commission, or USITC). This is called a Sunset Review; a negative determination of likelihood, either with respect to dumping or injury, will result in the duties expiring, the "sun" setting, as it were.

The WTO Appellate Body (AB) ruling that is the subject of this chapter resulted from a challenge by Japan to a number of aspects of Commerce's approach to the Sunset Review undertaken with regard to anti-dumping duties that had been imposed on certain steel

* We thank participants at ALI meetings, where we presented this paper, for helpful comments.

imports. Japan challenged both the general administrative practice of the Commerce Department as codified in that department's Sunset Policy Bulletin, and also the methodologies actually applied by Commerce in this particular investigation, in coming to its conclusions.

2 Legal issues

2.1 When can legal norms "as such" be challenged as violations of WTO rules, independent of their application?

In the Panel proceeding below, Japan argued that the United States Department of Commerce (USDOC) Sunset Policy Bulletin "as such" violated provisions of the *Anti-Dumping Agreement.* The Panel below made the finding that it did not have the jurisdiction to consider the Sunset Policy Bulletin "as such," because the Bulletin was not a mandatory measure and only mandatory measures could give rise to a violation of a WTO Agreement. Japan appealed these findings of the Panel.

In considering Japan's appeal, the AB observed that the wording of the Panel report appeared to confuse or conflate different issues: first of all, whether, in general, a measure must mandate a course of conduct in order to be subject to a WTO dispute settlement complaint; second, whether, in particular, when the measure challenged is a legal instrument "as such," it must be mandatory in order to be challengeable; third, whether, even if challengeable, a legal instrument "as such" must mandate official conduct violating WTO rules in order to be found in breach of those rules.

The AB then proceeded to treat these issues as analytically distinct. On the first issue, the AB held, citing DSU 3.3, that any measure that impaired benefits accruing to another WTO Member directly or indirectly could be the subject of a dispute complaint. "In principle, any act or omission attributable to a WTO member can be a measure of that Member for purposes of dispute settlement proceedings."[Footnote omitted]

This finding is obviously correct: neither the relevant WTO treaty provisions on dispute settlement limit state responsibility in the WTO to measures that mandate a course of conduct, nor do the general background rules of state responsibility as reflected in the International Law Commission (ILC) Articles and the jurisprudence of international tribunals impose this kind of limitation.[1] Moreover, restricting state responsibility in the WTO to acts of states that mandate a course of conduct would render unenforceable, or severely circumscribe, many provisions in the WTO treaties. For example, the Technical Barriers to Trade Agreement imposes a variety of obligations on WTO Members that concern *voluntary standard*-setting activities both domestic and international; these obligations are clearly distinguished from those that apply to mandatory regulatory measures: "regulations." Also, many subsidy measures that fall within the Subsidies and Countervailing Measures (SCM) Agreement do not mandate a course of conduct; a subsidy is defined in the Agreement as a financial contribution that confers a benefit. While some subsidy measures mandate a course of conduct (for instance, export performance), many do not.

On the second issue, whether legal instruments must mandate conduct that violates a WTO treaty provision in order to be challengeable "as such," the AB began by stating the rationale for allowing challenges to "instruments of a Member containing rules or norms . . . , irrespective of how or whether those rules or norms are applied in a particular instance." According to the AB, "the disciplines of the General Agreement on Tariffs and Trade (GATT) and the WTO, as well as the dispute settlement system, are intended to protect not only existing trade but also the security and predictability needed to conduct future trade. This objective would be frustrated if instruments setting out rules or norms inconsistent with a Member's obligations could not be brought before a Panel once they have been adopted and irrespective of any particular instance of application of such rules or norms." [Footnote omitted.]

The AB thus clearly endorsed a default rule that rule- or norm-creating instruments may be challenged "as such" in a WTO dispute settlement. This default rule is subject only to any treaty provision of contrary effect. The AB then went on to consider whether the AD Agreement contained any such provision of contrary effect; the AB noted that in the *US-1916 Act* case it had already decided this question in the negative. In this connection, the AB noted that Art. 17.3 of the AD Agreement provided for consultations – the first stage of

[1] See ILC Art. 2: state responsibility is incurred by any "action or omission" that is attributable to a state and that is a breach of an international obligation. There is no distinction between mandatory and other acts of states. In the *Iran Hostage* case, the International Court of Justice suggested that in some circumstances mere governmental encouragement or endorsement of the conduct of private actors could give rise to state responsibility.

dispute settlement – when a Member considered that measures taken by another Member impaired benefits accruing to it under the treaty, without in any way qualifying or restricting the concept of "measures." Secondly, the AB observed that Art. 18.4 of the AD Agreement required Members to take all necessary steps "of a general or particular character" to ensure that their "laws, regulations and administrative procedures" conformed to the AD Agreement.

In the AB's view, this provision not only makes it clear that the AD Agreement contemplates no departure from the default rule of state responsibility for rules and norms "as such," but in addition, that the AD Agreement takes a broad view of the nature of such rules or norms; the language "administrative procedures" suggesting to the AB that any "administrative instrument issued by an executive agency pursuant to statutory and regulatory provisions" (para. 84, AB report) can be challenged "as such" under the AD Agreement.

Now the AB went on to consider the third issue: does a legal instrument being challenged "as such" have to mandate a course of official conduct violating the WTO rules, in order for the instrument "as such" to be found in breach of those rules? The AB noted that the "mandatory/discretionary distinction" had been used as an "analytical tool" by panels in determining whether "legislation as such" violated a particular WTO rule. The AB considered that it had, in previous cases, skirted the issue of whether mandatoriness was a necessary criterion for finding that "legislation as such" violated a WTO treaty. While stating that it was going to continue to skirt the issue, the AB nevertheless observed that the import of the "mandatory/discretionary distinction," like that of any other "analytical tool" would vary from case to case. In other words, depending on the treaty provision at issue, and the nature of the measure, whether the legislation as such mandated a violation of the WTO rules might or might not be of decisive importance in finding a violation. This accords with the approach to the mandatory/discretion distinction in the *Section 301* case, where the Panel held that, at least in respect of some provisions of WTO treaties, "legislation as such" could constitute a violation even if it was not, strictly speaking, "mandatory." In any case, by placing such emphasis on the status of the mandatory/discretionary distinction as an "analytical tool," the AB is telling us what the distinction is not: it is not a metarule that overrides or precludes the determination of state responsibility based on a reading of WTO treaty provisions. Again, this seems to endorse, if only implicitly, the jurisprudence of the

Section 301 Panel, which regarded the mandatory/discretionary distinction as merely one, albeit important, heuristic for determining whether, in a particular case, a specific provision of a WTO treaty creates state responsibility for legal instruments "as such," independent of their application. In sum, although the AB explicitly denied that it was going in this case to "pronounce generally upon the continuing relevance or significance of the mandatory/discretionary distinction"(para. 93), it ended up giving important guidance on the legal status or character of that distinction.

After these general remarks about the mandatory/discretionary distinction, the AB went on to review the Panel's characterization of the Sunset Policy Bulletin as not "a legal instrument that operates so as to mandate a course of action." (Panel Report, para. 7.126). It appears that one reason that the Panel characterized the Sunset Policy Bulletin as "non-mandatory" was the Panel's view that the Bulletin did not operate independently from other legal instruments, namely the Statute and Regulations. Here it is very difficult indeed to understand the Panel's reasoning. The Panel was trying to determine whether a particular instrument mandated a course of action in the US legal system: it then seems to have invented a test which, as far as we know, is entirely alien to US administrative law, and one that, in fact, would be fatal to all delegated rulemaking – for all such rules depend by definition on authority delegated from some higher statutory framework, and thus are not independent or autonomous, as the Panel appeared to understand these terms.

Surprisingly, the AB did not explicitly address or overturn the Panel's finding that, to be mandatory, a legal instrument must be independent or autonomous, and not a derivative from some other legal framework. Instead, the AB noted language in the introductory provisions of the Bulletin indicating that the Bulletin addresses "methodological or analytical issues not explicitly addressed by the statute and regulations." (AB Report, para. 95). The AB appears to have understood the Panel's test as one that went to whether a legal instrument has different *content* from other instruments, not whether its *authority* is derivative from those other instruments. But the Panel's point seemed to be this: delegated rulemaking cannot be challenged "as such" at the WTO – one must either make a claim of WTO violation against the legislation delegating the rulemaking authority "as such," or a claim against individual acts derivative from that legislation that violate WTO law. "Policies" are either mandated by the legislation as such, and then the legislation as such is challengeable, or they are the products of delegated discretion under the legislation, in which case only individual acts of discretionary authority may be challenged.

The main problem with the Panel's approach, obviously informed by a rigid view of the mandatory/discretionary distinction – a rigid view that the AB clearly rejects in general – is that it doesn't reflect the way in which public law actually operates in the United States[2] and indeed in other jurisdictions as well.[3] As Peter Strauss observes, in the United States system, material such as "statements of policy, interpretations, staff manuals, and instructions that affect members of the public … has the force and effect of law in most cases…"(p. 806).

Moreover, as Nina Mendelson[4] points out, even though agencies are creatures of statute, a statute may grant to an agency the discretion to bind itself, i.e. to create rules that are mandatory and that the agency *must* follow in its future activity, but whose binding character flows from the agency itself. At the same time, as Mendelson also notes, agencies may issue policy statements, interpretations, and other material that the agency clearly indicates are not binding on its future actions. In sum, while agencies derive their power to determine what delegated rule- and policymaking will be binding or not from their statutory mandates, they exercise that power under very loose legislative constraint in many cases. Thus, the Panel's notion that a mandatory legal instrument must be one independent or autonomous from higher legislation simply misunderstands what determines whether agency policymaking is mandatory or binding.

In sum, it is regrettable that the AB did not take the occasion to overrule explicitly the Panel's finding that to mandate of itself a course of conduct, a legal instrument must be independent or autonomous from other legislation.

The AB did, however, go on to find fault with other aspects of the Panel's characterization of the Sunset Policy Bulletin as non-binding.

[2] Strauss, P. L. Publication Rules in the Rulemaking Spectrum: Assuring Proper Respect for an Essential Element, **53** *Admin. L. Rev.* 803 (2001).

[3] See the criticism by Howse and Neven of a panel report that adopted a similarly rigid approach where the question was the practice of the Canadian Export Development Corporation, "Canada-Export Credits and Loan Guarantees for Regional Aircraft (WT/DS222/R): A Comment," ALI Reports 2003.

[4] Mendelson, N. A. "Agency Burrowing: Entrenching Policies and Personnel Before a New President Arrives" **78** *NYU. L. Rev.* 557, 573–576 and accompanying footnotes (2003). See also, Bressman, L. S. "Schecter Poultry at the Millenium: A Delegation Doctrine for the Administrative State," **109** *Yale L.J.* 1399 (2000).

First of all, the AB held that the Panel had over-relied on wording in the introductory sections of the Bulletin that referred to its role as "guidance" and did not conduct "any in depth consideration of the impugned provisions of the Bulletin."(AB Report, para. 95). Here the AB was in part right and in part wrong. If what the AB meant was that the language "providing guidance" was sufficient in itself to establish the non-binding or non-mandatory character of the Sunset Bulletin, then the AB was right. If what it meant was that in all cases the introductory description of a policy instrument's role would not be dispositive of whether it was mandatory, then the AB was probably wrong. Consider, for instance, the FAA's Advisory Circular on Minimum Flightcrew: the circular is stated to be "... not mandatory... It is for guidance purposes only." Had similar wording been used in the introductory section of the Sunset Policy Bulletin, the Panel would surely not have had to read any further to make a determination of non-mandatoriness. But it is important to note that, as with this aviation circular, where a policy statement is intended to be non-mandatory, the language of the instrument tends not to leave matters at stating that it is for guidance; usually there is *additional* wording to indicate the non-mandatory character of the instrument; in other words, agency practice suggests that agencies do not believe the courts will infer non-mandatoriness from the word "guidance" *on its own.* And this does suggest that the AB was right, *in this case*, that the Panel could not leave matters at considering the introductory wording of the Bulletin in isolation.

Then what other factors or considerations ought the Panel to have taken into account (besides of course the wording of the impugned provisions themselves)? One factor was whether the agency should "treat" the "rules" in the Bulletin as "binding." The AB appeared to take seriously in this regard Japan's notion that the consistent following of the Policy Bulletin in agency decisions could be evidence that the agency considered the Bulletin to be "binding." The Panel had relied on a statement by the United States in its memorial and oral argument, to the effect that the agency could depart from the Sunset Policy Bulletin as long as it gave reasons for doing so and was not acting in an arbitrary and capricious manner, as an indication that the Policy Bulletin was not mandatory; the AB suggested that the Panel should have considered whether the *conditions* for deviating from the Policy Bulletin were such as to make it "mandatory."

The AB also suggested that the Panel ought to have compared the contents of the Sunset Policy Bulletin with "contents of the corresponding statutory and regulatory provisions." The AB also suggested that in considering the specific provisions of the Bulletin impugned by Japan, the Panel ought to have looked at whether those provisions were "normative" in nature.

The approach of the AB tracks very closely the US case law. Thus in *Doe v. Hampton*, the DC Circuit made a number of observations that are similar or identical to those of the AB in its critique of the Panel's findings: (1) the focus must be on individual provisions of the legal instrument; even if most of the provisions are non-binding, some may nevertheless be mandatory; (2) the intent of the agency to be bound is a crucial consideration; (3) the intent of the agency is to be "ascertained by an examination of the provision's language, its context, and any available extrinsic evidence."[5]

Having found that the Panel erred in rejecting Japan's claim that the Sunset Policy Bulletin "as such" violated the AD Agreement on the basis that the Sunset Policy Bulletin was not "mandatory," the AB went on to consider whether it should "complete the analysis."

The AB first considered Japan's claim that a provision of the Sunset Policy Bulletin violated the AD Agreement because it stipulated that the agency was to make a determination of the likelihood of future dumping on an order-wide, rather than a company-by-company basis. Here Japan's argument was that the provisions of Art. 11.3 of the AD Agreement were governed by Art. 6.10, which required that "as a rule," and where practicable, individual margins of dumping be assessed for each producer exporter or producer concerned. The AB agreed with the United States that this provision addressed itself essentially to the initial investigation and did not imply that a likelihood determination in a sunset review had to be done on a company-by-company basis. As the AB noted, since there is no requirement in the first place under the AD Agreement to calculate dumping *margins* in making a sunset review, the provisions of Art. 6.10 invoked by Japan were, in this respect, simply not applicable to sunset reviews.

Having found that there was nothing in the AD Agreement that required a company-by-company determination of likelihood in a sunset review, the AB then said it would "return to the measure at issue,..." As a matter of judicial economy, if the AB were applying the mandatory/discretionary distinction, it would have stopped before its "return to the measure at issue." Once the AB found that nothing

[5] *Doe v. Hampton*, 566 F.2d 265, 280–281 (1977).

in the AD Agreement required a company-by-company approach, Japan's claim failed, regardless of whether the provision in the Sunset Policy Bulletin setting out "an order-wide" approach was mandatory. If it was mandatory, it was not mandating anything contrary to the AD Agreement.

Yet the AB went on to make a point of the fact that the Sunset Policy Bulletin section in question stated that "the Department will make its determination on an order-by-order basis." The AB noted that the Bulletin did not provide any exception to this provision and that the use of the word "will" suggested that the agency was strictly limiting its discretion. The AB further observed that other provisions of the Bulletin used the more qualified phrase "normally will." Finally, the AB pointed to the fact that the United States itself had not suggested that the agency could deviate from an order-wide approach, or that it had ever done so in practice.

But the AB did not say what these facts pointed to – whether they established that the provision of the Sunset Policy Bulletin was mandatory or whether they established that the provision, because of its likely impact on future behavior, would be capable in principle of "as such" violating relevant provisions of the AD Agreement, whether or not it was "mandatory" in the strict sense.

Japan had also claimed that the Sunset Policy Bulletin violated the AD Agreement because certain rules or guidelines in the Policy Bulletin "restrict USDOC in a sunset review, to considering only two factors, namely historical dumping margins and import volumes, and set forth mechanical rules creating a bias in favor of an affirmative likelihood determination."(AB Report, para. 170). While the Policy Bulletin also allowed other factors to be considered when there was "good cause," Japan considered that a showing of good cause for consideration of other factors was, in practice, a very significant hurdle, such that the process was, in Japan's words, "biased."

In deciding whether to complete the analysis, the AB formulated the legal question it would have to answer if it were to do so, as "whether [the provisions concerned] instruct USDOC to treat dumping margins and/or import volumes as determinative or conclusive, on the one hand, or merely indicative or probative, on the other hand, of the likelihood of future dumping." (AB Report, para. 178).

The AB noted that the use of the adverb "normally" in the Sunset Review Bulletin suggested that the agency *could* take into account other considerations in making its determination; on the other hand,

Japan asserted that, in fact, this never did occur in practice. The United States contested Japan's factual claim here, arguing that it had "terminated many duties at the stage of sunset review," (AB Report, para. 183), and that statistics that suggested that importers and foreign producers always lost when at the sunset review stage could not substitute for an examination of the manner in which the evidence was weighed in each individual case by the agency. The AB then noted that, clearly, there were contested facts, and these could not be resolved by referring to any factual finding of the Panel below; since the AB then could only complete the analysis by engaging in fact-finding itself, the AB found that it could not complete the analysis.

The AB's refusal to complete the analysis shows its rejection of the mandatory/discretionary distinction as a mechanical metarule of state responsibility. If the AB viewed the mandatory/discretionary distinction as such a rule, it could easily have completed the analysis: in and of itself, the presence of the qualifier "normally" in the relevant provisions of the Sunset Bulletin would have constituted sufficient evidence that the provisions in question were "discretionary," i.e. as a formal matter, the agency *could* deviate from the guidelines. By contrast, the AB did not regard the clear grant of a margin of discretion through the qualifier "normally" as dispositive of whether the Sunset Bulletin "as such" engaged state responsibility under Art. 11.3 of the AD Agreement.

Beyond legal form, the crucial question for the AB is whether *in fact* a treaty provision gives rise to, or is likely to give rise to, a "consistent pattern" of conduct or practice in violation of the WTO treaty norms. In most respects, this approach seems to be an embrace of the spirit, if not the methodology as well, of the *Section 301* ruling. Legal pluralism triumphs over positivism: formal legality does not exhaust, and may actually misrepresent, normative impact – the capacity to influence and structure a pattern of human conduct.

There is an odd Leo-Strauss-like esotericism to the manner in which the AB deals with the mandatory/discretionary distinction in this case. The AB shouts from the rafters that it will *avoid* dealing with the validity and meaning of the distinction, and then, implicitly or surreptitiously, through the way in which it criticizes the Panel below, and then how it makes its decisions on completing the analysis, relegates the distinction, at least as understood through the positivist lenses of many Panel rulings pre-*Section 301*, to virtual oblivion. Sometimes one can appreciate the subtlety and even obscurity of the AB – such techniques may be justifiable where the legitimacy stakes are very high and there is a serious political conflict underlying different positions in the case (*Asbestos*, *Generalized System of Preferences* (*GSP*)) – but why here? Why not come out and say directly that whether there is formal mandatoriness or an element of discretion is simply one ingredient, and not always the most important one, of an inquiry into state responsibility for compliance with specific provisions of the WTO treaties?

2.2 Is the Sunset Policy Bulletin an "administrative procedure" within the meaning of Art. 18.4 of the AD Agreement?

Instead of turning to the specific obligations at issue to determine the nature of state responsibility, and allowing the nature of those obligations to control the relevance of the mandatory/discretionary distinction, the Panel below did the opposite: it read the distinction *into* the text, as if it were a metarule that structured state responsibility with respect to *all* WTO treaty provisions, regardless of the text itself. Thus, in interpreting Art. 18.4 of the AD Agreement, which requires Members to "take all necessary steps, of a general or particular character" to ensure that their "laws, regulations and administrative procedures" are in conformity with the obligations in the AD Agreement, the Panel held that the Sunset Policy Bulletin could not be an "administrative procedure," on account of the Panel's previous holding that the Bulletin was not "mandatory."

In addressing this finding, the AB first noted that "Taken as a whole, the phrase 'laws, regulations and administrative procedures' seems to us to encompass the entire body of generally applicable rules, norms and standards adopted by Members in connection with the conduct of anti-dumping proceedings."(AB report, para. 87). The AB further noted that, "If some of these measures could not, as such, be subject to dispute settlement under the *Anti-Dumping Agreement*, it would frustrate the obligation of 'conformity' set forth in Article 18.4." The AB went on to note that the Panel had defined an administrative procedure as "a pre-established rule for the conduct of an anti-dumping investigation" (Panel report, para. 7.134); the AB did not find this definition as in error, but rather it objected to the Panel's assumption that a "rule" meant a "mandatory rule." Instead, according to the AB, the Panel needed to consider the "normative nature of the provisions of the Sunset Policy Bulletin and to compare the type of norms the Commerce Department was required to publish in formal regulations with the type of norms it could set out in policy statements." The question, then, for the AB was whether the normative *effects* of the Bulletin were similar or analogous to those of formal rulemaking.

3 Economic issues

We identify and evaluate two key economic questions that arise in the AB's Report on the US Sunset Review of Anti-Dumping Duties. *First*, how is dumping calculated in the Sunset Review? And *second*, how is the likelihood of continued or renewed dumping assessed? We consider each question in turn.

3.1 How is dumping calculated in the Sunset Review?

A first issue confronted by the AB in *US Sunset Review* is to assess the range of appropriate methods for calculating the dumping margins for use in a Sunset Review of anti-dumping orders. The particular methodology at issue in this case is "zeroing."

In determining the likelihood of continued dumping in its Sunset Review, the United States utilized dumping margins that had been calculated as part of its administrative review which, as we discuss further below, is an administrative procedure for adjusting the level of anti-dumping duties that is separate from the Sunset Review. There is no WTO requirement that dumping margins must be used to determine the likelihood of continued dumping in Sunset Reviews (p. 46, 127). Nevertheless, the AB found that, if a methodology for calculating margins were ruled illegal for use in one part of the administration of anti-dumping law, then this methodology could not legally be used in another part of the administration of anti-dumping law, even if WTO rules did not mandate that margins must be an input in this other part of the administration of anti-dumping law (p. 47, 130). But as the AB did not have the facts to establish that the United States had actually used, in its administrative review calculations, the particular zeroing methodology that had been found illegal in EC – Bed Linen, the AB concluded that it was unable to rule on whether the margins used by the United States in its Sunset Review were in fact inconsistent with WTO law (p. 51, 138).

As for the economic issues raised by the use of a zeroing methodology when calculating dumping margins, an economic assessment of the legitimacy of zeroing can be found in Janow and Staiger (2003), and the same discussion applies here. We therefore refer readers to the relevant portions of that paper.[6] The broad conclusion in that paper, however, is that it is difficult to evaluate formally the economic merits of zeroing, because there is not an accepted understanding of why dumping is to be "condemned" in the first place. This conclusion applies equally well to a consideration of the merits of zeroing in the context of margin calculations for the determination of the existence of dumping, as in the EC – Bed Linen case, or in the context of margin calculations for use in the determination of the likelihood of continued or renewed dumping, as in the Sunset Review that is the focus of the present analysis.

3.2 *How is the likelihood of continued or renewed dumping assessed?*

A second issue confronted by the AB in *US Sunset Review* is to assess the range of appropriate methods for calculating the likelihood of continued or renewed dumping. The first question is whether or not the likelihood determination must be made on a company-specific basis or can rather be made on an order-wide basis (p. 51, 139). The AB found as a matter of WTO law that it can be made either way (p. 56, 155). The second question is whether the rules set out in the Sunset Policy Bulletin establish a procedure for determining likelihood that is biased against a finding that the anti-dumping order can be revoked (p. 63, 170). We consider each question in turn.

First, should the likelihood determination be made on a company-specific basis, or can it be made on an order-wide basis? At one level, it is difficult to assess the economic merits of permitting the likelihood determination to be made on an order-wide basis rather than a company-specific basis, without knowing the factual basis on which the likelihood determination is to be made in a particular case. For example, if the likelihood of continued or renewed dumping could be judged on the basis of common factors (such as exchange rate movements) that are outside the control of the individual companies named in the dumping order, then determining the likelihood of continued or renewed dumping on an order-wide basis by assessing whether the common factors that originally led to dumping are still in place would seem sensible. On the other hand, if the likelihood of continued or renewed dumping depends importantly on factors that are under the control of the individual companies named in the dumping order, then

[6] See pp. 124–128 of Janow, M. E. and Staiger, R. W. EC-Bed Linen, in H. Horn and P. C. Mavroidis, (eds.), *The WTO Case Law of 2001*, Cambridge University Press, 2003.

determining the likelihood of continued or renewed dumping on an order-wide basis introduces a "public good" dimension that has the potential to create a significant *free-rider* problem among the companies named in the anti-dumping order. This free-rider problem could in turn thwart the effectiveness of the Sunset Review process mandated in Art. 11.3 of the AD Agreement.

The simple point is, under a company-specific determination, each firm can internalize the benefit (termination of definitive anti-dumping duties) of potentially costly actions that would eliminate its reason for dumping and lead to a favorable Sunset Review, whereas under an order-wide determination, all firms are lumped together and each can "free ride" on the decisions of others to take these potentially costly actions.[7] The free-rider problem can in turn reduce the likelihood that any firm will actually undertake the costly actions which might lead to the elimination of dumping and the associated anti-dumping duties, and in this way can thwart the effectiveness of the Sunset Review process.

[7] We observe that, even in the presence of order-wide Sunset Reviews, it would still be possible for individual companies named in an anti-dumping order to take actions which could eliminate the actual duties that they pay. This possibility is provided for in Art. 9 of the WTO AD Agreement, which stipulates that anti-dumping duties shall be no more than the margin of dumping, which typically (except as provided in Art. 6.10) varies from company to company. It might then be wondered whether the potential free-rider problem associated with order-wide Sunset Reviews that we have described above has significance: After all, a company can always take actions that eliminate the anti-dumping duties it faces, and what more could it gain from a favorable Sunset Review at that point anyway? There are two problems with this sanguine view. *First*, as we discuss further below, the results found by Blonigen, B. A. and Park, J. H. Dynamic Pricing in the Presence of Anti-dumping Policy: Theory and Evidence, *American Economic Review* **94**(1), March 2004, pp. 134–154, suggest that the details of the administrative review processes under which the duty adjustments provided for in Art. 9 are made can (at least in the case of the administrative review process in the United States) create strong disincentives for companies to actually take actions to reduce the duties they face. And *second*, even if a company has succeeded in taking actions which eliminate its dumping margin and therefore the anti-dumping duty that it faces, it can still gain from a favorable Sunset Review, because a favorable Sunset Review terminates the administrative review process and, hence, the continuing risk of future positive-margin calculations and the implied anti-dumping duties. These so-called "investigation effects" have been shown to have significant impacts on trade volumes and prices (For example, see Staiger, R. W. and Wolak, F. A. Measuring Industry-Specific Protection: Anti-dumping in the United States, *Brookings Papers on Economic Activity: Microeconomics*, 1994, pp. 51–118, and Krupp, Corinne M. and Pollard, P. S. Market Responses to Anti-dumping Laws: Some Evidence from the US Chemical Industry, *Canadian Journal of Economics*, **29**(1), February 1996, pp. 199–227).

An analogy with reduced prison sentences for "good behavior" serves to illustrate the point. Imagine a prison in which the inmates faced the possibility of reduced jail sentences in exchange for good behavior, but where the behavior of inmates was assessed on a prison-wide basis and where the fate of all prisoners was determined as a group: either collectively their behavior was deemed good enough to warrant early release for all, or collectively their behavior was not deemed good enough to warrant such preferential treatment. Especially in a large prison with many inmates, such a collective evaluation sets up a very difficult public good problem for the inmates, and it is likely that (i) behavior would not improve much as a result of this incentive program, owing to the potential for "free-riding" on the good behavior of others, and as a consequence (ii) the inmates would not enjoy early release. But now suppose that each inmate is evaluated individually and, with evidence of good behavior, is given an individual early-release date. Under this alternative system, the public good aspect of the first system described above is eliminated. And because each inmate now internalizes the benefits of his own actions (i.e. good behavior brings early release, bad behavior prolongs jail time), it is far more likely under this alternative system that the behavior of substantial numbers of inmates would improve and those inmates would be released early.

Returning now to the case of dumping, it is sometimes maintained, for example, that companies dump on foreign markets when they have excess capacity and wish to sustain high prices in a protected domestic market. If conditions of excess capacity caused the dumping which led to the initial anti-dumping duties, then it would be sensible in a Sunset Review to assess whether conditions of excess capacity still remain when determining the likelihood of continued or renewed dumping. Consider then, the different outcomes that would likely arise in a Sunset Review depending on whether this review were carried out on a company-specific or an order-wide basis.

If this determination were made on a company-specific basis, then any company that took steps to reduce its capacity to a level consistent with the elimination of (its own) dumping could expect a favorable Sunset Review. In such a circumstance, it might be expected that the majority or even all firms would undertake the costly actions necessary to eliminate their own dumping, and the Sunset Review would be effective as a means to phase out anti-dumping duties and the dumping that triggered these duties.

On the other hand, if the determination were made on an order-wide basis, then any company that took steps to reduce its capacity to a level consistent with the elimination of (its own) dumping would raise only *fractionally* the probability of a favorable Sunset Review, because the order-wide determination would depend on the overall threat of continued or renewed dumping from all companies named in the original anti-dumping order, and hence on all of the capacity choices of the other named companies as well. In this circumstance, it might be expected that the majority or even all firms would *fail* to undertake the costly actions necessary to eliminate their own dumping, and the Sunset Review would fail to be effective as a means to phase out anti-dumping duties and the dumping that triggered these duties.[8]

As our discussion has illustrated, at one level it is difficult to assess the merits of permitting the likelihood determination to be made on an order-wide basis rather than a company-specific basis, without knowing the factual basis on which the likelihood determination is to be made in a particular case. But at a general level, we suggest that this difficulty is persuasive in indicating that a cautious view of the merits of permitting the likelihood determination to be made on an order-wide basis rather than a company-specific basis is called for. In particular, based on the concerns raised and discussed above, an argument can be made that the WTO legal text should be changed to require company-specific likelihood determinations in those Sunset Reviews where such determinations are feasible and not excessively costly relative to order-wide likelihood determinations, thereby introducing a presumption in favor of company-specific likelihood determinations in Sunset Reviews. We suggest, for the reasons discussed above, that this change could enhance the effectiveness of the Sunset Review process mandated in Art. 11.3 of the AD Agreement, and thereby hasten the phasing out of anti-dumping duties and the dumping that triggered these duties.

We now turn to the second question raised above: Do the rules set out in the Sunset Policy Bulletin establish a procedure for determining likelihood that is biased against a finding that the anti-dumping order can be revoked? In considering this question, the AB noted (p. 63, 172)

[8] The recent empirical results of Olson, Kara M., Free Riders Among the Rent-Seekers: A Model of Firm Participation in Anti-dumping Petitions, April 15, 2004, unpublished manuscript, document important free-rider effects in the context of the anti-dumping filing behavior of US companies, suggesting that the kinds of free-rider effects emphasized above in the context of order-wide Sunset Reviews could also be quantitatively important.

that the USDOC "normally will" make an affirmative determination regarding the likelihood of continued or renewed dumping if any of these three conditions hold: (i) dumping continued at any level above 0.5% after the issuance of the order; (ii) imports ceased after the issuance of the order; or (iii) dumping was eliminated after the issuance of the order and import volumes declined significantly. The logic of these rules is apparently a simple one: if dumping is still ongoing in the presence of anti-dumping duties, or if it has stopped but import volumes have declined significantly (or even ceased) as a result, then if definitive anti-dumping duties are terminated, dumping will likely continue (case (i)) or resume (cases (ii) and (iii)).

The AB had no problem concluding that the rules followed by the USDOC, as described just above, offered "indicative or probative" guidance for determining likelihood, but said that these rules should not be deemed "determinative or conclusive." (p. 65, 178). The AB then observed that there was insufficient evidence to conclude that the language in the Sunset Policy Bulletin made these rules determinative and conclusive, and so there was no as-such illegality associated with them (p. 69, 190). And the AB concluded that the USDOC's reliance on margins and import levels to determine likelihood in this case was sufficiently justified to point to likely future dumping, and so found that there was no as-applied WTO illegality associated with them. (p. 74, 205).

At a basic level, a meaningful assessment of the likelihood of continued or renewed dumping requires an understanding of two things: (i) what conditions led to dumping in the first place; and (ii) whether those conditions have changed in a way that removes the original reason for dumping. Somewhat astonishingly, neither of these two elements appears to play any real role in the USDOC's methodology for determining likelihood, or in the AB's assessment of the legitimacy of the USDOC's methodology.

Interestingly, because of the details of the administrative review process under US anti-dumping law (and presumably also of the administrative review processes of other countries that share these details), the continued existence of dumping margins in the face of anti-dumping duties is *not* necessarily indicative that dumping will continue if the anti-dumping duties are terminated. Specifically, an implication of the analysis of Blonigen and Park (2004) is that the administrative review process associated with US anti-dumping law can *increase* the incentive of a firm to engage in dumping, once it is faced with anti-dumping duties and is subjected to the administrative review process. This means that, even if the conditions that led the firm to dump originally are no longer in place, the firm may continue dumping as long as it is the subject of the administrative review process, *because* of the *dynamic disincentive* to stop dumping which is set up by the administrative review process itself under US anti-dumping law. And so, a firm that is currently dumping might, in fact, choose to stop dumping if the anti-dumping order were lifted. Blonigen and Park offer a theoretical model that is consistent with this kind of prediction, and then examine the data and find empirical support for their model. This suggests that the indicators used by the USDOC for determining the likelihood of continued or renewed dumping are problematic and unreliable.

To understand the findings of Blonigen and Park (2004), it is necessary to appreciate a few details of the way in which the administrative review process proceeds under US anti-dumping law. Under the US administrative review process, anti-dumping duties are potentially recalculated each year in light of the *past* year's pricing data. This means that, under US law, the amount of the anti-dumping duty that a company must pay is assessed on a *retrospective* basis. If it is found under an administrative review that the dumping duties faced by a firm in the previous year were higher than the dumping margins reflected in its actual pricing behavior during that year, then the firm is refunded the difference, and the duties for the current year are reduced to reflect this new (i.e. last year's) margin information. And conversely, if it is found under an administrative review that the dumping duties faced by a firm in the previous year were lower than the dumping margins reflected in its actual pricing behavior during that year, then the firm is billed for the difference and the duties for the current year are increased to reflect this new (i.e. last year's) margin information.

Presumably, the administrative review process under US anti-dumping law is put in place to allow firms "time off for good behavior," in the sense that it offers dumping firms an incentive to stop dumping and free themselves from anti-dumping duties. Yet notice that the retrospective nature of the assessed anti-dumping duties under the administrative review process makes it especially costly in the short run for a firm to actually get out from under anti-dumping duties once these duties have been initially imposed on it. The reason is that, to be free of duties beginning with next year's administrative review (and to receive the refund of duties paid this year), the firm must raise its price during this year to eliminate the dumping margin *while still facing the existing anti-dumping duties for the year*. This implies that its price to importers (and domestic consumers) during the current year must be pushed doubly high — so that, for example, a foreign company that faces a 40% anti-dumping duty this year must raise its price to importers and domestic consumers by an additional 40% for this year — and its sales during the current year must thereby be pushed commensurately low, if it is to rid itself of anti-dumping duties beginning with the next administrative review.

What we have just described is the *dynamic disincentive* to stop dumping which is set up by the administrative review process under US anti-dumping law. Evidently, especially for firms that do not care too much about future profits and are more focused on short-term profits, shedding existing anti-dumping duties under the US administrative review process can be very costly.

Interestingly, in their empirical work, Blonigen and Park (2004) find that the majority of firms do not decrease their dumping margins through the administrative review process, and a significant percentage actually increase their dumping margins over the review process. Blonigen and Park then argue that this can be explained formally as a consequence of the dynamic incentives set up under the US administrative review process. In particular, due to the retrospective nature of the assessed anti-dumping duties under the US administrative review process, as described just above, firms that do not care too much about the future and are concerned mostly with short-term profit levels will find it advantageous to *raise* their margins each year and dump more aggressively under the administrative review process, in order to offset the rising anti-dumping duties, until they are eventually driven out of the market by prohibitive anti-dumping duties. In fact, in their benchmark formal model, Blonigen and Park identify a critical rate at which a firm discounts future profits, and show that a firm that discounts future profits at a rate higher than this critical rate will choose to dump and then choose to raise its dumping margin in each year of the administrative review, while a firm that discounts future profits at a rate lower than this critical level will choose not to dump in the first place. In an extended formal model in which firms face uncertainty about the likelihood of initially being caught dumping, Blonigen and Park then show that some of the lower-discount-rate firms will now also be induced to take a risk and dump but, unlike their higher-discount-rate counterparts, these lower-discount-rate firms, if caught, will then use the administrative review process to lower or even eliminate their dumping margins and thereby escape from anti-dumping duties through time.

It can now be seen that the results of Blonigen and Park (2004) cast serious doubt on the methodology of the USDOC for determining the likelihood of continued or renewed dumping. In particular, an implication of their results is that the following scenario is not implausible: (i) a firm initially faces conditions that lead it to begin dumping, and is then caught and faces initial anti-dumping duties; (ii) the original conditions that led the firm to choose to dump then change in a way that would remove the firm's incentive to dump if it could make the choice of whether to dump anew; but (iii) under the administrative review process that is subsequently triggered, the dynamic disincentive to stop dumping keeps the firm dumping into the future. Clearly, under such a scenario, interpreting existing dumping activity under the US administrative review process as indicative of the likelihood that dumping will continue if the anti-dumping duties were terminated (and along with their termination, the termination of the administrative review process) is problematic.

In light of this discussion, we return to our initial observation that a meaningful assessment of the likelihood of continued or renewed dumping requires an understanding of two things: (i) what conditions led to dumping in the first place; and (ii) whether those conditions have changed in a way that removes the original reason for dumping. We have suggested that neither of these two elements appears to play any real role in the USDOC's methodology for determining likelihood, or in the AB's assessment of the legitimacy of the USDOC's methodology. But if the Sunset Review provided for in Art. 11.3 of the AD Agreement is to have meaning, then it must require that a meaningful assessment of the likelihood of continued or renewed dumping is carried out.

It is important to point out that an assessment of the conditions that have led the companies named in an anti-dumping order to dump is not required by Art. 9.1 of the AD Agreement for the original imposition of anti-dumping duties. So our discussion indicates that a different criterion should be applied across Arts. 9.1 and 11.3. But we see no necessary inconsistency in this. While a requirement *could* have been included in the AD Agreement that the particular reasons for dumping must be articulated as a condition for imposing anti-dumping duties under Art. 9.1, there is no logical necessity that such a requirement must be included. By contrast, we argue here that an understanding and articulation of the conditions that led to dumping is *logically necessary* to assess the likelihood of continued or renewed dumping, and therefore is an implied condition for extending definitive anti-dumping duties beyond the five-year termination date that Art. 11.3 otherwise dictates.

Thus we suggest that, while Art. 9.1 permits the imposition of anti-dumping duties without any assessment of the conditions that have led the companies named in the anti-dumping order to dump, the fundamental logic of Art. 11.3 indicates that an assessment of the conditions that led to dumping – and an evaluation that these conditions have not now changed – must be provided if a member government wishes to extend the definitive anti-dumping duty beyond the five-year termination date that Art. 11.3 otherwise dictates. We suggest that the AB erred in not requiring the United States to provide such an assessment as part of its Sunset Review.

4

United States – Continued Dumping and Subsidy Offset Act of 2000 (WT/DS217/AB/R: DSR 2003:I,375)

HENRIK HORN*

Institute for International Economic Studies, Stockholm University

PETROS C. MAVROIDIS*

Columbia Law School, New York and University of Neuchâtel, Switzerland

1 Introduction

On January 16, 2003, the WTO Appellate Body (AB) issued its report on the appeal by the United States (US) of the Panel decision in *United States – Continued Dumping and Subsidy Offset Act of 2000.*[1] The report concerns the consistency of the *United States Continued Dumping and Subsidy Offset Act* of 2000 (the "CDSOA," or the so-called *Byrd Amendment*) with several WTO provisions. This legislation requests the federal state to distribute proceeds from antidumping and countervailing duties to all US economic operators that have supported a request previously submitted to the *ratione materiae* competent US authority to investigate alleged dumping or subsidization. The appeal was directed against the Panel's finding that the *Byrd* legislation was inconsistent with the US obligations under the WTO *Antidumping Agreement* (AD), and the *Agreement on Subsidies and Countervailing Measures* (SCM). A total of 11 complainants (Australia, Brazil, Canada, Chile, the European Community, India, Indonesia, Japan, Korea, Mexico, and Thailand), and five additional third parties (Argentina,

* We thank Wilfred J. Ethier, Mark Koulen, Jasper-Martijn Wauters, and participants at the ALI conference organized in Geneva on April 12, 2005 for very helpful discussions.

[1] The AB report is WTO Doc. WT/DS217/AB/R and 234/AB/R.

Costa Rica, Hong Kong (China), Israel, and Norway), evidence the interest among WTO Members in the issues at stake in the dispute.

The subject matter of the dispute was not the application of the *Byrd* legislation in a particular instance, but the legislation as such, irrespective of any application. The AB dealt with two substantive issues:

1. To what extent does the *Byrd Amendment* constitute a specific action against dumping, impermissible under Arts. 18.1 AD and 32.1 SCM?
2. To what extent does the United States, by transferring duty payments made by exporters to the market to domestic firms, comply with the obligations under Arts. 5.4 AD and 11.4 SCM?

The AB, partially accepting the Panel's findings under Art. 18.1 AD, condemned the *Byrd Amendment* for being an offset payment that is neither a definitive antidumping duty, nor a provisional measure or a price undertaking. Since according to the AB, only these three forms of duties are permissible as specific action against dumping under the WTO AD Agreement, and since the *Byrd Amendment* is a measure to this effect, the AB concluded that the legislation violates US obligations under Art. 18.1 AD. Applying an identical rationale, the AB found that the *Byrd Amendment* also contravenes the SCM since, when used against subsidies, it counteracts subsidization in a different manner than what is permitted under the SCM. But the AB reversed the Panel's findings that the contested legislation violates Arts. 5.4 AD and 11.4 SCM by rendering the prescribed test of the support for an antidumping application meaningless. Neither did the AB accept the argument that the United States had acted in bad faith by enacting legislation that (in the Panel's view) is biased in favor of artificially supporting petitions to investigate. Having found that the United States was partially acting inconsistently with their obligations, the AB recommended that the United States bring its measures into compliance with its obligations.

In Sections 2 and 3 we summarize and discuss the adjudicating bodies', and in particular the AB's, analysis of the two main issues mentioned above.[2] Section 4 examines possible alternative legal bases

[2] We concentrate on the substantive issues raised before the AB. The AB also dealt with some procedural issues, most of which concerned the question whether some claims were properly before it or not (plus, an issue regarding submission of new evidence).

for attacking the *Byrd* legislation. Section 5 briefly summarizes our main findings.

2 Does the *Byrd Amendment* violate Arts. 18.1 AD and 32.1 SCM?

Article 18.1 AD reads:

> No specific action against dumping of exports from another Member can be taken except in accordance with the provisions of GATT 1994, as interpreted by this Agreement.

To this sentence a footnote is added:

> This is not intended to preclude action under other relevant provisions of the GATT 1994, as appropriate.

Article 32.1 SCM contains an equivalent provision in the context of subsidies.

The adjudicating bodies address three requirements in Art. 18.1 AD: whether the *Byrd Amendment* is a "specific" action (see Section 2.1), whether it acts "against" dumping (Section 2.2), and if it is a specific action against dumping, whether it is nevertheless lawful, being "in accordance with the provisions of GATT 1994" (Section 2.3).

2.1 Adjudicating bodies' interpretation of "specific"

The AB summarizes the Panel's reasoning as follows (§§227–228 of the AB report):

> Having decided that our ruling in *US – 1916 Act* was not dispositive of the issues in the present case, the Panel developed the following standard to determine whether a measure is a specific action against dumping or a subsidy: a measure will constitute specific action against dumping or a subsidy if: (1) it acts "specifically" in response to dumping or a subsidy, in the sense that the measure may be taken *only* in situations presenting the constituent elements of dumping or a subsidy; and (2) it acts "against" dumping or a subsidy, in the sense that the measure has an *adverse bearing* on the practice of dumping or on the practice of subsidization. (italics in the original, footnote omitted)
>
> Applying this standard to the CDSOA, the Panel, as a preliminary matter, determined that the CDSOA is a "specific action related to" dumping or a subsidy. According to the Panel, the CDSOA meets the first condition of the standard because CDSOA payments may be made

> *only* in situations where the constituent elements of dumping (or of a subsidy) are present. The Panel also pointed out that CDSOA offset payments follow automatically from the collection of anti-dumping (or countervailing) duties, which in turn may be collected only following the imposition of anti-dumping (or countervailing duty) orders, which in turn may be imposed only following a determination of dumping (or subsidization). The Panel thus determined that the CDSOA is a specific action related to dumping (or subsidization) because there is a "clear, direct and unavoidable connection" between the determination of dumping (or subsidization) and CDSOA offset payments.

The AB concurs with the Panel's finding:

> In our view, the Panel was correct in finding that the CDSOA is a specific action related to dumping or a subsidy within the meaning of Article 18.1 of the *Anti-Dumping Agreement* and Article 32.1 of the *SCM Agreement.* It is clear from the text of the CDSOA, in particular from Section 754(a) of the Tariff Act, that the CDSOA offset payments are inextricably linked to, and strongly correlated with, a determination of dumping, as defined in Article VI:1 of the GATT 1994 and in the *Anti-Dumping Agreement,* or a determination of a subsidy, as defined in the *SCM Agreement.* The language of the CDSOA is unequivocal. *First,* CDSOA offset payments can be made *only* if anti-dumping duties or countervailing duties have been collected. *Second,* such duties can be collected *only* pursuant to an anti-dumping duty order or countervailing duty order. *Third,* an anti-dumping duty order can be imposed *only* following a determination of dumping, as defined in Article VI:1 of the GATT 1994 and in the *Anti-Dumping Agreement. Fourth,* a countervailing duty order can be imposed only following a determination that exports have been subsidized, according to the definition of a subsidy in the *SCM Agreement.* In the light of the above elements, we agree with the Panel that "there is a clear, direct and unavoidable connection between the determination of dumping and CDSOA offset payments", and we believe the same to be true for subsidization. In other words, it seems to us unassailable that CDSOA offset payments can be made only following a determination that the constituent elements of dumping or subsidization are present. Therefore, consistent with the test established in *US – 1916 Act,* we find that the CDSOA is "specific action" related to dumping or a subsidy within the meaning of Article 18.1 of the *Anti-Dumping Agreement* and of Article 32.1 of the *SCM Agreement.*
>
> (§242, italics in the original, footnote omitted)

2.2 *Adjudicating bodies' interpretation of "against"*

The second issue to be resolved is whether the *Byrd Amendment* is not only "related" to dumping, but acts "against" dumping. The AB distils the view of the Panel as follows:

> ... the Panel affirmed that Article 18.1 of the *Anti-Dumping Agreement* (and Article 32.1 of the *SCM Agreement*) concerns measures that act against dumping as a practice (or subsidization as a practice), and do not require that the measure at issue must act against the imported dumped (or subsidized) product, or entities connected to, or responsible for, the dumped (or subsidized) product, such as the importer, exporter, or foreign producer. The Panel added that the term "against" in Article 18.1 of the *Anti-Dumping Agreement* and Article 32.1 of the *SCM Agreement* encompasses measures having a direct, as well as indirect, adverse bearing on the practice of dumping (or subsidization).
>
> Two considerations led the Panel to find that the CDSOA operates "against" dumping (or a subsidy), in the sense that it has an adverse bearing on dumping (or a subsidy). First, according to the Panel, the CDSOA acts against dumping (or a subsidy) by conferring on affected domestic producers, which incur qualifying expenses, an offset payment subsidy that would allow them to establish a competitive advantage over dumped (or subsidized) imports. Second, the Panel was of the view that the CDSOA has an adverse bearing on dumping (or a subsidy) because it provides a financial incentive for domestic producers to file anti-dumping (or countervail) applications, or at least to support such applications, in order to establish their eligibility for offset payments.
>
> (§229–230, italics in the original, underlining added, footnote omitted)

Concerning the consequence of the legislation that the Panel emphasizes – the direct effect on competitive conditions – the AB states the following:

> We note that the United States challenges what it views as the Panel's incorporation of a "conditions of competition test" in Article 18.1 of the *Anti-Dumping Agreement* and in Article 32.1 of the *SCM Agreement.* In our view, in order to determine whether the CDSOA is "against" dumping or subsidization, it was not necessary, nor relevant, for the Panel to examine the conditions of competition under which domestic products and dumped/subsidized imports compete, and to assess the impact of the measure on the competitive relationship between them. An analysis of the term 'against', in our view, is more appropriately centred on the design and structure of the measure; such an analysis does not

> mandate an economic assessment of the implications of the measure on the conditions of competition under which domestic product and dumped/subsidized imports compete.
>
> (§257 of the report, op. cit., italics in the original, underlining added, footnote omitted)

We are not entirely certain whether this is a dismissal of the US' argument that the Panel is effectively undertaking a "conditions of competition test," or whether it is to say that the Panel overdid it, by making such a test. The conclusion is in any event the same: no such test is needed.

The AB firmly rejects the Panel's second argument for why the *Byrd Amendment* violates Arts. 18.1 AD and 32.1 SCM – that it provides the domestic industry with a financial incentive to submit antidumping petitions. In the AB's view, an incitation to act upon one's right is as such not a violation:

> . . . the finding of the Panel that the CDSOA is a measure against dumping or a subsidy is also based on the view that the CDSOA provides a financial incentive for domestic producers to file or support applications for the initiation of anti-dumping and countervailing duty investigations, and that such an incentive will likely result in a greater number of applications, investigations and orders. We agree with the United States that this consideration is not a proper basis for a finding that the CDSOA is "against" dumping or a subsidy; a measure cannot be against dumping or a subsidy simply because it facilitates or induces the exercise of rights that are WTO-consistent. The Panel's reasoning would give Article 18.1 of the *Anti-Dumping Agreement* and Article 32.1 of the *SCM Agreement* a scope of application that is overly broad. For example, the Panel's reasoning would imply that a legal aid program destined to support domestic small-size producers in anti-dumping or countervailing duty investigations should be considered a measure against dumping or a subsidy within the meaning of Article 18.1 of the *Anti-Dumping Agreement* and of Article 32.1 of the *SCM Agreement*, because it could be argued that such legal aid is a financial incentive likely to result in a greater number or applications, investigations and orders.
>
> (§258, italics in original, underlining added, footnote omitted)

So why, then, does the *Byrd Amendment* violate Arts. 18.1 AD and 32.1 SCM according to the AB? The central passage in the report reads:

> Recalling the other two elements of the definition of "against" from the *New Shorter Oxford Dictionary* relied upon by the United States,

namely "of motion or action in opposition" and "in hostility or active opposition to", to determine whether a measure is "against" dumping or a subsidy, we believe it is necessary to assess whether the design and structure of a measure is such that the measure is "opposed to", has an adverse bearing on, or, more specifically, has the effect of dissuading the practice of dumping or the practice of subsidization, or creates an incentive to terminate such practices. In our view, the CDSOA has exactly those effects because of its design and structure.

The CDSOA effects a transfer of financial resources from the producers/exporters of dumped or subsidized goods to their domestic competitors ... there is no statutory or regulatory requirement as to how a CDSOA offset payment to an affected domestic producer is to be spent, thus indicating that the recipients of CDSOA offset payments are entitled to use this money to bolster their competitive position *vis-à-vis* their competitors, including the foreign competitors subject to anti-dumping or countervailing duties.

All these elements lead us to conclude that the CDSOA has an adverse bearing on the foreign producers/exporters in that the imports into the United States of the dumped or subsidized products (besides being subject to anti-dumping or countervailing duties) result in the financing of United States competitors—producers of like products—through the transfer to the latter of the duties collected on those exports. Thus, foreign producers/exporters have an incentive not to engage in the practice of exporting dumped or subsidized products or to terminate such practices. Because the CDSOA has an adverse bearing on, and, more specifically, is designed and structured so that it dissuades the practice of dumping or the practice of subsidization, and because it creates an incentive to terminate such practices, the CDSOA is undoubtedly an action "against" dumping or a subsidy, within the meaning of Article 18.1 of the *Anti-Dumping Agreement* and of Article 32.1 of the *SCM Agreement.*"

(§§254–256, italics in the original, underlining added, footnotes omitted)

2.3 The AB's interpretation of whether the legislation is "in accordance with the provisions of GATT 1994"

Having found that the *Byrd Amendment* is a specific action against dumping, the remaining question the AB addresses is whether it is "in accordance with the provisions of GATT 1994." The AB here finds that, for the *Byrd Amendment* payments to be legal, they have to belong to one of the categories of measures mentioned in Art. VI.2 GATT; they must hence take the form of either definitive antidumping duties, or provisional measures, or price undertakings. Since the *Byrd* payments do not fall under any of these three categories, they are illegal (a similar, but somewhat more involved reasoning is undertaken for the case of subsidies).[3]

2.4 Discussion

As mentioned above, the Panel found two reasons why the *Byrd* payments act "against" dumping in violation of Art. 18.1: one was that potential dumpers would choose to dump less in order to prevent the competitiveness of US firms being enhanced – what we for ease of exposition, will refer to as the *competitiveness effect* – and the other that exporters would dump less since the payments would encourage more antidumping filings, and support for such filings – to be denoted the *filings effect*. The AB hence accepts the Panel's reasoning concerning the competitiveness effect, but rejects the argument built on the filings effect.

In the following discussion, we make several claims. *First*, the AB treats in an incoherent manner the legal issues surrounding the two effects of the *Byrd* legislation that, in the Panel's view, violate Art. 18.1 AD. In particular, had the AB applied to the competitiveness-effect argument the same type of reasoning that it applied to the filings-effect argument, it would then have rightly found the contested legislation to be perfectly consistent with US obligations under the WTO, as we conclude in Section 2.4.1 of this Chapter, below. *Second*, the AB's treatment of the competitiveness-effect argument is deficient, as shown below in Section 2.4.2: the AB does not make clear what is required for an economic theory to strike down legislation; it makes claims concerning economic effects without performing an economic analysis; moreover, its economic theory itself is questionable. Finally, the AB *de facto* does not employ its own judge-made standard of review to strike down the legislation, which it has employed in previous cases when faced with claims concerning legislation's inconsistency with the WTO. Consequently, the AB (as well as the Panel) strikes down the *Byrd Amendment* on flimsy grounds, as we discuss in Section 2.4.3. Additionally, in the same Section, we go through the negotiating

[3] The same reasoning applies *mutatis mutandis* for the AB's findings in the context of the SCM. In the remaining part of this chapter, we will discuss only the AB's findings with respect to claims under the AD Agreement. Its findings are, in principle, identical with respect to claims under the SCM. We will refer to the latter only when necessary to explain issues that are specific to this Agreement.

history to show that one can legitimately inquire into the actual *ratio legis* of Art. 18.1 AD, since its legislative intent is far from clear.

2.4.1 The AB's incoherent treatment of dissuasive effects

Consider first the AB's treatment of the Panel's *competitiveness-effect* argument. The AB accepts the claimed economic relationship; we will discuss *infra* its rationale for doing this. The AB then argues that the *Byrd Amendment* is WTO-inconsistent, since it has the aforementioned alleged dissuasive effect on dumping, and this effect does not stem from one of the three instruments allowed under Art. VI GATT to dissuade dumping. This reasoning is also employed in the AB's discussion of whether the intent behind the legislation matters. On this score, the AB states:

> . . . The text of the CDSOA provides sufficient information on the structure and design of the CDSOA, that is to say, on the manner in which it operates, to permit an analysis whether the measure is "against" dumping or a subsidy. Specifically, the text of the CDSOA establishes clearly that, by virtue of that statute, a transfer of financial resources is effected from the producers/exporters of dumped or subsidized goods to their domestic competitors. This essential feature of the CDSOA constitutes, in itself, the decisive basis for concluding that the CDSOA is "against" dumping or a subsidy—because it creates the "opposition" to dumping or subsidization, such that it dissuades such practices, or creates an incentive to terminate them.
>
> (§259, underlining added, footnote omitted)

That is, it suffices that the measure dissuades dumping for it to be "against" dumping.

Now, we turn to the AB's view on the *filings-effect* argument. It is not clear to us whether the AB accepts the view that, as a matter of economic implications, the *Byrd* scheme actually reduces the number of filings, and the support for filings. When later discussing the alleged violation of Art. 5.4 AD, the AB seems to accept a US claim that there are no such effects, partly since filings would typically be supported anyway. On the other hand, when discussing the filings effect, the AB does not question the existence of the effect; if the AB had found it entirely implausible, it would presumably have added this argument to its objection against the Panel's acceptance of the filings-effect argument. However, from the point of view of this discussion it does not matter whether the AB believes in this effect or not, since the reason for rejecting the Panel's ruling is different: in its view, it does not matter whether there is a filings effect on dumping since

> a measure cannot be against dumping or a subsidy simply because it facilitates or induces the exercise of rights that are WTO-consistent. The Panel's reasoning would give Article 18.1 of the *Anti-Dumping Agreement* and Article 32.1 of the *SCM Agreement* a scope of application that is overly broad . . .
>
> (§258)

These lines, together with the example of legal aid (see below), are the *whole* explanation offered by the AB for the finding that the filings effect does not make the *Byrd* legislation illegal. Partly due to the marked terseness of this explanation, we must admit having severe difficulties understanding exactly what the AB means here.

First, a "textual" reading of this statement gives rise to several questions. For instance, the statement refers to "rights that are WTO-consistent." Does this mean that in the set of rights that the AB is discussing here, there are those that are WTO-*in*consistent? And who has argued that the *Byrd* legislation is illegal by facilitating WTO-consistent rights, as the quote seems to suggest? These questions may perhaps arise due to unfortunate drafting. But it definitely seems odd to us that a court that normally puts heavy emphasis on the "ordinary meaning of words," interprets the term "against" such that a measure need not be "against" dumping even though it is specifically designed to dissuade dumping, and also has this effect. For some unknown reason, the AB here decides not to adhere to its principle of relying on the "ordinary-meaning-of-the-words" interpretation.

Second, and more importantly, we do not understand why the AB does not apply the same type of test to the competitiveness effect that it uses to exonerate the filings effect. It indeed seems to us that such an argument could be as applicable in the context of the competitiveness effect: just as Members have the right to facilitate the filings of anti-dumping petitions under the WTO Agreement, they have *the right to subsidize domestic firms*. The *Byrd Amendment* can be seen as a vehicle for facilitating the exercise of this right, by providing a scheme for the distribution of funds. Of course, such subsidization is possibly actionable, but it is not illegal when measured against the background of the current SCM. It follows that there is no fundamental difference from the point of view of Art. 18.1 AD between the two sources of illegality found by the Panel. Just as the filings effect was exonerated under

Art. 18.1 AD, since it facilitates the exercise of WTO-consistent rights, so should the competitiveness implication of the legislation be exonerated, *removing the sole basis for the AB to strike down the Byrd legislation.*

Note that we are not arguing that it is necessarily unwarranted to treat the two alleged effects of the legislation differently in general. What we claim is that the AB has not convincingly explained why this should be done.

Third, as mentioned above, the AB uses a hypothetical program that provides legal aid to smaller firms for filing antidumping petitions, as an example to demonstrate the unreasonableness of using the filings effect as a basis to declare the *Byrd* legislation illegal. As quoted earlier:

> . . . the Panel's reasoning would imply that a legal aid program destined to support domestic small-size producers in anti-dumping or countervailing duty investigations should be considered a measure against dumping or a subsidy within the meaning of Article 18.1 of the *Anti-Dumping Agreement* and of Article 32.1 of the *SCM Agreement*, because it could be argued that such legal aid is a financial incentive likely to result in a greater number or applications, investigations and orders.
>
> (§258, italics in original)

As can be seen, the AB does not explicitly state that a prohibition of such a hypothetical program would be an undesirable outcome, but we take this to be implicit in the statement quoted above. Now, we agree with the AB that it seems plausible that such a program would make import competing firms more willing to request anti-dumping measures, and that it would thus have a dissuasive filings effect, like that of the *Byrd* legislation. But it also seems likely that this legal aid program will give rise to a *competitiveness effect.* For instance, some of these firms will presumably file petitions regardless of such an aid program; but because of income flowing from the legal aid program, they can use the financial resources that they would have spent on lawyers to invest and thus enhance their competitiveness. As far as we can see, this line of reasoning is almost identical to the argumentation in the case of the *Byrd payments.* Hence, for exactly the same reason that the AB finds the latter illegal due to the competitiveness effect, it should find *the legal aid program illegal as well.*

2.4.2 The evidence for the existence of the competitiveness effect

The AB's finding of an illegality is based on a claim that the *Byrd* legislation impacts on the incentives to dump. Central to the dispute should therefore be the *evidence* before the AB that led it to strike down the legislation. In our view, the AB's treatment leaves a lot to be desired in this respect.

2.4.2.1 No discussion of what should be required for an economic theory to strike down legislation A distinguishing feature of the dispute is the fact that the AB's (as well as the Panel's) finding is not based on any empirical verification. Instead, the AB's whole case rests on an *economic theory*. The theory essentially goes as follows: recipients of *Byrd* payments are allowed to use these payments to become more competitive in the marketplace, and, as a result, exporters have incentives to dump less:

> ... the recipients of CDSOA offset payments are entitled to use this money to bolster their competitive position *vis-à-vis* their competitors...
>
> (§255, underlining added)
>
> ... foreign producers/exporters have an incentive not to engage in the practice of exporting dumped or subsidized products or to terminate such practices...
>
> (§256, underlining added)

A fundamental conceptual issue that this raises is the question of what should be required of such an economic theory in order for it to serve as an appropriate basis for a finding of an illegality, in particular when striking down legislation as such. One can easily see that there are a number of important aspects involved. For instance, what *degree of certainty* should an adjudicating body have that the alleged effect will arise in some particular industry? How plausible should the theory be as a description of this industry? Another type of question is: to what extent does the alleged effect have to arise *across industries* in order for a finding of an illegality? This question seems especially pertinent in light of the fact that the issue at stake is legislation, and not only specific applications of legislation. The AB has, in its own case law when distinguishing between mandatory and discretionary legislation, established the principle that, for legislation to be illegal as such, it must systematically require authorities to implement WTO-inconsistent measures. For the *Byrd* legislation to be condemned with this principle being respected, it must hence first be established that the *Byrd* legislation is mandatory, in the sense that the *ratione materiae competent US authority* has no discretion and must make the payments whenever the legislation's statutes are fulfilled, a position which seems reasonable. The second part is much more questionable, however: the AB must maintain that its theory is descriptive of the effect of the legislation *across industries.* As will be argued below, there are good reasons to believe that this is highly unlikely to be the case.

We thus find the AB report wanting in its failure to discuss this basic question of what should be required in order for an alleged, but empirically unverified, theory to strike down legislation.

2.4.2.2 The AB advances an economic theory but no economic analysis The AB's theory is clearly a statement about the effect of the contested legislation on the *conditions of competition.* At the same time, the AB dismisses the need for an analysis of the conditions of competition. To repeat:

> In our view, in order to determine whether the CDSOA is 'against' dumping or subsidization, it was not necessary, nor relevant, for the Panel to examine the conditions of competition under which domestic products and dumped/subsidized imports compete, and to assess the impact of the measure on the competitive relationship between them...
>
> (§257)

How does the AB then determine the economic effects of the legislation without undertaking an economic analysis? The AB here uses a type of language it has employed in the context of Art. III GATT disputes:

> ... An analysis of the term 'against', in our view, is more appropriately centred on the design and structure of the measure; such an analysis does not mandate an economic assessment of the implications of the measure on the conditions of competition under which domestic product and dumped/subsidized imports compete.
>
> (§257, underlining added)

The central concept of "design and structure" is given some precision in §259, according to which

> ... [t]he text of the CDSOA provides sufficient information on the structure and design of the CDSOA, that is to say, on the manner in which it operates ... (underlining added)

Despite this reference to the revealing "structure and design" of the legislation, we simply fail to understand how an economic analysis of the competitive effects of the legislation can be avoided, when these effects are determined to be crucial to its illegality. Indeed, the AB actually undertakes a very brief economic analysis itself, after having dismissed the need for the Panel to do this, when it claims that the transfer of financial resources will have a certain impact on pricing decisions by exporters. It might perhaps be claimed that the economic effects of the legislation are so obvious that there is no need for an analysis. But this does not seem to be the position of the AB (even though we are uncertain about this). Instead, our reading is that there is some more fundamental reason why the "design and structure" of the legislation directly reveals to the AB its economic effects, but we do not understand what this is.

As a matter of fact, we do not understand the point of looking at the design and structure at all. The AB writes that:

> ...we believe it is necessary to assess whether the design and structure of a measure is such that the measure is "opposed to", has an adverse bearing on, or, more specifically, has the effect of dissuading the practice of dumping...
>
> (§254, underlining added)

But why should one look at something as vague as the "design and structure" in order to assess whether the measure has certain effects? Why not look directly at the *effects of the measure*? We do not think that this is just a play with words. The AB somehow (and we do not understand why) seems to feel that, by concentrating on the "design and structure" of the measure, it can make a shortcut in the determination of the *effects* of the measure, thus avoiding having to undertake a more traditional economic analysis.

2.4.2.3 The AB's economic theory is questionable As pointed out above, we do not know what criteria the AB believes should be fulfilled in order to strike down legislation, nor do we know how the AB views the degree of generality of the competitiveness effect argument. All we know is that this argument suffices, in the AB's view. One possibility is that, in the AB's view, for the legislation to be illegal, it suffices that the alleged effect arises in *certain* markets. In this case, the AB's economic theory may be reduced to a weak statement:

> "It is *not completely unlikely* (or it is likely) that the competitiveness effect is at play against *some* potential dumper in the US market."

If this is the correct interpretation of the AB's position, we can conclude that its economic theory seems acceptable without much further reasoning, since the competitiveness effect reasoning seems sufficiently plausible to arise at least somewhere. The problem with this interpretation is, however, that it relies on an extremely weak criterion to strike down the legislation.[4]

Another possibility might be that the AB believes that its theory is much more general. For instance, it might implicitly be concluding that:

> "The competitiveness effect describes the *typical* (or average) reaction by potential dumpers in the US market."

If this is the AB's position, the lack of economic analysis is much more troublesome. In our view, there are then good reasons to believe that the claim is factually incorrect. At the very least, it is sufficiently questionable to need some serious justification, as we will show below. To simplify matters, we will discuss the theory's two parts separately, even though a more satisfactory analysis would take account of the interaction between the two.

Will the legislation lead to enhanced competitiveness of domestic firms? Central to any reasonable economic analysis of the legislation's effect would be the link domestic firms perceive between their actions and the payments. If payments are seen by these firms as windfall gains, that is, as effectively unrelated to their actions in their respective markets (but of course depending on their expressed support for AD investigations, as required by the legislation), standard economic reasoning would suggest that they have *no* effect on the competitiveness of domestic firms. The payments would then only increase firms' financial wealth, without affecting their profit-maximizing decisions with regard to pricing or investment, the argument roughly being that the latter depend on demand and production cost conditions, and not on the financial wealth of the firm.[5] On the other hand, if firms perceive that the magnitude of the payments received are related to their pricing and investment decisions, the existence of the payment scheme may impact on domestic firms' behavior and thus their behavior *vis-à-vis* foreign competitors.

[4] And, as will be shown *infra*, it also runs afoul of the AB case law on this score.

[5] Grossman and Mavroidis (2004) argue that the AB made a crucial mistake in the *US – Lead Bismuth II* dispute by failing to appreciate a very similar type of distinction.

One would also want to know the likely *magnitude* of any such effects. In order for the legislation to affect the investment and pricing decisions of domestic firms, those firms must believe that these decisions affect the amount of payments they will eventually receive. However, it seems plausible that such links must often be seen as very weak. To start with, whenever an individual domestic firm has a limited market share, the impact of its decisions on the funds eventually to be distributed is likely to be very small. There is also likely to be considerable uncertainty concerning the payments it will receive. The payments will be affected by how the legislation affects dumping decisions by foreign firms (since this will affect the amount of money being available for redistribution), as well as the decisions of other domestic firms (since this will affect claims for the available money). Without pretending to have undertaken a satisfactory economic analysis, we note that these observations suggest that the legislation should often be expected to have negligible impact on pricing and investment decisions.

Despite being central to an economic analysis of the impact of the legislation, how domestic firms view the link between their competitiveness-related decisions and the payments receives very little discussion by the AB. The AB points out that the "qualifying expenditures" for which the *Byrd payments* are made must, according to the US legislation,

> ... be related to the production of the same product that is the subject of the related order or finding...
>
> (§255, underlining added)

But there is no discussion of the nature of the requirement that expenditures must "be related to the production." The AB also points to the related aspect of the payments that, once received, firms are allowed to use the payments in whatever fashion they want. But while related, the question of what can be done with the payments once received is not the same as the question of what it takes to receive the payments in the first place. If anything, the fact that firms are free to do whatever they wish with the payments, suggests that the payments will *not* affect the market behavior of domestic firms: if investments into enhanced competitiveness are profitable, why would firms wait for the payments to undertake them? And to the extent that the dumping allegations occur in industries that are no longer internationally competitive, shouldn't one expect that firms in such industries may find it more profitable to invest outside the industry, in which case the payments would actually foster exit from the industry? If so, the legislation would presumably tend to serve as an *encouragement* to dumping, rather than the opposite.

Will the possible enhanced competitiveness of domestic firms induce less dumping? Let us now, for the sake of the argument, accept the first part of the competitiveness effect theory – the idea that the *Byrd* legislation will serve to enhance domestic firms' competitiveness – and consider its second part – the notion that the enhancement of the competitiveness of domestic firms induces exporters to dump less. It is here natural to distinguish between two types of potential effects resulting from the legislation.

First, in their pricing decisions, exporters must trade off gains from lower prices against the increased likelihood of triggering antidumping procedures. The immediate impact of the legislation on this balancing act seems likely to be similar to that which is suggested by the competitiveness effect claim: that the prospect of facing, on top of the antidumping duty, enhanced competitiveness among domestic firms, should tend to act as an extra inducement not to dump.

Again, the magnitude of this effect may be limited if there are several or more exporters. Each exporter would realize that, while the magnitude of the antidumping duties it may trigger is determined fully by its dumping margin, the link between its dumping margin and the enhanced competitiveness of domestic firms is likely to be much weaker. Also, the enhanced competitiveness will tend to affect all the exporters equally, which provides another reason why the competitiveness effect is likely to have a limited magnitude.

The effect just described builds on the impact of the *threat* of *Byrd* payments. But suppose that this effect is not sufficiently strong to entirely deter dumping, so that some payments will *actually occur*. What will be the effect of this? According to the AB's theory, firms will invest these payments in order to enhance their competitiveness, which would be reflected in a lowering of prices by domestic firms. The natural response of exporters would then be to also cut prices, in order to meet this intensified competition. However, if exporters cut their prices, they tend to dump *more*, and not less, as maintained by the AB. It hence seems necessary to distinguish between the effects of the legislation when it deters dumping, from its effects when it does not suffice to deter dumping. Differently put, the legislation as such seems to dissuade dumping, while its application has the opposite effect.

Conclusion concerning the AB's economic theory The point here is not to argue that it would be impossible to construct an economically reasonable argument why the payments may be used to enhance the competitiveness of domestic firms. Throwing the right ingredients into the brew (such as an imperfectly working capital market and limited access to outside investment opportunities), one could indeed construct such arguments.[6] Given the size of the toolbox of present day economics, it is possible to construct a theoretically unobjectionable argument to show just about *anything*, so something more is needed in order for a theory to be of practical interest: it requires arguments for why the theory is a *plausible* description. Nor do we maintain that the AB's conclusion that the overall effect is to discourage dumping is wrong – this we simply do not know. Instead, we believe that the links between transfer payments and intensified competition, as well as between intensified competition and disincentives to dump, are much more complex than what seems to be acknowledged by the AB. There are also reasons to suspect that there are other economic implications of the legislation that the AB neglects.[7] Just a scratching of the economic surface of the *Byrd legislation* suggests to us that the AB's argument is highly questionable, if meant to represent "typical" implications of the contested legislation, or at the very least, needs significant support in terms of economic analysis. We therefore find it remarkable that the AB explicitly states that an economic analysis is not necessary at the same time that it makes its pronouncement on the effect of the legislation on competitive conditions. We believe that the AB in this central respect applied too low a standard of review.

[6] A different line of defense of the claimed competitiveness effect would be to argue that it is not really the competitiveness of firms that is enhanced, but rather the depth of their financial pockets, and that with the payment they can escape bankruptcy. This might plausibly be the case in certain circumstances. But it begs the question as to why the firms do not use the financial resources to invest in more profitable activities than those in the industry.

[7] For instance, as argued by Collie and Vandenbussche (2004), an essential aspect of the *Byrd* legislation is that it is likely to give a larger weight to tariff revenue in the government's duty determination, since the revenue now accrues to the lobbying industry, rather than the general taxpayer. Consequently, it may induce the government to use the leeway it has in determining the level of AD duties, to increase these as a result of the legislation. This raises the intricate question of whether the adjudicating bodies should take into account such effects. (The effects referred to here differ from those affecting the willingness of firms to file and support AD complaints that the AB dismissed as a basis for a finding of an illegality, arguing that the United States was in this respect only exercising its lawful rights.)

2.4.2.4 The AB violates its own standard for striking down legislation We attempted to demonstrate above that the competitiveness effect, as argued by the AB, cannot lightly be assumed to be the typical effect of *Byrd* payments. We should recall, however, that the legal challenge in the instant case is against legislation and not an application thereof. According to the standing case law, for an article of legislation to the be deemed to be WTO-inconsistent, it must *be shown* to *consistently* yield WTO-inconsistent outcomes. This has not been the case with respect to the *Byrd* legislation.

This discussion has, of course, to do with the distinction between mandatory/discretionary legislation and to what extent the latter can be properly challenged before a WTO adjudicating body. The earlier case law suggested that this was not the case. The subsequent case law has led to misunderstandings in the literature as to what the appropriate standard in similar cases actually is. We will try to briefly review the more recent case law and show that it should not be understood to condone a finding of illegality in cases where, as in the instant case, a piece of legislation *only in certain circumstances* could lead to a behavior inconsistent with the WTO.

In its *US – Section 211 Appropriations Act* opinion,[8] the AB distanced itself from the manner in which the Panel before it had applied the distinction between mandatory and discretionary legislation. In the AB's view this was a functional distinction that was not to be applied in a mechanistic fashion. However, the AB stated (§259) that

> ...where discretionary authority [was] vested in the executive branch of a WTO Member, it [could not] be assumed that the WTO Member [would] fail to implement its obligations under the WTO Agreement in good faith...

Its latest pronouncement was made in the *US – Corrosion-Resistant Steel Sunset Review* dispute in which the AB addressed a US practice established in the context of that country's review of the need for a continued imposition of antidumping duties.[9] The AB did state that, in certain circumstances, practices can also be challenged, but not that the mandatory/discretionary legislation is obsolete. The AB argued (§89) that Panels are not

> ...obliged, as a preliminary jurisdictional matter, to examine whether the challenged measure is mandatory...

[8] See WTO Doc. WT/176/AB/R. [9] See WTO Doc. WT/DS244/AB/R.

However, the AB did maintain (§89) that this distinction is fully pertinent when it comes to assessing whether the measure at hand is (or is not) WTO-consistent. In the case at hand, confronted with evidence suggesting that the contested US Bulletin was codifying practice that led to the same (WTO-inconsistent) outcome in dozens of cases (and with no evidence to the contrary), the AB held that the US practice was WTO-inconsistent although the Bulletin in which it was codified was not legally binding on the US administration.

These two cases suggest that non-binding instruments as well can be challenged before the WTO, but they have to predictably lead to WTO-inconsistent results. In other words, the likelihood that an illegality will be committed does not suffice for a piece of legislation to be adjudged WTO-inconsistent.

The most recent pronouncement on this score is evidenced in the panel report *Korea – Commercial Vessels*[10] where the Panel, citing the case law mentioned *supra*, explicitly upheld the distinction between mandatory and discretionary legislation and refuted an argument advanced by the European Community (EC) to the effect that there had been a *revirement de jurisprudence* on this score as a result of the AB jurisprudence in *US – Corrosion-Resistant Steel Sunset Review* (§§7.60 – 7.63).

It follows that in the present case, the AB consequently failed in two respects: one the one hand, it applied a deficient economic analysis to verify whether the *Byrd* payments had the alleged competitiveness effect; on the other, it misapplied its own standard for finding a violation.

2.4.3 Some reasons suggesting a limited intended ambit of Art. 18.1 AD

We have thus far considered the internal consistency of the AB's reasoning, and the evidentiary standard it implicitly applies. We will now turn to a more general interpretation of Art. 18.1 AD, and the question of its intended role in the Agreement. We will here make a few reflections suggesting that the adjudicating bodies may have given the provision an overly wide ambit.

Following its *US – AD Act of 1916* jurisprudence, the AB has understood Art. 18.1 AD to be a self-standing provision: there is no requirement that a Member have violated any one of the obligations

[10] See WTO Doc. WT/DS273/R of 7 March 2005.

embedded in Arts. 2–17 AD, for a violation of Art. 18.1 AD to occur.[11] Indeed, in the present case, the AB even rejects the Panel's findings under Art. 5.4 AD and argues that Art. 18.1 AD can by itself signal the inconsistency of a specific measure with the AD Agreement. In our view, the AB does not provide an adequate motivation for this far-reaching interpretation of Art. 18.1.

It would seem natural, when confronting an alleged violation of Art. 18.1 AD, to start by observing that the interpretation of the provision is far from self-evident. The requirement that Members should not take actions against dumping that are not in accordance with the GATT 1994, seems, at least under a textual reading, superfluous, since *no* actions should be taken in violation of the GATT 1994, regardless of whether addressing dumping or not. The footnote explaining that "[t]his is not intended to preclude action under other relevant provisions of the GATT 1994, as appropriate" is no doubt meant to limit the unclear scope of the requirement in the main text, and as such does not add much precision to the provision, nor does the qualification "as appropriate" add clarity. This is not to say that it is impossible to find a meaning by "reading between the lines." But Art. 18.1 AD is far from being a self-interpreting provision, and its implementation has to take this into account.

Since a purely textual interpretation of Art. 18.1 is difficult, the context, and the object and purpose, must play a prominent role in the interpretation of its ambit. One can here note that the provision is given a rather obscure place in the Agreement: it is put together with some other diverse obligations in a "Final Provisions" article, toward the end of the Agreement. This placement does not seem to suggest that the provision is intended to have a very important role. The provision rather seems to be one of several "leftovers" from the negotiation table.

Turning to the preparatory work that led to the inclusion of the provision, a version of this provision appeared in the original GATT/ITO discussions. Art. IV.7 of the 1947 version of the GATT reads as follows:

> No measures other than anti-dumping or countervailing duties shall be applied by any contracting party in respect of any product of the territory of any other contracting party for the purposes of offsetting dumping or subsidization.

[11] Assuming that there is an overlap between Arts. 1 and 18.1 AD.

This provision seems to underline the idea that dumping should not be dissuaded through other means than AD duties.

As a matter of positive law, however, this provision never saw the light of day, since it was not incorporated in the final Art. VI GATT 1947. Oddly, we find the only expressed understanding for its rationale in a statement justifying its exclusion: The sub-committee dealing with the final draft of the GATT decided to delete the provision, but it

> . . .did so with the definitive understanding that measures other than the compensatory anti-dumping or countervailing duties may not be applied to counteract dumping or subsidization except in so far as such other measures are permitted under other provisions of the Charter.[12]

This passage denotes a rationale for this provision that, to some extent, has been overtaken by the footnote to Art. 18.1 (footnote 24) in the current AD Agreement: in principle, parties should address dumping only through anti-dumping measures, and subsidies only through countervailing duties.

We find the provision in Art. 18.1 AD for the first time in the Tokyo Round AD Agreement (as Art. 16.1), but we have not been able to uncover even a trace of its negotiating history, either in the Tokyo Round,[13] or when it was incorporated into the Uruguay Round AD Agreement. The absence of any meaningful discussion on the rationale for this provision probably indicates a combination of two facts: *first*, that the Tokyo and Uruguay Round negotiators accepted the rationale offered at a previous stage, and, *second*, that the provision was not seen as being very important to the Agreement. It seems that the provision, when read with others (for example, Art. XIX GATT dealing with safeguards action) helped clarify the ambit of permissible action undertaken under contingent protection instruments.

The analysis above suggests that at least two rationales could be advanced as plausible explanations for the advent of Art. 18.1 AD: it could be that negotiators agreed with the original rationale (offered already in the preparatory work from 1947); or, it could be that the

[12] See the Archives, Reports of committees and principal sub-committees, Interim Commission for the ITO, Geneva, September (1948) at p. 74, §25.

[13] Indeed, a series of documents reflecting the negotiating history refers to the provision in terms more or less identical to the final draft terms, without referring at all to the rationale for its inclusion, see GATT Docs. MTN/NTM/W/168 of 10 July 1978, W/208 of 15 December 1978, and W/210 of 19 December 1978.

same provision kept its value in order to address practices that emerged post 1947, and that could not have been anticipated.

A good illustration of what the provision may have aimed at is probably the "anti-circumvention" provision in EC antidumping law. In the GATT years, the EC was condemned for using the anti-circumvention provision in its antidumping legislation to impose duties on finished items (cars), parts and components of which were allegedly dumped: Art. 13.10 of the EC antidumping regulation (2423/88) constituted the subject matter of the litigation and it relevantly provided:

> Definitive anti-dumping duties may be imposed, by way of derogation from the second sentence of paragraph 4(a), on products that are introduced into the commerce of the Community after having been assembled or produced in the Community ...

Such use was deemed necessary by the EC, since, otherwise, it would be left without any weapons to counteract this form of dumping (the EC namely could not satisfy the "likeness" element, as it appears in the injury analysis, since a part of a car and a car are not like products).

During the Panel proceedings in *EEC – Regulation on Imports of Parts and Components* that were requested by Japan, the EC did not advance detailed arguments in defense of its law under Art. VI GATT, but stated that were the panellists to take the view that its provision was consistent with Art. VI GATT, it would not disagree. We quote from the Panel's report:[14]

> The Panel further noted, that the United States, as an interested third party, had argued that Article VI of the General Agreement provided to a certain extent a legal basis for measures to prevent what it considered to be circumvention of anti-dumping duties. At one point in the proceedings the EEC stated that, if the Panel were to find that the anti-circumvention duties were justifiable under Article VI, 'it would not disagree' with such an approach... However, the EEC presented no arguments in support of a justification of its measures under Article VI. (§5.11)

The EC measures were found to be in violation of the GATT anyway (Art. III), without the Panel ever discussing their consistency with Art. VI GATT. This issue was left in limbo. During the Uruguay Round negotiations, negotiators could not agree on this issue and therefore

[14] GATT Doc. BISD 37S/132ff., adopted on 16 May 1990.

referred it to the WTO Anti-Dumping Committee for further deliberations. But no action has been taken on this front since then. As a result, it is still an open question whether anti-circumvention provisions are consistent with Art. VI GATT. However, the fact that a formal decision was taken during the Uruguay Round suggests that, at least on January 1, 1995, anti-circumvention provisions were very much a concern.

To conclude, there are several reasons to suggest that it is far from clear what the rationale behind Art. 18.1 AD actually is. When confronted with so much uncertainty, we would expect the AB to at least pay some attention to the circumstances surrounding the negotiation of this provision, and not, instead, jump to conclusions on its ambit based on an obscure text.

3 Does the *Byrd Amendment* violate Arts. 5.4 AD and 11.4 SCM?

The second issue raised in the appeal is whether the *Byrd Amendment* violates Art. 5.4 AD and the identical provision Art. 11.4 SCM. These provisions regulate the standing requirements for a petition to be examined by a domestic investigating authority entrusted with the administration of antidumping and subsidies/countervailing laws. Article 5.4 AD reads:

> An investigation shall not be initiated pursuant to paragraph 1 unless the authorities have determined, on the basis of an examination of the degree of support for, or opposition to, the application expressed by domestic producers of the like product, that the application has been made by or on behalf of the domestic industry. The application shall be considered to have been made "by or on behalf of the domestic industry" if it is supported by those domestic producers whose collective output constitutes more than 50 per cent of the total production of the like product produced by that portion of the domestic industry expressing either support for or opposition to the application. However, no investigation shall be initiated when domestic producers expressly supporting the application account for less than 25 per cent of total production of the like product produced by the domestic industry (footnote omitted).

3.1 *The divergent views of the panel and the AB*

The AB explains its understanding of the Panel's findings that the *Byrd Amendment* violates Arts. 5.4 AD and 11.4 SCM in the following terms:

> The Panel found that the CDSOA provides a financial incentive for domestic producers to file or support applications for the initiation of anti-dumping or countervailing duty investigations, because offset payments are made only to producers that file or support such applications. According to the Panel, the CDSOA will result in more applications having the required level of support from domestic industry than would have been the case without the CDSOA, and that "given the low costs of supporting a petition, and the strong likelihood that all producers will feel obliged to keep open their eligibility for offset payments for reasons of competitive parity, . . . the majority of petitions will achieve the levels of support required" under Article 5.4 of the *Anti-Dumping Agreement* and Article 11.4 of the *SCM Agreement.*
>
> (§277, italics in original, footnote omitted)

The Panel hence argues that the *Byrd Amendment* violates this provision, by making the quantitative test it requests meaningless.

The AB starts its examination of the Panel's argument by emphasizing that it does not accept the Panel's sole focus on the "object and purpose" of Arts. 5.4 AD and 11.4 SCM. Beginning with a textual analysis, it notes that Arts. 5.4 and 5.11 AD do not require authorities to look at the motives for firms' support for applications (something the Panel would most likely also agree with):

> . . . those provisions require no more than a formal examination of whether a sufficient number of domestic producers have expressed support for an application. . .
>
> (§286)
>
> . . . it is the "quantity", rather than the "quality", of support that is the issue.
>
> (§283)

The AB thus concludes that the text of Arts. 5.4 AD and 11.4 SCM does not support the Panel's reasoning.

Turning to the Panel's discussion on the "object and purpose" of these provisions, the AB dismisses the Panel's finding of an illegality on the basis of four arguments (the relative importance of which is not revealed). The AB argues, *first*, that the *Byrd* payments do

> . . . not change the fact that investigating authorities are required to examine the "degree of support" that exists for an application and that an application shall be considered to have been made "by or on

> behalf of the domestic industry" only if sufficient support has been "expressed"...
>
> (§289)

Hence, the presence or absence of the *Byrd* payments does not change, in the AB's view, the legal nature of the duty bestowed upon the United States to ensure respect of the statutory thresholds. *Second*, when performing this task, investigating authorities are not required by law to enquire into the motives of particular economic operators to support a petition (§291). *Third*, the challenged payments do not necessarily entail coercion to support filings; economic operators are still free to choose whether they will support a petition or abstain from doing so (§293). *Fourth*, empirical evidence from the United States suggests that the *Amendment* has not had the effect of increasing the number of initiations of investigations, since the United States argued that it was rare for domestic producers in the United States not to have sufficient industry support anyway and no counterargument to this proposition was raised. On the basis of these observations, the AB reverses the Panel's determination, and finds that the *Byrd* payments do not violate the "object and purpose" of Arts. 5.4 AD and 11.4 SCM.

The Panel also found that the United States had not acted in good faith, by rendering the substantive provision in Arts. 5.4 AD and 11.4 SCM a mere formality which would always be complied with as a result of the financial incentives provided to US domestic industry to support petitions to impose antidumping or countervailing duties.

The AB rejects this reasoning. It acknowledges the relevance of the good faith principle in the WTO legal order, by pointing to prior jurisprudence which made reference to it (§296). But the AB also maintains that a violation of the good faith principle requires more than a simple demonstration of a violation of a WTO provision (§298), and it concludes, without further explanation, that it does not share the Panel's view that the United States had not acted in good faith.

3.2 Discussion

We agree with the AB that a textual reading does not support a complaint under Art. 5.4 AD or 11.4 SCM. We are less convinced by the analysis of the "object and purpose" and "good faith" argument, however.

Looking at the "structure and design" of the legislation, it is hard to come to any other conclusion than that the *sole* purpose of the *Byrd Amendment*, is to encourage firms to support filings for antidumping investigations. Indeed, this feature importantly contributes to why it is a "specific" action against dumping. But, as far as we can see, the AB somehow sidesteps a direct confrontation with this central aspect of the legislation, in its analysis of how it squares with the "object and purpose" of Arts. 5.4 AD and 11.4 SCM, and in the dismissal of the good faith argument.

It seems reasonable to assume that these provisions were meant to have some practical significance, and in particular, that the specific levels for support that are stipulated in Arts. 5.4 AD and 11.4 SCM presumed that governments did not actively affect the process whereby the support is expressed.[15] Presumably, the support should be "real." It also seems reasonable to assume that the *Byrd* legislation provides a significant incentive to support filings. Consequently, it seems inescapable to conclude that the legislation adversely affects the intention behind Art. 5.4 AD, rendering it a meaningless hurdle against investigations being initiated with very limited industry support.

One natural possibility would thus be to see the *Byrd Amendment* as undermining the "object and purpose" of Art. 5.4, as argued by the Panel. But the AB dismisses this on what we see as flimsy grounds.

First, the argument in §279 that the existence of the *Byrd* legislation does not change the US authorities' duty to examine the degree of support that exists for an application, is hard to understand. The most sense we can make of it is to interpret it as saying that, in practice, the authorities have to change their method of counting the support for an application after the adoption of the contested legislation. Methods that sufficed in its absence are no longer useful in order to reveal whether the "true" support exceeds, for instance, 50%. We would be sympathetic to an argument along these lines, at least as a matter of theory. However, nothing in the AB report suggests that this is what it meant, and we can only understand the AB's argument as a formalistic reply without any clear implication for how the investigation concerning the support for applications should be done in practice.

Second, we also find the argument in §291, that authorities do not have to look into the motives of firms supporting applications,

[15] This conclusion is reinforced by the fact that the AD Agreement provides for the possibility that a WTO Member can *ex officio* initiate an antidumping investigation (see *infra*).

to be quite uninformative. The practical problems with this approach would, of course, be almost insurmountable, as pointed out by the AB. But this does not suffice as an argument to allow the test required under Art. 5.4 AD (and Art. 11.4 SCM) to become a mere formality, without at least acknowledging the problems that the AB encounters in giving it a meaningful interpretation. To our way of thinking, the AB fails to properly account for the context of this legal provision. A WTO Member can, of course, initiate an investigation *ex officio.* Doing so, it does not need any input from the private sector. Since governments have the institutional possibility to act *ex officio,* the "upon-request" route must indeed be the outcome of an autonomous private decision to this effect, and not a government-mandated/influenced decision. We would here have welcomed a discussion of "where to draw the line" in terms of government involvement in the *formation* of private support to a petition. By referring to the irrelevance of motives, the AB closed outright the door to a legal review of what the *bona fide* implementation of Art. 5.4 AD (and Art. 11.4 SCM) actually amounts to.

Third, the AB seems to contest the empirical claim that the *Byrd* legislation induces firms to support more applications, when it maintains that all applications would find support even in its absence. This latter argument is based on the US claim that it is "rare" that support is missing, and that during one particular year (the one before the implementation of the legislation), all applications were supported. This reasoning raises a number of questions. What is "rare" – 5% of cases, 15%, or what percentage of cases? How "rare" is acceptable? How representative was the particular year that the United States refers to? Why does the legislation include a requirement that firms have to have supported filings in order to be eligible for payment, if there is no scope to increase such support? After all, legislators should have realized that this would be a highly contentious aspect of the legislation.

It should also be noted that the US argument sidesteps an important aspect by essentially stating that, *given* that an application is filed, it is typically supported even absent the *Byrd* legislation, and that the legislation consequently does not change the picture at all. But there is presumably a self-selection with regard to applications. If firms know that an application will not find support, they will probably not set it in motion. What the US argument thus fails to account for is how the *Byrd* legislation influences the propensity to *file* applications.

Turning to the "good faith" argument we can only note that the AB does not in *any* way explain its position. It simply states that it does not share the view of the Panel, since a "good faith" argument needs to be based on something more than an illegality. The AB does not specify in any way what (or how much) more is required for such a violation to occur.

To conclude, we believe that Arts. 5.4 AD and 11.4 SCM were inserted to reduce the risk of "abusive" initiations of investigations, since initiations of investigations, irrespective of their final outcomes, can have a negative impact on the exporters. It is clear from the "design and structure" of the *Byrd* legislation that it is meant to influence filings for antidumping petitions, and that it has such an effect. In our view, it is therefore unsatisfactory that the AB did not sufficiently address the Arts. 5.4 AD and 11.4 SCM claim under this prism. Although not a necessity, it seems much more plausible to claim that the typical effect of the legislation is to stimulate filings or support for filings, than to claim that the competitiveness effect argument describes the typical reaction on behalf of potential dumpers.

4 Other possible lines of attack on the *Byrd* legislation

As discussed above, the AB deals with allegations that the *Byrd Amendment* violates Arts. 18.1 AD and 5.4 AD (and the corresponding provisions in the SCM). We will here discuss some other potential lines of attack. Of course, the AB, due to the *non ultra petita* maxim, can respond only to claims made by the parties to the dispute.

First, a natural objection to the legislation seems to be that it provides subsidies to the domestic industry. WTO Members importing from US companies that have benefited from *Byrd* payments could therefore have reacted by imposing countervailing duties (CVDs), provided the other conditions for this imposition were met. But one could possibly also make an argument that the *Byrd* payments, being subsidies, can be counteracted irrespective of whether the beneficiaries sell in the US market or abroad. The requirements in Arts. 1 and 2 SCM concerning the existence of a specific subsidy seem to be met: since money leaves the US budget, and goes to specific companies, the payments are specific. With regard to "benefit," the WTO case law does not demand a sophisticated analysis. Under the so-called "private-investor" test, the WTO case law indicates that the term captures any action mentioned under Art. 1.1 SCM that might even potentially and indirectly affect the decisions by the beneficiaries. Consequently, it is not necessary that the effects of the subsidies in terms of pricing decisions be shown, for a benefit to be deemed conferred. It suffices that the beneficiaries have received something from the government which they would not have received from the market. In the case of the instant dispute, domestic firms received the *Byrd* payments, and the WTO judge had no need, according to case law, to ask how these payments affected exporters.[16] Since the subsidy was not prohibited, it must have been actionable. To our knowledge, only Mexico made the argument concerning subsidization before the Panel, but did not pursue it to its logical conclusion.

There are limits, however, as to how much can be achieved through this legal argument. Assuming the money has been transferred to specific companies, a successful complainant would need to demonstrate adverse effects (Art. 5 SCM) or serious prejudice (Art. 6 SCM) resulting from the payments at hand. In short, the complainant would need to show that as a result of the subsidization, it suffered loss of market share, either in the US or in a third market.

What we have described so far, however, is not a line of attack against the *Byrd* legislation as such, but rather an attack against actual payments. Attacking the *Byrd* legislation as such under the SCM will present potential complainants with a mountain to climb.

To start with, potential complainants would have to satisfy the specificity requirement, since, in principle, *Byrd* payments are generally available. However, payments will be made to companies operating in the same sector where an antidumping investigation will be initiated each time. Hence, an argument can be made that, although payments are generally available, the *intent* of the legislator is to limit, *each time* payments occur, the beneficiaries to a particular sub-set of all potential

[16] Grossman and Mavroidis (2004) argued that the only understanding of the term "benefit" in Art. 1.1 of the SCM that is consistent with what seems to them the aims and objectives of those who drafted the Agreement, is that it must, somehow, affect the competitive conditions of the players in a given market. They view the main objective of the SCM to be to discourage subsidies that threaten harm to competing producers in importing countries. It therefore makes little sense to interpret "benefit" in terms of the financial wealth of the owners of a firm. Rather, the potentially adverse effects of a subsidy on producers in an importing country can be avoided only if a subsidy is deemed to exist whenever a government's financial contribution impacts the *competitive situation* in an industry. But for better or for worse, given the case law understanding of the term "benefit," it is not necessary to consider the effects on competition in order to classify *Byrd* payments as a subsidy in the sense of the SCM.

beneficiaries. Legislative intent is probably the most appropriate criterion to show whether a subsidy is *de facto* specific. On the other hand, there is no guarantee in the *Byrd* legislation that *Byrd* payments will eventually take place. If at all, the only guarantee is that an antidumping investigation will be launched (assuming that the statutory thresholds will always be met as a result of the incentive to support petitions, an assumption unsupported by empirical evidence, as we have already stated above). The "subsidy" that will always be provided is hence the antidumping investigation itself.[17] One could argue that antidumping investigations (even those that do not lead to the imposition of duties) have measurable effects in the market which favor the domestic industry, so a precise legal argument will have to be drafted along these lines.[18] Were, however, this avenue to be privileged, the complainant will have to control for the fact that it will be breaking new ground arguing that the initiation of an antidumping investigation is itself a subsidy since it represents a cost to government which confers an advantage to specific beneficiaries.

A non-violation complaint is a second possibility. The legal argument here would be that, following the change of concessions, an action occurred (*Byrd* legislation) that could not have been reasonably expected and that resulted in nullification and impairment of benefits for the complaining party. The complaining party would have an easy task to demonstrate that the *Byrd Amendment* could not have been reasonably expected: as established in the *Kodak – Fuji* report (WT/DS44/R), in case an action takes place after a concession has been negotiated, there is a presumption that the complainant could not have reasonably anticipated it.[19] The *prima facie* more difficult task would be to show nullification and impairment. One possibility would be for the complainant to demonstrate that its exporters are, because of the *Byrd Amendment*, subjected to a higher number of antidumping investigations than they would be otherwise (in the absence of the legislation). The nullification and impairment would materialize not in the higher number of investigations *per se*, but in the likelihood to face antidumping duties more frequently.

[17] We acknowledge our discussions with Alan Sykes on this issue.

[18] One could also argue that the subsidy is exhausted in the payment, without inquiring into the nexus between the payment as such and its origins in the antidumping investigation.

[19] This opinion was upheld by the AB in its *Asbestos* jurisprudence; see WTO Doc. WT/DS135/AB/R.

A third avenue for attacking the *Byrd* legislation would be to focus on its effect on the competitive position of exporting firms (rather than on their incentives to dump, which is at the core of the Panel's Art. 5.4 AD argument). In the dispute at hand, the AB makes explicit reference to all the interpretative tools referred to in the Vienna Convention on the Law of Treaties (VCLT) and to which it has made reference in all its case law so far: the text, context, object, and purpose of the treaty. Yet, it once again fails to take proper account of the context, which denotes through which *specific means*, the *specific ends* assigned to the *treaty-regime* will be achieved. An alternative way in which the *Byrd Amendment* could be found illegal, would thus put more emphasis on the context of the AD Agreement.[20]

The context of the Agreement is at least the rest of the Agreement, legally speaking. The most important provision to understand the function of the AD Agreement is Art. 3.1 AD (Arts. 5 and 15.1 SCM). There it is clearly stated that WTO Members are allowed to counteract dumping (or subsidies) provided that they demonstrate that their domestic industry producing the like (to the dumped/subsidized) product has suffered injury as a result of dumping (subsidy). The purpose is therefore not to prevent dumping from occurring – had this been the case, it could have been declared illegal as such – but to *allow importing countries to insulate themselves from the effects of dumping.*

How far, then, can a country go in order to insulate itself? The importing country has to establish that material injury has occurred as a result of the dumping. But once this is done, the magnitude of the permissible duty is independent of the magnitude of the injury. Instead, the maximum antidumping duty is the full dumping margin. But, *any worsening of the competitive position of the dumping firm beyond this maximum amount is not permissible under the AD Agreement.*

Consequently, *Byrd* payments would affect the competitive position of exporting firms, for two reasons: *First,* dumping firms would face more severe consequences from their dumping than what is intended under the AD Agreement. Not only would the full dumping margin be offset through the duty, but also, on top of this, the dumping firms would face a deterioration of their competitive position due to the payments. As far as we can see, this "over-punishment" of dumping

[20] The following borrows from Bhagwati and Mavroidis (2004).

firms would be a sufficient ground to declare the *Byrd Amendment* illegal under the AD. Of course, this argument relies on the assumption that the payments *de facto* change the competitive position, which as a matter of economics is far from being a foregone conclusion, as discussed above.

Second, enhanced competitive positions of domestic firms will not only affect dumping exporters, but also *other* exporters to the market, and the detrimental effect on these exporters may possibly serve as a basis for a finding of an illegality under the SCM.

5 Concluding remarks

Our main observations concerning the AB's determination in the *Byrd* legislation dispute have been the following:

First, we believe that the AB is inconsistent in its treatment of the two reasons advanced by the Panel to support its findings that the *Byrd* legislation violates Art. 18.1 (and 32.1 SCM). Had the AB applied the same criterion to the competitiveness effect argument as it applied to the filings effect argument, it would not have found the contested legislation to be WTO inconsistent.

Second, the economic theory that the AB uses for striking down the legislation is inadequately motivated, and it is not clear how general the AB believes the theory to be.

Third, we doubt the validity of the theory, if it is meant to describe the typical impact of the contested litigation across industries.

Fourth, the AB strikes down the legislation as such on much weaker grounds than what it has established as a requirement in its case law.

Fifth, we believe that the AB should have undertaken a more comprehensive discussion of the claims under Art. 5.4 AD (and 11.4 SCM).

Finally, with regard to the outcome of the dispute, we believe that the reasons advanced by the AB do not suffice to establish that the legislation is inconsistent with Art. 18.1 AD (and 32.1 SCM). It seems to us that the question of whether the *Byrd* legislation violates Art. 5.4 AD (and Art. 11.4 SCM) is a more promising avenue for establishing an illegality: the text would give only very limited support for such a finding, but the legislation is likely to have the effect of rendering the test prescribed in these provisions meaningless, and it therefore seems to violate the object and purpose of the provision.

Post scriptum

Remarkably, a more recent Panel (*European Communities – Measures affecting trade in commercial vessels*, WTO Doc. WT/DS301/R of 22 April 2005), when confronting the issue of the interpretation of Art. 32.1 SCM, seems to follow a different path from the one taken by the AB in the instant case. Delving into the negotiating history of this provision, it reaches the conclusion (as we also do) that this provision was originally meant to ensure that GATT contracting parties will not use measures other than, say, antidumping, to counteract dumping, unless such measures are permitted under the GATT (footnote 326 in the report, op. cit.). It then goes on to

> ... conclude that a subsidy provided in response to another Member's subsidy – that is to say, a counter-subsidy – will not, merely because of its impact on conditions of competition, constitute specific action against that subsidy and therefore be proscribed by the SCM Agreement. Rather, there must be some *additional* element, inherent in the design and structure of the measure, that serves to dissuade, or encourage the termination of, the practice of subsidization.
>
> (§7.164, op. cit., italics in the original)

The reason for this conclusion is that

> ... if the mere fact that a subsidy granted by a Member to its domestic producers mitigates, or is intended to mitigate, the competitive impact of a subsidy granted by another Member to its domestic producers were sufficient to treat the subsidy granted by the first Member as action 'against' the subsidy of the second Member, this would create a new type of substantive disciplines on the provision of subsidies in addition to the disciplines already contained in Parts II and III of the SCM Agreement. Subsidies that in themselves are not prohibited because they are not subsidies of the kind covered by Article 3, and which do not necessarily even produce the effects that are the basis for a successful challenge under Articles 5 and 6 of the SCM Agreement, would nevertheless be prohibited because they are granted in reaction to subsidies of other Members. The Panel considers it unlikely that the drafters, having created a structure for the Agreement under which prohibited subsidies are regulated by Part II of the Agreement and actionable subsidies by Part III, would have then inserted a very significant additional prohibition in the concluding provisions of the Agreement.
>
> (§ 7.161)

It should be noted that the challenged action in this ship-building case bears a striking similarity to the *Byrd Amendment*: the European Community designed a device to subsidize its domestic producers each time Korea would subsidize its own producers in the ship-building sector.

References

Bhagwati, J. and Mavroidis, P. C. (2004). Killing The Byrd Amendment With The Right Stone, *World Trade Review* **3**: 119–127.

Collie, D. R. and Vandenbussche, H. (2004). *Anti-dumping Duties and the Byrd Amendment* (mimeo).

Grossman, G. and Mavroidis, P. C. (2004). United States – Imposition of Countervailing Duties on Certain Hot-Rolled Lead and Bismuth Carbon Steel Products Originating in the United Kingdom: Here Today, Gone Tomorrow? Privatization and the Injury Caused by Non-Recurring Subsidies. In H. Horn and P. C. Mavroidis, eds., *The American Law Institute Reporters' Studies – The WTO Case Law of 2001*. Cambridge University Press, Cambridge, UK.

5

European Community – Antidumping Duties on Malleable Cast Iron Tube or Pipe Fittings from Brazil (WT/DS219/AB/R: DSR 2003:VI, 2613)

HENRIK HORN*
Institute for International Economic Studies, Stockholm University
PETROS C. MAVROIDIS*
Columbia Law School, New York and University of Neuchâtel, Switzerland

1 Introduction

This chapter addresses the Appellate Body (AB) report on *European Community – Antidumping Duties on Malleable Cast Iron Tube or Pipe Fittings from Brazil.*[1] The underlying Panel determination was appealed by the complainant Brazil only. Following the approach it took before the Panel, Brazil raised a number of issues concerning the antidumping investigation by the European Community (EC). The five substantive issues were:

1. Whether the Panel correctly found that the EC acted consistently with its obligations under the Antidumping (AD) Agreement when not accounting for the devaluation of the Brazilian currency (see Section 2 of this chapter);
2. whether the Panel correctly found that the EC treated "low-volume" imports consistently with its international obligations (Section 3);

* We are grateful to David Palmeter, and especially to Jasper-Martijn Wauters, for numerous discussions on the issues addressed in this chapter.

[1] WTO Doc. WT/DS219/AB/R, 22 July, 2003.

3. whether the Panel correctly found that the absence of separate findings of "growth" factors in the EC final determination is consistent with the EC's WTO obligations (Section 4);
4. whether the Panel correctly found that there is no need to examine individually the impact of factors for which the cumulative impact has been assessed (Section 5); and
5. whether the Panel correctly found that the EC fully respected its obligations in its treatment of the causality element (Section 6).

The main procedural issues raised concerned the Panel's finding that a certain document was properly before the EC investigating authority and also its finding concerning the EC's disclosure obligations with respect to this document (Section 7).

Before commencing our discussion of the AB determinations, let us emphasize that, when addressing the normative issue of what the AB in our view should have decided on the issues appealed, we will not put into question the purpose of the AD instrument, which we interpret to be to insulate an importing country from the effect of international price discrimination. As is often pointed out, it is not easy to reconcile this purpose with economic theory, and there is a significant empirical body of literature demonstrating various (from an economic–efficiency point of view, often adverse) "side effects" from, e.g. antidumping investigations. It is therefore not an easy task to determine economically desirable interpretations of provisions of such an agreement. Consequently, we simply take the desirability of counteracting international price discrimination for granted.

2 How should have devaluations been treated during the period of investigation (POI)?

The contested antidumping investigation lasted for a year and led to the establishment of a dumping margin of 34.8%.[2] Approximately three months before the investigation's conclusion, the Brazilian Real was devalued by 42%. The first substantive issue discussed in the dispute was how this devaluation should have been taken into account by the EC.

[2] For a more comprehensive account of the facts, see §§ 66ff of the AB report.

2.1 *The Panel's findings*

Brazil argued before the Panel that the EC violated its obligations under the AD Agreement (Art. 2.4.2 AD) by not sufficiently accounting for the Real's devaluation. The Panel rejected this argument, holding that the EC had to choose one of the two methods for price comparison included in Art. 2.4.2 AD. In § 7.106 of its report, the Panel dismissed the Brazilian argument in the following terms:[3]

> [W]e see no foundation in the text of the Agreement . . . for a requirement that an investigating authority re-assess its own determination made on the basis of an examination of data pertaining to the [POI] prior to the imposition of an anti-dumping measure in the light of an event which occurred during the [POI]. We decline to read such a provision into the text.[4]

2.2 *The issues before the AB*

Brazil presented a somewhat different argument before the AB, emphasizing the wording of Art. VI.2 GATT, which states that the purpose of AD duties is to offset dumping. In Brazil's view, this wording makes it plain that what is being addressed through AD duties is current rather than past behavior, and that therefore the whole investigation process should be geared towards this end.

Brazil also argued that it did not have to establish the legal relevance of the GATT to the AD Agreement, since numerous panel and AB reports before had made it clear that AD duties must be imposed in accordance with both Art. VI.2 GATT, as well as various provisions of the AD Agreement. More specifically, Brazil claimed that, in order to fulfill the purpose of AD duties (to offset dumping), Art. VI.2 GATT should serve as a guide to select among the methodologies for price comparisons laid down in Art. 2.4.2 AD. In other words, investigating authorities are not *always* free to choose the methodology for price comparison. There could be cases where their discretion is prejudged. One such case is when devaluation has occurred in the

[3] The Panel report is reflected in WTO Doc. WT/DS218/R of 7 March 2003 (hereinafter the Panel report).

[4] POI stands for period of investigation (in this instance, the antidumping investigation).

country of the exporter. In the instant case, Brazil maintained that the EC should have:

(i) used only post-devaluation data, since pre-devaluation data are irrelevant; and
(ii) compared the weighted average normal value, pre-devaluation, to specific export transactions, post-devaluation.

Brazil found support for its claim in the second sentence of Art. 2.4.2 AD, which reads:

> Subject to the provisions governing fair comparison in paragraph 4, the existence of margins of dumping during the investigation phase shall normally be established on the basis of a comparison of a weighted average normal value with a weighted average of prices of all comparable export transactions or by a comparison of normal value and export prices on a transaction-to-transaction basis. A normal value established on a weighted average basis may be compared to prices of individual export transactions if the authorities find a pattern of export prices which differ significantly among different purchasers, regions or time periods, and if an explanation is provided as to why such differences cannot be taken into account appropriately by the use of a weighted average-to-weighted average or transaction-to-transaction comparison.

In Brazil's view, in a devaluation scenario, an antidumping authority should only compare a weighted average to prices of individual transactions. Hence, in such cases, investigating authorities do not have the luxury to choose between the two methodologies embedded in the first sentence of Art. 2.4.2 AD; they must always opt for the methodology reflected in its second sentence.

In the AB's view, the argument by Brazil raises two issues (§ 74 of the AB report):

> First, we must determine whether Article VI.2 of the GATT 1994 imposes an *obligation* on an investigating authority to select a particular comparison methodology under Article 2.4.2 of the *Anti-Dumping Agreement.* Second, if we find such an obligation to exist in Article VI.2, we must determine whether the facts of this case required the European Commission, pursuant to Article 2.4.2, to compare weighted average normal value for the entire POI with prices of individual export transactions from the post-devaluation period of the POI. (emphasis in the original)

Hence, the AB would examine whether the EC violated its obligations in this *specific* instance, only if it first found that as *a matter of principle* Art. VI.2 GATT imposes an obligation on WTO Members to select a particular methodology among those provided for in the first sentence of Art. 2.4.2 AD.

2.3 *The AB's response*

The AB upheld the Panel's findings in this respect for the following reasons (§ 84):

First, Art. VI.2 GATT does not, in the AB's view, lend support to the Brazilian argument. Art. VI.2 GATT, the AB notes, reads:

> In order to offset or prevent dumping, a contracting party may levy on any dumped product an anti-dumping duty not greater in amount than the margin of dumping in respect of such product.

In the AB's view, this provision aims to ensure that the dumping margin will never be exceeded (§ 75). In fact, specific provisions of the AD Agreement are more explicit and underscore the *effet utile* of Art. VI.2 GATT: for example, Art. 9.3 AD makes it clear that if the duties imposed exceed the dumping margin, there is an obligation to refund, and duties cannot, according to Art. 11 AD, remain in place longer than necessary to counteract dumping (§ 81). In short, Art. VI.2 GATT aims to ensure that the dumping margin will constitute the ceiling of duties imposed and does not prejudge the methodology used to determine the dumping margin.

Second, as a matter of legislative technique, the AB noticed the level of detail in other provisions figuring in the AD Agreement. In the AB's view, had the founding fathers wanted to impose one methodology over another, be it only in specific cases, they would have done so in an explicit manner (§ 77).

Third, the AB played with a couple of counterfactuals. In one scenario, devaluation occurs on the last day of the POI. In the AB's view, in such a case, the argument put forward by Brazil would oblige the investigating authority to discard the vast majority of transactions and perhaps focus on only one in order to establish the dumping margin, an outcome the AB finds undesirable, since it would go against the obligation to employ representative data (§ 78). By the same token, if at the end of the POI there is re-evaluation of the currency of the exporter, one would end up with a different, paradoxical outcome (§ 79).

2.4 Discussion

We disagree with the AB's determination, and instead believe that a major structural change in the conditions under which pricing decisions are made should be taken into account by the investigating authority, as explained below.

2.4.1 How does the exchange rate affect the calculated dumping margin?

Let us start by briefly examining whether a (significant) devaluation is likely to affect calculated dumping margins. To this end, we will use a highly stylized example in which a Brazilian firm sells its product at home and in the EC market. The price in the home market is 5 Reais, while the price in the EC market is 3 Euros. The exchange rate is 1 Real/Euro. The firm is thus dumping (5 Reais charged in the home market compared to 3 in the EC, or 5 Euros compared to 3).

The Real is now devalued, the new rate becoming 2 Reais/Euro. Suppose first that the firm retains prices constant in Reais. The price in Euros would then fall in direct proportion to the deterioration of the value of the Real, that is, from 3 to 1.50. In this case there would be *no* change in the dumping margin, since the price in Reais would remain the same as before.

In an alternative scenario, the Brazilian firm instead maintains its *local* price in the EC constant, that is, the Euro-denominated price. The price in the EC market, expressed in Reais, will then increase in direct proportion to the devaluation, from 3 to 6 Reais. Since this will exceed the price charged in the Brazilian market, dumping will have ceased to exist.

As can be seen from these two examples, the reaction of the Brazilian firm to devaluation matters crucially for the calculation of dumping margins. The two scenarios can be seen as polar cases. One should normally expect something in between to occur, that is, that the price in the EC market falls, but by less than the full amount of the devaluation – that there is less than full exchange rate "pass-through."[5] The price in the EC market, *expressed in Reais*, will then increase, thus partly reducing the dumping margin, as long as the local Brazilian price remains constant. More generally, the optimal reaction by the Brazilian firm will depend on the competitive conditions in the EC market.

[5] See, for instance, the survey by Goldberg and Knetter (1997).

2.4.2 Could and/or should the EC have used only post-devaluation data?

The fact that a devaluation may importantly affect the incentives to dump raises the general question of how such changes should be taken into account, if they occur during the POI. In particular, will the purpose of the AD agreement be served if duties are imposed in a situation where dumping has occurred during part of the POI, but has ceased during the POI due to a structural change in market conditions?

It seems highly reasonable to view the general purpose of the AD to be to *affect market outcomes*: this much is clear from Art. VI.2, which states that the purpose is "to offset or prevent" dumping, and from Art. 11.1 AD, which states that

> [a]n anti-dumping duty shall remain in force only as long as and to the extent necessary to counteract dumping which is causing injury.

By the same token, Arts. 11.2 and 11.3 AD make it plain that it is ongoing and not past injury that will be counteracted through the imposition of antidumping duties. Moreover, Art. 9.3 AD states that at no point in time will the level of antidumping duties exceed the dumping margin. Indeed, a WTO Member could be obliged to reimburse duties received if, as a result of changes in the normal value or other factors affecting the extent of the dumping margin, the duties imposed are higher than the actual dumping margin (Art. 9.3.3 AD).

Given that the purpose *is* to affect market outcomes, we can distinguish between the use of AD duties to offset ongoing dumping, or as retaliation for past dumping (this possibly serving as a deterrent against future dumping).

If the AD allows duties to be imposed as retaliation, the Brazilian argument does not seem to have much merit – having established dumping, the EC is correct to impose duties. But we do not see this as a plausible interpretation. It seems more appropriate to view AD duties as instruments for correcting ongoing dumping. Members should therefore not be allowed to impose duties when dumping no longer exists, since there is then nothing to "offset or prevent."[6]

[6] Indeed, if AD duties were meant to counteract already-incurred injury, then a lump-sum payment (equivalent to the amount of the injury suffered) would be most appropriate. This, of course, is not the case. In fact, the AD agreement includes a very elaborate scheme to ensure that variations in future dumping margins will not be over-penalized. Everything in the agreement indicates that duties are conceived to be a means to ensure that dumping will not occur in the future.

Assuming that our understanding is correct, the next question is whether devaluation may be of such a nature as to make part of the POI simply irrelevant in determining whether antidumping duties serve their objective function, that is, to stop ongoing and future injurious dumping. This is how we understand the argument by Brazil in this respect: since devaluation occurred during the last three months of the POI, all previous comparisons are now irrelevant for the purpose of imposing antidumping duties. We have sympathy for this point, but before explaining why, we want to stress that we simply cannot tell whether in this dispute a dumping margin was actually established for the post-devaluation period. Brazil argued that this was indeed the case, but the Panel and the AB have neither endorsed nor rejected this point.

There are several reasons why we have sympathy for Brazil's claim. First, it could perhaps be argued that the practical significance of its claim is questionable, since, even if the duties are imposed with the full understanding that the dumping has ceased, they will eventually be reimbursed. However, we do not believe that such a reimbursement, even if made to the full amount of duties paid, would fully compensate the exporter. The exporting firm, when duties are imposed on it, typically cannot lower its price to keep the price in the importing country constant in terms of the local currency, and as a result will lose market share. It may be very costly for the firm to regain its market share when the duties are eventually lifted. It is therefore not at all immaterial (from the firms' perspective) whether the importing country is barred from imposing duties or is allowed to do so but required to reimburse the duties received at some future date. Hence, Brazil's claim does concern an issue of practical significance.

Second, to see the unreasonableness of the EC position, assume that a significant devaluation occurred in the second month of a one-year-long POI. Assume further that, after the devaluation, dumping has ceased. A very formalistic and, we dare say, contextual, reading of the POI would argue in favor of using both pre- and post-devaluation data to calculate the dumping margin. But is such a calculation consonant with *bona fides*? How can the EC authority, in the face of data suggesting that for the 11 most recent months of investigation no dumping has been found, still impose duties because a dumped transaction occurred at the beginning of the POI? How is the very purpose of antidumping duties served through such practices?

The opposite scenario should of course also be addressed: what if the devaluation occurred in the last part of the POI? Indeed, this scenario is not that far from what actually occurred in the present case. We believe that in such a situation, an investigating authority should either continue investigating or drop the process altogether. The first alternative is very much an option: the length of the POI is not mandated in the AD Agreement; even assuming that the suggested length for the POI is legally binding (as it appears to be in an Antidumping Committee [ADP] Recommendation),[7] nothing in the ADP Recommendation obliges investigating authorities to stop investigating after six months. Indeed, the POI is but a tool to serve the overall objective that the

[7] See WTO Doc. G/ADP/6. On this issue, past case law is far from coherent. The panel report on *United States – Antidumping Measures on Certain Hot-Rolled Steel from Japan* (WTO Doc. WT/DS184/R of 28 February 2001) takes the view that the ADP Recommendation on the length of the POI on injury is a *nonbinding instrument*. Accordingly, in the Panel's view, all obligations of investigating authorities with respect to the length of the POI have to be found in the AD Agreement itself. We quote footnote 152 of the report:

> We note that the Committee on Anti-Dumping Practices recently adopted a recommendation which provides that "the period of data collection for injury investigation normally should be at least three years". Committee on Anti-Dumping Practices, Recommendation concerning the Periods of Data Collection for Anti-Dumping Investigations, adopted by the Committee on 5 May 2000, G/ADP/6. We note, however, that this recommendation was adopted after the investigation at issue in this dispute had been completed. Moreover, the recommendation is a non-binding guide to the common understanding of Members on appropriate implementation of the AD Agreement. It does not, however, add new obligations, nor does it detract from the existing obligations of Members under the Agreement. See G/ADP/M/7 at para 40, G/ADP/AHG/R/7 at para. 2. Thus, any obligations as to the length of the period of investigation must, if they exist, be found in the Agreement itself.

The Panel on *Argentina – Definitive Antidumping Duties on Poultry from Brazil* (WT/DS241/R of 22 April 2003), takes an opposite view, showing considerable *deference* towards the ADP Recommendation on the length of the POI when evaluating the injury:

> Furthermore, we note that the issue of periods of review has been examined by the Anti-Dumping Committee. It has issued a recommendation to the effect that, as a general rule, "the period of data collection for injury investigations normally should be at least three years, unless a party from whom data is being gathered has existed for a lesser period, and should include the entirety of the period of data collection for the dumping investigation" (emphasis added). It would appear, therefore, that the period of review for injury need only "include" the entirety of the period of review for dumping. There is nothing in the Anti-Dumping Committee's recommendation to suggest that it should not exceed (in the sense of including more recent data) the period of review for dumping.
>
> (§ 7.287, emphasis in the original).

imposition of antidumping duties is intended to serve. It should be used for this purpose and for this purpose only. A significant devaluation is a strong indication, in and of itself, that dumping may cease. Extending the POI will allow an investigating authority to ensure that this has indeed been the case. At any rate, by not extending the POI, an authority risks punishing the exporter for behavior that is not current behavior, let alone future behavior. In other words, it risks using the AD Agreement for a purpose other than that which it is supposed to serve. This is *abus de droit* and should be explicitly discouraged.

Would the text of Art. VI.2 GATT and the AD then allow the interpretation proposed by Brazil, if found desirable on more general grounds? The AB did not address the question of whether the EC *could* have taken account of only the last part of the POI: The Brazilian claim concerned an obligation in Art. VI.2 for the EC to use a particular methodology, and not an obligation stemming from Art. 2.4.2 AD. Having dismissed the existence of such an obligation stemming from Art. VI.2 GATT, the AB did not have to deal with the question of whether the method suggested by Brazil was permitted under Art. 2.4.2 AD.

As far as we can see, however, nothing would *prevent* the EC from taking into account the devaluation if they so wanted. As stated in Art. 2.4.2 AD:

> A normal value established on a weighted average basis *may be compared to prices of individual export transactions* if the authorities find a pattern of export prices which differ significantly among *different... time periods*... (emphasis added)

Then, was the EC *obliged* to take the devaluation into account? This is less clear. The AB asserts (§ 76) that the phrase "to offset or prevent dumping" in the Art. VI.2 sentence,

> In order to offset or prevent dumping, a contracting party may levy on any dumped product an anti-dumping duty not greater in amount than the margin of dumping ...

should be read to mean only that duties cannot exceed the dumping margins. But this interpretation seems to make the phrase void of meaning. To illustrate, suppose that this phrase did not exist, and that the sentence in Art. VI.2 instead read:

> A contracting party may levy on any dumped product an anti-dumping duty not greater in amount than the margin of dumping ...

In our view, this would not make any difference to the ambit of the provision. The AB's interpretation thus seems to deprive the words "to offset or prevent" of any impact, and is therefore questionable as such. In addition, it seems reasonable to see the purpose of AD duties in the GATT to be to offset *existing* and future dumping (as opposed to past dumping), and the reading suggested by Brazil would be compatible with this.

Still, Art. 2.4.2 AD, first sentence, does not establish a hierarchy among the two methodologies that in principle can be used, and the second sentence clearly explains that the methodology embedded there should primarily be understood as an additional weapon in the arsenal of the investigating authority (as Brazil seems to suggest). Moreover, it is clear that, according to this provision, its use is a matter of discretion – it is stated that the second method "may" be employed.

Furthermore, even assuming that in the cases mentioned in this second sentence there is an obligation to use the transaction-to-weighted-average methodology, Brazil seems not to have explained why this should always be the case in a devaluation scenario. As noted above, it is not self-evident that a devaluation will affect dumping margins, even if it is likely to do this.

2.4.3 Specific remarks on the AB report

(1) The AB maintains in § 76 that:

> [t]he precise rules relating to the determination as to whether there is dumping ... are set out in Article 2 of the *Antidumping Agreement* ...

This is obviously correct insofar as it goes. However, this raises the question of what to do when the rules, detailed as they are, threaten to lead to the imposition of AD duties in a situation where dumping no longer occurs. As noted above, the AB asserts that this would violate Art. 11.1 AD. However, we fail to see what would prevent such duties from being imposed in any event, if only to be later reimbursed. A mechanical application of the methodology described in Art. 2 AD would lead to such imposition, regardless of whether it is obvious to anyone that there is no longer any dumping to offset or prevent.

(2) The AB discusses in §§ 74–77 whether Art. VI.2 GATT obliged the EC to use a specific methodology, and to use data only from the post-devaluation period, when determining the export prices.

It concludes in § 77 that this is not the case. If it wanted to, the AB could have stopped here. But it continues with a discussion of what it sees as unreasonable implications if one were to adopt Brazil's suggestion of letting the POI be sensitive to changes in market conditions.

First, the AB claims that Brazil's proposal would lead to the unreasonable consequence that "… the determination would have to be based on the data of a very short period of time" (§ 78). An alternative and, in our view, a much more reasonable conclusion would be that, faced with a major structural change that is likely to have a major impact on any assessed dumping margins, the investigating authority would have to wait for some time to collect data to ensure that dumping also occurs after the structural change. After all, the data before it, limited as it is, might suggest that there is no longer dumping. It does not seem unreasonable to request the importing country to restrain its trigger-happiness in such a case.

Second, while noting that the AD does not stipulate any particular length of the POI, the AB emphasizes the importance of not opening a door for importing countries to manipulate its length. We fully agree with this, of course. But consistency is desirable only so long as it leads to reasonable outcomes, and that seems questionable in this case. The AB argues that in the case of a revaluation, the investigating authority could make an affirmative finding of dumping based on data covering a very short period of time. We are not convinced that this need occur, however. It does not seem unreasonable to request of an affirmative finding that the data on which it is based cover a sufficiently long period to be deemed representative of the current situation.

(3) The AB notes in § 82 that neither the EC nor the Panel had confirmed the Brazilian claim that any dumping that may once have existed had ceased with the devaluation. The AB here argues that one cannot take for granted the consequence of devaluation:

> The lasting impact of a devaluation will therefore have to be determined on the basis of objective and reliable post-devaluation data …
>
> (§ 82)

This seems entirely sensible, in our view. But it raises the question of whether a Member, knowing that a very significant devaluation has occurred, and lacking data on its impact, should be permitted to impose

AD duties based on older, and most likely not very informative, data. More data can be collected only through extra time in the POI.

2.5 Conclusion

The argument that the POI may have to be adjusted to take into consideration fundamental changes in market conditions seems highly reasonable, and doing so would not seem to violate the AD or the GATT. It should be noted, however, that accepting this general principle does not mean taking a stand on whether, in this specific dispute, any dumping had ceased to exist.

The adjudicating bodies were, in our view, probably right to dismiss Brazil's claim, since Brazil did not clearly make the point that devaluation, as such, should oblige an investigating authority to defer imposition of duties until more reliable data has been collected. But we would, on more principled grounds, have preferred to see a different outcome.[8]

3 How should data from periods with "low sales" be treated?

A second issue on appeal concerned the use of data from a period with "low sales." The relevant provisions in the AD follow. Article 2.2 AD reads:

> When there are no sales of the like product in the ordinary course of trade in the domestic market of the exporting country or when, because of the particular market situation or the low volume of the sales in the domestic market of the exporting country,[2] such sales do not permit a proper comparison, the margin of dumping shall be determined by comparison with a comparable price of the like product when exported to an appropriate third country, provided that this price is representative, or with the cost of production in the country of origin plus a reasonable amount for administrative, selling and general costs and for profits.

Footnote 2, appearing in the body of Art. 2.2 AD, reads:

> Sales of the like product destined for consumption in the domestic market of the exporting country shall normally be considered a sufficient quantity for the determination of the normal value if such sales constitute 5 per cent or more of the sales of the product under consideration to the importing Member, provided that a lower ratio should be

[8] It seems to us that Brazil could have used a non-violation complaint as well to make this point.

acceptable where the evidence demonstrates that domestic sales at such lower ratio are nonetheless of sufficient magnitude to provide for a proper comparison.

Finally, Art. 2.2.2 AD deals with the calculation of selling, general and administrative (SG&A) costs and profit in the context of constructed price:

For the purpose of paragraph 2, the amounts for administrative, selling and general costs and for profits shall be based on actual data pertaining to production and sales in the ordinary course of trade of the like product by the exporter or producer under investigation. When such amounts cannot be determined on this basis, the amounts may be determined on the basis of:

(i) the actual amounts incurred and realized by the exporter or producer in question in respect of production and sales in the domestic market of the country of origin of the same general category of products;
(ii) the weighted average of the actual amounts incurred and realized by other exporters or producers subject to investigation in respect of production and sales of the like product in the domestic market of the country of origin;
(iii) any other reasonable method, provided that the amount for profit so established shall not exceed the profit normally realized by other exporters or producers on sales of products of the same general category in the domestic market of the country of origin.

3.1 The Panel's findings

In the dispute, the EC discarded actual normal prices, and instead employed constructed normal prices. The WTO Members are requested by Art. 2.2 AD to do this if, *inter alia*, the total volume of sales of the exporting firm is low in its domestic market (defined as such if sales in the home market are less than 5% of the sales destined to the market of the WTO Member investigating the allegations of dumping). However, when constructing the price, the EC used data from "low-volume" sales to calculate the SG&A costs as well as the profit margin.

The Panel found (§ 7.137, *op. cit.*) that the EC did not violate its obligations under the AD Agreement, since low-volume sales are made in the ordinary course of trade and the relevant provision (Art. 2.2.2, see *infra* in subsection 2.2.3) explicitly requires WTO Members, when constructing the normal value, to use data relating to transactions in the ordinary course of trade.

3.2 *The AB's findings*

Brazil contested this finding by the Panel. In its view, the EC could not use data it had previously discarded. Instead, when constructing the price, the EC should have used data other than that existing in the "low-volume" sales to calculate SG&A and profit:

> The issue before us, therefore, is whether an investigating authority must exclude data from low-volume sales when determining the amounts for SG&A and profits under the chapeau of Article 2.2.2, having disregarded such low-volume sales for normal value determination under Article 2.2.[9] (§ 92).

The AB summarizes its interpretation of Art. 2.2 AD as follows:

> Article 2.2 makes clear that an alternative basis for deriving "normal value" must be relied upon by an investigating authority where one of three conditions exists:
>
> (a) there are no sales in the exporting country of the like product in the ordinary course of trade; or
> (b) sales in the exporting country's market do not "permit a proper comparison" because of "the particular market situation"; or
> (c) sales in the exporting country's market do not "permit a proper comparison" because of their low volume.
>
> Where one of these conditions exists, Article 2.2 further specifies two alternative bases for the calculation of "normal value":
>
> (a) third-country sales, that is, the comparable price of the like product when exported to an "appropriate" third country, provided the price is "representative"; or
> (b) constructed normal value, that is, the sum of:
>
> (i) the cost of production in the country of origin;
> (ii) a "reasonable amount" for SG&A; and
> (iii) a "reasonable amount" for profits. (§§ 94-5)

[9] We should probably note here that, whereas the reader can admire the clarity of expression in the quoted paragraph, this is not likely the case with the remaining paragraphs of this subsection. In particular, § 86 of the report is a monument of self-contradiction.

The AB upholds the Panel's findings concerning the use of "low-volume" sales data for the construction of a normal price, for the following reasons:

1. In the AB's view, the absence of explicit language in the body of Art. 2.2.2, second sentence, AD prohibiting the use of data taken from "low-volume" sales in the calculation of SG&A and profit when constructing the price must mean something: if such use is not prohibited, it is by inference allowed (§ 98).
2. The AB also finds support for its reading of Art. 2.2.2 by examining the absence of specific language in that Article within the context of the AD Agreement: the AD Agreement is characterized, in the AB's view, by its very detailed expression. Thus, the absence of specific language supporting Brazil's claim is evidence of the negotiators' intention not to disallow practices similar to those employed by the EC (§ 99).
3. Prior case law supports the AB's interpretation (§ 100).
4. "Low-volume" sales are sales in the ordinary course of trade and the EC action is hence in full compliance with Art. 2.2.2, first sentence, AD (§ 101).

3.3 *Discussion*

The adjudicating bodies' reasoning is logical so long as the relevant provisions are read in isolation from their context: Art. 2.2.2 AD refers only to the "ordinary course of trade" (OCT), and as long as the transactions are in the OCT, they should consequently be included in a calculation under this provision. But while this interpretation is logical when Art. 2.2.2 AD is read without regard to its context (the remaining provisions of the AD Agreement), it is somewhat unsatisfactory in that it sidesteps the more fundamental issue raised by Brazil: under what circumstances may information that is discarded under one provision be used under another?

Starting at a more technical level, the determination by the adjudicating bodies rests on their interpretation and application of the OCT concept. This concept is essentially treated as independent of the concept of "low sales." A highly textual reading of the AD supports this view: Art. 2.2 AD allows for the possibility of low sales volumes being in the OCT in its first sentence:

> When there are no sales of the like product in the ordinary course of trade in the domestic market of the exporting country *or* when, because of.... the low volume of the sales in the domestic market of the exporting country, such sales do not permit a proper comparison... (emphasis added, footnote omitted)

Furthermore, the only guidance the AD Agreement provides concerning the interpretation of OCT is reflected in Art. 2.2.1 AD, which states the minimum sales volume necessary for an investigating authority to be allowed to discard data showing (roughly speaking) pricing below cost in the domestic market, as being *not* in the OCT. Hence, as far as the text is concerned, any other situation would be in the OCT, including situations with low sales volume. One may even argue that Art. 2.2.1 AD, strictly speaking, implies that with sufficiently low sales volumes, the transactions *must* be regarded as being in the OCT, since the condition for discarding them is not fulfilled. Yet another argument to this effect would be that Art. 2.2. AD implies that transactions can *either* be non-OCT *or* be low-volume, but *not both*, since the Article does not include an "and." Hence, if the data is low-volume, it must be in the OCT.

In our view, this highly textual reading is not the appropriate way of evaluating Brazil's claim. By virtue of the principle of effective treaty interpretation (the guiding interpretative principle, as recognized by the AB in its case law in all reports since 1995), it simply cannot be that data which is not useful (reliable) under Art. 2.2 AD, suddenly becomes, without any further scrutiny, useful under Art. 2.2.2 AD.

Before describing this view in more detail, we want to point out that the issue at stake, more generally, concerns the incentives for the investigating authority to construct prices *based on* actual data, rather than to use actual data *as such*. The price-construction route has a couple of significant attractions for such authorities: once data on SG&A and profits are considered to be in low volumes, Art. 2.2 AD permits the export price to be compared with the cost of production in the country of origin, plus a reasonable amount for SG&A and for profits. The computation shall, with regard to the latter two price components, "*be based on*" actual data from the ordinary course of trade. Hence, the investigating authority can deviate from the data supplied and construct a price with all the discretion that the notion "be based on" allows. This is likely in practice to give an opportunity to manipulate the established dumping margin upwards and save administrative resources by avoiding the undertaking of a thorough determination of the actual price. But such a practice would violate the "object and purpose" of the AD to perform a fair price comparison (as explicitly enshrined in Art. 2.4 AD), and an interpretation of the provisions in Art. 2 AD must take these possibilities into account.

3.3.1 The purpose of the "low-volume" concept

According to a textual and contextual reading of the AD Agreement, once the requirements of any one of the three grounds (mentioned in Art. 2.2 AD) justifying a rejection of normal value have been met, an investigating authority can construct the price. In so doing, it must:

(i) respect the requirements of Art. 2.2.1.1 AD as far as the construction of the *production cost* is concerned; and
(ii) respect the requirements of Art. 2.2.2 AD as far as the construction of *SG&A* and *profit* are concerned.

These requirements are applicable here, since, according to Art. 2.2 AD, a constructed price is composed of the abovementioned three elements, that is, production cost, SG&A, and profit.

There are at least two possible reasons why the AD includes the "low-volume" provision. One is that an exporter may deliberately charge lower prices in the domestic market than what would be motivated from the point of view of demand and production cost considerations in this market, in order to escape a dumping finding in the export market. Such behavior is costly in itself, but if the profits in the domestic market are very small anyway relative to those in the export market, such behavior might be profitable.

The other reason that occurs to us for including the "low sales" provision is to prevent the use of data that is not representative due to a limited number of observations on transactions. Market prices are influenced by a number of factors, and for this reason, may fluctuate depending on the particular economic "shocks" that hit the market at any particular moment. When prices fluctuate, it is necessary to compute some form of average price to use as a comparison.

This average can be computed with a high degree of confidence when the computation is done on the basis of a large number of observed transactions, collected from a period during which there are no structural changes affecting the industry, and when the data is applied to a subsequent period in which the structural factors remain the same. However, with very few transactions to base the calculation upon, random factors will have a large impact on the calculated normal price. Article 2.2 AD can be seen as recognizing this fact in its acknowledgment of the possibility that, because of low volumes, it may not be possible to compute a "proper" normal price.

We find it difficult to dismiss either of these two explanations for the "low sales" criterion completely. Speaking in favor of the first interpretation (which does as such not contradict the second), is the fact that a low volume is defined as a fraction of sales, rather than some absolute number, which would be more relevant with regard to the number of observations argument. However, we take for granted that the antidumping instrument in the WTO should only be used when there is a high degree of certainty concerning the existence of dumping (its imposition should be fair as *per* Art. 2.4 AD). To ensure that this is indeed the case, it is of paramount importance that, during the dumping investigation, the investigating authority employ reliable data. Indeed, the AD Agreement says as much when it states in the body of Art. 2.2 AD "... such sales do not permit a proper comparison." We thus tend to see the desire to base AD measures on statistically reliable calculations as an overriding concern of the AD, and that the specific provisions of the agreement must be read in light of this concern.

3.3.2 The AB's neglect of the term "like" in Art. 2.2.2 DSU

Viewing the purpose of the low-sales-volume concept as motivated by a desire to use statistically reliable data, the outcome of the dispute with regard to the low-volume argument by Brazil is clearly unsatisfactory. If data is of insufficient quality to be used for a certain purpose, the *very same data* cannot become reliable for the same purpose under another provision.

Technically speaking, the problem with the adjudicating bodies' determination is, as we see it, their neglect of the term "like product" in Art. 2.2.2 AD, which is highly suggestive of the circumstances under which the provision would be applied. To recall, the first sentence reads:

> For the purpose of paragraph 2, the amounts for administrative, selling and general costs and for profits shall be based on actual data pertaining to production and sales in the ordinary course of trade of the *like product* by the exporter or producer under investigation. (emphasis added)

In the GATT/WTO context, this concept invariably refers to a comparison of *separate* products. It is used to limit the ambit of provisions to situations where these distinct products have very similar (or possibly identical) features. Indeed, the term "like product" is defined in Art. 2.6 AD as follows:

> Throughout this Agreement the term "like product" ("produit similaire") shall be interpreted to mean a product which is identical, i.e. alike in all respects to the product under consideration, or in the absence of such a product, *another* product which, although not alike in all respects, has characteristics closely resembling those of the product under consideration. (emphasis added)

In the present dispute, the adjudicating bodies – the Panel offering a full analysis and the AB confirming – first examined what the term "like product" meant in the context of the AD Agreement. Then, the Panel and the AB adopted a very formal reading of this provision, maintaining that data from the same product, previously discarded under Art. 2.2 AD, could now be used in the context of an Art. 2.2.2 AD. Indeed, they might have argued, what could be more "like" than sheer identity? However, to the best of our knowledge, nowhere in WTO law is the concept used to refer to the *same physical item.*

Why is this of significance here? Because the methodology employed by the EC, and accepted by the AB, is to interpret the requirement in Art. 2.2.2 AD that the SG&A and profit data should stem from a like product to allow the EC to use data from the *very same* product. This fundamentally violates the notion that likeness involves a comparison of physically separate products. If negotiators intended the Art. 2.2.2 AD calculation to be done with data from the same transactions that were discarded under Art. 2.2 AD, would they not have made this explicit in the agreement? It is striking how differently the AB interprets silence in different provisions: sometimes it means something, and sometimes it means nothing, but the reasons for the particular position taken in this regard are not explained.

Of course, one cannot exclude the possibility that some price-elements (like the SG&A and/or profit) can legitimately be used, even if the price (comprising, we repeat, production costs, SG&A, and profits) as such has been discarded. But whereas *all* information concerning all price elements of *another but like* product can be legitimately used (since information concerning a non-investigated transaction, by definition does not suffer from the flaws enshrined in Art. 2.2 AD), *only a sub-set* of the information can be used when it stems from the *physically identical product.* For, if one were to take the opposite point of view, one would have to *ipso facto* accept that improper data under Art. 2.2 AD suddenly becomes proper under one of its subparagraphs that aims to "flesh out" how investigating authorities should behave when making use of the institutional possibility offered to them under this provision. The more plausible interpretation is that negotiators understood Art. 2.2.2 AD to be applicable in situations where, because the use of certain data on transactions is likely to be beset with statistical problems due to the limited number of observations, or due to special circumstances, Members could use SG&A and profit data from *other* transactions, as long as these transactions involved products with sufficiently similar features (hence, the reference to the "like" good).

To conclude, when determining the SG&A as well as profits, the investigating authority cannot, in our view, use the same data discarded under Art. 2.2 AD. It has to use data from other transactions.

3.3.3 The AB's interpretation of the intent of negotiators

A central point in the AB's argument is the fact that Art. 2.2.2 AD lacks the reference to low-volume sales that is contained in Art. 2.2 AD, and that this difference cannot be disregarded:

> Considering that the treaty negotiators covered in great detail various aspects of the constructed value calculation, the omission of any reference to low-volume sales in the chapeau of Article 2.2.2 is telling.
>
> (§ 99)

To this paragraph there is a footnote stating that:

> [u]nlike the *Tokyo Round Anti-Dumping Code*, the present *Anti-Dumping Agreement* identifies low-volume sales as a basis for constructing normal value, including the footnote to Article 2.2 specifically defining low-volume sales in the home market in relation to a proportion of sales made in the importing Member. (Footnote 2 to Article 2.2 of the *Anti-Dumping*

> *Agreement*) This reinforces our view that a reference to "low-volume" sales should not be implied when such reference is not expressly stated.

The AB here claims that the lack of explicit reference to low-volume sales in Art. 2.2.2 AD must signal a desire on the part of the negotiators of the agreement that the two situations be treated differently in this respect. But *why* would negotiators on the one hand expressly recognize the possibility that data collected during periods of low volume may be unreliable, and that therefore a different method may be used to find the normal value, but then allow that the same problem arises in this alternative method, which was chosen in order to prevent this problem? The AB might respond that it is bound by the text when ruling on Brazil's appeal, and this is what the text says (even though this might also be challenged). But to interpret the *intent* of the negotiators to allow for this illogical construction seems to go too far. A much more likely reason for the construction seems to be that the problem with poor data (which is a generic problem when the data only includes a few observations) is already addressed in Art. 2.2 AD.

3.3.4 What should the AB have done?

We do not know for certain what data Brazil supplied to the EC. One possibility is that the EC was first provided with data directly specifying prices, and when these were discarded, it obtained data that would allow the EC to construct the price on the basis of information on production costs, SG&A, and normal profits. If this is what actually occurred, the EC procedure could in principle be defended at least from a normative point of view. It could possibly be argued that the price data is less reliable from a statistical point of view than the constructed price data.[10]

On the other hand, the case would look very different if the EC denounced the *same* data as not useful for a computation directly under Art. 2.1 AD, as it employs for the calculation under Art. 2.2.2 AD. (There are other instances in the report that lead us believe this is what actually occurred, such as Recitals 170–172.) This would be a strong indication that the EC is choosing to construct a price,

[10] Such a situation may arise when the statistical problems with the data mainly stem from disturbances on the demand side, such as fluctuating demand. In such a situation, it is possible, at least in principle, that a more reliable "normal" price could be obtained by aggregating price elements, where the profits would be "normal" profits, as opposed to realized profits.

rather than to use the price supplied by Brazil, for the abovementioned non-legitimate reasons. In order to determine the reason for the EC's choice, we would need to know exactly *which* data it retained, and which it discarded.

We emphasize again that we do not know why the EC chose to construct the price. What we miss in the AB's analysis, however, is a discussion of what is required for a price to be "constructed" in an appropriate fashion. There is a tension between data first being discarded under one provision, and then being used under another provision that is more attractive to the investigating authority. In our view, the AB did not appropriately take into account the possibility of an importing country misusing the constructed-price route.

More specifically, we believe that, had the AB sufficiently accounted for the rationale for, and the context of, Art. 2.2.2 AD, it would have been led to an opposite conclusion from what it decided. Should the AB, in light of Brazil's claim, have first examined *what* data was at stake? In this part of the discussion, it should have made a distinction between price and price elements. It should then have proceeded to examine whether the EC used some or all three of the elements discarded under Art. 2.2 AD. It would then naturally have moved to a discussion of whether previously discarded data could still be legitimately utilized, and if yes, under what conditions, in the context of an antidumping investigation. If this were indeed the case, the AB would have found that the only scenario which allows a WTO Member to use previously discarded data is the scenario we indicated *supra*: when a subset of the discarded data is used. Otherwise, under Art. 2.2.2 AD, a WTO Member would have to construct the price utilizing data from a non-investigated, but like product.

4 Did the EC take proper account of the "growth factor"?

Brazil complained before the Panel that the EC's final determination did not contain a separate examination of whether there was injury to industry *growth*. Article 3.4 AD mentions "growth" among the factors indicating injury, and, according to consistent case law, all factors mentioned in Art. 3.4 AD must be examined by an investigating authority. The EC counterargument was that *implicitly*, the EC had examined growth and this conclusion was obvious when reading the determination.

4.1 The Panel's findings

The Panel held that, while investigating authorities must perform a substantive examination of all factors mentioned in Art. 3.4 AD, they do not have to provide separate findings for each individual factor. The Panel found that the test of Art. 3.4 AD could still be satisfied even in the absence of explicit separate findings, as long as an adjudicating body could conclude that a substantive review of all factors mentioned in Art. 3.4 AD had indeed occurred. In pertinent part, the Panel found:

> The facts on the record of the investigation and taken into account in the EC injury analysis indicate to us that, in its examination of other injury factors – in particular, sales, profits, output, market share, productivity and capacity utilisation – satisfy us that, in addressing developments in relation to these other factors in the manner that it did in this particular investigation, the European Communities implicitly addressed the factor of "growth."
>
> We therefore find that the European Communities did not violate its obligations under Article 3.4 in its treatment of "growth" and that it at least addressed each of the listed Article 3.4 factors.
>
> (§§ 7.310–311 of the Panel report, *op. cit.*)

4.2 The AB's findings

Brazil appealed the Panel's finding concerning the EC's treatment of the "growth factor." The AB explained its understanding of the issue before it as follows:

> The participants in this appeal do not dispute that it is mandatory for investigating authorities to evaluate all of the fifteen injury factors listed in Article 3.4 of the *Anti-Dumping Agreement*. One of the fifteen factors expressly listed in Article 3.4 is the "actual and potential negative effects on … growth." The issue raised by Brazil in this appeal is whether the requirements of Article 3.4 were satisfied in this case, even though the factor "growth" was evaluated only "implicitly" and no separate record of its evaluation was made.
>
> (§ 156, italics in the original)

The AB upheld the Panel's findings in this respect on two grounds (§ 166): on the one hand, it held the view that Art. 3.4 AD does not prejudge the *manner* in which the factors listed there will be examined.

They all have to be examined, but an implicit, albeit verifiable, review suffices by and large (§§ 160–1); on the other hand, in the AB's view, growth is a *sui generis* factor anyway, in the sense that it is to be found implicitly in a series of other factors mentioned in Art. 3.4 AD (§ 162).

For example, when reviewing pertinent parts of the EC final determination, the AB mentioned specifically the following passage from the EC Provisional Regulation:

> The examination of the above mentioned injury factors shows that the situation of the Community industry deteriorated. In particular, the Community industry experienced a decline in production, production capacity, sales and market share. Moreover, the Community industry suffered a significant loss of employment and a decline in investments, as well as an increase of stocks. As to the capacity utilization, its increase depended on the reduced production capacity.
>
> (§ 165)

In the AB's view, the "declines" and "losses" observed in the final determination with respect to several of the factors examined in this case are necessarily related to "growth" as well. In the AB's view (§ 165):

> To put it more precisely, the negative trends in these factors point to a lack of "growth." This, in turn, supports the conclusion that the European Commission evaluated this injury factor.

4.3 *Discussion*

The purpose of Art 3.4 AD is presumably to ensure that anti-dumping duties are not imposed on the basis of a very narrow definition of injury, in a situation where most other effects of the dumping are positive for the importing country. This seems reasonable as such, as long as Members have not agreed on a more precise definition of the concept injury.

The difficulty with this approach, however, is that as long as no guidance is given for how to weigh the different components, it becomes rather useless to go through each and every one of them. The lowering of prices by foreign competitors should, except under very special circumstances, result in declines in domestic firms' sales, profits, output, market share, employment, wages, ability to raise capital, cash flow, etc. Do not these effects suffice for all practical purposes to establish injury? We are thus not convinced by the case law that makes it compulsory for an investigating authority to examine all factors listed in Art. 3.4 AD.

There is also a redundancy in the list provided in Art. 3.4 AD in another respect: industry growth is obtained using data on industry production at two different points in time. The list already includes *actual* and *potential* output (and sales), and should therefore implicitly take account of the industry growth factor.

We therefore agree with the AB's determination from a more conceptual point of view. We are also broadly in agreement at a more textual level. The AD does not specify the manner in which the analysis of the 15 factors in Art. 3.4 AD is to be conducted and reported. On the other hand, in order for the requirement to examine all factors to have any practical bite, it is probably necessary that the findings with respect to each and every one be published. But this would be a pure formality, in the absence of rules for how such analysis should be conducted and, as mentioned above, for how the different findings are to be aggregated.

Finally, due to the nature of the list in Art. 3.4 AD, it does not serve any purpose to impose, as an obligation *per se*, a requirement of going through all the factors mentioned there, as the AB has time and again done in its case law, other than as some sort of an administrative (bureaucratic) checkup. The factors mentioned in Art 3.4 AD reveal their true purpose only when they are placed in the context of the non-attribution exercise: by virtue of Art. 3.5 AD, a WTO Member wishing to impose duties must first ensure that injury has been caused by dumped imports and not by factors other than dumped imports. The examination of the state of the industry, as mandated by Art. 3.4 AD, should hence serve this perspective.

5 Individual examination of the impact of cumulated factors

A third substantial issue raised by Brazil was its claim that an investigating authority, when opting for cumulation in accordance with Art. 3.3 AD, first had to assess the impact of imports from each and every WTO Member individually before reviewing their combined effect.[11]

[11] Under this provision, an investigating authority can cumulate the effect of dumped imports from various sources and lawfully impose duties, even if, had the investigation's assessment had been conducted on a state-by-state, individual basis, the *de minimis* thresholds established in the agreement would not have been met.

5.1 The Panel's findings

The Panel rejected Brazil's claim as follows:

> The text of this provision [Article 3.3] contains no additional requirement that authorities shall also consider whether there has been a significant increase in imports country-by-country before progressing to a cumulative assessment.[12]

5.2 The issue before the AB

Brazil appealed this Panel finding on two grounds:

First, according to Brazil, the Panel erred in its interpretation of Art. 3.3 AD. Brazil maintained its original point that for cumulation to be lawfully carried out under the AD Agreement, an investigating authority had to first examine the impact of imports from each and every WTO Member under investigation individually. Brazil found supporting evidence for such a reading of the pertinent legal provision (Art. 3.3 AD) in its immediate context, i.e. in Art. 3.2 AD (§ 105). The AB reformulated the Brazilian claim in the following terms:

> The issue before us is whether an investigating authority must first analyze the volumes and prices of dumped imports on a country-by-country basis under Article 3.2 as a pre-condition to cumulatively assessing the effects of the dumped imports under Article 3.3.
>
> (§ 107)

Second, Brazil also argued that import volumes and prices could not be cumulated: in its view, as expressed by the AB,

> ... import volumes and prices cannot be considered as "effects" of imports; on the contrary, import volumes and prices "are precisely the factors which may cause the effects envisaged by Article 3.4." Brazil therefore argues that import volumes and prices cannot be cumulated under Article 3.3. It submits that the Panel's contrary interpretation of Articles 3.2 and 3.3 would permit an investigating authority to impose anti-dumping duties on products from a country when those products, in contrast to those from other countries, may not be causing injury to the domestic industry.
>
> (§ 105)

[12] See § 7.234 of the Panel report, *op. cit.*

5.3 *The AB's response*

The AB rejected *in toto* Brazil's arguments in this respect (§ 118). With regard to the question of whether for cumulation to be lawfully performed, an assessment of the impact of the exports of individual firms is required, the AB started its analysis by first laying out the relevant legal framework, that is Art. 3.3 AD:

> Where imports of a product from more than one country are simultaneously subject to anti-dumping investigations, the investigating authorities may cumulatively assess the effects of such imports only if they determine that *(a)* the margin of dumping established in relation to the imports from each country is more than *de minimis* as defined in paragraph 8 of Article 5 and the volume of imports from each country is not negligible and *(b)* a cumulative assessment of the effects of the imports is appropriate in light of the conditions of competition between the imported products and the conditions of competition between the imported products and the like domestic product. (italics in the original)

The AB disagreed with Brazil's claim on both textual and contextual grounds. With respect to the text, the AB noted that there is no explicit requirement in the body of Art. 3.3 AD requesting investigating authorities to perform individual assessment of imports before cumulating them (§ 110). As the AB noted:

> The text of Article 3.3 expressly identifies three conditions that must be satisfied before an investigating authority is permitted under the *Anti-Dumping Agreement* to assess cumulatively the effects of imports from several countries. These conditions are:
>
> (a) the dumping margin from each individual country must be more than *de minimis*;
> (b) the volume of imports from each individual country must not be negligible; and
> (c) cumulation must be appropriate in the light of the conditions of competition
>
> (i) between the imported products; and
> (ii) between the imported products and the like domestic product.
>
> By the terms of Article 3.3, it is "only if" the above conditions are established that an investigating authority "may" make a cumulative assessment of the effects of dumped imports from several countries.
>
> (§ 109)

With respect to the contextual argument, the AB examined Art. 3.2 AD, the provision cited by Brazil in support of its argument, which reads as follows:

> With regard to the volume of the dumped imports, the investigating authorities shall consider whether there has been a significant increase in dumped imports, either in absolute terms or relative to production or consumption in the importing Member. With regard to the effect of the dumped imports on prices, the investigating authorities shall consider whether there has been a significant price undercutting by the dumped imports as compared with the price of a like product of the importing Member, or whether the effect of such imports is otherwise to depress prices to a significant degree or prevent price increases, which otherwise would have occurred, to a significant degree. No one or several of these factors can necessarily give decisive guidance.

Once again, in the AB's eyes, nothing in the body of Art. 3.2 AD supported the conclusion drawn by Brazil that an individual assessment before cumulation was required.

As to the second claim advanced by Brazil, the AB essentially rejected it because, in its view, throughout Art. 3 AD, the terms "effects" and "factors" seemed to have been used interchangeably.

5.4 *Discussion*

Brazil's claim that an individual assessment is required for cumulation to lawfully take place is unsupported by the text of the Agreement – The body of Art. 3.3 AD clearly reflects one obligation only: to cumulatively assess the effect of imports. There is no prerequisite to first individually assess them as well. Hence, as a matter of positive law, we agree with the AB.

As to Brazil's second claim, that import volumes and prices cannot be cumulated, we can observe that the plain language of Art. 3.5 AD (which lays out the injury factors) contradicts the claim advanced in this respect: import volumes and prices are among the "factors" explicitly laid down.

At a more normative and general level, the question of how to deal with cumulation would be of no concern if *any* dumping margin could be targeted through an antidumping duty. However, the first sentence of Art. VI.1 GATT lays down the reason for an antidumping measure – to prevent injury to a domestic industry. There are thus *two* factors limiting the maximum permitted size of the antidumping duty: the dumping margin, as well as the injury *caused by this exporter's dumping.* It is then necessary not to attribute to a particular exporter injury that is caused by other exporters (or by other factors). But how to attribute such harm to individual exporters is not a straightforward matter.

For instance, suppose that a firm in country A and a firm in country B each sell a highly substitutable product to country C, and that the cost and demand conditions in the two countries are the same, so that they sell at the same price in their respective home markets. Suppose that the injury to C is measured in terms of jobs lost. If only one exporter dumps, domestic employment in the sector is reduced by 500 jobs, but if both dump, the reduction in jobs is 800. How would the attribution be done in such a case? Or suppose that it suffices that only *one* country dump for the entire domestic industry to be wiped out, and both dump. One might then possibly argue that one of the firms is not adding to the injury. But which one? As can be seen, the question of attribution is far from trivial.

It is far beyond the scope of this chapter to suggest how to undertake an individual attribution analysis. The more general point, however, is that it is often not possible to perform an analysis on a country-by-country basis. As is so often the case when conducting an economic/statistical analysis, it is necessary to include all factors at the same time in order to determine how they interact, and the contribution to injury by each.

6 Causality analysis

Brazil complained before the Panel that the EC did not honor the causality requirement laid down in Art. 3.5 AD, in two important respects:

First, the EC did not take into account the relatively higher cost of production for EC producers (compared to that of Brazilian producers) as a cause of injury. In Brazil's view, the EC should have taken this factor, which was "known" to the investigating authority, into account.

Second, the EC did not perform a cumulative assessment of how all factors other than dumped imports contributed to injury. Although the EC did examine such factors individually and reached the conclusion that they were not responsible for the injury caused, in Brazil's view, the EC was further required to perform a cumulative assessment in addition to the individual assessment of such factors.

6.1 *The Panel's findings*

The Panel rejected both claims by Brazil. The first claim was rejected on two grounds: Brazil had raised the "high-production-cost" factor during a stage of the investigation other than the stage during which the causality requirement was being discussed. As a result, the factor was not "known" to the EC investigating authority when it should have been, i.e. during the stage when the causality requirement was being discussed. Second, when this factor was raised, the EC had indeed examined it and dismissed its relevance in light of the marginal difference in production costs between Brazilian and EC producers (§ 7.362 of the Panel report, *op. cit.*).

As to the second claim, it may be appropriate to cite *verbatim* the Panel's findings:

> In its determination, the European Communities identified certain factors, other than dumped imports, that were potentially causing injury to the domestic industry including imports from third countries not subject [to] the investigation; decline in consumption and substitution. *With respect to each of these factors individually*, the European Communities conducted a separate examination and found either that it "is not such as to have contributed in any significant way to the material injury suffered by the Community industry" (decline in consumption); that it made "no significant contribution" (export performance) or that "no significant influence" could have resulted (own imports of the product concerned), that it cannot have significantly contributed to injury (substitution), or (in the case of imports from the countries not subject to the investigation) "even if imports from other third countries may have contributed to the material injury suffered by the Community industry, it is hereby confirmed that they are not such to have broken the causal link between the dumping and the injury found." The European Communities concluded that any other factors that may have contributed to the injury to the domestic industry were "not such as to have broken the casual link" between dumped imports and injury.
>
> These aspects of the EC determination indicate to us that the European Communities *analysed individually the causal factors concerned and identified the individual effects of each of these causal factors.* With respect to each of the factors, the European Communities concluded that the extent of the contribution to injury was not significant, or, in one case, extrapolated that, even if the effect were significant, it would not be such as to "break the causal link" between dumped imports and

> material injury. The European Communities' overall conclusion was that none of these factors had an effect that was such to have broken the causal link between dumped imports and material injury.
> We are certainly aware of the theoretical possibility that a causation methodology which separates and distinguishes between individual injury factors may not accommodate the possibility that multiple "insignificant factors" might *collectively* constitute a significant cause of injury such as to sever the link between dumped imports and injury. However, the EC methodology – which we understand to separate and distinguish between the effects of each of these causal factors and the dumped imports including through an examination as to whether the extent of the effects of each causal factor are such that it is necessary to separate and distinguish its effects – does not leave the effects of those factors entirely lumped together and indistinguishable.
> (§§ 7.367–369 of the Panel report, emphasis in the original)

Brazil appealed both findings.

6.2 *The AB's findings*

The AB understood the first issue before it to be as follows:

> The issue before us is whether, under Article 3.5, the alleged higher cost of production of the European Communities industry, raised by the Brazilian exporter solely in the context of the European Commission's dumping and injury determinations, was a "known factor[] other than the dumped imports which at the same time [was] injuring the domestic industry," thereby requiring examination by the European Commission.
> (§ 173)

And the AB described the second issue thus:

> The issue before us, therefore, is whether the non-attribution language of Article 3.5 requires an investigating authority, in conducting its causality analysis, to examine the effects of the other causal factors *collectively* after having examined them *individually*.
> (§ 187, emphasis in the original)

The AB rejected both claims advanced by Brazil, albeit on different grounds than those of the Panel. The AB discarded the Panel's conclusion that, unless Brazil raised the factor at each and every stage of the investigation, the factor at hand was not "known" to the investigating authority. In the AB's view, the fact that the factor was raised at some stage made the factor known throughout the investigation (§ 177).

However, since the EC had dismissed its relevance (in light of the aforementioned minute differences in cost structure among Brazilian and EC producers), the AB held that the EC no longer had to account for this factor during the investigation process.

The issue of whether there was an obligation to cumulate was more complicated. The AB rejected the claim advanced by Brazil on burden-of-proof grounds (§ 195); the AB accepted that, in principle, there could be cases where a cumulative assessment of the injury from factors other than dumped imports might be necessary (§§ 191–2). In its view, however, Brazil had not demonstrated why this was indeed the case in the instant matter. In the absence of specific proof to this effect, the AB upheld the Panel's findings (§ 194).

To reach this conclusion, the AB first recalled the pertinent part of Art. 3.5 AD, which is the applicable legal provision in this context:

> The authorities shall also examine any known factors other than the dumped imports which at the same time are injuring the domestic industry, and *the injuries caused by these other factors must not be attributed to the dumped imports.* (emphasis added by the AB in its report)

In the AB's view, this language was necessary for non-attribution purposes, and non-attribution was the objective of the causality requirement (§ 188). The AB interpreted the non-attribution requirement in the following way:

> Non-attribution therefore requires separation and distinguishing of the effects of other causal factors from those of the dumped imports so that injuries caused by the dumped imports and those caused by other factors are not "lumped together" and made "indistinguishable."
>
> (§ 188, footnote omitted)

At the same time, however, the AB noted that although the AD Agreement was explicit as to the *ends* sought through Art. 3.5 AD (non-attribution), it was silent as to the *means* to be used in pursuance of the stated ends:

> We underscored in *US – Hot Rolled Steel*, however, that the *Anti-Dumping Agreement* does not prescribe the *methodology* by which an investigating authority must avoid attributing the injuries of other causal factors to dumped imports:
>
> We emphasize that the particular methods and approaches by which WTO Members choose to carry out the process of separating and distinguishing the injurious effects of dumped imports from the

> injurious effects of the other known causal factors are not prescribed by the *Anti-Dumping Agreement.* What the Agreement requires is simply that the obligations in Article 3.5 be respected when a determination of injury is made.
>
> Thus, provided that an investigating authority does not attribute the injuries of other causal factors to dumped imports, it is free to choose the methodology it will use in examining the "causal relationship" between dumped imports and injury.
>
> (§ 189)

The AB did not delve into details of the methodology the EC employed in the present case. Having established the purpose of the causality requirement, as well as the absence of an obligation to use a specific methodology to reach the stated purpose, the AB went on to accept that, in principle, the Brazilian claim was valid. In the absence, however, of any specific arguments to substantiate its claim, the AB upheld the Panel's findings, albeit on different grounds: while the Panel saw no obligation to cumulate at all, the AB saw an obligation to cumulate in some unspecified situations. Implicitly, therefore, the AB admitted that there was no generic obligation imposed on WTO Members to cumulate the effects of factors other than dumped imports when performing their causality analysis; an individual examination of the effects of known factors sufficed.

6.3 Discussion

With respect to Brazil's first claim, we believe that the AB decision is correct, but could have been taken one step further. The Panel's finding that factors have to be raised in each separate stage of the investigation to be known to the investigating authority makes no sense, and it imposes a considerable burden on exporters who might not even know at which precise stage of the investigation they are since the AD Agreement does not impose any specific obligations in this respect. As a result, the "staging" of the procedure is a matter within the discretion of the investigating authority, and diversified practice among jurisdictions in this respect cannot *a priori* be excluded.

But the decision's shortcoming, as we see it, is that it does not address the fact that, after years and years of antidumping practice, GATT/WTO case law still accepts the notion that only factors raised by the parties are "known" to the investigating authority. This approach serves only to make life easy for investigating authorities and might throw into question the soundness of the findings as such. Take, for example, the present case: should not the EC authority, even in the absence of a submission by the Brazilian exporter, *motu proprio* ask its own domestic industry questions concerning its cost structure? It is remarkable that case law turns a blind eye to the fact that an investigating authority must first *investigate* before it judges the appropriateness of the imposition of antidumping duties. The AB, strictly speaking, did not have to deal with this issue, so we raise it simply as an *obiter dictum.*

On the second issue, however, a number of points can be raised. One can first note that Brazil was apparently arguing that, with respect to *other* factors that may explain injury, the EC should have taken into account not only their individual impact, but also their *aggregate* effect on injury.

First, we can note here that it is necessary in an economic/statistical analysis to take into account the interaction between different explanatory variables, for the reason indicated in our discussion of the "cumulation" issue.

Second, there are problems with the reliance on the inherently difficult concept of "causality" in several of the WTO agreements; indeed, legal analysis outside the confines of WTO law is typically quite weak in its treatment of causality: Roman law distinguished between *causa adequata* (where the issue is to what extent a factor by itself is sufficient to cause injury) and *conditio sine qua non* (where the issue is to what extent a particular factor is necessary for injury to occur). In legal practice, both tests have found application within qualitative narratives. Some laws (like, for example, the EC antitrust law) *sometimes* require very demanding causality tests: in its *Wood Pulp* judgment for example, the Court of Justice of the EC imposed a "but for" test on anyone wishing to demonstrate that a certain practice had its origins in a cartel type of behavior. According to this test, unless all other factors potentially explaining the behavior had been previously rejected, no explanation based on a cartel theory would have been demonstrated.[13]

The WTO case law is taking its first steps on this (quintessentially philosophical) issue. In the present dispute, the AB (probably wisely) refused to lay out how it understands causality in precise, operational

[13] This test is, of course, very demanding on the investigating authority and, if taken to its logical extreme, might lead to a proliferation of too few findings of illegalities, and hence underenforcement of the contract.

terms. What we find troubling, however, is the AB's argument that the EC methodology is acceptable, since the AD does not specify any particular methodology to follow:

> In contrast, we do not find that an examination of *collective* effects is necessarily required by the non-attribution language of the *Anti-Dumping Agreement.* In particular, we are of the view that Article 3.5 does not compel, *in every case*, an assessment of the *collective* effects of other causal factors, because such an assessment is not always necessary to conclude that injuries ascribed to dumped imports are actually caused by those imports and not by other factors.
>
> (§ 191, emphasis in original)

What we fail to see is how it can be known that an analysis of "collective" effects would not add information concerning the sources of injury *without conducting the analysis.*

In the AB's defense, it can be said that Brazil did not seem to explain in its appeal the *reasons* why the EC methodology was deficient. The AB, applying the *in dubio mitius* principle, was not prepared to question the EC action in the absence of at least a presumption that what the EC did was not enough. This may be correct from a formal point of view. But the AB here escaped the need to address the causality issue more fully by hiding behind a rather small tree.

7 The handling of documents in AD proceedings

The Panel faced two claims by Brazil concerning the handling of documents: first, that a certain document (called "EC-12") was not properly before the EC investigating authority, and second, that the EC was under the obligation to disclose it anyway. Document EC-12 was an internal note for file and included evidence that the EC had properly examined the injury factors enshrined in Art. 3.4 AD.

7.1 The Panel's findings

The Panel rejected both claims by Brazil (§§ 7.45–46 of the Panel report, *op. cit.*). The Panel found that the document was properly before the investigating authority and that the EC was under no obligation to disclose it. The Panel reached its first conclusion following a series of questions that it addressed to the EC on the matter. The Panel reached the second conclusion by finding that, since the EC had made available to interested parties the raw data used to prepare EC-12, the EC's position that disclosure of EC-12 would be unwarranted in the absence of additional information was legitimate. Brazil appealed both Panel findings.

7.2 The AB's findings

The AB faced two complaints by Brazil:

First, Brazil appealed the Panel's finding that EC-12 was properly before the investigating authority, claiming that this finding constituted an erroneous interpretation of Arts. 17.6, 3.1 and 3.4 AD.

Second, Brazil appealed the Panel's finding that the EC was under no obligation to disclose EC-12, claiming that this finding constituted an erroneous interpretation of the EC's obligations under Arts. 6.2 and 6.4 AD.

We address each claim in turn.

7.3 Discussion

7.3.1 When is a document properly before an investigating authority?

Brazil made three claims in this respect: the first was that the Panel's finding constituted an erroneous interpretation of Art. 17.6. The second and the third claims concerned violations of Arts. 3.1 AD and 3.4 AD, respectively. But these were in effect one and the same claim (since Art. 3.4 is a specification of the generic obligation embedded in Art. 3.1 AD). Following the AB's approach, we will examine them jointly.

We start with Brazil's claim under Art. 17.6 AD, which reads in relevant part:

> In examining the matter referred to in paragraph 5:
>
> (i) in its assessment of the facts of the matter, the panel shall determine whether the authorities' establishment of the facts was proper and whether their evaluation of those facts was unbiased and objective. If the establishment of the facts was proper and the evaluation was unbiased and objective, even though the panel might have reached a different conclusion, the evaluation shall not be overturned …

The issue before the AB was whether the Panel's assessment of the facts was proper, under Article. 17.6(i) of the *AD Agreement*, when it found that Exhibit EC-12 formed part of the record of the underlying antidumping investigation.

The AB first noted that the standard of review it applied to such claims was quite deferential towards the Panel's and, as its prior case law made clear, the AB would not interfere lightly with the Panel's discretion to act as the assessor of facts. This standard of review entailed, *ipso facto*, a high burden of proof for the complainant to meet in alleging that the Panel did not lawfully exercise its discretion when it found that the establishment of facts by the EC was proper (by including EC-12 in the record before the investigating authority).

The AB then described in detail Brazil's claim in this respect. In the AB's view, Brazil found fault with the Panel's position because the Panel relied solely on the EC assertion that EC-12 was properly before it (§ 126). Hence, in essence, Brazil reproached the Panel for laxity when dealing with this issue.

The AB rejected the Brazilian claim. In its view, ample record evidence demonstrated that the Panel did not rely solely on the EC assertion; it asked the EC a series of questions, and the EC offered evidence demonstrating that, throughout the investigation, it had relied on EC-12 (§§ 126–7). In the absence of any contrary evidence supplied by Brazil, which, as stated above, bore the burden of proof in this respect, the AB felt that it should not disturb the Panel's findings (§ 128).

Turning to Brazil's claims under Arts. 3.4 and 3.1 AD, Brazil argued that the information included in EC-12 was not contemporaneous with the investigation. In the AB's words:

> [Brazil] asserts that the issue here is that there was no verifiable evidence of the contemporaneous character of Exhibit EC-12 and, therefore, the European Communities was not entitled to rely on that document to evidence its compliance with Articles 3.1 and 3.4 of the *Anti-Dumping Agreement*.
>
> (§ 129, italics in the original)

In line with its prior findings in its *Thailand – H Beams* report (to which we refer *infra*), the AB dismissed Brazil's argument.[14] In the AB's view, Art. 3.4 AD did not at all prejudge the manner in which the information (i.e. the injury factors laid down one by one in the body of this provision) was to be reviewed: investigating authorities were

[14] Appellate Body Report, *Thailand – Anti-Dumping Duties on Angles, Shapes and Sections of Iron or Non-Alloy Steel and H-Beams from Poland*, WT/DS122/AB/R, adopted 5 April 2001.

required by virtue of this information to review certain information, and there was no additional obligation.[15]

7.3.2 Should EC-12 have been disclosed to interested parties?

The AB upheld Brazil's claim that the EC-12 document should have been disclosed to interested parties. To reach this conclusion, the AB first referred to Art. 6.4 AD, which reads:

> The authorities shall whenever practicable provide timely opportunities for all interested parties to see all information that is relevant to the presentation of their cases, that is not confidential as defined in paragraph 5, and that is used by the authorities in an anti-dumping investigation, and to prepare presentations on the basis of this information.

The AB critically distanced itself from the Panel's findings in this respect when it dismissed the rationale offered in support of the final finding in the Panel report, namely that it was for the investigating authority to judge whether the information at hand was relevant and, if so, to disclose it. In the AB's view, it was for the interested parties to do this (§ 145). Moreover, the AB stated that since the investigating authority's evaluation of certain injury factors was set out exclusively in EC-12, this information was in fact used by the EC in its investigation, and the EC was thus obligated to disclose it to interested parties (§ 147).

Finally, the AB agreed with the argument presented before it that a violation of Art. 6.4 AD leads *ipso facto* to a violation of Art. 6.2 AD (§ 149). For these reasons it reversed the Panel's findings and held that the EC, by not disclosing EC-12, violated its obligations under Arts. 6.2 and 6.4 AD (§ 150).

7.3.3 The AB did not address the core issue

We believe that the AB essentially avoided responding to the core of the Brazilian claim, by adopting an overly formalistic reading of some AD provisions, and by failing to offer an overall approach as to what needs to be done, in light of current legislative constraints, when similar claims are being formulated. Let us first recount the facts:

1. Art. 3.4 AD lays down all factors demonstrating injury that must be reviewed by an investigating authority;

[15] As we will try to develop in Art. 2.6.4, the AB, through this finding, essentially avoided responding to the real issue.

2. EC-12 is the sole evidence that the EC did, in fact, examine the factors reflected in Art. 3.4 AD;
3. The EC did not disclose EC-12 to the Brazilian exporters under investigation.

Brazil, for all practical purposes, alleges that EC-12 has been "cooked." It also complains that the document has not been disclosed to its exporters. The AB agrees with the second claim because, in its view, anything that the exporter claims is relevant should be disclosed to the exporter. The AB avoids responding to the former allegation by asserting that all Art. 3.4 AD requires WTO Members to do is to examine the list of factors mentioned there, without prejudging the manner of examination.

But, of course, the real issue is whether the EC actually examined those factors or whether it simply produced an *ex post facto* justification under the name EC-12. The AB did not respond to the allegation that the EC did the latter.

7.3.4 How could Brazil have known the content of EC-12?

This is not the first time that WTO adjudicating bodies have faced similar claims. In *Thailand – H Beams*, Poland complained before the Panel that it was indiscernible from Thailand's final determination how that country had complied with the various requirements of the AD Agreement. Thailand then produced a document that explained in excruciating detail what had happened during the investigation that led Thailand to believe that an imposition of duties was in good order. The Panel in this dispute dismissed the document's relevance on the ground that absence of production equals absence of examination. Thailand appealed, and the AB (in our view, probably rightly so) rejected the Panel's finding. In the AB's view, the possibility that this information had indeed been used by the Thai authorities could not, as a matter of principle, be excluded outright simply because the document reflecting it had not been produced to the interested parties. In other words, the AB dissociates the obligation to notify from the obligation to review, without delving into the question whether, in the AD's institutional balance, interested parties should be notified of the content of a review, or to what extent an investigating authority can use information, relating to a review of the factors mentioned in Art. 3.4 AD, that at the same time can legitimately be kept away from interested parties.

What is the institutional balance embedded in this interpretation of the AD Agreement? On the one hand, an investigating authority must publish a final determination that contains in sufficient detail all issues of law and fact *considered material* by the investigating authority (Art. 12.2 AD). Clearly, the words "considered material" leave room for discretion, and therefore it cannot be ruled out that some information used in the proceedings to reach the final determination may be excluded from the public announcement.[16] On the other hand, Art. 6.4 AD obliges investigating authorities to disclose all information requested by interested parties.[17]

Assuming that parties had access to the same information, one could possibly argue that, to the extent that some information was not requested under Art. 6.4 AD, it was not judged material by the interested party at hand, and therefore all such subsequent claims on this score should fail on this ground. But access to information is in practice not symmetric, and such symmetry is nowhere reflected in the institutional balance of the AD Agreement. Instead, AD investigations take place within an adversarial system, where the umpire (the investigating authority) will be asked to administer conflicting information in a due-process manner. The AD Agreement nowhere imposes on the authority the obligation to immediately disclose to the exporter, for example, information submitted by the domestic industry. One should thus expect that the parties often have very different access to information.

Hence, an interested party can protect its rights under Art. 6.4 AD only in a limited manner: it can request information on issues about which, in one way or another, it has knowledge. With respect to the other issues, the only information it will (eventually) get will be through the public notice. But, as argued, an investigating authority does not have to disclose all information, by virtue of Art. 12.2 AD. Hence some relevant information might never be transmitted. Article 6.9 AD is not of much help either: according to this provision, an

[16] For the purposes of our argument here, we do not need to deal with the situation where the excluded information, in the case of a challenge, is subsequently judged material by a WTO Panel. We will return to this point when discussing our suggested approach.

[17] For the purposes of our argument here, we do not need to deal with disclosure obligations in regard to submitted confidential information. Indeed, in the case at hand, there was no such argument advanced by Brazil.

investigating authority must always, before a decision is made, inform interested parties of the *essential facts* on which the decision is based. Once again the term "essential facts" leaves room for discretion.

So, the AB was effectively beating around the bush when ruling under Art. 6.4 AD. On the one hand, the AB finding in this respect is one step toward making the due-process clause more effective. Regrettably, however, it does not go the full nine yards. To do that, we submit, the AB would have to address Art. 12.2 AD in a meaningful, contextual manner.

The *Pipe Fittings* Panel essentially wholeheartedly adopted the AB's *Thailand – H Beams* determination. The AB upheld the Panel's finding and, as mentioned *supra*, reversed only the Panel's findings with respect to the disclosure requirement.

If there were an excuse for the AB determination in the *Thailand – H Beams* case (since Poland did not argue that the Thai document was indeed "cooked"), there is no such excuse here: Brazil did, in fact, argue that EC-12 was not properly before the EC investigating authority because, in all likelihood, it did not exist at the time of the investigation. Brazil also argued that this conclusion was warranted by the fact that the document was not produced to Brazil: the disclosure obligations are thus, in Brazil's eyes, the institutional safeguard to guarantee that documents will not be "cooked."

Viewed against this background, the AB rulings are a half-measure: on the one hand, the AB emphasized the importance of Art. 6.4 AD, insisting that it is not up to the investigating authority to decide which information is relevant. But the AB failed to take the bigger picture into account: how is Brazil to know exactly what has been used as input in the investigation, other than through communications/notifications to its exporters? The AD, as we established above, does not require that *all* information be transmitted by the investigating authority. But the AD approach could have been substantially helped, had the AB re-thought its findings in *Thailand – H Beams* and elaborated on its reasoning there. In short, we believe that through a more appropriate allocation of the burden of proof, concerns similar to those of Brazil in the present case can be taken care of.

8 Concluding remarks

To conclude, let us just note that in line with our prior writings in this context, our main source of discontent with this AB report is the often acontextual interpretation of some of the key terms of the AD Agreement. We believe that, read in their context, several provisions should have been interpreted differently than what was done by the AB. Consequently, in our view, the AB, in this case following unpersuasive reasoning, ended up with the wrong outcome.

References

Goldberg, P. K. and Knetter, M. M. 1997. "Goods markets and exchange rates: what have we learned?" *Journal of Economic Literature* **35**: 1244–1272.

6

United States – Final Determination with Respect to Certain Softwood Lumber from Canada (AB-2003-6, WT/DS257/AB/R)

HENRIK HORN
Institute for International Economic Studies, Stockholm University
PETROS C. MAVROIDIS
Columbia Law School, New York and University of Neuchâtel, Switzerland

1 Introduction

This note addresses the Word Trade Organization (WTO) dispute *United States – Final Countervailing Duty Determination With Respect To Certain Softwood Lumber From Canada* (WT/DS257); denoted "*Softwood Lumber IV*" below. The issues discussed by the Panel and the Appellate Body (AB) in this dispute are very closely related to those examined by the Panel in *United States – Preliminary Countervailing Duty Determination With Respect To Certain Softwood Lumber From Canada* (WT/DS236); to be referred to as "*Softwood Lumber III*." This dispute was not appealed, and the AB thus did not have the opportunity to provide its view on the issues raised in the dispute. The fundamental character of several of the issues at stake in both these disputes makes the AB's determination in *Softwood Lumber IV* particularly interesting.

The Panel in *Softwood Lumber IV* – "the Panel" if not stated otherwise – saw itself as facing seven claims by Canada:

(1) The United States Department of Commerce (USDOC) erred in determining that "stumpage" is a financial contribution in the form of the provision of a good by provincial governments.

(2) The USDOC erred in finding that the Canadian provincial stumpage programs confer a benefit.
(3) Even if stumpage does provide subsidies, the USDOC erred in not conducting a pass-through analysis in determining subsidization of softwood lumber in the case of certain upstream transactions for inputs.
(4) The USDOC failed to determine that the programs are *specific* subsidies within the meaning of Art. 2 of the Agreement on Subsidies and Countervailing Measures (SCM).
(5) The USDOC inflated the subsidy amount by using an inaccurate factor to convert the US log measurements into cubic meters.
(6) The United States did not comply with its obligations under Art. 12 *SCM* in regard to two aspects of the investigation, which concerned the change in the choice of benchmark state from the preliminary to the final determination, and the use of information based on a letter of the Maine Forest Products Council.
(7) The *Byrd Amendment* payments distorted the assessed support for the investigation, in violation of Art. 11.4 SCM.

The Panel found the following:

(1) The USDOC's determination that provision of stumpage constitutes a financial contribution in the form of the provision of a good or service was not inconsistent with Art. 1.1(a)(1)(iii) *SCM.*
(2) The USDOC's determination of the existence and amount of benefit to the producers of the subject merchandise was inconsistent with Art. 14 and 14(d) *SCM.*
(3) The USDOC's failure to conduct a pass-through analysis in respect of upstream transactions for log and lumber inputs between unrelated entities was inconsistent with Art. 10 *SCM* and Art. VI:3 of GATT 1994.
(4) The USDOC's determination that the provincial stumpage programs are specific was not inconsistent with Art. 2.1(c) *SCM.*

The Panel refrained from adjudicating on claims (5) and (6) for reasons of judicial economy, and Canada essentially withdrew claim (7).

Both Canada and the United States appealed certain findings by the Panel, giving the AB the opportunity to address claims (1)–(3) above.

In this note, we will examine the AB's determination in regard to issues (2) and (3), concentrating on what we see as new elements in relation to *Softwood Lumber III*; we discussed the latter dispute in Horn and Mavroidis (2005). We will, however, refrain from discussing issue (1) – whether stumpage programs provide goods in the sense of the *SCM* – even though it may have broken some new legal ground. We simply find the issues addressed in this context to be of such a legal/technical nature that they lack more general interest. Let us just note that for reasons explained in Horn and Mavroidis (2005), we find it clear that from the point of view of the object and purpose of the *SCM* (if not the text and context), the stumpage programs must be seen as "providing goods," and that they may thereby confer a benefit. We thus fully agree with the AB determination in this regard:

> . . . we *uphold* the Panel's finding, in paragraph 7.30 of the Panel Report, that USDOC's "[d]etermination that the Canadian provinces are providing a financial contribution in the form of the provision of a good by providing standing timber to timber harvesters through the stumpage programmes" is not inconsistent with Article 1.1(a)(1)(iii) of the *SCM Agreement.*
>
> (§ 76, italics in original)

We will discuss the AB's findings in regard to the calculation of benefit in Section 2 of this note, and address the pass-through issue in Section 3. Section 4 states our conclusion.

2 The AB's findings on alternative benchmarks

In establishing the magnitude of the benefit allegedly provided by the stumpage programs, the United States employed prices on stumpage contracts in various US states. The United States justified the procedure by arguing that, although the use of Canadian private stumpage prices would have been the preferred option to calculate the amount of benefit, in this particular case it was not possible to use such prices as the benchmark, since they were distorted and suppressed by the very measure under investigation. According to the United States, the trade-distorting potential of the government's provision of a good can be identified only by reference to an independent market price, i.e. a price that is unaffected by the very trade distortion the test is designed to identify.

The Panel explicitly accepted that the United States might have a point, as a matter of economic logic. It would therefore be desirable to use other private-sector prices than those prevailing in the allegedly subsidizing country, in certain special situations. But the *SCM* does not allow for this possibility in situations other than those in which *no* market price exists in the investigated country. In cases where market prices exist, WTO Members have to rely on them, even if the market at hand is small. The Panel felt that, economically irrational as this outcome may be, it did not have the mandate to modify the unambiguous terms of the Agreement:

> . . . we do not believe that it would be appropriate for this Panel to substitute its economic judgement for that of the drafters. The Appellate Body has repeatedly emphasized, and we cannot but agree, that under Article 31 of the Vienna Convention on the Law of Treaties the interpretation of a treaty must be based on the text, as a proper interpretation is first of all a textual interpretation. For all the reasons set forth above, we do not consider that Article 14(d) can, consistent with customary rules of interpretation of public international law, be understood in the manner urged by the United States. We consider that our task is to interpret the applicable provisions as they exist and apply the text of the Agreement to the facts before us, not to rule on the economic logic of the text as it stands.
>
> (§ 7.59, footnote omitted)

2.1 The US appeal

The Panel's finding was appealed by the United States. In the AB's words, the US claim was the following:

> The United States argues that the Panel's interpretation of Article 14(d) is "completely at odds" with the concept of "benefit", as used in Article 1.1 of the *SCM Agreement* and as interpreted by the Appellate Body. The United States refers to the Appellate Body's interpretation of the term "benefit" in Article 1.1(b) in *Canada – Aircraft*, where it said that a government financial contribution confers a benefit if the "'financial contribution' makes the recipient 'better off' than it would otherwise have been, absent that contribution", and that the marketplace provides the appropriate basis for comparison. According to the United States, the Panel's interpretation would not permit an investigating authority to determine whether the recipient is better off than it would have been absent the financial contribution. In addition, the United States contends

> that the term "market conditions" in Article 14(d) "can only mean a market undistorted by the government's financial contribution." Therefore, the United States submits that USDOC could rightfully reject the prices of private transactions in Canada as a benchmark.
>
> (§ 80, italics in the original)

Consequently, the United States requested the AB to reverse the Panel's findings in this respect. The AB understood its task in the following terms:

> The initial issue before us is whether an investigating authority may use a benchmark, under Article 14(d) of the *SCM Agreement*, other than private prices in the country of provision for determining if goods have been provided by a government for less than adequate remuneration. If our answer were to be in the affirmative, two additional questions would arise: (i) what are the specific circumstances under Article 14(d) in which an investigating authority may use a benchmark other than private prices in the country of provision; and (ii) assuming such circumstances exist, what alternative benchmarks may an investigating authority use to determine whether goods were provided by a government for less than adequate remuneration.
>
> (§ 82, footnote omitted)

2.2 *The AB's findings*

The AB partitions the claim by the United States into several distinct issues.

2.2.1 *Can* alternative benchmarks be used?

The first question addressed is *whether* Art. 14(d) of the SCM permits investigating authorities to use a benchmark other than private prices in the country of provision. The AB here first examines the text, and finds that the Panel made an erroneous interpretation of the phrase "in relation to" in Art. 14(d) *SCM*:

> . . . The Panel reasoned that the phrase "in relation to" in the context of Article 14(d) means "in comparison with". . .. As we see it, the phrase "in relation to" implies a comparative exercise, but its meaning is not limited to "in comparison with". The phrase "in relation to" has a meaning similar to the phrases "as regards" and "with respect to". These phrases do not denote the rigid comparison suggested by the Panel, but may imply a broader sense of "relation, connection, reference". Thus, the use of the phrase "in relation to" in Article 14(d) suggests that, contrary to

> the Panel's understanding, the drafters did not intend to exclude any possibility of using as a benchmark something other than private prices in the market of the country of provision.
>
> (§§ 88–89)

The AB then moves to the context of Art. 14(d) *SCM*:

> The chapeau of Article 14 requires that "*any*" method used by investigating authorities to calculate the benefit to the recipient shall be provided for in a WTO Member's legislation or regulations, and it requires that its application be transparent and adequately explained. The reference to "*any*" method in the chapeau clearly implies that more than one method consistent with Article 14 is available to investigating authorities for purposes of calculating the benefit to the recipient. The Panel's interpretation of paragraph (d) that, whenever available, private prices have to be used *exclusively* as the benchmark, is not supported by the text of the chapeau . . .
>
> (§ 91)

In addition, a wider interpretation of the concept "in relation to" is mandated also due to the object and purpose of Art. 14 *SCM*. The AB here relies on the argument that government subsidies may distort private-sector prices, if the private sector is sufficiently small relative to the government sector:

> . . . the determination of the existence of a benefit is a necessary condition for the application of countervailing measures under the *SCM*. If the calculation of the benefit yields a result that is artificially low, or even zero, as could be the case under the Panel's approach, then a WTO Member could not fully offset, by applying countervailing duties, the effect of the subsidy as permitted by the Agreement.
>
> (§ 95)

On the basis of these findings, the AB concludes that the Panel's interpretation of Art. 14(d) is overly restrictive. Other prices than those in the country of provision *can* be used as benchmarks even when the latter prices exist.

2.2.2 *When* can alternative benchmarks be used?

The second issue decided by the AB is: *when* may an investigating authority use a benchmark other than private prices in the country of provision? The United States argued in its appeal that this possibility is not restricted to situations where no privately determined domestic price exists at all, but also applies to situations where such prices exist, but are distorted by the subsidy. The AB here argues that:

> . . . there may be little difference between situations where the government is the sole provider of certain goods and situations where the government has a predominant role in the market as a provider of those goods. Whenever the government is the predominant provider of certain goods, even if not the sole provider, it is likely that it can affect through its own pricing strategy the prices of private providers for those goods, inducing the latter to align their prices to the point where there may be little difference, if any, between the government price and the private prices. This would be so even if the government price does not represent adequate remuneration. The resulting comparison of prices carried out under the Panel's approach to interpreting Article 14(d) would indicate a "benefit" that is artificially low, or even zero, such that the full extent of the subsidy would not be captured, as the Panel itself acknowledged. As a result, the subsidy disciplines in the *SCM Agreement* and the right of Members to countervail subsidies could be undermined or circumvented when the government is a predominant provider of certain goods. (§ 100)
>
> It appears to us that the language found in Article 14(d) ensures that the provision's purposes are not frustrated in such situations. Thus, while requiring investigating authorities to calculate benefit "in relation to" prevailing conditions in the market of the country of provision, Article 14(d) permits investigating authorities to use a benchmark other than private prices in that market. When private prices are distorted because the government's participation in the market as a provider of the same or similar goods is so predominant that private suppliers will align their prices with those of the government-provided goods, it will not be possible to calculate benefit having regard exclusively to such prices. (§ 101)

But the AB also cautions that the possibility of using alternative benchmarks is very limited:

> . . . We agree with the United States that "[t]he fact that the government is a significant supplier of goods does not, in itself, establish that all prices for the goods are distorted". Thus, an allegation that a government is a significant supplier would not, on its own, prove distortion and allow an investigating authority to choose a benchmark other than private prices in the country of provision. The determination of whether private prices are distorted because of the government's predominant role in the market, as a provider of certain goods, must be made on a case-by-case

> basis, according to the particular facts underlying each countervailing duty investigation.
>
> (§ 102)

On the basis of this reflected reasoning, the AB concludes that:

> … an investigating authority may use a benchmark other than private prices of the goods in question in the country of provision, when it has been established that those private prices are distorted, because of the predominant role of the government in the market as a provider of the same or similar goods.
>
> § (§ 103, underlining added)

The AB thus reverses the Panel's finding and determines that prices other than private-sector prices in the country of provision may be used:

> … when it has been established that those private prices are distorted because of the predominant role of the government in the market as a provider of the same or similar products …
>
> (§ 103)

2.2.3 *Which* alternative benchmarks can be used?

The AB reports that at the oral hearing, Canada suggested three possibilities:

> … (i) a benchmark constructed using a methodology similar to that provided in Article 2.2 of the *Agreement on Implementation of Article VI of the General Agreement on Tariffs and Trade 1994* (the "*Anti-Dumping Agreement* "); (ii) a proxy estimated on the basis of costs of production; and (iii) a methodology that examines whether government prices are consistent with market principles …
>
> (§ 105)

The United States instead proposed world market prices available in the country of provision, or an examination of the consistency of the contested measures with market principles. The AB agreed to these proposals in very general terms. But it refrained from taking any more definite stands, since the issue before it was limited to whether the method actually employed by the US authority was legal.

2.2.4 The legality of the method employed by the United States

The Panel's finding that the method employed by the United States – to use prices from neighboring US states as benchmarks – was illegal under Art. 14(d) *SCM*, was based on an interpretation of this Article that the AB had hitherto rejected. The AB therefore reversed the Panel's finding. Having reversed this finding, the AB would have been required to determine the legality of the US method *de novo*. But it refrained from doing this, since, in its view, it lacked the necessary factual information that would have allowed it to complete such a legal analysis.

2.3 Discussion

As a matter of economic logic, we fully agree with the AB that alternative benchmarks are necessary in cases where the government significantly influences private prices, directly or indirectly. As emphasized by the AB, when undertaking such calculations, it will be necessary to adjust the benchmark prices, in order to appropriately account for various differences between different markets, such as differences in production costs, transport costs, costs of capital, or differences in taxation that may directly or indirectly affect any price comparison, etc. But while as a matter of principle it is necessary to use alternative benchmarks, it will in practice most likely be very hard to determine these in a satisfactory fashion. As we discussed in Horn and Mavroidis (2005), there are fundamental difficulties with the *SCM* in this respect.

While we are sympathetic to the AB's findings from this perspective, although concerned about its practical aspects, we see a legal problem with the AB's textual analysis. The AB seems to be drawing very far-reaching conclusions from the distinction it draws between the Panel's interpretation of "in relation to" as meaning "in comparison with," and their own, wider interpretation of "relation, connection, reference." From this wider interpretation, the AB infers that:

> ... the drafters did not intend to exclude any possibility of using as a benchmark something other than private prices in the market of provision.
>
> (§ 89)

We fail to see that such an interpretation of the drafters' intentions could be read from the three words "relation, connection, reference." If the drafters intended the term "in relation to" to be of such an indicative nature, why were they not more explicit on this score, by including a term such as "*inter alia*"? If silence means something (as the AB has time and again told us), then clearly in this case it must mean that the founding fathers had no wish to provide alternative benchmarks.

We are thus led to conclude that the Panel's interpretation is more correct than that of the AB, from a textual point of view. This is what prompted us, in our report of last year, to recommend a formal amendment of the *SCM* in this respect. As we see it, the AB's finding is effectively impermissible judicial activism, since the AB's interpretation of Art. 14(d) *SCM* amounts to a formal amendment of the provision. As Art. X of the Agreement Establishing the WTO makes plain, this is the exclusive privilege of the *Herren der Verträge*, the WTO Membership. We believe that even an authentic interpretation (as per Art. IX of the Agreement Establishing the WTO) is legally impossible here, since, what is requested is not a specification of a term, but, instead, a complete turnaround of the situation (by providing for the possibility, nonexisting in the current text, to use alternative benchmarks every time a situation similar to that of the instant case is present).

3 When is a pass-through analysis necessary?

The third substantive issue that the AB addresses concerns the need for analysis of the pass-through of any subsidy to log production, to downstream lumber production. Canada claimed before the Panel that in instances where the recipient of the (alleged) subsidy is at arm's length from the subject of the countervailing duty – the lumber producer – the United States was required to conduct a pass-through analysis. The United States, on the other hand, claimed that there was no such necessity when the subsidy determination was made on an aggregate basis.

In the view of the Panel,

> [t]he heart of the pass-through issue is whether, where a subsidy is received by someone other than the producer or exporter of the product under investigation, the subsidy nevertheless can be said to have conferred benefits in respect of that product ...
>
> (§ 7.91 Panel report)

The Panel concluded that this cannot be taken for granted. With regard to the US argument that the analysis was performed on an aggregate basis, the Panel responded:

> Thus, contrary to the US argument, the question of pass-through has to do with correctly identifying the subsidy amount attributable to the

> subject merchandise entering the US (the numerator). The fact that the US conducted the lumber investigation on an aggregate basis does not prevent and cannot cure the overall numerator (the aggregate subsidy amount from the stumpage programmes) from being overstated where upstream transactions for inputs between unrelated entities are present and subsidies have not been passed through.
>
> (§ 7.98)

The Panel consequently found in favor of Canada.

3.1 The US appeal

The United States appealed the Panel's determination, claiming that no pass-through analysis of subsidization to log production for the production of softwood lumber was necessary in two specific situations involving arm's-length relationships:

(1) where a tenured timber harvester owns a sawmill and processes some of the logs it harvests into softwood lumber, but at the same time sells, at arm's length, some of the logs it harvests to unrelated sawmills for processing into lumber; and
(2) where a tenured timber harvester processes logs it harvests into lumber and sells, at arm's length, some or all of this lumber to lumber re-manufacturers for further processing.

3.2 The AB's findings

The AB first points out that, according to the text General Agreement on Tariffs and Trade (GATT) 1994 and the *SCM*, as well as according to case law,

> ... where countervailing duties are used to offset subsidies granted to producers of input products, while the duties are to be imposed on *processed* products, and where input producers and downstream processors operate at *arm's length*, the investigating authority must establish that the benefit conferred by a financial contribution directly on input producers is passed through, at least in part, to producers of the processed product subject to the investigation.
>
> (§ 146, italics in original)

The AB also dismisses the argument by the United States that:

> ... no pass-through analysis was required with respect to arm's length sales of logs and lumber by tenured timber harvesters owning sawmills,

> to unrelated sawmills and re-manufacturers, because Article 19.3 recognizes that exporters who are not investigated individually may nevertheless be subject to countervailing duties; accordingly, it is not necessary, in an aggregate investigation, to determine whether individual producers or exporters actually received subsidies.
>
> (§ 148)
>
> ...[w]here the producer of the input is not the same entity as the producer of the processed product, it cannot be presumed, however, that the subsidy bestowed on the input passes through to the processed product. In such case, it is necessary to analyze to what extent subsidies on inputs may be included in the determination of the total amount of subsidies bestowed upon processed products. For it is only the subsidies determined to have been granted upon the *processed products* that may be offset by levying countervailing duties on those products.
>
> (§ 140)

The AB agrees with the United States that Members are allowed to perform an investigation on an aggregate basis. But it nevertheless rejects the US claim that a pass-through analysis is for this reason not required:

> ... country-wide or company-specific countervailing duty rates may be imposed under Part V of the *SCM Agreement* only *after* the investigating authority has determined the existence of subsidization, injury to the domestic industry, and a causal link between them ...
>
> (§ 154, italics in original)

3.2.1 Sales of *logs* at arm's length by timber harvesters/sawmills to independent lumber producers

We now turn to the first of the two situations that the United States wanted the AB to examine: where *logs* are sold by vertically integrated harvesters/primary lumber producers to independent primary lumber producers. The United States claimed that in such a case there was no need for a pass-through analysis, because the harvester/sawmill *was* a producer of the product subject to the investigation by processing *some* logs into softwood lumber in its own sawmill.

The AB understands the United States to be arguing that the arm's-length sales may be cross-subsidizing the harvester/lumber producer's own primary lumber production:

> ... We understand the United States to argue that benefits, initially attached to logs, but retained by a harvester/sawmill when the logs are

> sold in arm's length transactions to unrelated buyers, may be used by such a vendor to "cross-subsidize" its own production of softwood lumber processed in-house from other logs . . .
>
> (§ 157)

But the AB does not accept this argument as a reason for not performing a pass-through analysis:

> . . . We agree, in the abstract, that a transfer of benefits from logs sold in arm's length transactions to lumber produced in-house from different logs *is possible* for a harvester that owns a sawmill. But whether, *in fact*, this occurs depends on the particular case under examination. In any event, these arm's length sales at issue concern logs, which are not products subject to the investigation. Accordingly, in cases where logs are sold by a harvester/sawmill in arm's length transactions to unrelated sawmills, it may *not* be assumed that benefits attaching to the *logs* (non-subject products) automatically pass through to the *lumber* (the subject product) produced by the harvester/sawmill. A pass-through analysis is thus required in such situations.
>
> (§ 157, italics in original)
>
> Indeed, we disagree with the proposition that, as long as an enterprise produces products subject to an investigation, *any* benefits accruing to the same enterprise from subsidies conferred on any different products it produces (which are *not* subject to that investigation), could be included, without need of a pass-through analysis, in the total amount of subsidization found to exist for the investigated product, and that may be offset by levying countervailing duties on that product. We conclude that the pass-through of the benefit cannot be presumed with respect to arm's length sales of logs by harvesters, who own sawmills, to unrelated sawmills, for further processing.
>
> (§ 158, italics in original)

The AB thus upheld the Panel's finding that the lack of pass-through analysis violated US obligations under Arts. 10 and 32.1 *SCM*, and Art. VI:3 of the GATT 1994.

3.2.2 Sales of *lumber* at arm's length by timber harvesters/sawmills to independent lumber re-manufacturers

The final issue addressed by the AB is the US claim that no pass-through analysis is needed in a case where a tenured timber harvester processes logs it harvests into lumber and sells, at arm's length, some or all of the lumber to re-manufacturers for further processing. The AB starts by emphasizing that in such a case:

> ... the products of *both* the harvesters/sawmills and the re-manufacturers are subject to the investigation ...
>
> (§ 161, italics in original)

The AB then quotes from the Panel report:

> ... some portion of any subsidy from stumpage is attributable to the harvester/sawmill's production of the lumber for re-manufacturing and some is attributable to the other products (including lumber) that the harvester/sawmill produces. Here, if the subsidies attributable to the lumber for re-manufacturing are not passed through to the re-manufacturer that purchases it, then those subsidies should not be included in the numerator of the subsidization equation, as in this situation it is the re-manufactured product, not the upstream lumber product, that is the subject merchandise under investigation.
>
> (§ 162)

The AB dismisses this reasoning as a confusing of pass-through questions that may arise when individual enterprises are investigated with questions arising when calculations are made on an aggregate basis:

> ... Once it has been established that benefits from subsidies received by producers of *non-subject* products (that is, inputs) have passed through to producers of *subject* products (primary and remanufactured softwood lumber), we do not see why a further pass-through analysis *between* producers of subject products should be required in an investigation conducted on an aggregate basis. In this situation, it is not necessary to calculate precisely how subsidy benefits are divided up between the producers of subject products in order to calculate, on an aggregate basis, the total amount of subsidy and the country-wide countervailing duty rate for those subject products.
>
> (§ 163, italics in original)

The AB notes that this procedure may result in the imposition of duties on shipments of re-manufactured softwood that is not being subsidized. But this is nevertheless "by the book":

> ... Article 19 of the *SCM Agreement* contemplates the imposition of a country-wide countervailing duty rate, even when a specific exporter is not subsidized, or when that country-wide rate does not match the

> precise amount of subsidization benefiting a specific shipment . . . [T]he possibility for an exporter not investigated individually to request, pursuant to Article 19.3, an expedited review to establish an individual countervailing duty rate for that exporter, also confirms that a country-wide duty rate may, in principle, be imposed. However, the pass-through question would not be the same when determining, through the review procedure provided for in Article 19.3, an individual countervailing duty rate for the exporter that requested the review. In such a review, it is likely that a pass-through analysis would be required to determine whether input subsidies on logs, having passed through to the production of softwood lumber inputs, have passed through *also* to remanufactured lumber produced from those inputs by the *particular exporter.*
>
> (§ 164, italics in original, footnote omitted)

The AB thus reversed the Panel's finding that the failure to conduct a pass-through analysis in respect of arm's-length sales of *lumber* by tenured harvesters/sawmills to unrelated re-manufacturers violates Arts. 10 and 32.1 *SCM* and Art. VI:3 GATT 1994.

3.3 Discussion

From an economic perspective, whether a pass-through analysis should be undertaken or not clearly depends on what the purpose of such an analysis would be, which in turn must reflect the purpose of the *SCM* and Art. VI GATT. But *if* the purpose is to prevent injury to import-competing industry, and the countervailing duty (CVD) should only just offset such injury, then it is *always* necessary to perform a pass-though analysis, regardless of the vertical structure of the industry in the allegedly subsidizing country. This is, of course, the purpose of CVDs. Contrary to what seems to be the prevailing view among the parties to this dispute, and also the adjudicating bodies, there is no guarantee that in the case of a vertically integrated structure, subsidies to upstream activities will affect downstream production (even though there is probably a presumption to this effect). And in the case of arm's-length relationships, it is entirely possible, if not likely, that there will be effects on downstream production from upstream subsidization.

The AB seems to agree with this view, since, if it thought that a pass-through analysis was unnecessary, presumably it would have said so, and suggested what should take place instead. But it did not. The reason it reversed the Panel's findings with respect to sales of lumber at arm's length by timber harvesters/sawmills to independent lumber re-manufactures is that in such cases, because duties can be imposed on an *aggregate* basis, there is a legislative presumption that exported softwood lumber from noninvestigated Canadian producers has been subsidized (Art. 19.3 SCM), and therefore there is no need for an additional investigation to the same effect. One may indeed question the reasonableness of this provision. But such a task was not before the AB, and for this reason we leave this issue aside. What can be noted, however, is that an aggregate procedure must by necessity be imprecise, and lead to duties on individual products that do not reflect the actual extent of subsidization. But it is hard to say anything about how such a calculation should be performed from an economic point of view. Also, economic operators who have not been subsidized can always request refund of duties, assuming they have proven that they never benefited from a subsidy. There is, by virtue of Art. 19.3 SCM, a reversal of the burden of proof, in the sense that, CVDs can be imposed without a prior demonstration of subsidization.

4 Concluding remarks

The Panel and the AB seem in this dispute to have moved in the direction of generally both desiring and requiring a pass-through analysis, in contrast to the Panel's position in *Softwood Lumber III*. As we have explained, we find such a move intellectually appealing. We also find the AB's approach refreshing in being less narrowly textual, and placing greater emphasis on context and purpose, even though, regrettably, this time the AB went too far in this direction. We find it hard to interpret Art. 14(d) SCM, as it now stands, so as to allow for alternative benchmarks of the type proposed by the United States to be used. While the Panel acknowledged this restriction imposed by the Agreement, the AB neglected it, and by taking on the role of the legislator, the AB thus contravened Art. 3.2 DSU.

References

Horn, H. and Mavroidis, P. C. (2005). United States – Preliminary Determination with Respect to Certain Softwood Lumber from Canada: What is a subsidy? In H. Horn and P. C. Mavroidis, eds., *Principles of World Trade Law: The World Trade Organization. The Case Law of 2002.* The American Law Institute and Cambridge University Press, Cambridge, UK.

7

United States – Definitive Safeguard Measures on Imports of Certain Steel Products (WT/DS259; WT/DS252; WT/DS248; WT/DS249; WT/DS251; WT/DS258; WT/DS254; WT/DS253: DSR 2003:VII, 3117)

GENE M. GROSSMAN
Princeton University
ALAN O. SYKES
University of Chicago

1 Introduction

Since the inception of the WTO, safeguard measures have regularly been the subject of dispute settlement proceedings. The latest in this chain of disputes concerns the definitive safeguard measures imposed by the United States on a wide range of steel products in 2002.

The safeguards investigation of steel imports was initiated under the US law by the US International Trade Commission (USITC) at the request of the United States Trade Representative (USTR) in June, 2001. The request covered four broad categories of steel products, which were divided into 33 categories by the USITC for purposes of data collection. Ultimately, the USITC defined 27 separate "industries" producing steel products within the scope of the investigation. For each of these industries, the USITC proceeded to determine whether imports had increased, and if so, whether increased imports were a substantial cause of serious injury or threat of injury. This analysis resulted in negative determinations for 15 industries, affirmative determinations for eight industries, and "divided" determinations (a 3–3 vote) for four industries.[1]

Under the US law, a negative determination by the USITC precludes any action by the President to impose a safeguard measure. Affirmative determinations and divided determinations are forwarded to the President for consideration of possible relief, along with remedial recommendations that the President is not bound to follow. As to some products, the USITC has recommended that imports from nations with which the United States has preferential trading arrangements – including Canada, Mexico, Israel, and Jordan – be exempted from any safeguard measures.

After the conclusion of an inter-agency review process, the President instituted ten distinct safeguard "measures" covering various steel products, which generally excluded imports from preferential trading partners. Eight WTO members (including the European Community) challenged the measures pursuant to the WTO dispute resolution process, and the proceedings were consolidated before a single Panel. The Panel ruled against the United States on all of the challenged measures, on multiple grounds. The Appellate Body affirmed the ruling in considerable part, leading to the eventual dismantling of the measures in December, 2003.

The issues before the Panel and the Appellate Body were by and large familiar ones, and their opinions broke little new ground. The Panel decision is by far the more interesting of the two, but in the end we view both opinions as simply the latest in a long line of unsatisfactory WTO decisions in the safeguards area. Our critique in this regard draws heavily on our prior work, along with the work of other American Law Institute (ALI) reporters. See Horn and Mavroidis (2003); Sykes (2003, 2004); Grossman and Mavroidis (2005).

Section 2 lays out some of the key legal issues in safeguards jurisprudence, and describes the state of the law prior to the steel dispute. Section 3 then considers the issues in the steel case, notes some interesting features of the Panel report, and shows how the Appellate Body decision added little to what had come before it. Section 4 offers some concluding thoughts about the future of safeguard measures in the WTO system and the need for coherent reforms.

[1] USITC, Certain Steel Products, Inv. No. TA-201-73, (USITC Pub. No. 3479, December, 2001), Vol. I (hereafter USITC Report).

2 Legal, historical, and economic background

The legal basis for safeguards in the General Agreement on Tarriffs and Trade (GATT) system originally was found in Art. XIX, which became outmoded with the passage of time in a way that created serious confusion regarding the legal prerequisites for the use of safeguards. With the advent of the WTO, a new Safeguards Agreement elaborated additional legal constraints on the use of safeguards, but failed to resolve many of the central puzzles that had arisen under Art. XIX. Appellate Body decisions since the inception of the WTO have only made matters worse, to the point that the legal requirements for the use of safeguards are largely incoherent, and no nation can employ them without the near certainty of defeat in the dispute resolution process, should they be challenged. This section briefly reviews Art. XIX, the evolution of national practice under GATT, and the legal developments since the adoption of the Safeguards Agreement and prior to the steel decision.

2.1 Article XIX and its interpretive puzzles

GATT Art. XIX provides in paragraph (1):

> If, as a result of unforeseen developments and of the effect of the obligations incurred by a contracting party under this Agreement, including tariff concessions, any product is being imported into the territory of that contracting party in such increased quantities and under such conditions as to cause or threaten serious injury to domestic producers in that territory of like or directly competitive products, the contracting party shall be free, in respect of such product, and to the extent and for such time as may be necessary to prevent or remedy such injury, to suspend the obligation in whole or in part or to withdraw or modify the concession.

2.1.1 Unforeseen developments

The first clause of Art. XIX provides that safeguard measures are permissible only following "unforeseen developments" associated with "the obligations incurred by a contracting party." What constitutes an "unforeseen development?" Unforeseen by whom, at what point in time? How does one determine the "effect of the obligations incurred?"

These questions had a natural answer at the outset of the GATT system. The original GATT negotiations concluded in 1947, with the expectation that GATT would be supplanted within a few years by a new institution to be called the International Trade Organization (which, of course, never came into being because of a shift in the political winds). The first clause of Art. XIX has a natural interpretation in the context of a trade agreement that was expected to be short-lived. The negotiators had made a number of trade concessions to each other in 1947, and Art. XIX provided for their suspension in the event that those concessions had an unforeseen, adverse impact on import-competing industries due to a surge in import competition. To the questions posed above, therefore, one might answer that an "unforeseen development" was some development that caused the increase in imports following a trade concession under the original GATT to be greater than reasonably expected. It had to be unforeseen by the GATT negotiators, at the time of the 1947 negotiations. And the import surge had to result from one of the original GATT trade concessions, in the sense that it would not have happened *but for* some such concession.

But how does one interpret the requirements of Art. XIX(1), first clause, in an agreement that remains in force after many years? Consider an import surge 30 or 40 years after the agreement was drafted. What would it mean to say that such a surge resulted from the "obligations incurred," particularly if those obligations were incurred decades earlier? Could any such surge have been "foreseen" given the passage of so much time? By whom and when? And how are the answers affected by the fact that GATT negotiations are ongoing, with new negotiating "rounds" every decade or so? The requirements of the first clause no longer have a straightforward interpretation in an agreement that lasts for decades rather than a few years, and that is characterized by an ever-changing set of commitments.

For these reasons, GATT practice evolved over time toward ignoring the requirements of the first clause in Art. XIX(1).[2] National laws to authorize safeguard measures soon made no mention of them. Section 201 of the US Trade Act of 1974, for example, simply requires the USITC to determine "whether an article is being imported into the United States in such increased quantities as to be a substantial cause[3] of serious injury, or the threat thereof."[4] There is no requirement that developments be "unforeseen" or that they result from earlier

[2] See McGovern (1986, p. 291).

[3] A "substantial cause" is a "cause that it is important and not less than any other cause." 19 U.S.C. § 2252(b)(1)(B).

[4] 19 U.S.C. § 2252(b)(1)(A).

trade concessions. At this writing, this statute remains the basis for safeguard measures under the US law.

Such a development is an understandable consequence of the difficulties in giving content to the first clause of Art. XIX in a long-lived agreement. But as shall become immediately apparent, the absence of this "anchor" for the remainder of Art. XIX(1) creates other problems.

2.1.2 Serious injury and causation

Under Art. XIX, it is not enough that an unforeseen import surge results from a trade concession. The import surge must go on to cause or threaten "serious injury." This phrasing raises other obvious interpretive issues – what is "serious injury?" How does one determine whether the "cause" of such injury (or threat thereof) is "increased quantities" of imports?

On the first question, the text appears deliberately vague. The drafters might have made reference to specifics in this regard – lost profits, unemployment, bankruptcies, and the like – but chose to leave the term undefined. Perhaps the best inference is that they did not want to constrain the concept unduly by attempting a definition, and that they would allow a variety of factors into the analysis.

On the question of causation, the logic was nevertheless fairly clear. The unforeseen import surge, resulting from the trade concession, had to be responsible for serious injury. Put differently, the serious injury had to be "caused" by the trade concession, via its effect on the level of import competition, in the usual *but for* sense of the term "cause." Within this framework, the "exogenous" variable is the trade concession, and the "increased quantities" of imports were those resulting from that concession. Likewise, the level of imports in the absence of the trade concession serves as the baseline against which to measure the "increase."

But now imagine reading out the first clause of paragraph one, as GATT members began to do many years ago. Then, one must simply have "such increased quantities [of imports] . . . as to cause or threaten serious injury," as is required, for example, by the US law. The baseline for the "increase," import levels prior to a recent trade concession, is no longer available. Further, the only apparent candidate for an exogenous variable is the "increased quantities" of imports, as there is no longer any background event from which these "increased quantities" result.

Two considerable problems arise as a result. *First*, how does one now determine whether there are "increased quantities" of imports at all – against what baseline is the increase to be measured?

Second, and more fundamental, how can one treat increased quantities of imports as an exogenous or "causal" variable? Elementary economics suggests that the forces of supply and demand will determine the quantity of imports, just as they do prices and domestic production. If imports and domestic products are perfect substitutes, for example, then the quantity of imports will equal the difference between domestic demand and domestic supply at the equilibrium price. That price, in turn, will be determined by the intersection between the domestic demand curve and the total supply curve, comprised of the sum of domestic supply and import supply. The exogenous factors in the economic framework are the determinants of domestic supply, domestic demand, and import supply. Domestic demand is affected by such things as domestic consumer tastes and incomes, domestic supply by the domestic costs of inputs into production and the state of available production technology, and import supply by the parallel factors that affect supply and demand in other countries. The quantity of imports is then a *result* of the interaction of these forces; it is not a causal variable at all.

Likewise, changes in the quantity of imports will be the *result* of changes in the determinants of domestic supply, demand, and the world price. Increased quantities of imports may result, for example, from a fall in the world price due to falling input costs abroad, to improved production technology abroad, or to weakening demand abroad. Increased quantities of imports can also result from an increase in domestic demand attributable, for example, to rising consumer incomes. Finally, increased quantities of imports can result from increasing costs of domestic production reflected in a leftward shift of the domestic supply schedule.

Against this backdrop, the question "did increased quantities of imports cause serious injury to a domestic industry?" is simply incoherent. Suppose, as an illustration, that the domestic industry suffers a decline due to rising costs. As domestic production falls at the world price, imports will increase to fill the rising gap between domestic demand and supply. Are "increased quantities" of imports the "cause" of this "injury?" Certainly not in the usual sense of the term "cause." By hypothesis, what has changed are the costs of domestic firms, and that change *results* in reduced domestic production and increased imports.

Hence, once the first clause of Art. XIX(1) becomes a nullity, it is by no means clear how nations should operationalize their reliance on Art. XIX. There is no longer any natural baseline against which to measure "increased quantities," and there is no longer any intelligible exogenous variable to assess as the potential "cause" of serious injury.

2.2 *The Safeguards Agreement*

For reasons that would take us afield here, relating primarily to the proliferation of "gray-area" measures such as voluntary export restraints during the later years of GATT, the Uruguay Round negotiators concluded a new Agreement on Safeguards. Unfortunately, the Agreement did little to resolve the puzzles raised by Art. XIX(1).

On the basic preconditions for reliance on Art. XIX, the Agreement largely parrots the US law in stating that a "Member may apply a safeguard measure to a product only if that Member has determined ... that such product is being imported into its territory in such increased quantities, absolute or relative to domestic production, and under such conditions as to cause or threaten serious injury to the domestic industry that produces like or directly competitive products."[5] Like the US law, it omits any reference to "unforeseen developments" or the "effect of the obligations incurred."

The only guidance as to the meaning of "serious injury" and to the analysis of causation is provided by Art. 4 of the Agreement, which states in pertinent part:

> 1. For purposes of this Agreement:
>
>   (a) "serious injury" shall be understood to mean significant overall impairment in the position of a domestic industry;
>   (b) "threat of serious injury" shall be understood to mean serious injury that is clearly imminent ...
>
> 2. (a) In the investigation to determine whether increased imports have caused or are threatening to cause serious injury to a domestic industry ... the competent authorities shall evaluate all relevant factors of an objective and quantifiable nature having a bearing on the situation of that industry, in particular, the rate and amount of the increase in imports of the product concerned in absolute and relative terms, the share of the domestic market

[5] Id. Art. 2(1).

taken by increased imports, changes in the level of sales, production, productivity, capacity utilization, profits and losses, and employment.

(b) The determination referred to in subparagraph (a) shall not be made unless this investigation demonstrates, on the basis of objective evidence, the existence of the causal link between increased imports of the product concerned and serious injury or threat thereof. When factors other than increased imports are causing injury to the domestic industry at the same time, such injury shall not be attributed to increased imports.

Plainly, this provision does not seriously address, let alone resolve, the conundrums presented by modern GATT practice under Art. XIX. It does not provide any guidance, for example, on what it means to say that increased imports are a causal variable, or any guidance on what is meant by "factors other than increased imports ... causing injury to the domestic industry at the same time." The concept of "serious injury" is left quite vague, and members must simply "evaluate" relevant factors. Further, although the Agreement nowhere refers to "unforeseen developments" and the "effect of the obligations incurred" as a predicate to safeguard measures, it does not specifically provide that Art. XIX(1), first clause, may henceforth be ignored.

Hence, fundamental questions regarding the legal prerequisites for safeguard measures remain unanswered by the WTO Agreement on Safeguards. These unresolved issues have found their way into WTO disputes.

2.3 Safeguards in Appellate Body jurisprudence prior to the steel case

2.3.1 The Resurrection of unforeseen developments

As indicated, GATT practice evolved toward ignoring the unforeseen developments requirement of Art. XIX, and the Safeguards Agreement says nothing about that requirement. But in its first important ruling in a safeguards dispute – *Korea – Dairy*[6] – the Appellate Body overruled the dispute Panel's findings in the case to the effect that formal compliance with Art. XIX(1), first clause, was no longer required. The Appellate Body instead held that a treaty interpreter "must give meaning and effect to all the terms of the treaty. An interpreter is not free to adopt a reading that would result in reducing whole clauses

[6] *Korea – Definitive Safeguard Measure on Imports of Certain Dairy Products*, WT/DS98/AB/R (1999).

or paragraphs of a treaty to redundancy or inutility."[7] Article XIX and the Safeguards Agreement are to be read cumulatively it said, and the first clause of Art. XIX remained a binding obligation.

As for the proper interpretation of the obligation imposed by Art. XIX(1), first clause, the Appellate Body opined: "[I]t seems to us that the ordinary meaning of the phrase 'as a result of unforeseen developments' requires that the developments which led to a product being imported in such increased quantities and under such conditions as to cause or threaten to cause serious injury to domestic producers must have been 'unexpected.' With respect to the phrase 'of the effect of the obligations incurred by a Member under this Agreement, including tariff concessions,' we believe that this phrase simply means that it must be demonstrated, as a matter of fact, that the importing Member has incurred obligations under the GATT 1994, including tariff concessions."[8] The Appellate Body went on to endorse the reasoning of the working party report in the old GATT *Hatter's Fur* case,[9] which stated: "... 'unforeseen developments' should be interpreted to mean developments occurring after the negotiation of the relevant tariff concession which it would not be reasonable to expect that the negotiators of the country making the concession could and should have foreseen at the time when the concession was negotiated."[10] This line of reasoning was repeated by the Appellate Body in *Argentina – Footwear*,[11] which also overruled the dispute Panel in the case.

Thus, the Appellate Body has fully revived the first clause of Art. XIX, and has held in these and subsequent decisions that national authorities have failed to demonstrate their compliance with it. *United States – Lamb*,[12] in particular, holds that WTO members must demonstrate their compliance with the Art. XIX(1), first clause, prior to the time that a safeguards measure is undertaken. The USITC's failure to consider the matter in its Lamb investigation was "not surprising" given the absence of any reference to it in the governing US statute, but that was no defense for the United States under WTO law.[13]

One can certainly quarrel with the legal soundness of these decisions. Given the uniform practice of ignoring Art. XIX(1), first clause,

[7] Id. ¶80. [8] Id. ¶84. [9] Sales No. GATT/1951-3 (Nov. 1951). [10] Id. ¶89.

[11] *Argentina – Safeguard Measures on Imports of Footwear*, WT/DS121/AB/R (1999).

[12] *United States – Safeguard Measures on Imports of Fresh, Chilled or Frozen Lamb Meat from New Zealand and Australia*, WT/DS178/AB/R (2001).

[13] Id. ¶73.

during the latter years of GATT, and its omission from the Safeguards Agreement, it is questionable whether the drafters of the Uruguay Round Agreements had any intention of reviving the obligation – had they wished to alter the established GATT practice in this respect, one might argue, they would have indicated so with clarity. The difficult interpretive issues that the clause raises in a long-lived agreement, which led to its irrelevance in GATT practice, might also have been noted as a basis for letting it remain dormant.

Having embraced the opposite view, the Appellate Body might have undertaken to explain coherently what Art. XIX(1), first clause, now requires. At what point in time must the events in question have been unforeseen – at the time of the last tariff concession? What if the last concession on the product in question was decades ago – could anything today have been foreseen? What if, over time, the product has been the subject of numerous tariff concessions – are expectations associated with the last concession the only relevant ones? Why or why not? How does one establish the expectations of trade negotiators as an evidentiary matter? What if there are many negotiators and their accounts of their expectations are incongruent? What if most of them are dead? This list of questions is assuredly incomplete.

With regard to the "effect of the obligations incurred," by contrast, the Appellate Body apparently offers a construction that enables this requirement to be trivially satisfied in every case – a member need simply show that it has incurred some obligations with respect to the product in question. It is hard to imagine how a dispute could arise without such an obligation, since a member with an unbound tariff could always raise it unilaterally without any need to rely on a safeguard measure. The Appellate Body evidently does not require members to demonstrate that "increased quantities" of imports are attributable directly to any recent trade concession. It suffices for them to argue that in the absence of a tariff binding, they would be able to raise tariffs to eliminate the import surge.

2.3.2 Increased quantities

As noted, Art. XIX originally contemplated that "increased quantities" of imports would be measured against baseline levels prior to 1947 GATT concessions. Having revived Art. XIX(1), first clause, therefore, one might perhaps have expected the Appellate Body to require a similar approach to establishing the baseline against which the existence of "increased quantities" is assessed, perhaps by looking to import levels prior to the most recent concession on the product in question. But it has not taken that approach.

In *Argentina – Footwear,*[14] the Appellate Body considered a case in which Argentina had adopted the approach embraced some years earlier by the USITC – a five-year "rule of thumb" for establishing the import baseline. The dispute Panel in the case concluded that it is "reasonable to examine the trend in imports over a five-year historical period."[15] But the Appellate Body focused on language from the second clause of Art. XIX(1) and its counterpart in Art. 2.1 of the Safeguards Agreement: "any product [that] is being imported into the territory of that contracting party in such increased quantities and under such conditions as to cause or threaten to cause serious injury." The phrase "is being imported," according to the Appellate Body, "indicates that it is necessary for the competent authorities to examine recent imports, and not simply trends in imports during the past five years – or, for that matter, during any other period of several years."[16] "In our view, the determination of whether the requirement of imports 'in such increased quantities' is met is not a merely mathematical or technical determination. In other words, it is not enough for an investigation to show simply that imports of the product this year were more than last year – or five years ago. Again, and it bears repeating, not just *any* increased quantities of imports will suffice. There must be '*such* increased quantities' as to cause or threaten to cause serious injury to the domestic industry in order to fulfill this requirement for applying a safeguard measure. And this language in both Art. 2.1 of the *Agreement on Safeguards* and Art. XIX:1(a) of the GATT 1994, we believe, requires that the increase in imports must have been recent enough, sudden enough, sharp enough, and significant enough, both quantitatively and qualitatively, to cause or threaten to cause 'serious injury.'"[17]

Thus, the Appellate Body insists that imports must have increased "recently." But how recently, and in what amount? The phrase "recent enough, sudden enough, sharp enough, and significant enough, both quantitatively and qualitatively, to cause or threaten to cause 'serious injury'" hardly provides useful guidance. The insistence on "not just any increase" but "such increased quantities" as to cause injury is equally unhelpful. And one must again confront the fundamental issue

[14] *Argentina – Safeguard Measures on Imports of Footwear,* WT/DS121/AB/R (1999).
[15] Id. ¶130. [16] Id. ¶130. [17] Id. ¶131.

that all of this verbiage avoids – what does it mean to say that increased quantities of imports "cause" injury when they are, as an economic matter, a *result* of a variety of possible developments? Far from lending badly needed clarification, the Appellate Body's treatment of the "increased quantities" requirement only adds to the confusion.

2.3.3 Serious injury

Like Art. XIX and the Safeguards Agreement, the Appellate Body has not attempted to define "serious injury" with any precision. Its focus has been primarily on the text of Art. 4.2, which simply provides: "the competent authorities shall evaluate all relevant factors of an objective and quantifiable nature having a bearing on the situation of that industry, in particular, the rate and amount of the increase in imports of the product concerned in absolute and relative terms, the share of the domestic market taken by increased imports, changes in the level of sales, production, productivity, capacity utilization, profits and losses, and employment." According to the Appellate Body, the text requires that all of the listed factors be "evaluated" in every case, and it has found safeguard measures wanting under the WTO law whenever a member has failed to discuss one or more of these factors in its official report on safeguard action.[18] The Appellate Body has further held that the obligation to evaluate "all relevant factors" may extend to factors not raised by any of the parties to the safeguards investigation.[19]

Otherwise, the Appellate Body has simply insisted that serious injury represents "significant overall impairment" as stated in Art. 4.1 of the Safeguards Agreement.[20] It characterizes this standard as "high" and

[18] See *Argentina – Safeguard Measures on Imports of Footwear*, WT/DS121/AB/R (1999), ¶121.

[19] See *United States – Definitive Safeguard Measures on Imports of Wheat Gluten from the European Communities*, WT/DS166/AB/R (2001), ¶55.

[20] To date, the Appellate Body has largely refrained from detailed commentary on the reasoning behind findings of "serious injury" by national authorities. The most notable exception is *United States – Safeguard Measures on Imports of Fresh, Chilled or Frozen Lamb Meat from New Zealand and Australia*, WT/DS178/AB/R (2001). The USITC had found lamb prices in the United States to be "depressed" even though they were generally higher than four or five years earlier. And it had found a threat of serious injury even though prices had risen toward the end of its period of investigation. The Appellate Body held these findings to be insufficient to support the USITC determination. Id. ¶¶157–59.

"exacting."[21] It is not necessary that every "relevant factor" reflect industrial decline, however, for serious injury to be present – "a certain factor may not be declining, but the overall picture may nevertheless demonstrate 'significant overall impairment.' "[22]

On the whole, therefore, the Appellate Body has provided relatively little guidance on the meaning of "serious injury," a situation that is perhaps understandable given the vagueness of the pertinent textual obligations. Beyond a requirement that all factors listed in the Safeguards Agreement be "evaluated" in each case, it remains unclear what conditions will support a finding of serious injury or threat, and what degree of deference on the matter will be afforded to national authorities.

2.3.4 Causation

The Appellate Body has addressed the causal relationship between increased quantities of imports and serious injury in several opinions prior to the steel case. None of them, however, provides clear answers to the conceptual difficulties identified in Section 1.

Argentina – Footwear briefly addresses the proper method for determining whether imports are the "cause" of injury. The dispute Panel in that case indicated that "if causation is present, an increase in imports normally should coincide with a decline in the relevant injury factors."[23] The Appellate Body agreed with the Panel that "in an analysis of causation, 'it is the relationship between the movements in imports (volume and market share) and the movements in injury factors that must be central to a causation analysis and determination.' " The Appellate Body further noted that "with respect to a 'coincidence' between an increase in imports and a decline in the relevant injury factors, [] the Panel simply said that this should 'normally' occur if causation is present."[24]

Hence, in its first important statement on the subject, the Appellate Body tips its hat to the notion that correlation and causation are not

[21] *United States – Safeguard Measures on Imports of Fresh, Chilled or Frozen Lamb Meat from New Zealand and Australia*, WT/DS178/AB/R (2001), ¶124.

[22] *Argentina – Safeguard Measures on Imports of Footwear*, WT/DS121/AB/R (1999), ¶139.

[23] *Argentina – Safeguard Measures on Imports of Footwear*, WT/DS121/AB/R (1999), ¶141.

[24] Id. ¶144.

the same, but implies that they "normally" go hand in hand. One has no sense that the Appellate Body is aware of (or at least troubled by) the profound conceptual difficulty in confounding the two in a setting where the ostensible "causal" variable is in fact endogenous.

The other Appellate Body opinions on causal analysis focus principally on the so-called "non-attribution requirement" of Art. 4.2 of the Safeguards Agreement. It provides that safeguard measures may not be employed unless the "investigation demonstrates, on the basis of objective evidence, the existence of the causal link between increased imports of the product concerned and serious injury or threat thereof. When factors other than increased imports are causing injury to the domestic industry at the same time, such injury shall not be attributed to increased imports." One question raised by this language during the course of various disputes has been whether the harm "caused" by increased imports (again suspending the issue of what it means to treat increased imports as causal) must by itself suffice to cause serious injury, or must simply contribute to serious injury, perhaps along with other factors. To this ill-posed question, the Appellate Body has responded that "the *Agreement on Safeguards* does not require that increased imports be 'sufficient' to cause, or threaten to cause, serious injury. Nor does that Agreement require that increased imports 'alone' be capable of causing, or threatening to cause, serious injury."[25]

Although increased imports need not account for all of the serious injury, the Appellate Body nevertheless underscores the importance of ensuring that injury caused by "factors other than increased imports" "not be attributed to increased imports." To make sense of these dual principles, one can only assume that the Appellate Body is concerned about situations in which increased imports have not made any causal contribution to serious injury, and where serious injury is nevertheless wrongly "attributed" to imports.

It has found fault with Members' "non-attribution analysis" on multiple occasions. In *United States – Wheat Gluten*,[26] the volume of imports had risen 38% during the five-year period of investigation

[25] *United States – Safeguard Measures on Imports of Fresh, Chilled or Frozen Lamb Meat from New Zealand and Australia*, WT/DS178/AB/R (2001), ¶170. See also *United States – Definitive Safeguard Measures on Imports of Wheat Gluten from the European Communities*, WT/DS166/AB/R (2001), ¶70.

[26] *United States – Definitive Safeguard Measures on Imports of Wheat Gluten from the European Communities*, WT/DS166/AB/R (2001).

employed by the USITC. Over the same period, the US productive capacity had grown 68%. Capacity utilization at US firms had fallen considerably along with profits, however, and the USITC had linked the decline in profitability to declining capacity utilization rates.[27]

One issue before the Appellate Body was whether the USITC had incorrectly "attributed" injury caused by the expansion of the US capacity to rising imports. On this question, the Appellate Body noted that, had the US capacity not risen over the period of investigation, its capacity utilization rate would have fallen only modestly even with the increased volume of imports.[28] Further, had imports maintained their market share over the period of investigation, capacity utilization rates still would have fallen significantly due to the increased capacity brought on line.[29] In the face of this evidence, the Appellate Body concluded that the USITC had not "adequately evaluated the complexities" and had not "ensured that injury attributable to other factors [was] not 'attributed' to imports."[30]

The Wheat Gluten opinion is problematic in a number of respects. *First*, as with the other Appellate Body opinions on causation, it does nothing to help with the question of how to conceptualize imports as a causal variable. *Second*, taking seriously for a moment the notion that imports are "causal," it was undisputed in the case that they had risen substantially during the period of investigation, while the profitability of domestic producers had fallen. Given the Appellate Body's earlier pronouncements that a correlation of this sort is "normally" present when a causal connection exists, and that imports need not account for all serious injury, one wonders why this evidence was not enough. The logic of the Appellate Body opinion seems to suggest that the problems suffered by US producers were caused by two factors – rising imports, and investment in new capacity that proved unnecessary. In the absence of either factor, US producers would have been considerably more profitable. Why, then, is it inappropriate to attribute at least part of the "serious injury" to imports?

Finally, and as the United States argued, much of the increase in capacity was put in place before imports began to increase.[31] The sequence of events thus suggested that US producers had invested in new capacity in anticipation of growth opportunities, but that imports had increased to capture those growth opportunities and render

[27] Id. ¶¶81, 84. [28] Id. ¶85. [29] Id. ¶86. [30] Id. ¶ 91. [31] Id. ¶87.

the new investment uneconomical. It could thus be argued that the unexpected surge in imports was the real "problem," and that investments in capacity were not a conceptually distinct cause of injury but rather a background predicate for the injury caused by imports. To this line of argument, the Appellate Body responded: "[T]he relevance of an 'other factor,' under Art. 4.2(b), depends on whether that 'other factor' was, or was not, 'causing injury' 'at the same time' as increased imports. Therefore, the possible relevance of the increases in capacity added during the period of investigation does not depend on the moment in time when the increases in capacity occurred, but on when the effects of those increases are felt, and whether they are 'causing injury' 'at the same time' as increased imports."[32] This response simply begs the question as to why domestic investments in new capacity should be considered an "other factor" distinct from imports as a cause of injury, if indeed the anticipated recoupment of those investments was frustrated by an unexpected import surge. The USITC had treated capacity investments as an alternative cause of injury to be sure (and dismissed them as less important), and the Appellate Body simply seemed to accept it as an "other factor" without reflection.

The decision in *United States – Lamb*[33] is similar in this last respect. The USITC had considered six factors other than the increased imports that might have contributed to serious injury: "the cessation of subsidy payments under the National Wool Act of 1954; competition from other meat products, such as beef, pork and poultry; increased input costs; overfeeding of lambs; concentration in the packing segment of the industry; and a failure to develop and maintain an effective marketing program for lamb meat."[34] The Appellate Body again seemed to accept these factors uncritically, and simply inquired whether the United States had done enough to ensure that injury caused by these factors was not "attributed" to imports. Once again it found the analysis of the USITC wanting, suggesting that it consisted of conclusory assertions without reasoned explanation.[35] Along the way, the Appellate Body added: "We emphasize that the method and approach WTO Members choose to carry out the process of separating the effects of increased imports and the effects of the other causal factors

[32] Id. ¶88.

[33] *United States – Safeguard Measures on Imports of Fresh, Chilled or Frozen Lamb Meat from New Zealand and Australia*, WT/DS178/AB/R (2001).

[34] Id. at ¶182, n. 57. [35] Id. ¶¶185–86.

is not specified by the *Agreement on Safeguards*. What the Agreement requires is simply that the obligations in Art. 4.2 must be respected when a safeguard measure is applied."[36] Evidently, Members can use any analytical method they wish that complies with Art. 4.2, yet the Appellate Body offers no counsel as to what the set of permissible methods might include.

Finally, in *United States – Line Pipe*,[37] the USITC had considered the possibility that decreased oil and gas drilling was a more important cause of injury than increased imports, and had concluded to the contrary. Once again, however, its analysis was deemed insufficient – the "cited parts of the USITC Report do not *establish explicitly*, with a *reasoned and adequate explanation*, that injury caused by factors other than the increased imports was not attributed to increased imports. The passage on page *I-30* of the USITC Report highlighted by the United States is but a mere assertion that injury caused by other factors is not attributed to increased imports."[38]

In sum, the Appellate Body decisions prior to the steel case, regarding the causal analysis required by the Safeguards Agreement, suggest the following principles: (a) correlation is typically the best evidence of causation; (b) the "other factors" considered by national authorities during the course of their investigations will be accepted uncritically without any reflection as to their logical relevance; and (c) the Appellate Body will not tell nations how to conduct their "non-attribution analysis," but will insist that it contain "reasoned and adequate explanation," which has so far been lacking in every case. In these decisions, the Appellate Body offers no theory as to how imports are to be viewed as causal, or as to how members should determine what constitutes a potential "other factor." It faults the lack of "adequate explanation" in the decisions of national authorities, yet its own explanation of the permissible role for safeguard measures could hardly be less instructive.

3 The steel dispute

The recent steel dispute raised all of the issues noted above, and others. The Panel decision hints at a partial resolution of the

36 Id. ¶181.

37 *United States – Definitive Safeguard Measures on Imports of Circular Welded Carbon Quality Line Pipe from Korea*, WT/DS202/AB/R (2001).

38 Id. ¶220.

"unforeseen developments" puzzle, but makes little progress on other fronts. The Appellate Body decision breaks no new ground at all, and holds the steel safeguards imposed by the United States to be illegal for predictable reasons in light of the prior cases.

3.1 The panel decision

The challenges to the US steel safeguard measures collectively attacked every aspect of their legal basis. The Panel exercised judicial economy to avoid addressing arguments regarding the definition of "industry" in the US investigation and the existence of serious injury. Its findings instead focused on four areas: the existence of "unforeseen developments" as a predicate for safeguards; the question of whether steel imports had increased in "such increased quantities" as to permit safeguards; the causal link between increased imports and injury; and the lack of "parallelism" between the injury analysis and the remedial measures.[39]

3.1.1 Unforeseen developments

The US law has yet to be amended to require that increased imports result from unforeseen developments, and the initial USITC decision in the steel case predictably paid little heed to the issue. But prior to the imposition of the steel safeguard measures in March 2002, the USTR requested additional information from the USITC regarding unforeseen developments, and received a supplemental report on that issue in February. Based, in large part, on this supplemental report, the United States argued before the Panel that four unforeseen developments had contributed to the influx of imports that had injured the US steel industry: the Asian financial crisis; the drop in demand for steel due to the dissolution of the Soviet Union; the unexpected strength of the US demand for steel; and the persistent appreciation of the US dollar.[40] Among other arguments, the complainants urged that none of these events were "unforeseen," and questioned whether they had resulted in increased imports sufficient to justify safeguards.

In assessing these issues, the Panel began by noting that the parties agreed that "the point in time at which developments should have

[39] *United States – Definitive Safeguard Measures on Imports of Certain Steel Products*, WT/DS248-49, 251-54, 258-59/R (July 2003) (hereafter Panel Rep.).

[40] Id. ¶10.40.

been unforeseen is that of the completion of the Uruguay Round."[41] The Panel allowed that the Asian financial crisis could constitute an unforeseen development "since it took place after the United States last negotiated its tariff concessions on the steel products covered by the investigation."[42] It noted that the same was true of the consequences for the steel market resulting from the dissolution of the Soviet Union, even though that process had begun prior to the end of the Uruguay Round. The ongoing strength of the US economy and the US dollar were harder to regard as unforeseeable, but the Panel concluded that these factors were not viewed by the USITC as unforeseen developments in themselves, but simply circumstances that contributed to the increase in imports that resulted from the developments in Asia and the Soviet Union. Thus, the United States prevailed on the proposition that unforeseen developments had affected the steel market to some degree.

According to the Panel's interpretation of the text of GATT Art. XIX, however, the unforeseen developments must produce increased imports that cause serious injury or threat. It was on this issue that the United States failed to persuade the Panel, in part because the USITC findings of injury were all contained in the original USITC report rather than its supplemental report – at no time prior to its affirmative injury findings did the USITC identify the increased imports that had resulted from the unforeseen developments and analyze their impact on the domestic industry. Such analysis was required, according to the Panel, for every line of steel products (every "industry") in which a safeguard measure was taken.[43] Instead, the USITC had simply asserted in its supplemental report, after the original injury findings had been made, that unforeseen developments had affected the steel market in a general way – to which the Panel stated, "in light of the complexity of the matter, a more sophisticated and detailed economic analysis was called for."[44]

The Panel's treatment of the unforeseen developments issue might prove helpful in suggesting how to operationalize this requirement in practice, but at the same time underscores that it is a potentially severe hurdle for any nation that seeks to employ safeguard measures. As to the questions posed earlier in this essay – unforeseen by whom? At what point in time? – the Panel suggests that the relevant actors

[41] Id. ¶10.74. [42] Id. ¶10.80. [43] Id. ¶ 10.128. [44] Id. ¶0.125.

are trade negotiators, and that the relevant time is the point when the member seeking to use safeguards "last negotiated its tariff concessions on the ... products covered by the investigation." The end of the Uruguay Round may be taken to have "reset the clock" on this latter issue, as GATT members formally withdrew from their old GATT obligations at the end of the Round and entered a new (WTO) treaty, even if the tariff bindings on many products did not change.

In deciding whether events were "unforeseen" by the negotiators at the relevant time, the focus in the first instance will be on whether the events in question took place before or after the conclusion of the negotiations. One can thus imagine the rules here evolving in a manner that is roughly consistent with the rules in nonviolation cases – a presumption might arise that negotiators foresee the results of events that take place before the conclusion of negotiations, and do not foresee the results of events that take place later.[45] As tariffs decline to minimal levels and more and more time passes since the last concession, the set of "unforeseen" events will presumably expand and unforeseen developments should become easier to identify.

The Panel's demand for linkage between unforeseen developments and particular import increases, and the further requirement that these imports be linked to serious injury or threat, is a substantially new interpretation of the obligations imposed by GATT Art. XIX(1). The great virtue of requiring such a linkage between unforeseen developments and injury, via the effect of unforeseen developments on import quantities, is that a coherent exogenous variable thereby resurfaces in the analysis – one asks not whether "increased imports" have caused injury in the abstract, but whether particular unforeseen developments have caused injury, via an effect on the relative competitive position of imported and domestic goods. The question that national authorities are asked to answer is once again economically intelligible, as it was at the outset of GATT.

But the new obligations inherent in the Panel's interpretation do pose some substantial analytical challenges. It is hardly clear what sort of "more sophisticated and detailed economic analysis" will suffice. Consider the steel case itself: By the Panel's reasoning, the United States should have ascertained precisely how much US imports had increased, in each of the 27 steel "industries," as a result of the

[45] See *Japan – Measures Affecting Consumer Photographic Film and Paper*, WT/DS44/R (1998), ¶10.79.

Asian financial crisis and the drop in demand for steel inside the old Soviet Union. It should then have analyzed whether this increase caused or threatened to cause serious injury to the relevant industry (as well as provided a convincing "non-attribution" analysis, discussed further below). On the surface, such an analysis seems to call for a global general equilibrium model of each segment of the steel market, so that the effect of events in particular overseas markets such as Asia and the former Soviet Union can be simulated with precision. If that sort of analysis is indeed required, the time and expense involved could be enormous. The accuracy of such exercises is also subject to considerable doubt because the results often turn on controversial assumptions. And for many industries, the data necessary to estimate the parameters for such models will be lacking, and modelers would have little choice but to fall back on simulations that rest on seat-of-the-pants guesses about relevant supply and demand elasticities, cross-elasticities of demand, and the like. The potential boon for consulting economists is readily apparent, but one must harbor no illusions that the task of undertaking such analysis is straightforward – if done properly, it is expensive, time-consuming, and inevitably fraught with the potential for serious error. Perhaps a future reviewing Panel would be satisfied with something less daunting (and thus less rigorous and even more error prone), but the question of what will suffice as a "reasoned and adequate explanation" of the linkage between unforeseen developments and injury remains unclear at best.

The problem of "non-attribution" might also appear to become more tractable under the Panel's interpretation of "unforeseen developments" – one might say that as long as the unforeseen developments cause increased imports, in turn resulting in injury or threat, then by definition injury has not been "attributed" to any factor other than imports. The task of identifying the other factors to which import-related injury must not be "attributed," and of assessing their impact, could arguably be put to the side. Conceptual issues still remain, however, as to what is permitted to "count" as an unforeseen development. Imagine, for example, an "unforeseen" shock in the domestic market for inputs into steelmaking that raises the cost of steel production in the United States. The US steelmakers raise their prices to cover costs, and imports flood into the US market to undercut the price increases and market shares of domestic firms. Such "increased imports" may surely be said to cause injury (relative to a counterfactual world in which the imports are not permitted to increase), and to result from the unforeseen developments in the domestic input market. But are safeguard measures appropriate when the root cause of injury is a shock in the domestic economy? Or would safeguards to remedy such injury be impermissible because the injury caused by the domestic shock is wrongly "attributed" to imports? Nothing in the WTO decisions thus far afford much help with such matters, an issue about which we will say more below in connection with the "non-attribution" problem.

3.1.2 Increased imports and the baseline question

Taking its cue from earlier Appellate Body decisions, the Panel held "that the use of the present tense in the verb phrase 'is being imported' in both Art. 2.1 of the Agreement of Safeguards and Art. XIX:(1)(A) of the GATT 1994 indicate[d] that it [was] necessary for the competent authorities to examine recent imports and that the increase in imports [had been] 'recent.'"[46] Further, "the emergency nature of safeguard measures call[ed] for an assessment of whether imports increased suddenly so that the situation became one of emergency."[47] And finally the Panel stated that, given its conclusion that "the competent authority [had to] have determined that imports increased suddenly and recently," it would "generally focus its analysis on the situation of imports in the more recent period that had preceded the end of the period of investigation."[48]

The Panel then proceeded to examine the data on import trends for each of the ten product categories covered by the challenged measures. In most instances, the Panel generated a graph representing the import volume and market share data over the five-year period of investigation employed by the USITC. Because the Panel's focus was on the "more recent period that [had] preceded the end of the period of investigation," the graph for each product category says much about how the Panel came out in each case. We produce four of the graphs (Figures 1–4) for purposes of illustration:

For both hot-rolled bar (Figure 1) and stainless steel rod (Figure 2), the Panel found that the USITC report did not contain a "reasoned and adequate" explanation of why imports had increased. Regarding hot-rolled bar, the Panel focused on the USITC's "failure to [have]

[46] Panel Rep. ¶10.159. [47] Id. ¶10.166. [48] Id. ¶10.175.

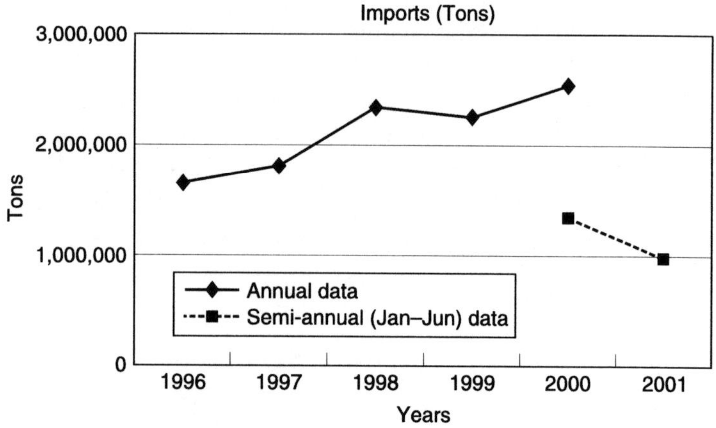

Figure 1 Hot-rolled bar

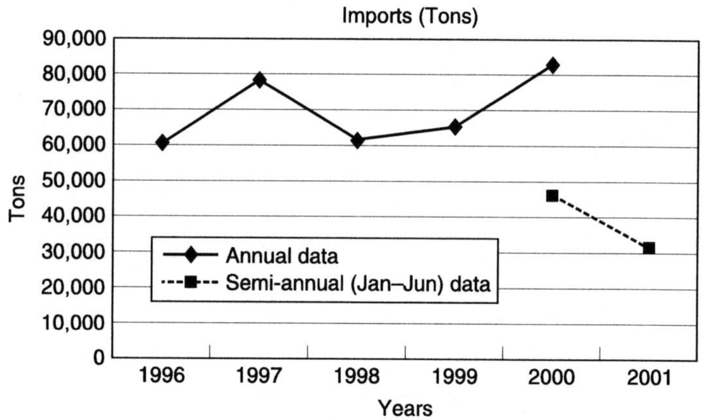

Figure 2 Stainless steel rod

account[ed] for the most recent data from interim 2001… " The Panel stated:

> The decrease from interim 2000 (1.34 million tons) to interim 2001 (952,392 tons) represented a decrease by 28.9%, whereas the increase in the year-to-year period before (1999 to 2000) that was characterized as "rapid and dramatic" was merely 11.9%. In light of this decrease in the most recent period, the Panel does not believe that the trend of imports from 1996 to 2000 (an increase by 52.5%) is sufficient to provide a basis

for a finding that, at the moment of the determination, hot-rolled bar "is being imported in such increased quantities."[49]

The analysis was similar in many respects for stainless steel rod:

> The USITC relied on the increase occurring between 1996 and 2000, with the largest increase from 1999 to 2000 (25%). The decline between interim 2000 and interim 2001 was acknowledged, but the USITC did not give an explanation why it nevertheless found that there was an increase of imports in absolute numbers. This failure is particularly serious since this decrease (by 31.3%) was sharper than the preceding increase, and, as a matter of proportion, offset the increase of the two preceding years.[50]

For rebar (Figure 3), by contrast, the Panel accepted the USITC finding of increased imports: "In light of the tripling of imports, the decrease over the last 18 months is not significant enough in order to stand in the way of a conclusion that rebar 'is being imported in such increased quantities.' "[51]

Likewise, as to stainless steel bar (Figure 4), the Panel found:

> [I]n the light of the significant increase from 1999 to 2000 (19.3 percentage points), the decline by 3.3 percentage points from interim 2000 to interim 2001 is, contrary to what the European Communities has

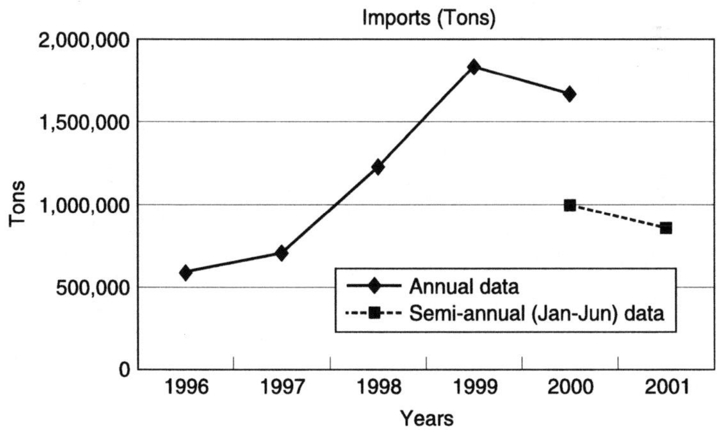

Figure 3 Rebar

[49] Id. ¶10.205. [50] Id. ¶10.267. [51] Id. ¶10.225.

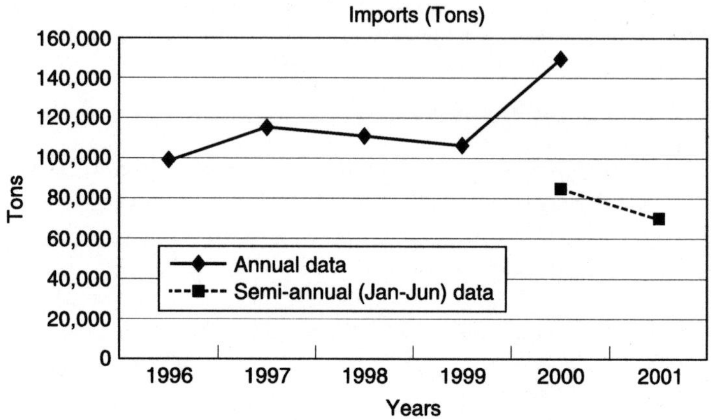

Figure 4 Stainless steel bar

> stated, insignificant. It simultaneously does not detract from a finding that imports, relative to domestic production, remain at high levels so that stainless steel bar "is being imported in (such) increased quantities."[52]

For two product categories, tin mill products and stainless steel wire, the Panel ruled that the United States failed to demonstrate the presence of increased imports because it had relied on the separate opinions of the USITC Commissioners who had defined the relevant "industries" in different ways. For example, some treated "tin mill products" as a separate industry, while another included tin mill products in a broader industry. The Panel was of the view that the separate findings reached in such a fashion could not collectively constitute a "reasoned and adequate" explanation for the finding of increased imports.

In sum, the Panel's reasoning generally focused on two issues: whether imports had risen substantially over the entire period of investigation (the five-year period ordinarily used by the USITC as its baseline), and whether any *recent* downtrend in imports had undercut the finding of an overall increase. Implicitly, recent trends carried more weight than the five-year trend, but a modest recent decline in imports

[52] Id. ¶10.254.

would not prevent a finding of increased imports if the five-year trend was more dramatically upward.

The Panel's approach is at least somewhat puzzling, for a couple of reasons. *First*, having held earlier that the United States should have linked import increases to the Asian financial crisis and the dissolution of the Soviet Union, one might have expected the Panel to suggest that the timing of those events defined the baseline for measuring the increase in imports. Instead, as under longstanding US practice, the Panel (and the complainants) seemed to have accepted that the arbitrary five-year baseline was permissible in principle: "The complainants do not challenge the choice of a five-year period of investigation *per se*. Complainants rather disagree with the fact that, generally, the USITC did not focus sufficiently on the situation of imports in the latest part of the period of investigation."[53] *Second*, had the United States in fact linked an increase in imports to unforeseen developments such as the Asian financial crisis and the dissolution of the Soviet Union, and had it shown that the extra imports *resulting from these developments* were sufficient to cause serious injury, would that not have been enough to establish a basis for safeguard measures? Why did the United States need additionally to show a sudden, sharp and significant increase in total imports? Should the right to safeguard measures have been eliminated, for example, if the effects of the unforeseen developments, working through increased imports, had been reinforced by a slowdown in the US demand, which might have caused additional injury but served to temper the growth in import volume?

The great emphasis on the most recent year or months of data is peculiar in another respect. The time series for imports of any good may exhibit significant volatility for a variety of reasons, and the notion that WTO members would wish to condition the right to use safeguards heavily on the most recent import fluctuations, which may be quite unpredictable when an investigation is initiated, seems odd even if it has some arguable textual basis. The preamble to the Agreement on Safeguards emphasizes the importance of "structural adjustment," much as the US law has long set forth the alternative goals of promoting industrial competitiveness or facilitating an orderly industrial contraction.[54] If these stated goals are to be taken seriously, they concern

[53] Id. ¶10.160. [54] See 19 U.S.C. § 2251(b).

measures to address long-term structural trends. Likewise, Art. 7 of the Safeguards Agreement provides that safeguard measures may be imposed for four years, with the possibility of an extension to eight years. The potential duration of the measures is also suggestive of the notion that they address long-term trends in industrial competitiveness. If this is right, why should the opportunity to utilize safeguard measures turn critically on recent import fluctuations rather than long-term import trends? One wonders whether the Panel here, and the Appellate Body generally, has turned the matter completely on its head.

3.1.3 Causation and the "non-attribution" problem

The Panel found fault with the USITC analysis of causation for nine of the ten "industries" covered by the US safeguard measures. In each instance, it held that the USITC had failed to demonstrate a causal link between increased imports and injury, that it had failed to ensure that injury caused by other factors was not "attributed" to imports, or both.

3.1.3.1 Demonstrating the causal link to imports Again taking its cue from prior decisions, the Panel suggested that a causal linkage between increased imports and injury might be established in one of two ways: through a "coincidence" analysis, or through an analysis of the conditions of competition. In the words of the Panel, a coincidence analysis examines the "temporal relationship between the movements in imports and the movements in injury factors."[55] Such coincidence is "normally" evident "if causation is present,"[56] although the suggestion that a temporal lag may exist between import increases and injury "may have merit in certain cases."[57] Where a clear coincidence exists, "no further analysis is required of the competent authority," save for a careful non-attribution analysis.[58] Where coincidence is lacking or an analysis of coincidence has not been undertaken, the competent authority must explain its absence and must show causation convincingly through other means.

According to the Panel, an analysis of the conditions of competition requires the competent authority to consider the factors enumerated

[55] Panel Rep. ¶10.299. [56] Id. §10.300. [57] Id. ¶10.310. [58] Id. ¶10.307.

in Art. 4.2(a) of the Safeguards Agreement: changes in import volume, import market share, domestic sales, production, productivity, capacity utilization, profits and losses, and employment. Other unenumerated factors may also be relevant.[59] In the Panel's view:

> [P]rice ... is an important, if not the most important, factor in analysing the conditions of competition in a particular market ... we consider that relative price trends as between imports and domestic products will often be a good indicator of whether injury is being transmitted to the domestic industry ... given that price changes have an immediate effect on profitability, all other things being equal.[60]

Against this backdrop, the Panel proceeded to consider the analysis of the USITC as to each of the challenged measures. In the important category of certain carbon flat-rolled steel (CCFRS), for example, it found:

> [T]here was no coincidence between, on the one hand, import trends and the situation of the domestic industry of CCFRS, as reflected in data for production, net commercial sales, productivity and capacity utilization of the domestic CCFRS ... There was [also] a lack of coincidence between import trends and declines in domestic operating margin ... We did discern coincidence, albeit lagged, between increased imports, on the one hand, and employment, on the other hand ... Having taken into consideration all of the foregoing, in the Panel's view, overall, coincidence did not exist.[61] ... Given a lack of coincidence between import trends and the injury factors, it was for USITC to provide a compelling explanation as to why a causal link was considered, nevertheless, to exist.[62]

The USITC's analysis of the conditions of competition for CCFRS was then found deficient as well. The Panel first suggested that the product category might be too broad for such an analysis to be undertaken at all in convincing fashion. Further, according to the Panel, the USITC had apparently relied heavily on evidence of import underselling and downward price trends for both imports and domestic products for two sub-products in the CCFRS category, without explaining "why pricing data for the other three items that constituted CCFRS [had] [not] been specifically considered." And, "while some of the domestically produced constituent items [had been] undersold

[59] Id. §10.318. [60] Id. ¶10.320. [61] Id. ¶¶10.374–75. [62] Id. ¶10.376.

by the import counterparts at particular points during the period of investigation, this [had] not necessarily [been] the case for the entire period of investigation."[63] Thus, the Panel concluded, the conditions of competition analysis failed to support the existence of a causal link between increased imports and injury.

As to other product lines, the Panel found the USITC's analysis more convincing. For fittings, flanges, and tool joints (FFTJ), the Panel examined the relation between imports and indicators of injury, and noted that "clear coincidence exist[ed] between the upward trend in imports and the downward trend in the injury factors, except for productivity." Because the USITC report had not analyzed this coincidence in detail, however, the Panel also found that a conditions-of-competition analysis was required to support the USITC's finding of a causal link.[64] In that regard, the Panel reviewed data assembled by the USITC showing that imported products had significantly undersold domestic products during the period of investigation, and on that basis concluded that the conditions-of-competition analysis supported the existence of a causal link.

In the case of hot-rolled bar, the Panel noted that the USITC had not undertaken a coincidence analysis. But as part of its analysis of the conditions-of-competition, the USITC had assembled data on market penetration by imports along with import and domestic prices. The data were presented in the following graph (Figure 5). Based on these data, the Panel concurred that a causal link was present – "[t]he USITC explained that domestic prices declined in an effort to mitigate the erosion of market share ... On the basis of the foregoing, overall, we find that the USITC's conditions of competition analysis was compelling."[65]

It would be unfair to fault the Panel for following the analytic lead of the Appellate Body and the USITC, but in doing so it followed them to the land of economic gibberish. The Panel insisted that the linchpin in the search for *causation* was a search for *coincidence.* The irony of that phrasing is glaring – the Random House English dictionary defines "coincidence" as "a striking occurrence of two or more events at one time apparently by mere chance." The most elementary statistics class teaches that correlation is not causation, and the problem is not ameliorated by relabeling correlation as coincidence.

[63] Id. ¶10.379. [64] Id. ¶10.516. [65] Id. ¶¶10.429–30.

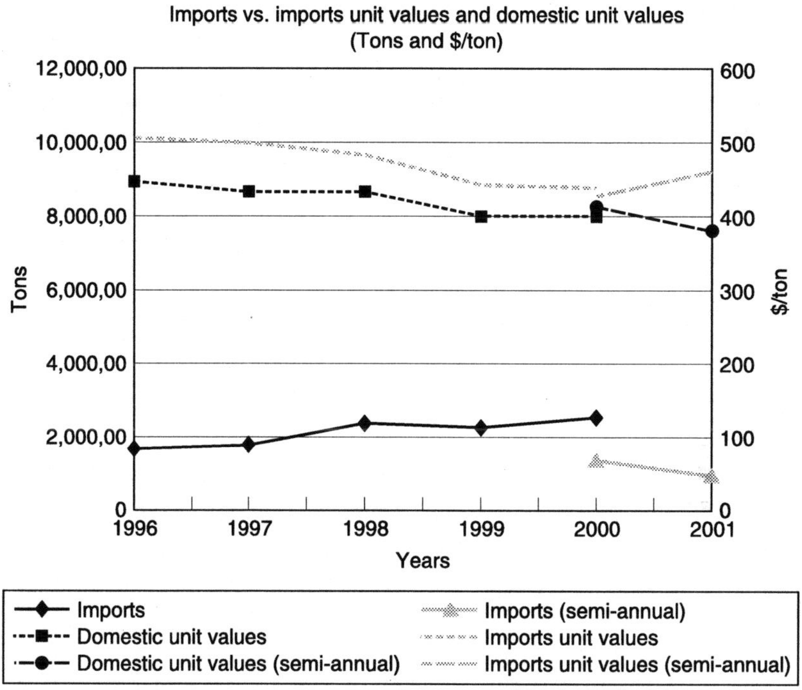

Figure 5 Hot-rolled bar

Further, as explained earlier, the problem is actually much more fundamental. It is not disreputable to examine correlation as an aid to an exploration of causation with appropriate caveats. But one can only do so when one variable is a logical candidate for the cause of the other. Import quantities do not *cause* anything – they are simultaneously determined along with prices, domestic output, domestic employment, and so on. It makes no more sense to say that increased imports caused a decline in domestic production, for example, than to say the exact opposite.

The Panel's analysis also involves internal inconsistency. On the one hand, it would require the complainant to identify "unforeseen developments" that are linked to increased imports which in turn have caused serious injury or threat. But on the other hand, it would prescribe a separate causation analysis in which the unforeseen developments play no role. If the Panel's requirements for establishing the existence of unforeseen developments have been met – namely, that the domestic industry experienced exogenous shocks that *caused* import volume to rise and conditions to deteriorate – must not the requirements for causality have been met as well? What additional information can the examination of coincidence provide?

The "conditions of competition" analysis that serves as an alternative to coincidence analysis is no more comforting. To the extent that the Panel, like the USITC, finds evidence of import "underselling" to be persuasive evidence of causation, an economist would respond that persistent underselling by imports is simply an evidence that they are of lower perceived quality for some reason. It says nothing about a causal link between anything and anything else. Likewise, to the degree that a high degree of correlation exists between the price series for imported and domestic goods, that fact is some evidence that the goods are reasonably close substitutes in consumption. Again, no inference of "causation" is supported, as indeed there is no intelligible causal variable under examination.

To be sure, cases will arise in which "coincidence" is relatively stronger or weaker. Cases will arise in which imported goods undersell domestic goods, and many cases will arise in which import and domestic price trends are highly correlated. It will thus be possible for importing nations to demonstrate "causation" with some regularity using the tests that the Panel applies. But if any relationship exists between that set of cases, and the set of cases in which safeguard measures are appropriate on some principled basis, it will arise only by "coincidence."

3.1.3.2 The non-attribution problem Following the lead of the Appellate Body, the Panel made clear that the presence of a "causal link" between imports and injury, as established above, was not enough to satisfy the requirements of the Safeguards Agreement. If other factors also contributed to injury, the "competent authorities [needed to] separate and distinguish the injurious effect of the increased imports from the injurious effects of the other factors."[66]

This exercise is required even though imports need not be solely responsible for injury, but must merely have contributed to it. A proper non-attribution analysis also determines the permissible scope of the safeguard remedy – the Appellate Body ruled in

[66] Id. ¶10.329.

United States – Line Pipe that safeguard measures may only remedy the injury attributable to increased imports, not that attributable to other factors.[67]

For a number of product lines, the Panel found the USITC's non-attribution analysis to be lacking. The Panel's approach, as in previous cases, was simply to accept at face value the "other factors" put forth by the respondents at the USITC, with no discussion as to how or why they were appropriate or inappropriate. The Panel then checked to see whether the USITC had confidently distinguished the injury attributable to the factor in question, and ensured that such injury was not attributed to imports.

We offer one illustrative example of the analysis: in the case of hot-rolled bar, as noted above, the Panel accepted the USITC's analysis of the conditions of competition as a basis for finding a causal link between increased imports and injury. But the respondents argued before the USITC that injury was caused, *inter alia*, by increased input costs for domestic producers, what the Panel termed increases in the costs of goods sold (COGS). The USITC acknowledged that COGS had risen during part of the period of investigation, but argued that import competition had suppressed prices and prevented domestic firms from recouping their higher costs. On that basis, the USITC concluded that imports were the more important cause of injury. The Panel evidently considered this analysis too cursory, and thus falling short of a "reasoned and adequate" explanation. The Panel hinted, however, that if the USITC had gone further in its analysis, it might have been able to defend its conclusion. In particular, the Panel noted that there was a general lack of "coincidence" between changes in COGS and operating margins for domestic producers. Had changes in COGS "played a significant role in the situation of the domestic industry," the Panel reasoned, "one would have expected operating margins to increase while COGS was decreasing."[68]

The Panel's discussion of the non-attribution requirement suffers from the same logical flaws as the treatment of the issue in prior cases. Its analysis of the COGS factor for hot-rolled bar illustrates the fundamental problem. An increase in input costs for domestic firms will lead them to institute price increases if they can. But, as may have been the case in the hot-rolled bar market, import competition

[67] Id. ¶10.338. [68] Id. ¶10.440.

may prevent such price increases. The price increases that are attempted by domestic firms, caused by rising input prices, may thus be the *cause* of greater import volumes, which restrain price increases and leave domestic firms in a weakened financial situation.

The Panel insists, however, that the injury attributed to rising COGS must be distinguished from the injury attributed to imports. As the above discussion makes clear, this task is **logically impossible**. If the imports themselves result from increases in COGS, how can the effects of the two possibly be distinguished? Putting it differently, the causal variable in this scenario is an increase in domestic input costs. The *result* is both an increase in imports, and a weakened financial situation for domestic firms. For the same reason, the proposition that a permissible safeguard measure can address the injury caused by increased imports, but not the injury caused by rising COGS, is also fundamentally incoherent.

The Panel's suggestion that one can analyze the importance of COGS by looking at the coincidence between changes in COGS and operating margins is silly. Other things being equal, increases in COGS will surely tend to lower operating margins, but many other factors in the market are variable over time, and the absence of a "coincidence" between changes in COGS and operating margins simply indicates that other things are happening simultaneously – a clear demonstration of why "coincidence" and causation are two different things. Obviously, the presence of other factors varying simultaneously cannot negate the fact that increases in input costs, other things being equal, are disadvantageous for domestic producers.

The ultimate issue here is a simple one – should safeguard measures be permitted when the cause of injury to a domestic industry, and the cause of rising imports, is a shock to the cost structure of domestic firms? There may be good reasons to answer this question yes or no, but the analysis of the Panel merely masks and confuses it.

3.1.4 Parallelism

The "parallelism" requirement stems from *Argentina – Footwear*. The Appellate Body there held that a correspondence must exist between the imports included in the analysis that led to the injury determination, and the imports covered by the safeguard measure.[69]

[69] Id. ¶10.590–91.

Thus, for example, if imports from Canada were part of the data on which the injury finding rests, imports from Canada cannot be exempted from any subsequent safeguards remedy.

The legal basis for the parallelism requirement is shaky. Pauwelyn (2004) criticizes the requirement and argues forcefully that the real issue is whether Art. XXIV of GATT, pertaining to the formation of customs unions and free trade areas, either requires or permits Members of such entities to exempt imports from other Members from safeguard measures. This question thus far has no clear answer.

Whatever its merits, the parallelism requirement is established in the cases, and the United States undertook to argue that it had complied. The original USITC determination had aggregated imports from all sources, however, while the eventual safeguard measures had largely excluded imports from NAFTA countries, Israel, and Jordan. The USITC was asked to revise its analysis to exclude these imports in its supplemental report to USTR. It did so, and reached the same conclusions for each industry.

The Panel took issue with the analysis for several reasons. In several instances, the USITC had not made clear that it had properly excluded imports from Israel and Jordan in its revised analysis. The USITC also failed to explain to the Panel's satisfaction why its findings had remained the same despite the fact that a smaller quantity of imports had been involved after the parallelism adjustments. In addition, the Panel held that the USITC was obliged to repeat its non-attribution analysis based on the revised import totals, and that it had failed to do so in the supplemental report.

In the interest of parallelism, therefore, the Panel would have the USITC revise its import data, and thereafter undertake the same conceptually-flawed analyses of coincidence, conditions of competition, and non-attribution. The excluded imports would become an "other factor" to which injury from the included imports could not be attributed. But such exercises are no more valuable with the revised data than with the original. Until a logically sound approach to the question of causation emerges, the requirement of parallelism is just a sideshow.

It is also somewhat peculiar that neither the Panel nor the prior pertinent decisions draw any connection between the parallelism issue and the unforeseen developments issue. If the United States is obliged by Art. XIX to draw a connection between injury and developments in Asia and the former Soviet Union, is it not possible that such injury was transmitted through an effect on imports from particular sources, rather than an effect on all imports or on world prices? Does the answer to that question have any implications for the permissible scope of the safeguard remedy, or for the possible exclusion of imports from particular sources?

3.2 The Appellate Body decision

The Appellate Body affirmed the Panel in most pertinent respects, or exercised judicial economy to avoid reaching the issues raised.[70] We can thus address its decision with considerable brevity.

3.2.1 Unforeseen developments

Much of the US appeal on this issue consisted of a challenge to the "standard of review" employed by the Panel – a requirement that the US competent authorities provide a "reasoned and adequate" explanation for their findings. The Appellate Body essentially affirmed the standard employed by the Panel, and we have no quarrel with the general principle that national authorities should set forth findings with enough clarity and logical reasoning for reviewing Panels to be able to assess them.

The Appellate Body also concurred with the Panel that a Member proposing to invoke safeguards must demonstrate that unforeseen developments have led to increased imports for each "industry" covered by a safeguard measure.[71] Here too it affirmed the finding that the USITC had failed to make such a showing with a "reasoned and adequate" explanation.[72] We have no quarrel with this principle either as a general matter. The treaty text requires the preconditions for safeguards to be met for any "product" covered by a safeguard measure. When, as in the steel case, national authorities determine that a number of different "products" are involved and proceed to define a number of separate "industries" to investigate, it is appropriate to require that the preconditions for safeguard measures be met in each industry.

But the Appellate Body opinion does not address the deeper issues raised by the unforeseen developments requirement. It expressly states that it offers no ruling on the question whether the developments

[70] *United States – Definitive Safeguard Measures on Imports of Certain Steel Products*, WT/DS248-49, 251-54, 258-59/AB/R (November, 2003) (hereafter App. Body Rep.).

[71] Id. ¶319. [72] Id. ¶326.

identified by the United States – the Asian financial crisis, the dissolution of the Soviet Union, and so on – actually constitute "unforeseen developments" as a legal matter.[73] It thus offers no guidance on how one determines what is "unforeseen," or what is permitted to "count" as an unforeseen development. Most importantly, it does not address the ultimate issue, raised implicitly by the Panel's analysis, as to whether national authorities must convincingly link all of the "serious injury" caused by "increased imports" to the underlying "unforeseen developments." If indeed they must, then the requisite analysis becomes somewhat better grounded in a coherent economic theory on the one hand, but the task of producing a "reasoned and adequate" justification for a safeguard measure becomes all the more daunting on the other.

3.2.2 Increased imports

Here, the Appellate Body reaffirmed the principle set forth in *Argentina – Footwear* that a mere increase in imports is not enough to satisfy the requirement of "such increased quantities" as to cause injury. It quoted with approval its prior reference to a requirement that "the increase in imports [] have been recent enough, sudden enough, sharp enough, and significant enough, both quantitatively and qualitatively, to cause or threaten to cause 'serious injury,' "[74] and found that the Panel had interpreted this standard correctly. In so doing, the Appellate Body did nothing in our view to clarify the practical application of the standard. Likewise, its decision does little to explain the logic behind the standard – why do the consequences of "unforeseen developments" not unfold slowly at times, so that the resulting increase in imports is not particularly sudden or sharp? And, at the risk of seeming repetitive, what sense does it make to fret about the time period over which increased imports may or may not have caused injury, when the law offers no coherent theory of how imports cause anything? On these fundamental conceptual issues relating to the increased imports requirement, the marginal contribution of the opinion is nil.

Regarding the Panel's findings with respect to specific product categories, the Appellate Body for the most part affirmed, to the extent that the Panel's findings were appealed by the United States.

[73] Id. ¶269. [74] Id. ¶345–46.

We critiqued the Panel's analysis at some length above on these issues, and will not repeat the discussion here.

The Appellate Body did reverse the Panel's findings with regard to tin mill products and stainless steel wire. Contrary to the Panel's conclusion, the Appellate Body held that the findings of different Commissioners, who had defined the industries in varying ways, could in principle suffice as a "reasoned and adequate" explanation for a finding of increased imports.[75] According to the Appellate Body, nothing in the treaty text precluded an aggregation of judgments in this fashion, nor was it logically inconceivable that analyses based on different conceptions of the "industry" might nevertheless justify a finding of increased imports. Having reversed the Panel on this point, however, the Appellate Body found it unnecessary to complete the Panel's analysis because it held the safeguard measures for tin mill products and stainless steel wire to be illegal on other grounds.[76] The reversal of the Panel here may be of some modest comfort to the United States, with its history of ITC Commissioners who often arrive at different definitions of the relevant "industry" in safeguards proceedings, but seems to be of modest conceptual importance.

In sum, as with its treatment of the unforeseen developments requirement, the Appellate Body decision adds nothing of significance to its previous decisions beyond tacit approval of the analysis conducted by the Panel on several of the product categories. Our thoughts on that analysis are set forth above.

3.2.3 Parallelism

The Appellate Body agreed with the Panel that the USITC had not shown that it had properly excluded imports from Canada, Mexico, Israel, and Jordan in reaching its findings. It emphasized especially that the USITC had not considered the excluded imports as an "other factor" in a proper non-attribution analysis.[77] We have no quarrel with the factual proposition that the USITC's reasoning on this front was murky, although the task of fixing the problem remains confounded by the absence of any coherent way to identify the impact of the relevant set of "increased imports," or to separate the injury caused thereby from injury caused by other factors. Until a conceptual framework

[75] Id. ¶¶416, 429. [76] Id. ¶431. [77] Id. ¶¶456.

for identifying the relevant exogenous variables and assessing their impact is articulated, it is simply not clear how to implement a requirement of parallelism. And in the absence of an intelligible theory as to when safeguard measures are appropriate and when they are not, it is impossible even to say whether a "parallelism" requirement makes sense.

3.2.4 Causation

Because its rulings on the unforeseen developments, increased imports, and parallelism issues sufficed for finding that each of the ten challenged measures violated WTO law, the Appellate Body declined to consider the Panel's analysis of the causation issue. It simply referred the parties to its prior rulings for further "guidance," rulings with which we have already taken issue.

In sum, unlike its prior rulings in the safeguards area, the Appellate Body ruling in the steel dispute offers virtually nothing of conceptual importance. To the extent that any important new law was made, it consisted of affirming the reasoning of the Panel on certain key points that have already been discussed extensively above. Nothing in the opinion resolves any of the conundrums raised by prior Appellate Body decisions.

4 Concluding commentary

Our review of the steel dispute suggests how difficult it will be for WTO members to use safeguards going forward without a prospect of near-certain defeat when a complaint is brought against them. Members must demonstrate the existence of unanticipated developments, argue persuasively that they were "unforeseen," convincingly trace their impact on increased imports, demonstrate that much of the import surge was sufficiently "recent," convincingly show the relation between the imports and serious injury to an appropriately defined "industry," and convincingly show that "other factors" did not cause the injury attributed to increased imports. And they must accomplish these things in a theoretical vacuum, where neither the treaty text nor the Appellate Body decisions to date offer any clear explanation of what it even means to say that "increased imports" have "caused" or threatened to cause serious injury, how one identifies the "other factors" that might be responsible for injury, and how one attributes injury among its various causes. Because it is unclear what the law requires as a conceptual matter, it is exceedingly difficult to comply with it, and one can hardly fault national authorities for their inability to offer a "reasoned and adequate" demonstration of their fidelity to the law.

To be sure, some observers may welcome these developments. For those who believe that safeguard measures are nothing more than wasteful protectionism, insurmountable hurdles to their use will have appeal. But the literature is in fact rather agnostic on the use of safeguards. Bagwell and Staiger (1990, 2002) suggest that safeguard measures may be understood as a device for reducing the pressure on nations to cheat on trade agreements, and thus can reduce the danger that the agreements may unravel. Sykes (1991) argues that the opportunity to employ safeguard measures *ex post* may facilitate more trade concessions *ex ante* in an environment where negotiators face political uncertainty about the consequences of their trade concessions. And the experience of the GATT suggests that if safeguard measures become unavailable, nations may return to arrangements such as voluntary export restraints that are even worse from the *ex post* standpoint because no standard restricts their use or limits their duration – the political pressures to protect troubled industries through trade policy will remain regardless of the state of the law, as will their potential to cause mischief.

It is thus plausible that safeguard measures have a constructive role to play in the trading system. If they are to play that role effectively going forward, however, the law must evolve in a way that makes clear to WTO members what circumstances are appropriate for safeguards, and how to go about demonstrating the existence of those circumstances. For the reasons given above, the treaty text is woefully deficient in this regard, and the decisions of the Appellate Body have only compounded the problem.

One way or another, what is needed is a fresh start. We can imagine it coming in two ways. First, the Appellate Body might change course dramatically, and initiate a "common law" evolution toward coherent standards for the use of safeguards, much as the US courts have done in fleshing out the vague and imprecise standards of the US antitrust laws. To do so, however, the Appellate Body would have to abandon its insistence on grounding every principle in treaty text, in favor of ascertaining the "object and purpose" of the Safeguards Agreement from other sources, perhaps even by some direct appeal to economic theory. Such a process would represent a major departure from the Appellate Body's usual approach to cases, however, and many might question the legitimacy of such a departure. Alternatively, the WTO membership might simply renegotiate the Agreement on Safeguards, with an eye toward resolving the fundamental issues that we have identified (and no doubt some that we have not). At this writing, neither possibility appears terribly likely in the foreseeable future.

Whatever the near-term likelihood of legal reform, the economic literature does offer some ideas on possible directions for change. A number of economic scholars advocate an interpretation of the legal prerequisites for safeguards that melds easily with basic price theory, an approach that actually surfaced briefly in the reasoning of a few USITC Commissioners.[78] Grossman (1986), Kelly (1988), and Irwin (2003) would divide the potential causes of injury into three groups: forces that cause shifts in the domestic supply schedule; forces that cause shifts in the domestic demand schedule; and forces that cause shifts in the import supply schedule. Any harm to the domestic industry that can be attributed to shifts in the import supply curve will be deemed to result from "increased imports;" any harm attributable to rising domestic costs that shift the domestic supply schedule will be deemed to result from causes other than increased imports. Likewise, harm due to shifts in domestic demand will be attributed to causes other than imports, unless the shift in demand is due to a price reduction on imperfectly substitutable imports. This approach also has the great virtue of economic coherence, shifting the inquiry to ask whether changing conditions of import supply, rather than increased quantities of imports, are causally responsible for injury. It does not, however, address the problem of what counts as an "unforeseen development," or whether such a requirement is desirable and appropriate. And we do not pretend that it would always be easy to implement as a practical matter. The data requirements for confident estimation of the pertinent supply and demand relationships may often be lacking, and the task of identifying and specifying those relationships can be controversial.

Critics may also argue that the import supply approach is not the only coherent way to implement a safeguards system, and may

[78] See US International Trade Commission, Wood Shakes and Shingles, Inv. No. TA-201-56, Pub. No. 1826 (1986) (views of Commissioners Liebeler and Brunsdale).

preclude safeguard measures in cases where WTO members might agree they ought to be permissible. The old GATT *Hatter's Fur* case noted above is instructive in this regard. The US position in that case was, that a decline in domestic demand for the types of hats produced by domestic firms was the "unforeseen development" that resulted in an import surge and that justified safeguards action. The working party appeared to accept this theory, at least in principle, while quibbling as to whether the facts supported it.

Sykes (2003) suggests a slightly different set of principles. Noting that the original structure of Art. XIX was aimed at protecting against the "unforeseen" consequences of trade concessions that might produce import surges, he suggests that safeguards may be appropriate when unanticipated shocks lead exporters to enjoy unanticipated prosperity while import-competing firms simultaneously suffer severe and unexpected declines. Such an approach could permit a safeguard measure on the facts of the *Hatter's Fur* case, for example. This approach too leaves many details to be worked out, most especially the issue of how to determine whether shocks are unanticipated, and is no more than an initial step toward articulating the role of safeguards in the system.

Our goal here is not to opine definitively on the proper logic of safeguards. That task, of course, is a matter for the WTO membership. We simply suggest that economically oriented scholars may offer some useful ideas for the reform of safeguards law, and that they can at least help to suggest what sort of framework will stand the test of logical coherence. Current WTO jurisprudence flunks that test miserably, and without reform will continue to present insuperable obstacles to the use of safeguard measures. We are unsure about the systemic consequences of this state of affairs, but are by no means confident that the consequences are benign.

References

Bagwell, K. and Staiger, R. W. (1990). A Theory of Managed Trade, *American Economic Review*, **80**: 779–795.

Bagwell, K. and Staiger, R. W. (2002). *The Economics of the World Trading System* (Cambridge, MA: The MIT Press).

Grossman, G. M. (1986). Imports as a Cause of Injury: The Case of the US Steel Industry, *Journal of International Economics*, **20**: 201–222

Grossman, G. M. and Mavroidis, P. C. (2005). United States – Definitive Safeguard Measures on Imports of Circular Welded Carbon Quality Line Pipe from Korea. In H. Horn and P. C. Mavroidis (eds.), *The WTO Case Law of 2002.* American Law Institute Reporters Series (Cambridge, UK: Cambridge University Press).

Horn, H. and Mavroidis, P. C. (2003). United States – Safeguard Measures on Imports of Fresh, Chilled or Frozen Lamb Meat from New Zealand and Australia: What Should be Required of a Safeguard Investigation?. In H. Horn and P. C. Mavroidis (eds.), *The WTO Case Law of 2001.* American Law Institute Reporters Series (Cambridge UK: Cambridge University Press).

Kelly, K. (1988). The Analysis of Causality in Escape Clause Cases, *Journal of Industrial Economics*, **37**: 187–207.

Irwin, D. (2003). Causing Problems? The WTO Review of Causation and Injury Attribution in US Section 201 Cases, *World Trade Review*, **2**: 297–325.

McGovern, E. (1986). *International Trade Regulation*, 2nd edn. (London: Gobefield).

Pauwelyn, J. (2004). The Puzzle of WTO Safeguards and Regional Trade Agreements, *Journal of International Economic Law*, **7**: 109–142

Sykes, A. O. (1991). Protectionism as a 'Safeguard': A Positive Analysis of the GATT 'Escape Clause' with Normative Speculations, *University of Chicago Law Review*, **58**: 255–305.

Sykes, A. O. (2003). The Safeguards Mess: A Critique of Appellate Body Jurisprudence, *World Trade Review*, **2**: 261–295.

Sykes, A. O. (2004). The Persistent Puzzles of Safeguards: Lessons from the Steel Dispute, *Journal of International Economic Law*, **7**: 523–564.

8

Mexico – Measures Affecting Telecommunications Services (WT/DS204/R) A Comment on "El mess in TELMEX"

DAMIEN J. NEVEN*

Graduate Institute of International Studies, Geneva and Centre for Economic Policy Research, London

PETROS C. MAVROIDIS*

Columbia Law School, New York and University of Neuchâtel, Switzerland

1 Introduction

This chapter reviews the panel report on *Mexico – Measures Affecting Telecommunication Services.* The Panel considered claims by the United States that Mexico acted inconsistently with its obligations in respect to the liberalization of its market for telecommunication services. It is the first Panel to consider solely the rules agreed upon in the General Agreement on Trade in Services (GATS). It is also the first Panel to deal with the telecommunication services industry and its complex layers of legislation, in particular the rules agreed to in the *Telecommunications Reference Paper* (TRP) on pro-competitive regulatory principles. Viewed from this perspective, this report is, because of its potential as a precedent, of particular significance.

This case essentially revolves around the question of under what conditions foreign telecom operators can terminate calls in Mexico. The United States argued that the Mexican regulation of termination charges was not in conformity with the obligations contained in the TRP. It argued in particular that the termination charges were not cost-oriented and that Mexico had set up a cartel of telecom operators.

* This chapter was prepared in the context of the project of American Law Institute project on the Principles of World Trade Law. We would like to thank Joseph Weiler, Aaditya Mattoo, Pierre Larouche, Gary Horlick, Henrik Horn, Alan Sykes, and Damien Gérardin for useful comments on a previous version of this chapter.

The following section of this chapter, Section 2, briefly discusses the Mexican regulation in dispute from an economic perspective and presents the legal framework of the dispute, focusing on the relevant provisions of the TRP. Section 3 analyzes whether and how the termination charges can be covered by the TRP. In this section, we *first* observe that the US operators do not supply cross-border services under mode 1, as the Panel stated in its report. Indeed, a cross-border (mode 1) supply of telecom services can hardly take place when both the supplier (a US telecom firm) and the consumer of the service (US subscribers) are situated in the same jurisdiction (as is the case here). Finding, as the Panel did, that US firms were supplying cross-border (mode 1) services does not accord with the basic definition of a mode-1 service. Rather, a southbound international call involves the purchase by US operators of termination services from Mexican carriers. Hence, the only cross-border transaction here is a transaction involving the sale of termination services by Telmex (the Mexican carrier asked to terminate southbound calls) to its North American clients (the US operators requesting termination of their calls in the Mexican market). The transaction involves Mexico exporting services, rather than the other way around. *Second*, we observe that Mexico did not enter into any commitment with respect to the export of termination services (under Art. XVIII GATS). *Third*, we discuss the issue of whether the Panel, had it properly defined the sales of termination services as a mode-1 export, could have imposed the disciplines of the TRP on the supply of that service. In this event, the Panel would possibly have taken the position that the TRP prevents the exercise of market power in export markets. We argue that such an approach would not be warranted: we find, with respect to both wording and context, that the TRP does not apply to cross-border supply of services but to mode-3 supply of services only.

Assuming, for the sake of argument, that termination charges for international calls are covered by the TRP, Section 4 discusses whether the termination fees charged by Telmex can be considered as cost-oriented. We argue that the Panel defined a benchmark for cost orientation, namely long-run average incremental cost, that is somewhat controversial. There are indeed a number of good reasons against the adoption of this standard, and it is surprising that a WTO panel, with no particular expertise or experience in this matter, should take responsibility for imposing a particular regulatory standard in such a complex field.

Section 5 discusses whether cartels fall within the scope of the TRP. We argue that the TRP should not be construed as containing an obligation with respect to cartels. Section 6 contains a brief summary of our findings and some conclusions.

2 Background

2.1 Regulation of termination charges

Within Mexico, local networks (the "last mile") are typically provided by the historic incumbent monopolist (Telmex). Long-distance services within Mexico (between cities or regions) have been opened to competition, and, at the time of the instant case, there were as many as 27 long-distance carriers operating in the country, including Telmex. Long-distance carriers could not, however, be controlled by foreign operators, ownership being limited to a 49% share (according to the Mexican telecom regulation, in line with appropriate specific limitations on commitments taken by Mexico within GATS). Nonetheless, some carriers were still partly owned by US operators or associated with them.

In this environment, the completion of international calls requires the linking of networks operated by different firms.[1] In order to offer outgoing calls to the United States, for instance, long-distance carriers in Mexico must connect to a firm operating in the United States. Similarly, in order to provide international service to their domestic subscribers, US operators need a connection to a Mexican operator in order to terminate the calls. From an economic point of view, the Mexican and US legs of an international call can be seen as strict complements; a call originating in the United States up to the Mexican border has no value if it is not associated with a Mexican termination; conversely, a call originating in Mexico up to the US border has no value, unless it is associated with a termination in the United States.

The connection between US and Mexican networks is subject to a specific regulation, referred to as the International Long Distance (ILD) rules.[2] We first describe these rules and subsequently discuss their economic significance.

[1] Given that, in addition, none of the Mexican carriers control a foreign network.

[2] "Rules for the provision of international long-distance service to be applied by the licensees of public telecommunications networks authorized to provide this service."

2.1.1 ILD rules

This regulation includes, for the purpose of our discussion, four important components:

First, it establishes a system of authorization/certification for the operation of the switches that connect domestic and foreign networks. These are referred to as international gateways. At the time of this case, there were 11 international gateways, which were operated by the Mexican long-distance carriers. That is also to say that some long-distance carriers did not operate an international gateway and had to subcontract the switching of their international calls to a carrier operating a gateway.

Second, the regulation stipulates (*Rule 2*, XII) that all gateway operators should charge the same rate for terminating calls in Mexico, referred to as the "settlement rate." Termination involves two separate operations, namely the international switch and the connection to the Mexican subscriber. The latter involves a local link and possibly a long-distance link.[3] The regulation also specifies that the same rate will apply, regardless of whether the international gateway operator terminates the call itself or transfers the call to another long-distance (and/or local) carrier. A symmetric pricing scheme is stipulated for outgoing calls: foreign operators must be paid a fixed fee for the termination of calls in their territory. Again, this fee is not dependent on the carrier that originates the call in Mexico.

Third, the regulation (*Rule 13*) determines how the (uniform) prices (for terminations in Mexico and abroad) are set; the Mexican operator with the largest market share of outgoing calls in a reference period is put in charge of negotiating the rates with the foreign operators. At the time of the instant case, Telmex had (by a wide margin) the highest market share and thus was in charge of negotiating termination fees.

Fourth, the regulation (*Rule 2*, XIII) allocates incoming calls among the international gateways. Each gateway operator has an allocation of *incoming* calls for any given month, which reflects its market share of *outgoing* calls during the previous month. If an operator receives calls in excess of its quota, it must redirect calls to other gateway operators

[3] The gateway operator is supposed to pay to the operator of the local loop an interconnection fee, which corresponds to the interconnection fee that is normally paid for national calls, as well as some (unspecified) percentage of the settlement rate.

in order to achieve the appropriate distribution of market share. In such a case, the termination charge that the gateway operator receiving the call has obtained from the foreign operator is passed through to the gateway operator to whom the call is transferred (less a fee that reflects the cost of switching and routing).

2.1.2 Some consequences of the ILD rules

From an economic perspective, the consequences of this regulation can be outlined as follows:

First, since no US firms can terminate calls in Mexico or control a gateway operator, all US operators must purchase termination from a Mexican operator when offering a call from the United States to Mexico.

Second, the price of termination services within Mexico is set in such a way that it is likely to mimic the price that would be set by a monopolist; the regulation envisions that the price is determined by a single firm (Telmex), with the knowledge that all others will apply the same price. The incentives of the firm in charge of setting the price will then mimic the incentives that a monopolist would have, at least if the share of overall demand that the firm can obtain is independent of the price. From this perspective, the market-sharing arrangement that supplements the pricing arrangement, in such a way that market shares are determined by shares in another market, is instrumental and indeed brings the incentives of Telmex closer to those of a monopolist in the pricing of termination services. Some discrepancies may still arise to the extent that termination services are differentiated or to the extent that the marginal costs of the different operators vary. In those circumstances, a hypothetical firm in charge of maximizing the overall profit (a monopolist) may want to differentiate prices among operators. The regulation envisages a single price and may thus fall short of maximizing the overall profit. Finally, the market-sharing arrangement on the basis of market shares in outgoing calls also consolidates the implementation of the monopoly solution, as it removes the incentives for secret price cuts with respect to the termination of incoming calls.

Third, the pricing of termination and allocation of incoming calls will affect incentives in the market for outgoing international calls. The profitability of a reduction in price in this market will be enhanced at the margins, and hence the regulation should lead to lower prices for outgoing international calls.

Fourth, the regulation also enforces a *monopsony* in the market for termination of calls in the United States. US operators face a single buyer. The classic theory of monopsony indicates that a single buyer will internalize the effect that an increase in the price paid for a marginal unit will have on infra-marginal ones, and, hence, will buy less than what would be purchased by a collection of small independent buyers. The classic theory of monopsony, however, assumes that the single buyer faces a well-defined supply curve. Under the circumstances, it may be more reasonable to assume that there is a relatively small group of firms selling termination services in the United States.[4] How the outcome of bargaining over termination rates will be affected by the presence of a few buyers, rather than a large collection of them, will vary depending upon the details of the bargaining. But it seems reasonable to presume that the implementation of a monopsony will lower the price of termination in the United States (relative to the price that would obtain with a set of independent buyers).

Fifth, the regulation clearly affects the incentives that US operators have to enter into agreements with Mexican firms, and in particular with Telmex, with respect to the routing of calls; US operators will be more or less indifferent regarding different Mexican partners with respect to calls into Mexico. Indeed, they will be charged the same price, regardless of the gateway operator that they choose. Neither can their choice be driven by quality considerations, as they have no control over the identity of the operator that will effectively terminate the call. Matters are different, however, with respect to the termination of calls into the United States. In this regard, agreements with larger Mexican operators are more attractive; even if the prices paid for termination in the United States will not vary from one operator to another, total revenues will increase in line with the volume of calls handled by the Mexican operator with whom they enter into an agreement. Mexican operators, however, are fairly indifferent as to their choice of a US partner: the market-sharing agreement for termination of calls from the United States effectively ensures that the total revenue they obtain

[4] According to Sidak and Singer (2004), the US market is highly concentrated, with an HHI index around 5000 during the 1990s (5842 in 1992, declining to 4162 in 1999, but increasing again to 6215 in 2000).

is not dependent on the size of their US partner. As indicated above, it is effectively determined by each operator's domestic market share. Hence, large Mexican operators are in a privileged position. They are attractive to US partners but have no marked preference for a particular US partner. They should accordingly be in a position to extract a high surplus for entering into a routing agreement. Interestingly, it would appear that it was a conflict between the US operators with respect to the choice of the Mexican partners that led to the dispute in the first place. According to Mardsen (2004), Sprint (a relatively small US operator) entered into a routing agreement with Telmex in the mid 1990s. AT&T and MCI had to settle for smaller Mexican partners and were dissatisfied with this outcome. According to Mardsen (2004), they called on the US Trade Representative (USTR) to help them gain better access. It is somewhat intriguing, however, that the United States did not directly challenge the practice that disadvantaged AT&T and MCI, relative to Sprint, namely the *buyers'* cartel: Telmex fixing the price at which termination in the United States would be bought by all Mexican operators. Rather, the United States challenged the export cartel, namely the cartel with respect to the export of termination services (such that Telmex would fix the price that applied to sales of termination services by all Mexican operators to US telecom firms). One can only conjecture that the United States anticipated that it had a stronger case against the export cartel than the buyers' cartel, and presumed that prohibition of the export cartel would also trigger the dissolution of the buyers' cartel.

2.2 *The legal framework*

For the Panel to find against Mexico, it first had to establish that the transaction at hand was covered by Mexico's commitments. In the GATS[5] framework, the obligations assumed by WTO Members are distinguished between general obligations and specific commitments. The former binds every WTO Member irrespective of specific commitments, whereas the latter reveals the extent of trade liberalization assumed. Mexico, for example, by virtue of the most-favored-nation clause (a general obligation), must, in principle, treat all telecoms operators originating in any WTO Member in a non-discriminatory manner.

[5] GATS stands for General Agreement on Trade in Services.

Were Mexico, however, to decide not to undertake any specific commitment in the field of telecoms, this contractual promise would amount to an empty shell (in terms of trade liberalization), since Mexico will be consistently honoring its promise by refusing access to all non-national-telecom carriers to its telecom market. Similarly, with respect to market access (Art. XVI GATS), WTO Members are committed to "accord services and service suppliers of any other Member treatment no less favorable than that provided for under the terms, limitations and conditions agreed and specified in its Schedule." In addition, according to Art. XVIII GATS, "Members may negotiate commitments with respect to measures affecting trade in services not subject to scheduling under Art. XVI .... Such commitments shall be inscribed in a Members' schedule." One hundred and fourteen WTO Members so far (counting the European Union members individually) have undertaken specific commitments in the field of telecommunications.

The WTO Members that have entered commitments must respect a complicated set of obligations. Besides the GATS, they will have to respect the following legal documents: (i) the Annex on Telecommunications; (ii) the regulatory principles reflected in the TRP; and (iii) the schedules of specific commitments.

Legally speaking, by virtue of Art. XXIX GATS, the Annexes to the GATS are an integral part of the GATS. Furthermore, by virtue of Art. XX. 3 GATS, the specific commitments entered into by WTO Members are an integral part of the GATS as well. The legal nature of the TRP is more convoluted. It was agreed to by the negotiators as a necessary step to further specify the obligations reflected in the other legal instruments. However, WTO Members did not have to adopt it as such. As a result, some did, some did not, and some adopted a portion of it. Consequently, there are many national "TRPs" with no identical content. To the extent adopted, a national TRP is part of a given WTO Member's commitments. So far 69 WTO Members have adopted the TRP either *in toto* or in part. The regulatory principles reflected in the TRP have been inscribed in schedules of specific commitments in accordance with Art. XVIII GATS (additional commitments).

The United States presented claims under both the Annex and the TRP. Because the TRP in any event incorporates the obligations reflected in the Annex, in the remaining part of the chapter we will focus on the claims made by the complainant under the TRP. There are three important sections of the TRP for the purposes of our discussion. *First*, the reference paper defines a "major supplier" in the following terms:

> A major supplier is a supplier which has the ability to materially affect the terms of participation (having regard to price and supply) in the relevant market for basic telecommunications services as a result of:
>
> (a) Control over essential facilities; or
> (b) use of its position in the market.

Second, Section 1 relates to competitive safeguards and reads as follows:

> 1.1. Prevention of anti-competitive practices in telecommunications
> Appropriate measures shall be maintained for the purpose of preventing suppliers who, alone or together, are a major supplier from engaging in or continuing anti-competitive practices.
>
> 1.2. Safeguards
> The anti-competitive practices referred to in the above paragraph shall include in particular:
>
> (a) Engaging in anti-competitive cross-subsidization;
> (b) using information obtained from competitors with anti-competitive results; and
> (c) not making available to other services suppliers on a timely basis technical information about essential facilities and commercially relevant information which are necessary for them to provide services.

Third, Section 2 focuses on interconnection and in relevant part reads as follows:

> 2. Interconnection
>
> 2.1. This section applies, on the basis of the specific commitments undertaken, to linking with suppliers providing public telecommunications transport networks or services in order to allow the users of one supplier to communicate with users of another supplier and to access services provided by another supplier.
>
> 2.2. Interconnection to be ensured
> Interconnection with a major supplier will be ensured at any technically feasible point in the network. Such interconnection is provided:
>
> (a) Under non-discriminatory terms, conditions (including technical standards and specifications), and rates and of a quality no less favourable than that provided for its own like services or for like services of non-affiliated service suppliers or for its subsidiaries or other affiliates;

(b) in a timely fashion, on terms, conditions (including technical standards and specifications), and cost-oriented rates that are transparent, reasonable, having regard to economic feasibility, and sufficiently unbundled so that the supplier need not pay for network components or facilities that it does not require for the service to be provided; and

(c) upon request, at points in addition to the network termination points offered to the majority of users, subject to charges that reflect the cost of construction of necessary additional facilities.

The United States claimed that the ILD rules discussed above were inconsistent with the obligations Mexico assumed by virtue of its TRP. In particular, the United States claimed that:

(i) international termination of calls fell within the scope of Mexico's commitments with respect to "interconnections" under Section 2 of the TRP;

(ii) Telmex should be considered as a "major supplier";

(iii) the interconnection rates charged by Telmex (and other gateway operators) to US suppliers were not "cost-oriented"; and, finally,

(iv) Mexico failed to ensure that Telmex and other gateway operators did not engage in anti-competitive practices, as these firms operated a cartel.

The Panel effectively accepted all the US claims, albeit only with respect to facilities-based services. In June, Mexico decided not to appeal and agreed to remove disputed ILD rules.[6] In effect, Mexico committed to a pricing of termination charges on the basis of commercial negotiations between US and Mexican operators. The United States was satisfied.

3 Crossing the border?

The United States focused its complaint on the termination in Mexico of calls originating in the United States. In order to evaluate whether

[6] WT/DS204/7 S/L/161. One can only offer conjectures as to why Mexico decided not to appeal. It would appear that the WTO ruling presented the Mexican government with an opportunity to liberalize the market (and reduce the power of Telmex) at limited political cost (the WTO being portrayed as an external constraint). The Mexican government (and its competition authorities) had previously tried to liberalize the market on their own initiative, but faced significant political pressures.

Mexico had undertaken a commitment with respect to this service, the Panel first sought to define the service and its mode of supply.

3.1 *Mode-1 supply of basic telecommunications services*

The United States claimed that its operators were providing cross-border telecommunication services (mode 1). In the US argument, Mexico's practices were unlawful because they contravened Mexico's commitments with regard to mode-1 supply of "basic telecommunications services"[7] from the United States to Mexico, through US carriers. This was **taken for granted** by the Panel. In § 7.42 of its report, we read:

> More generally, a supplier of services under the GATS is no less a supplier solely because elements of the service are subcontracted to another firm, or are carried out with assets owned by another firm. What counts is the service that the supplier offers and has agreed to supply to a customer. In the case of a basic telecommunications service, whether domestic or international, or supplied cross-border or through commercial presence, the supplier offers its customers the service of completing the customer's communications. Having done so, the supplier is responsible for making any necessary subsidiary arrangements to ensure that the communications are in fact completed. The customer typically pays its supplier the price of the end-to-end service, regardless of whether the supplier contracts with, or uses the assets of, another firm to supply the services.

This passage, which is contained under the heading "(b) Are the services at issue supplied cross-border?," appearing on page 144 of the Panel report, leaves no doubt that the Panel was indeed contemplating a transaction whereby a US carrier supplies cross-border telephone services to its customers, and not the sale of termination services from Mexico to the United States. Indeed, with respect to this latter element of the telephone service, the Panel makes the point that it is immaterial whether it is being subcontracted (out-sourced) by the US carrier.

The definition of mode 1 in GATS is not a model of clarity. However, the intention of the parties must be that the supplier of a service and its consumer are not physically present in the same territory.

[7] That is, public voice telephony, circuit-switched data transmission, and facsimile services, both "facilities based" and by a "commercial agency."

This is what distinguishes mode 1 from the three other modes of supply. Article. I.2 GATS reads:

> For the purposes of this Agreement, trade in services is defined as the supply of a service:
>
> (a) from the territory of one Member into the territory of any other Member.

The Scheduling Guidelines (WTO Doc. MTN.GNS/W/164, dated September 3, 1993) underscore the need to ensure a common understanding of what each mode of supply covers and refer to telecoms as one means for supplying cross-border services from the supplier to the consumer:

> It is important to have a common understanding of what each mode covers. To this end, further examples and explanations are given below.
>
> (a) Cross-border supply
>
> International transport, the supply of a service through telecommunications or mail, and services embodied in exported goods (e.g. a computer diskette, or drawings) are all examples of cross-border supply, since the service supplier is not present within the territory of the Member where the service is delivered.

Examples of cross-border supply offered either in the scheduling guidelines, or indeed in the actual schedules themselves, refer to transactions in which the supplier of the service and the consumer are physically present in two different territories, neither of them moves, and yet a service is being supplied. For example, an attorney at law established in Geneva, Switzerland, sends, by e-mail, his legal advice to a client who resides in Brussels, Belgium.

If one applies this line of reasoning to the transaction considered by the Panel, we are led to conclude that US operators do not provide a cross-border service under mode 1, since both the supplier (US carrier) and the consumer (US residents) are indeed physically present in the same territory.

3.2 *Mode-1 export of services?*

As indicated above, an international call from the United States to Mexico can be seen as the bundle of two strict complements, namely a routing from the US subscriber to the border and a termination within Mexico. The US operator sells the bundle to a US subscriber and purchases one element of the bundle (one input) from a Mexican operator. From this perspective, Mexican operators are thus selling one service (termination) to a foreign firm. In other words, they are producing a service using domestic inputs and selling it to a foreign undertaking.[8] This is literally a mode-1 type of supply, but in this perspective the supplier is the Mexican operator that terminates the call (and not the US operator, as deemed by the Panel).[9]

Hence, the Panel ends up imposing a discipline on the exports of Mexican services, making sure in particular that such services are sold at prices that reflect cost. This raises at least two questions: *first*, it raises the question whether from a legal perspective the GATS framework imposes a discipline on exports. *Second*, it raises a fundamental question about the distinction between exports and imports in the case of telecom services. Indeed, the perspective that we have taken so far relies on what could be seen as a convention, namely that the consumer of a southbound call is the US subscriber.

The GATS allows for additional commitments with respect to exports under Art. XVIII. Some countries have indeed entered into additional commitments with respect to exports, in the case of maritime services, for instance. Mexico, however, has not entered into any commitment with respect to exports. Arguably, the Panel should have observed this and simply dismissed the case.

[8] This is a perfectly legitimate scenario in the GATS context: according to Art. XXVIII(i) GATS: " 'service consumer' means any person that receives or *uses* a service" (emphasis added).

[9] One can also wonder whether US firms could be seen as supplying services in Mexico if they could open subsidiaries in Mexico that would complete the calls. In that circumstance, US firms would compete with domestic suppliers (for termination) and from that perspective, they could be seen as supplying services through mode 3. Still, they would not be selling to Mexican customers, and at least from this perspective they could not be seen as exporting a service to Mexico. It is not clear to us whether both elements are required (the provision of a service in competition with domestic suppliers and the sale to a domestic customer). Anyhow, it is clear that Mexico has never committed to allowing US firms to open subsidiaries (as recognized by the Panel) and hence had not committed to allowing supply through mode 3. Of course, if US firms were in addition allowed to sell outgoing calls in Mexico, they would clearly be offering a service through mode 3. This seems to imply that imports of telecom services can only be supplied through mode 3 and that supply requires an access to the local network for foreign firms, as well as the authorization to sell services domestically. This analysis, however, hinges on the principle that the calling party pays for the call. The issue is further discussed below.

The Panel was thus set on a misleading course from the very beginning when it ruled that the US operators were supplying cross-border telecommunications services. The panel (§ 7.30) did not reflect on the nature of the services provided by the US operators and offered a superficial discussion of the modes of supply; the Panel was satisfied that a call originating in the United States was supplied cross-border simply because, according to the "ordinary meaning of words," it was "supplied from the territory of one member into the territory of another." The Panel did not pause to reflect on the fact that the ordinary meaning of words did not provide guidance with respect to the direction in which the services flowed.

Interestingly, the approach that we take here has actually been put forward in the context of the negotiation (as we discovered *ex post*). Had the Panel spent more time delving into the negotiating documents, it would have come across similar points of view. Australia, for example, tabled a proposal that is along the same lines. On page 4 of its proposal,[10] we read:

> Australia considers that cross-border supply applies to services such as telecommunications termination services whereby a service provider in the territory of one member delivers or terminates a telephone call to a service provider in the territory of another member. Under Article I of the GATS the service provider receiving the call is supplying a (termination) service to a service provider in another country.

As indicated above, the Mexican regulation allowed for the operation of a buyers' cartel (a cartel in the purchase of termination services in the United States) in addition to the sellers' cartel that the Panel focused on. Hence, the rules allowed for a restriction of competition in the import of termination services, and it may have been more natural for the Panel to focus on those restrictions. However, the Panel is, as usual, restricted to considering the claims put forward by the parties, and since the United States did not focus on the buyers' cartel, that was not within the scope of what the Panel could review.

The Panel's approach also has far-reaching consequences. Indeed, the Panel has effectively outlawed export cartels. This may be attractive from an economic perspective. Indeed, export cartels lead to the

[10] See WTO Doc. S/NGBT/W/3/Add. 14 of 21 October 1994. See also the Australian communication on scheduling for termination in services in WTO Doc. S/NGBT/W/16 of 10 November 1995.

distortions that are associated with the exercise of market power (in terms of allocative and possibly productive efficiency). These distortions are also often considered significant from an empirical perspective (see, for example, Jenny 2003). The institutional consequences are, however, significant; for instance, a consequence of the Panel approach is that the exemption of export cartels in the United States under the Webb-Pomerene Act appears to be in contravention of the obligations of the United States under the GATS. One wonders whether the signatories of the GATS meant to impose such a discipline, given that the implementation of competition rules (including rules on export cartels) is not pursued further within the WTO, at least for the time being.

3.3 Exports and imports of telecom services

As indicated above, the sale of southbound international calls by US telecom suppliers to US subscriber cannot be seen as a mode-1 supply of services into the Mexican market to the extent that the buyers are located in the United States (the same territory as that of the supplier). This approach emphasizes the location of the party who pays for the service in order to distinguish between domestic and international transactions. However, a call could conceivably be seen as a service for which both the calling party and the receiving party are willing to pay, and the question of who pays for the service could be seen as a matter of convention.[11] In this framework, a US operator that connects a US calling party with a Mexican correspondent is providing a service to the Mexican party. The US operator is effectively supplying a service to Mexican consumers, using US factors or production, so he can be seen as providing a cross-border supply under mode 1, as well as purchasing Mexican services (to terminate the call).

This raises two issues: *first*, it is apparent that the distinction between exports and imports of telecom services relies on the location of the party who pays for the services (the consumer being considered the one who pays). Still, neither the GATS (broadly speaking) nor the WTO case law seems to have singled out the identity of the party who pays to define the identity (and location) of the party who consumes a service. *Second*, one can only feel a little uncomfortable with a substantive distinction (which triggers the application of the GATS)

[11] This is the so-called "calling party principle" or CPP.

that relies on a convention (namely, the convention that the calling party pays).

One can then wonder what the Panel's analysis would have been if the recipients of southbound calls had been considered consumers of the services provided by the US telecom operators. According to this approach, the conditions under which a US operator could buy the Mexican termination service would affect its ability to offer a service to Mexican consumers. Because the routing of the call to the border and the termination of that call in Mexico are a complement, a restriction on the export of termination services, for instance an export cartel that increased the price of termination, would increase the cost of supplying the service by the US operators and thereby reduce the amount of services sold to Mexican consumers (and their US correspondents). The export restriction would act as an import barrier. Accordingly, there may have been a case for preventing export restrictions under the GATS because of their potential effect on imports, for instance under a market-access provision.[12] This logic, however, is not spelled out by the Panel.

3.4 *Mexico's concession: the routing requirement*

Having accepted that US firms were providing cross-border telecommunication services, the panel observed that, in its schedule, Mexico has committed to provide market access for such services, subject only to a routine requirement[13] (that calls be routed to a Mexican operator with a concession).

Mexico, in its schedule of commitments, inserted a routing restriction according to which all international traffic would have to be routed through the facilities of an enterprise that had a concession. It then defined under what conditions a concession could be granted under Mexican law. In the Panel's view, in order to respond to the US claim, it would first have to assess the consistency of the routing restriction with Art. XVI.2 GATS (the legal basis invoked by the complainant).

[12] Of course, any restriction on exports that are used in the production of a commodity abroad for which there is an import demand will have that effect. But the strict complementarity between the two components of the call makes the effect sharper.

[13] In addition, the Panel observed that Mexico's commitment applies only to cross-border services supplied by facilities-based operators, and not by operators using capacity leased from another operator.

The Panel (§§ 7.80–7.86) makes a *prima facie* defensible argument[14] distinguishing between facilities- and non-facilities-based trade and goes on to find that the Mexican routing restriction makes it clear that non-facilities-based carriers cannot supply telecoms services: a "facilities-based service operator" is a telecommunications service provider owning, as opposed to leasing, networks used to provide telecommunications services. On the other hand, "comercializadoras" (non-facilities-based) are in fact "resale-based service suppliers," leasing bulk-rate plant (i.e. transmission) capacity from facilities-based carriers and using that capacity to provide services to individual customers or groups of customers at prices high enough to make a profit, yet sufficiently below the equivalent rates of the facilities-based carriers to attract customers. Hence, in the Panel's view, the routing restriction is tantamount to telecom carriers having to interconnect with facilities-based carriers in Mexico, since interconnecting with non-facilities-based carriers is not an option.

Having decided this[15] (i.e. that the United States could legitimately expect Mexico to honor its concession with respect to facilities-based suppliers), the panel next examined to what extent Mexico had honored its commitment under the TRP (and Section 5 of the Annex) to provide reasonable (i.e. cost-oriented) rates with respect to access pricing (interconnection).

Indeed, as discussed above, the full picture of Mexico's telecom commitments includes not only the routing restriction, but its

[14] There are many aspects of the argument, however, with which we disagree. For example, the Panel seems to adopt the idea that only limitations of the six types mentioned in Art. XVI.2 GATS can lawfully be entered into a schedule of concessions. However, the plain textual reading of Art. XVI GATS leads to the exact opposite outcome: (1) the expressions "terms" and "conditions" appearing in Art. XVI.1 GATS, which are not repeated in its § 2, are terms distinct from the term "limitation" (which also appears in § 1). Hence, in our view, § 2 is only an elaboration of § 1 with respect to "limitations," but that still additional "terms" and "conditions" could be lawfully inserted in a schedule. (2) Footnote 8 to Art. XVI GATS (actually to its § 1), which clearly indicates that the movement of capital under mode 1 and (partially) under mode 3 must be allowed. But that would imply that a restriction on capital movements could be introduced with respect to modes 2 and 4, although those restrictions do not fall squarely within any of the six measures in § 2 of Art. XVI GATS. The Panel summarily discards such arguments by paying more attention to documents of ambivalent legal value (scheduling guidelines) rather than to the text of Art. XVI GATS itself.

[15] Mexico did not go down without a fight on this issue. In its view, the routing restriction made it impossible for any carrier to supply cross-border telephone services to customers

obligations under the Annex and the TRP. It is also clear that the evaluation of the routing restriction was a *passage obligé* for the Panel: coming to a conclusion on the precise ambit of Mexico's commitments with respect to facilities-based service is the necessary first step toward establishing Mexico's obligation to guarantee cost-oriented rates. Had the panel, for example, concluded that Mexico had undertaken no commitments on mode 1, the rest of the analysis would have been redundant.

3.5 Applying the TRP to mode-1 supply of services

Hence, the Panel saw the routing restriction as the basis for the additional interconnection commitments contained in the reference paper (Section 2). Given that the TRP does not explicitly mention interconnection with respect to cross-border services, the Panel then relies on various other means and contextual elements to evaluate whether it does indeed cover such types of interconnection. The Panel took the view that commitments under the TRP are applicable to international interconnection,[16] i.e. in a transaction where the supplier of telecom services has no commercial presence in the market where it will supply the services at hand. In other words, the panel has indeed ruled that, with respect to mode 1 (cross-border), WTO Members have to abide by the TRP.[17]

The Panel made this finding despite the fact that the so-called regime of accounting rates had been explicitly excluded in the course of the negotiation, as expressed by the Report of the Group on Basic Telecommunications (15 February 1997). The regime of accounting

in Mexico, unless the foreign carrier was also established in Mexico and carried a concession. Hence, assuming that AT&T also controlled a carrier in Mexico that had lawfully been granted a concession by Mexico, it could sell telephone services to customers in both the United States and Mexico. This point is probably not the strongest in Mexico's defense of the case: the routing restriction imposed the obligation to *route* incoming calls to facilities-based carriers, which meant that anyone, and not only those having invested in Mexico, could, in principle, route calls to facilities-based operators in Mexico. Hence, Mexico's defense did not address the heart of the issue here, that is, under what conditions such transactions would take place.

16 We find no evidence in the negotiating history where this term (i.e. "international interconnection") has been used. For a very comprehensive of the context surrounding the negotiating history of the TRP, see Bronckers and Larouche (2005). The authors provide a very detailed account of the circumstances surrounding the negotiation and of the regulatory framework as such.

17 Of course this obligation binds only those WTO Members that adopted the TRP.

rates is a regime that was widely used by different countries before deregulation, such that the price for termination of international calls was determined only on the basis of net flows, typically between historic operators and on the basis of agreed rates. The regime implemented by Mexico under ILD rules can be seen as a variation of an accounting-rate regime that accommodates the presence of several operators. The Panel, however, found that the Report of the Group on Basic Telecommunications referred only to accounting-rate regimes that violate MFN provisions.

We find this approach hard to sustain. The TRP was negotiated and conceived to address a situation where telecom services would be supplied through commercial presence. For reasons having to do with the fact that (a) not all WTO Members had, at the time of the advent of the Telecoms Agreement, adequate competition statutes in place, and (b) because some WTO Members had already de-monopolized trade in services and hence obligations would de facto be assumed by private entities, it was felt that a contractual arrangement was necessary to make sure that telecoms liberalization would be effectively pursued.[18] This is the role of the TRP.

Both the text and the concessions assumed under the TRP make it clear that it was conceived to address a mode-3 supply of service and nothing else.

Interconnection (access pricing) is the centerpiece of the TRP. According to § 2.2(a), WTO Members must provide interconnection:

> under ... terms, conditions ... and rates and of quality no less favourable than that provided for its own like services ...

The term "like services" has consistently been interpreted by WTO Panels dealing with GATS-related issues from the consumers' perspective: to the extent that consumers treat two services interchangeably, the services at hand will be considered like.[19] For consumers, of course, it is highly unlikely that a phone call between two points in Mexico City and a phone call from Mexico City to Athens, Georgia, are interchangeable. Viewed from the supply side, the outcome does not differ: for Telmex, for example, it is impossible to establish comparability between the two phone calls mentioned above, since Telmex will need to

[18] See Hoekman *et al.* (1998) and Mavroidis and Neven (2000) on this issue.

[19] See for example, the Panel and the Appellate Body(AB) reports on *EC – Bananas* (WTO Doc. WT/DS/27).

purchase termination services from a US carrier, the cost of which does not necessarily have to correspond to that charged by Mexican carriers when terminating calls. Moreover, it could very well be the case that the United States has entered no such commitments at all; hence, comparability will never be established. The only case where comparability can always be established is when we compare a phone call between two points in Mexico City supplied by Telmex and the same phone call supplied by, for example, AT&T.

The application of the TRP to mode-1 exports raises further issues. For instance, it is hard to make sense of the requirement with respect to *universal service* (§ 3 of the TRP) in the case of mode-1 exports. It would effectively amount to a requirement for Mexican telecom operators to sell termination services to foreign suppliers so that all foreign subscribers can call Mexico. This would be absurd, as Mexican suppliers have no way to ensure that every foreign subscriber can call Mexico, as this is largely determined by the policy of foreign suppliers.

Consider further § 1.1 of the TRP, which informs the rest of the document as to the nature of the obligations assumed. It reads:

> Appropriate measures shall be maintained for the purpose of preventing suppliers who, alone or together, are a major supplier from engaging in or continuing anti-competitive practices.

Assuming that it is applicable to export transactions, this provision would *ipso facto* mean that some national competition laws would have to be drastically amended. Typically, competition statutes use domestic consumer welfare as the proxy to distinguish between what is and what is not permissible in terms of market behavior. Cartelizing export markets is not much of a concern, since they involve higher profits for domestic firms (at the expense of foreign buyers) and cannot be expected to hurt domestic consumers. A good example is offered by the US competition laws: the *US Webb–Pomerene Export Trade Act* of 1918, for all practical purposes, exempts US export cartels from antitrust persecution by US authorities. Has the United States, by agreeing to telecom liberalization under the GATS, *ipso facto* agreed to abolish this act? This would be a far-fetched conclusion indeed.

Once again, the commitments under § 1 make perfect sense when viewed as commitments regarding behavior in the domestic market.

It is not only the text, but also the manner in which the text has been understood by WTO Members when scheduling their commitments, that lends intellectual support to this line of thinking: we found not one single export commitment (e.g. selling termination services irrespective of the commercial presence of the foreign carrier in the domestic market)[20] in the schedules of concessions of those WTO Members that undertook commitments in the field of telecoms. Hence, subsequent practice, an interpretative element mentioned explicitly in Art. 31 of the Vienna Convention on the Law of Treaties (VCLT),[21] leads to the same conclusion.

The Panel's attitude is indeed problematic here. By contrast, were one to understand the obligations imposed by the TRP as limited to a mode-3 type of telecom supply (commercial presence), then the whole document makes eminent sense. It essentially amounts to an obligation to impose minimum competition-law requirements to incumbents, in full respect of the territoriality principle conferring jurisdiction.

The Panel is thus right only if the requirement to supply services at cost-oriented rates under § 2.2(b) of the TRP is interpreted outside its context (i.e. without taking any account of all other obligations mentioned in the TRP). This is not, however, a mode of interpretation consonant with Art. 31, on which, the panel, paradoxically, relied.

Overall, we find good reasons to think that the disciplines embedded in the TRP should not be applied to the provision of mode-1 cross-border services. *First*, this implies that even if the case before the Panel concerned termination services supplied on a cross-border basis by Mexican carriers to US customers, the panel should still have declined to apply the TRP and should have dismissed the case. *Second*, it also implies that if the Panel had been confronted with another claim by the United States, namely that Telmex was exercising buyer power in the purchase (imports) of termination services from the United States (for northbound calls), it should also have dismissed the case.

[20] In fact, if at all, the negotiating record seems to suggest that WTO Members did not wish, for some time at least, to rock the boat with respect to such transactions. This is what the agreed Memorandum on Accounting Rates essentially boils down to.

[21] From early on, when ruling on the first dispute submitted to it, the AB made it clear that the WTO judge has no choice but to follow the VCLT when interpreting the WTO agreement, and this by virtue of Art. 3.2 DSU.

4 Cost-oriented rates

In what follows, we assume that the interconnection provision of the reference paper applies to the international termination of calls and review the Panel's approach in the implementation of this provision.

The Panel first inquired whether Telmex could be considered a "major supplier." The Panel acknowledged that a relevant market had to be delineated in order to perform this assessment and concluded that the relevant market was the market for the termination of calls into Mexico. Telmex was found to be a major supplier in light of the fact that it could "affect the terms of participation" in the market. The Panel then examined whether termination rates were cost-oriented. The Panel discussed what cost-orientation may entail and, relying again on supplementary sources, found that long-run average incremental cost could be seen as an appropriate benchmark. The Panel indicated (§ 7.177):

> We find that the increasing and wide-spread usage of incremental cost methodologies among WTO members supports the interpretation of the term "cost-oriented" as meaning the cost incurred in supplying the service, and the use of long term incremental cost methodologies, such as those required in Mexican law, is consistent with this meaning.

The Panel then reviewed the evidence submitted by the United States, in particular the evidence showing that the price for termination of international calls was much higher than the price for terminating calls within Mexico, even if one allows for the additional cost incurred in the international gateway. Taking these domestic termination rates as an appropriate benchmark for what long-run incremental cost may be, and having observed that international rates were "substantially" higher, the Panel concluded that the international rates were not cost-oriented.

From an economic perspective, the Panel's focus on properly defining the relevant market is welcome; by so doing, the Panel reduces the risk that it may find that a firm alone or together with others is a "major supplier" in a market in which market power could not be extracted. Unfortunately, the Panel did not spell out in detail how the relevant market should be delineated, simply referring to the importance of demand substitution.

As indicated above, the Panel found that the termination of international calls is a relevant market because buyers cannot undertake an international call without termination (there is no substitute). This analysis raises at least two issues:

First, the Panel did not inquire about the possibility of substitution through calls in the opposite direction; faced with an increase in termination charges, which is passed on to the final US consumers, it is possible that US buyers will drastically reduce their demand and convince their Mexican correspondents to call them. This approach, which has been discussed in the telecom literature,[22] suggests that southbound calls may be substitutable for northbound calls.[23] This pattern may be important among so-called closed user groups. If the substitution is large enough (at the level of the overall market and not only for some closed user groups), it may imply that there is no relevant market for the termination of calls into Mexico, but rather a market for point-to-point services between Mexico and the United States. This issue is not discussed by the Panel.[24]

Second, one can wonder whether the Panel should not have made a distinction between the international switch (the interconnection itself) of the incoming calls and the termination in the domestic network. These two components can, in principle, be unbundled, and, in fact, they are, when gateway operators transfer excess calls to other long-distance carriers. So, the Panel should probably have distinguished between the two relevant markets. If it had done that, it obviously would have found that Telmex and the other long-distance carriers were major suppliers in both. However, this approach suggests that the Panel could have raised another concern with respect to the termination offered by Telmex and other suppliers, namely the extent to which it was unbundled (since Art. 2.2(b) stipulates that interconnection should be "sufficiently unbundled").

Having delineated the market, the Panel considers, as indicated above, whether Telmex is a major supplier and whether rates are cost-oriented. This discussion is somewhat odd under the circumstances of the case; given that the regulation will lead to prices that will mimic monopoly prices, a discussion of whether Telmex is a major supplier would appear to be somewhat besides the point (the belabored

[22] See for instance, Hausman (2002).

[23] If northbound calls are taken as a substitute for southbound calls, the distinction between imports and exports of basic telecom services disappears.

[24] Even though it was apparently raised by Mexico, see Sidak and Singer (2004) on this issue.

discussion of Telmex's market share is, from that perspective, a little surrealistic). Similarly, to the extent that, among all market structures, monopoly will lead to prices that least reflect costs, the discussion of whether rates set by Telmex are cost-oriented may not be necessary.

It is, however, worth commenting briefly on the Panel's analysis with respect to cost orientation, as it may establish some precedent.[25] *First*, as indicated above, the wording of Art. 2 induces the Panel to find reference in the field of regulation; the Panel considers as a benchmark the level at which prices could be regulated if termination is considered as a bottleneck facility. The Panel draws an immediate analogy to domestic interconnection and the access prices to local networks, which are often bottleneck facilities. The Panel also finds some guidance from the recommendations of the International Telecommunications Union with respect to the determination of accounting rates, i.e. when there is a single international gateway – which is therefore a bottleneck facility. However, these references are certainly not the only useful references, given that international termination is somewhat unlikely to be a bottleneck facility (as long as access to the last mile is regulated).

Second, assuming that the regulated rates provide useful guidance, it appears that the choice of long-run average incremental cost as a proper benchmark and the presumption that the same rates should be applied for a given service regardless of the users can be discussed. The reference to long-run incremental cost (a forward-looking concept) can be recommended only if there is no issue with respect to the financing of the existing infrastructure, or in other words, when there is no risk of important stranded costs. In addition, in the presence of public-service obligations in some segments, the use of long-run average incremental costs cannot be recommended. It does not seem that the panel should prejudge the issue of whether Mexico should be imposing some public-service obligations.[26]

Moreover, it is not clear that rates should not be differentiated across segments; there is a great deal of literature on the regulation of access prices (see for instance, Armstrong [2002], for a survey) and this

[25] The approach followed by the Panel to define a "major supplier" is discussed in the next section.

[26] Of course, in the case at hand, it is not clear why the Mexican regulator should distribute rents to long-term carriers that are not assuming public-service obligations. Only Telmex is arguably assuming such obligations, in particular with respect to the provision of a local network in remote areas.

literature emphasizes three concerns, namely: (i) the need to reflect the marginal cost of providing access; (ii) the need to finance the infrastructure (in particular in the presence of large fixed and common costs); and (iii) the provision of appropriate incentive for entry (when entrants operate with lower margins than the incumbent, they may profitably enter even though they are less efficient). The optimal access prices will then typically balance the allocative inefficiency that is induced by an increase in access charges in excess of marginal cost and the improvement in productive efficiency that such an increase induces by limiting the excess entry. One of the main insights of these pricing schemes is, however, that the markup over marginal cost should vary among market segments; markups should be higher in markets where the elasticity of demand is low (in the spirit of Ramsey prices).

To be fair, it is true that few regulatory authorities have found it practical to calibrate access charges according to demand elasticities, so that access charges often reflect average costs (for some hypothetical use of capacity). Still, adopting a suboptimal practice as a legal norm in the context of the WTO is not necessarily appropriate, as regulators' ability to calibrate access charges may improve over time. Furthermore, if the reference to average cost is commonly accepted among regulators in developed countries, it is not clear whether this practice is equally attractive for developing countries (see for instance, Laffont 1998).

5 Abuse of dominant cartels?

Finally, the Panel considered whether Mexico had maintained appropriate measures to prevent "suppliers who are, alone or together a major supplier from engaging in or continuing anti-competitive practices."

In deciding whether Telmex was alone a major supplier (in the context of the interconnection discussed in the previous section), the Panel simply used the definition provided by the reference paper. In particular, the fact that Telmex could materially affect the "terms of participation in the market with respect to price" was sufficient to conclude that it was a major supplier. Given that Telmex was, following the ILD rules, in charge of negotiating common prices for termination, this seems relatively uncontroversial. The Panel further found that Telmex and the other operators were *together* also a major supplier, simply because the implementation of the ILD rules involved the fixation of common prices by all gateway operators.

Clearly, Telmex and the other gateway operators had the ability in the context of the ILD rules to materially affect prices.

The Panel then defined what was meant by anticompetitive practices. Its first source of inspiration was the dictionary, from which it learned that an anticompetitive practice was "an action that lessens rivalry or competition in the market" (§ 7.230). From the (non-exhaustive) list of anticompetitive practices provided by the reference paper, the Panel concluded that, since "anti-competitive cross-subsidization" was listed, pricing actions could be a concern (§ 7.232). The Panel further observed that, since the definition of what was a major supplier included its ability to "materially affect prices," anticompetitive practices should focus on prices (§ 7.233). That was enough for the Panel to conclude that horizontal price-fixing should be considered an anticompetitive practice in the reference paper. Final confirmation of its approach was given by the Havana Charter, which recognized that price-fixing could adversely affect international trade; and the fact that the Organisation for Economic Cooperation and Development (OECD) had adopted a recommendation calling for strict prohibition of cartels; the fact that, in the WTO working group on trade and competition policy, "reference had been made to the pernicious effect of cartels"; and the fact that, in the competition legislation of certain Members, anticompetitive practices included price-fixing.

The approach followed by the Panel is not convincing. The fundamental, quintessential obligation of all WTO adjudicating bodies is not to undo the balance of rights and obligations as struck by the negotiating partners (Art. 3.2 DSU). To put it bluntly, panels cannot invent obligations, given the institutional risk that this would entail. In case of legitimate doubt, it is probably more appropriate for the judge to raise the issue and leave the decision to the principals (*die Herren der Verträge*).

The WTO Members decided not to undertake any explicit obligations vis-à-vis their partners regarding cartels. With respect to cartels, WTO Members have adhered to a contractual arrangement in which they must consult when a complaint to this effect has been launched (Art. IX GATS). They accepted nothing more beyond this obligation. This provision is evidence that the negotiating partners were indeed aware of the danger that restrictive business practices originating in cartels might present for trade in services. The non-inclusion of such practices in the TRP was thus a matter of choice rather than a simple omission.[27]

In its chapeau, § 1.2 of the TRP also makes it clear that what follows is an indicative list of restrictive business practices (RBPs).[28] It then enumerates three anticompetitive practices, and cartels are not included. The Panel acknowledged this point as well (§ 7.231).

An indicative list is a clear-cut case of an incomplete contract that the judge will be called upon, eventually, to complete. The inclusion of certain practices in the indicative list of § 1.2 of the TRP can be seen as reflecting the judgment of the contract's authors with respect to the prevalence of type-II errors (false negatives), if the practice is not systematically addressed (i.e. the possibility that if such a practice is not constrained, it will often be harmful). By contrast, the fact that some practice is not included must reflect the judgment that, if not constrained, such a practice will not be systematically harmful. This perspective has clear implications for the standard of review that should be applied in case an additional practice is included in the list. Moreover, the identity of the practices included in the list could give guidance to the judge as to which transactions could be added to the existing list.[29]

Had the Panel approached the list of § 1.2 in this manner, it would have noticed that the first and second examples in the indicative list cannot concern cartel-type behavior. At the same time, while with respect to the third example cartel-type behavior cannot be excluded, it is highly unlikely that the drafters of the treaty wanted to sanction such behavior through this example.

The Panel chose to disregard this avenue and instead build its case that cartel-type behavior was punishable through the TRP by looking at the Mexican legislation, the Havana Charter, and some OECD documents. However, because the Havana Charter never entered into force, its legal value is largely symbolic (by virtue of Art. XXIX GATT), and the OECD documents are non-binding contracts. The fact that Mexico

[27] Concurring on this issue, Marsden (2004).

[28] We use the term "RBPs" as equivalent to the term "anti-competitive practices" appearing in the TRP.

[29] From this perspective, it is also useful to note that the reference paper imposes a discipline only to particular firms, namely those that are "large" (dominant). A discipline with respect to cartels typically applies to all firms and hence does not fit well in this context. Indeed, most competition regimes rely on this distinction and have separate provisions for cartels (e.g. Art. 81 ECT) and the abuse of dominance (Art. 82, ECT).

punishes cartels through its domestic legislation is simply irrelevant: as stated above, the United States punishes cartels when they cartelize the US economy, but does not do so when they cartelize the world. What matters is the nature of obligations assumed under the WTO.[30]

Arguably, provisions like Art. 82 ECT on the abuse of dominance (or the analysis of monopolization under Section 2 of the Sherman Act) are also sources from which the panel should have sought some inspiration: in particular, the TRP requires a threshold finding that firms are "major suppliers" before practices may be evaluated, and in that respect, it is similar to Art. 82 ECT, in which dominance must first be established before an analysis may be undertaken as to whether observed conduct constitutes an abuse. In addition, as discussed above, the TRP was conceived as an instrument to control the conduct of historic incumbent operators, a task that is undertaken under provisions like Art. 82 ECT.[31]

Under provisions like Art. 82 ECT (or Section 2 of the Sherman Act), a distinction is usually drawn between exploitative and exclusionary practices.[32] The former designation refers to the exploitation of market power at the expense of buyers and includes business practices like price discrimination, in addition to, the profitable price increases permitted by the firms' own-demand elasticities. The latter refers to business practices aimed at foreclosing or marginalizing competitors and includes predation as well as other practices like tying and bundling.

Exploitative abuses are normally not pursued under Section 2 of the Sherman Act because preventing firms from exploiting the market power that the successful development of their business has conferred on them might reduce the very incentive to develop that business and compete in the first place. Similarly, the European Commission (EC) and European Union (EU) courts have been very reluctant to sanction exploitative abuse. From that perspective, the Panel's approach, which is sanctioning the mere exploitation of market power, appears to be rather bold.

[30] We do not equate the WTO with a self-contained contract, but we find it implausible to assume that all national law is binding on WTO Members anyway, even in the absence of specific international commitments to this effect.

[31] This is acknowledged by the panel (at § 7.237): "members agreed . . . to implement a pro competitive regulatory framework designed to prevent continued monopoly behavior, particularly by former monopoly operators, and abuse of dominance by these or any other major suppliers."

[32] See, for instance, or Fox (2002).

There is another dimension in which the panel's approach appears to diverge from the antitrust practice. Art 82 ECT allows for the fact that "one or more undertakings" may hold, and abuse, a dominant position. The practice has focused on single-firm dominance and unilateral conduct as potentially abusive, but the EU has also developed the concept of collective dominance, in narrow circumstances. A similar approach is followed under Section 2 of the Sherman Act. Admittedly, the limited use of collective dominance that is found in the EU and the United States is partly due to the fact that both antitrust regimes rely on different provisions (Art. 81 and Section 1) in order to sanction conduct involving several firms, and in particular, price-fixing. Of course, unlike antitrust authorities, the panel could not rely on another provision to sanction horizontal price-fixing, which is clearly present and presumably damaging in the present case. And the prospect that sanctioning exploitative abuse may discourage investment and reduce the incentive to compete hardly matters in the presence of a cartel.

Still, it is striking that the Panel did not approach the case from the perspective of collective dominance. Such an approach may have had some merit. Indeed, structural links among companies would be easy to show in a case like this, where it is the legislator that in fact established the cartel. On the other hand, the abuse-of-dominance scenario should not be discarded altogether: in this case, there is one leading player (Telmex) that has by law received assurance of non-competition from other minor players (since prices will be set at an industry level). Depending on the specifics of the case, on which we have no additional information, it could be that this law contributes to abuse by the dominant player.

There is a final issue that deserves comment, namely whether practices that are required under domestic law can be sanctioned by the TRP. Mexico, and the EU as a third party, argued that this is not the case; according to them, if a Member decides not to allow competition in a particular segment of the telecommunications sector, there is simply no scope for an anticompetitive practice. Following the EU submission, "it is not possible to restrict competition where competition is not allowed." The United States disagreed, naturally arguing that, if Mexico were free to introduce legislation that compels firms to engage in anticompetitive practices, the TRP would be meaningless. The issue is thus whether the TRP should be seen as a constraint on regulation or a constraint on additional measures (for instance, competition policy) that may be taken, given that regulation takes precedence.

This Panel found that the TRP acts as a constraint on regulation so that business practices that are required by domestic law can be found to be anticompetitive under the TRP. In so doing, the Panel effectively set aside the so-called "state doctrine" in antitrust. According to this doctrine, business practices that are required by states (domestic or foreign) fall outside the reach of antitrust rules. Such a doctrine may be justified when competition law is implemented at the same time as other laws promulgated by the same government (even if the implicit precedence given to other laws could be disputed). In this case, one authority decides according to its own preference how two of its instruments should be managed. But it is hard to justify the doctrine in the context of the TRP, which results from an international agreement, relative to domestic regulation: these are different authorities, and it is not clear why the domestic authority should be given the right to manage the implementation of domestic regulation and the international agreement. Indeed, the opposite would seem to be appropriate, given that the international agreement is a constraint on the domestic government to start with. Hence, it does indeed seem appropriate to reject the state doctrine.

6 Conclusion

The Panel's decision in this case had the effect of prohibiting a price-fixing agreement that was in all likelihood damaging in terms of overall welfare. This agreement was clearly improving welfare in Mexico (increasing the profit of gateway operators) at the expense of the US firms and consumers. From this perspective, the outcome can be seen as satisfactory.

However, the Panel achieved this result through a sequence of interpretations and assessments that seems controversial: *first*, by accepting a transaction such as the one under dispute as a mode-1 supply of services, the panel *ipso facto* accepted that a supply of service where the supplier of the service and its consumer are physically in the same territory is also covered by commitments under mode 1. This conclusion, however, is unwarranted in light of the definition of mode 1, the concessions made under mode 1, and the willingness of WTO Members to ensure that mode 1 will have a horizontal meaning irrespective of the service to which it applies. Our analysis still highlights the difficulty in distinguishing exports and imports in the field of telecommunications and the importance of additional guidance in this matter. *Second*, even assuming that the dispute before the panel was presented as a dispute concerning the conditions under which Mexico would supply termination services under mode 1 to the US carriers, the Panel should not have assumed that the TRP was applicable to such transactions. A careful, contextual reading of this document supports the view that it covers supply of services under mode 3 only. This is not to say that Mexico could not have assumed similar obligations for its sales of termination rates to US carriers with no commercial presence in the Mexican market. However, in the present case no such commitments were entered into. This is a factual issue, and the Panel, by making a legal issue out of it, undid the balance of rights and obligations as struck by the negotiating partners. *Third*, even assuming that the TRP applies, the Panel should not have concluded that interconnection rates were not "reasonable, cost-oriented rates" on the basis of the evidence before it. The Panel took a rather definite view on regulatory principles which involve complex and controversial issues. This ruling may thus have important systemic consequences. *Fourth*, even assuming that the reference paper applies, the Panel should not have concluded that cartels are punished by the TRP, knowing in addition that this approach was not necessary for it to reach its finding on this score.

Overall, the Panel's review of the competition-law component of this dispute leaves much to be desired. Based on the evidence before it, the Panel would have been on much safer ground had it requested additional information. Indeed, Art. 13 DSU empowers panels with very important discovery competencies. Sadly, this panel refused to make use of this institutional facility. This is regrettable, especially in a case like this, where recourse to expertise, in light of the current endowments of the WTO, is especially necessary.

References

Armstrong, M. (2002). The theory of access pricing and interconnection, In *The Handbook of Telecommunications Economics*, Caves, et al., eds. Chapter 8 Vol. I., Elsevier Science: North Holland, pp. 295–384.

Bronckers, M. and Larouche, P. (2005). The GATS Mimeo.

Fox, E. (2002). What is harm to competition? Exclusionary practices and anticompetitive effects, *Antitrust Law Journal*, **70**: 371–413.

Hausman, J. (2002). Mobile Telephone. In *Handbook of Telecommunications Economics*, Caves, et al., eds. Vol. I, Elsevier Science: North Holland, pp. 563–604.

Hoekman, B., P. Messerlin and Mavroidis, P.C. (1998). Regulation, competition policy and market access negotiations: lessons from the telecommunications sector. In *Competition and Trade Policies*, Einar Hope ed. Routledge: New York, pp. 115–139.

Jenny, F. (2003). International Cooperation on competition: myth, reality, and perspective, *Antitrust Bulletin*, **48**: 973–1003.

Laffont, J.-J. (1998). Competition, information and development, *Annual World Bank Conference on Development Economics*, pp. 237–268.

Mardsen, P. (2004). Trade and competition. WTO decides first competition case – with disappointing results, *Competition Law Insight*, **16**(3), pp. 3–9.

Mavroidis, P.C. and Neven, D.J. (2000). The WTO agreement on telecommunications: it's never too late. In *The Liberalization of State Monopolies in the European Union and Beyond*, D. Geradin, ed. Kluwer: London, pp. 307–318.

Sidak, G. and H. Singer. (2004). Überregulation without economics: the world trade organization's decision in the US–Mexico arbitration on telecommunication services Mimeo.

9

European Communities – Conditions for the Granting of Tariff Preferences to Developing Countries (WT/DS246/AB/R)

GENE M. GROSSMAN
Princeton University

ALAN O. SYKES
University of Chicago

1 Introduction

The WTO case brought by India in 2002 to challenge aspects of the European Communities' Generalized System of Preferences (GSP) brings fresh scrutiny to a policy area that has received little attention in recent years – trade preferences for developing countries. The idea for such preferences emerged from the first United Nations Conference on Trade and Development (UNCTAD) in 1964. The ensuing negotiations led to Resolution 21(ii) at the second session of UNCTAD in 1968, acknowledging "unanimous agreement" in favor of the establishment of preferential arrangements.[1] Tariff discrimination violates the most-favored nation (MFN) obligation of General Agreement on Tariffs and Trade (GATT) Art. I, however, and thus the legal authority for preferential tariff schemes had to await a GATT waiver of this obligation, which came in 1971. The waiver was to expire after 10 years, but the authority for preferences was extended by the GATT Contracting Parties Decision of November 28, 1979 on Differential and More Favorable Treatment, Reciprocity and Fuller Participation of Developing Countries, popularly known as the "Enabling Clause,"[2] and now incorporated into the law of the WTO along with the GATT itself.

[1] See OECD Secretary General (1983). [2] GATT, 26th Supp. BISD 203 (1980).

While trade discrimination favoring developing countries is the essence of any GSP scheme, India's WTO complaint raised the question of what type of discrimination is permissible – must all developing countries be treated alike, or can preference-granting nations discriminate among them based on various sorts of criteria? The European system challenged by India afforded more generous preferences to the least-developed countries, to developing nations that undertook certain measures to protect the environment and labor rights, and to 12 nations involved in efforts to combat drug trafficking. India originally challenged the environmental, labor and drug-related preferences, but later limited its complaint to only the drug preferences. A WTO Panel ruled in India's favor in late 2003.[3] The WTO Appellate Body affirmed the ruling in India's favor in early 2004,[4] although it modified the Panel's findings in a way that seemingly authorized some differential treatment of developing countries based on their "development, financial and trade needs."

The purpose of this chapter is to review the current state of the law in the WTO system, and to ask whether economic analysis can offer any wisdom about the proper extent of "discrimination" through GSP measures. As shall become clear, the issues are challenging ones, both from a legal and an economic standpoint. There are good economic reasons to be concerned about discrimination and reciprocity in GSP schemes, and respectable legal arguments that they should be strictly limited. GSP benefits are "gifts" of a sort, however, and tight limitations on their terms may put an end to them altogether. It is exceedingly difficult to say whether discrimination and reciprocity in GSP schemes make the trading community worse off or better off over the long haul.

Section 2 of this chapter provides a legal and a historical background, including a description of the GSP schemes currently in place in the United States and Europe, and a thorough review of the recent Panel and Appellate Body decisions. Section 3 evaluates the Appellate Body decision from a legal perspective and considers its possible implications for aspects of the US and European GSP schemes that were not challenged by India. Section 4 examines trade preferences from an

3 European Communities – Conditions for the Granting of Tariff Preferences to Developing Countries, WT/DS246/R (December 1, 2003) (hereafter Panel Rep.).

4 European Communities – Conditions for the Granting of Tariff Preferences to Developing Countries, WT/DS246/AB/R (April 7, 2004) (hereafter AB Rep.).

economic perspective, inquiring into the soundness of the GSP concept as a whole and asking whether some forms of "discrimination" are somehow better than others.

2 Legal background

Resolution 21(ii) at UNCTAD II in 1968 called for the establishment of a "generalized, non-reciprocal, non-discriminatory system of preferences in favour of the developing countries, including special measures in favour of the least advanced among the developing countries." It further stated that such preferences had three objectives: to increase the export earnings of developing countries, to promote their industrialization, and to accelerate their rates of economic growth.

From the outset of serious negotiations within UNCTAD, however, it was clear that the "non-discriminatory system of preferences" envisioned by Resolution 21(ii) would in fact embody considerable elements of "discrimination." Indeed, Resolution 21(ii) on its face contemplates discrimination in favor of the least-developed countries. Further, the theory behind GSP was that it would reduce the reliance of developing countries on exports of primary products and promote industrialization. Accordingly, it was understood that manufactured goods would be the main beneficiaries of preferences, and that agricultural products would be treated less favorably.[5] This "discrimination" across sectors inevitably produces a kind of *de facto* discrimination across beneficiaries – some beneficiaries have far greater capacity to produce the manufactured goods that are designated for preferential treatment than others.

Beyond these features built into the conception of the system, political factors intruded heavily on the willingness of nations to grant preferences across the board. Some developing countries were seen as ideologically unacceptable recipients of preferences, many produced manufactured goods in politically sensitive import sectors such as textiles and footwear, and the possibility of import surges was a matter of significant concern. Thus, it quickly became clear that if GSP schemes were to be politically viable in the major developed nations, they would have to contain substantial additional limitations as to product coverage and beneficiaries, and be accompanied by safeguards to address

[5] See OECD Secretary General (1983).

politically unacceptable increases in imports. No mechanism existed for coordinating the evolution of national schemes on such matters, and thus each developed rather differently.

Along the way, some preference-granting countries began to condition GSP benefits on the willingness of beneficiary nations to cooperate on various policy margins, either by rewarding cooperation with greater preferences or punishing its absence by withdrawing them. The conception of GSP as a "non-reciprocal" program thus came under considerable pressure as well.

2.1 *GSP scope and conditionality in the United States and Europe*

UNCTAD reports that there are currently 16 national GSP schemes notified to the UNCTAD secretariat – Australia, Belarus, Bulgaria, Canada, the Czech Republic, the European Community, Hungary, Japan, New Zealand, Norway, Poland, the Russian Federation, the Slovak Republic, Switzerland, Turkey, and the United States.[6] They differ in significant detail, and interested readers may consult the UNCTAD website for the particulars of various systems. Our purpose here is simply to show how the more important schemes are riddled with provisions that might be viewed as "discrimination" or "reciprocity," and for that purpose it will suffice to consider only the schemes of the United States and the European Communities.

2.1.1 GSP in the United States

The GSP of the United States was first enacted in the Trade Act of 1974 and took effect in 1976. It is presently authorized through 2006 and will then expire unless renewed by an act of Congress.

The statute has three sections – a general grant of authority to the President to extend preferences,[7] a section on the designation of beneficiary countries,[8] and a section on the designation of eligible products.[9] Regarding the designation of beneficiary countries, the statute begins with a short list of developed countries that are ineligible. It next forecloses beneficiary status to eight other categories of nations: (1) "communist" countries (with exceptions); (2) countries

[6] See http://www.unctad.org/Templates/Page.asp?intItemID=2309&lang=1, last accessed September 1, 2004.

[7] 19 U.S.C. § 2461. [8] 19 U.S.C. § 2462. [9] 19 U.S.C. § 2463.

that are parties to an "arrangement" which withholds "supplies of vital commodity resources from international trade" (aimed at OPEC); (3) countries that injure US commerce by affording preferences to other developed countries; (4) countries that expropriate the property of US citizens, including intellectual property, without just compensation; (5) countries that fail to enforce binding arbitral awards in favor of US citizens; (6) countries that aid or abet terrorism or fail to take "steps to support the efforts of the United States to combat terrorism"; (7) countries that have not taken steps "to afford internationally recognized worker rights"; and (8) countries that fail to fulfill their "commitments to eliminate the worst forms of child labor." The last five exclusions can be waived by the President in the "national economic interest."[10]

The President has the discretion to confer beneficiary status on any nation not excluded by the above factors, and the statute provides additional factors that the President must take into account in exercising this discretion.[11] The President must consider, along with the prospective beneficiary's interest in the program, its level of development, and its treatment in the GSP schemes of other donor countries, whether the country provides "equitable and reasonable access to [its] markets and basic commodity resources" and "adequate and effective protection of intellectual property rights," whether it has taken steps to reduce investment-distorting practices and barriers to trade in services, and whether it takes steps to afford internationally recognized worker rights. The statute also provides for "mandatory graduation" of "high income" countries, without defining the term "high income."[12] At the low-income end of the spectrum, it also allows the President to designate least-developed beneficiary nations, and to extend to them preferences that are not extended to other developing nations.

Pursuant to these provisions, quite a number of nations that have become highly successful exporters, such as Hong Kong, Singapore, and Malaysia, have now been "graduated" from the US scheme due to their "high-income" status. Several nations have had their GSP status suspended temporarily due to problems in their worker-rights practices, including Nicaragua, Paraguay, and Chile. Some of the benefits to Argentina were suspended in 1997 over an intellectual property

[10] 19 U.S.C. § 2462(b). [11] 19 U.S.C. § 2462(c). [12] 19 U.S.C. § 2462(e).

dispute, and some of the benefits to Pakistan were suspended at one time but later restored in return for cooperation in anti-terror efforts. Beneficiary status has also been denied to a number of nations with whom the United States has had poor political relations (e.g. Cuba, Iran, North Korea, Syria).[13] It is assuredly possible that geopolitical considerations play a broader role *sub rosa* in many of the decisions regarding beneficiary status, and there is no mechanism to ensure that the various criteria are applied in careful and even-handed fashion.

We will not dwell at length on the provisions for the designation of eligible products, as they are unlikely to be at the heart of any dispute over "discrimination" or "reciprocity" (although they might be said to cause *de facto* discrimination as indicated). Because they are relevant to an assessment of the economic effects of the system, however, we note three important details. *First*, many sensitive items are excluded by statute from the GSP system, such as certain textile and apparel products, watches, electronic products, steel products, footwear and leather products, certain agricultural products, and "any other articles which the President determines to be import-sensitive."[14]

Second, a product from a particular beneficiary becomes ineligible for coverage if there is no longer a "competitive need" (unless it comes from a least-developed beneficiary). When imports of a product from a single beneficiary exceed a certain monetary threshold (currently $ 115 million), *or* 50% of all US imports of the article in a calendar year, it must be removed as an eligible product unless the President executes a "waiver."[15]

Third, all items are subject to rules of origin. In general, a product will not be deemed to originate in a beneficiary nation unless it meets a 35-percent value-added test – the value of the input products produced in the beneficiary nation, plus the value of processing in that nation, must equal 35% of the value of the finished good.[16]

2.1.2 GSP in the European communities

The European approach to GSP has evolved considerably over time. The system in place through 1994 relied heavily on quantitative limits

[13] See generally UNCTAD, Generalized System of Preferences: Handbook on the Scheme of the United States of America (2003); UNCTAD, Generalized System of Preferences: List of Beneficiaries (2001).

[14] 19 U.S.C. § 2463(b). [15] 19 U.S.C. § 2463(c–d). [16] 19 U.S.C. § 2463(a)(2).

for the importation of duty-free or reduced-duty industrial and agricultural products. The arrangement challenged by India, which is now authorized through the end of 2005, relies to a much greater extent on "tariff-modulation" and "special-incentive" arrangements, coupled with provisions for country and sectoral graduation as well as an "everything-but-arms" arrangement for least-developed countries.[17]

The tariff-modulation arrangement classifies goods into "very-sensitive," "sensitive," "semi-sensitive," and "non-sensitive" products. Roughly speaking and with a few exceptions, beneficiary countries then receive tariff reductions of 15%, 30%, 65%, and 100%, respectively, off the usual MFN rate for goods in each category. Least-developed countries, however, receive duty-free treatment on goods in all categories except armaments. Countries can be completely graduated from the system based on a "development index," and individual exports from particular countries can also be graduated based on a combination of considerations relating to the development index and to the beneficiary's market share or degree of specialization in a particular product.

"Special-incentive arrangements" provide additional margins of preference to nations that apply for them and prove their eligibility. A labor arrangement applies to developing countries that have adopted the substance of the standards required by several International Labor Organization Conventions relating to, *inter alia*, forced labor, collective bargaining rights, non-discrimination principles, and child labor. An environmental-incentive arrangement applies to goods originating in countries with tropical forests that can establish their adherence to international standards regarding the sustainable management of tropical forests.

The special arrangements supporting measures to combat drugs are made available to 11 South or Central American countries, plus Pakistan, that are involved in efforts to reduce drug trafficking. They too provide additional margins of preference on a range of products, essentially exempting goods from sector-specific graduation rules that would otherwise apply to them.

[17] See generally Council Regulation (EC) No. 250/2001 of 10 December 2001 applying a scheme of generalized tariff preferences for the period from 1 January 2002 to 31 December 2004; UNCTAD, Generalized System of Preferences: Handbook on the Scheme of the European Community (2002).

Finally, the scheme contains a number of "temporary-withdrawal and safeguard" provisions. The most important are aimed at import surges, and allow preferences to be suspended after an investigation of such developments. Other provisions for temporary withdrawal apply to situations where the beneficiary country has been shown to have tolerated slavery, violated worker rights, exported goods of prison labor, failed to take appropriate means to control drug trafficking, engaged in fraud with respect to rules of origin, engaged in "unfair trade practices," or infringed on the objectives of certain fishery conventions.

The policies favored by the European system differ somewhat from the policies encouraged by the United States, although there are notable similarities. Both systems certainly exhibit a significant degree of "discrimination" and "reciprocity" in their design and in their application that goes well beyond simply the more favorable treatment of least-developed nations that was envisioned by UNCTAD Resolution 23(ii).

2.2 India's complaint and its legal basis

As noted earlier, India's original complaint before the WTO challenged the labor, environmental, and drug-related preferences in the European GSP scheme, but India later restricted its challenge to the drug-related preferences. Its decision to restrict the scope of its complaint has resulted in an Appellate Body decision that leaves open many questions about the permissible scope of "discrimination," as shall be seen.

The legal foundation for India's challenge begins with GATT Art. I, which requires that any "advantage, favour, privilege or immunity" granted by one member nation to the product of another and relating, *inter alia*, to "customs duties and charges of any kind," must also be granted "immediately and unconditionally" to like products originating in other member nations. This principle is commonly termed the "most-favored nation" (MFN) obligation of GATT.

Any GSP scheme, of course, involves tariff discrimination by the preference-granting nation. It thus requires some derogation from the legal prohibition in Art. I, which was first allowed under a 10-year waiver approved by the GATT membership in 1971. During the Tokyo Round, however, GATT members negotiated an agreement to make the authority permanent, embodied in the so-called "Enabling Clause."

The relevant text of the Enabling Clause provides:

1. Notwithstanding the provisions of Article I of the General Agreement, contracting parties may accord differential and more favourable treatment to developing countries, without according such treatment to other contracting parties.
2. The provisions of paragraph 1 apply to the following:

(a) Preferential tariff treatment accorded by developed contracting parties to products originating in developing countries in accordance with the Generalized System of Preferences,[3 (original footnote)]
. . . .

(d) Special treatment of the least developed among the developing countries in the context of any general or specific measures in favour of developing countries.

3. Any differential and more favourable treatment provided under this clause:

(a) shall be designed to facilitate and promote the trade of developing countries and not to raise barriers to or create undue difficulties for the trade of any other contracting parties;
(b) shall not constitute an impediment to the reduction or elimination of tariffs and other restrictions to trade on a most-favoured-nation basis;
(c) shall in the case of such treatment accorded by developed contracting parties to developing countries be designed and, if necessary, modified, to respond positively to the development, financial and trade needs of developing countries.

3(original footnote) As described in the Decision of the CONTRACTING PARTIES of 25 June 1971, relating to the establishment of "generalized, non-reciprocal and non discriminatory preferences beneficial to the developing countries."

The Enabling Clause plainly allows nations to depart from the MFN obligation to provide more favorable tariff treatment to goods from developing countries, and to provide even more favorable treatment for goods from the least-developed countries. Its text is otherwise silent on the range of goods to be covered by preferences, on the permissibility of other forms of "discrimination" among beneficiaries, and on the acceptability of attaching conditions ("reciprocity") to preferential benefits. Footnote 3, however, states that the

"Generalized System of Preferences" contemplated by the Enabling Clause is the system contemplated in the 1971 waiver, which in turn referred back to the "generalized, non-reciprocal, and non-discriminatory" system of preferences discussed under the auspices of UNCTAD.

Footnote 3 raises a number of issues not directly addressed by India's complaint. What is meant by the requirement of "generalized" preferences – does this obligation place any limits on the exclusion of particular products from GSP schemes? What does the obligation to provide "non-reciprocal" preferences imply about the imposition of conditions for the granting of preferences?

India's complaint put these issues to the side and focused instead on the requirement of non-discriminatory preferences. According to India, when a nation grants a preference on a particular product, it must extend that preference to all developing countries, subject only to the proviso that least-developed nations can receive greater preferences. Because the drug-related preferences in the European scheme afford special benefits to 12 enumerated beneficiaries that are not co-extensive with the set of least-developed nations, India contended, the preferences failed the requirement of non-discrimination under the Enabling Clause and in turn violated GATT Art. I.

2.3 The European response and the Panel decision

Before the Panel, Europe's first response was a formalistic claim that the Enabling Clause did not create an exception to Art. I of GATT, but removed GSP schemes altogether from the coverage of Art. I. The distinction was important, according to Europe, because India's complaint alleged a violation of Art. I but not of the Enabling Clause *per se*, and the Panel should only adjudicate claims brought before it. The Panel quickly put this issue to the side (over a dissent), however, and read the Enabling Clause as an exception to the MFN obligation of Art. I – *but for* the exception, preferences would violate Art. I, and therefore India's allegation of an Art. I violation squarely raised the proper issue. Further, following WTO precedent on "exceptions" to primary obligations, the Panel held that Europe had the burden of demonstrating that its program fell within the exception afforded by the Enabling Clause.[18]

[18] Panel Rep. ¶¶7.31–7.54.

Once the Panel ruled that GSP preferences fell under Art. I, the Panel had little difficulty in concluding that India made out a *prima facie* case of a violation.[19] The Panel then turned to the question whether Europe could invoke the Enabling Clause and thereby establish its "affirmative defense." On this front, Europe had three main arguments. *First*, it pointed to paragraph 3(c) of the Enabling Clause, which provides that differential treatment shall "be designed and, if necessary, modified, to respond positively to the development, financial and trade needs of developing countries." Europe argued that different developing countries have different "development, financial and trade needs," and that this provision authorized (and indeed required) preferences to be modified to respond to those differing needs, inevitably producing differences in the preferences across beneficiaries.

Second, Europe argued that India misinterpreted the requirement in footnote 3 that preferences be "non-discriminatory." For Europe, "discrimination" involved arbitrary differences in the treatment of similarly situated entities – as long as differences in treatment could be justified by a legitimate objective, and the differences were reasonable in pursuit of that objective, no "discrimination" should be found.[20]

Third, Europe argued that paragraph 2(a) of the Enabling Clause, which authorizes "preferential tariff treatment accorded by developed contracting parties to products originating in developing countries," did not require preference-granting nations to afford preferences to *all* developing countries. Had the drafters meant to require that preferences be extended to all, Europe suggested, they could have inserted the word "all" into the text.

India's response to the first and third arguments was that the term "developing countries" in paragraphs 3(c) and 2(a) should be read as *all* developing countries, i.e. developing countries as a group. Preferences should respond to the "development, financial, and trade needs" of those countries as a group, claimed India, and should not vary in accordance with any individual needs. In India's view, paragraph 2(a) likewise provided no authority for picking and choosing among developing countries. This proposition is reinforced by footnote 3 and its reference to non-discriminatory preferences, according to India,

[19] Panel Rep. ¶¶7.55–7.60.

[20] Robert Howse advances another line of argument that Europe did not pursue in the case. He suggests that the "obligations" in footnote 3, particularly the obligation to afford "non-discriminatory" preferences, were never intended to have binding legal effect but were merely aspirational. For a thorough vetting of this perspective, see Howse (2003).

which should be read to require formally identical treatment subject only to the exceptions specifically contemplated by the Enabling Clause.

The Panel addressed each of Europe's arguments separately, but its analysis of all three was strikingly parallel. The Panel found that the relevant portions of the text of the Enabling Clause were ambiguous. Following the Vienna Convention, it then turned to the context of the treaty text, its object and purpose, and other aids to interpretation. It noted that the Enabling Clause referred back to the waiver granted in 1971, which in turn made reference to "mutually acceptable" preferences. The "mutually acceptable" preferences were apparently those negotiated under the auspices of UNCTAD and embodied in the "Agreed Conclusions" that eventually emerged from the ongoing negotiations in UNCTAD. The Panel thus concluded that the Enabling Clause should be interpreted to permit the sort of preferential system contemplated by the UNCTAD negotiators, memorialized in the Agreed Conclusions, and incorporated by implicit reference into the 1971 waiver.

The Panel then reviewed the Agreed Conclusions at some length. It found that they anticipated some limitations on product coverage – most manufactured goods would be covered, with limited exceptions, with only case-by-case coverage for agriculture. But, according to the Panel, nothing in the negotiating history seemed to contemplate discrimination among developing countries on the basis of their development or other "needs," except for the special treatment of least-developed nations. The only other potential limitations on coverage addressed by the UNCTAD negotiations concerned measures to withdraw preferences or to set quantitative ceilings when exporters achieved a certain competitive level, along with safeguard measures to address import surges.

On the basis of these findings, the Panel accepted India's suggestion that the phrase "developing countries" in paragraph 2(a) referred to *all* developing countries,[21] and implicitly as well its suggestion that the reference to "developing countries" in paragraph 3(c) was to developing countries as a group. According to the Panel, paragraph 3(c) did not authorize differences in preferences except those contemplated by the UNCTAD negotiators.[22] Finally, the Panel found no basis in the

[21] Panel Rep. ¶7.174. [22] Panel Rep. ¶7.116.

text or relevant negotiating history for Europe's suggestion that the requirement of "non-discriminatory" preferences was satisfied as long as differences in treatment resulted from objective criteria relating to legitimate objectives. Rather, footnote 3 "require[d] that identical tariff preferences under GSP schemes be provided to all developing countries without differentiation," excepting only the differential treatment expressly contemplated in the Agreed Conclusions.[23]

Europe's final line of defense was an effort to invoke GATT Art. XX(b), which allows measures "necessary to protect human ... health." The Panel was not persuaded, questioning whether the drug-related preferences were genuinely aimed at the protection of human health in Europe, questioning their "necessity," and questioning whether they amounted to an arbitrary discrimination among beneficiary nations where similar conditions prevail in violation of the chapeau to Art. XX.[24] Europe did not appeal these findings.

2.4 The Appellate Body decision

The Appellate Body affirmed the proposition that the Enabling Clause is an exception to GATT Art. I. India had the burden of raising the question whether Europe's system was consistent with the Enabling Clause and did so; Europe then had the burden of proving its consistency.

Europe did not appeal the Panel's interpretation of paragraph 3(c) of the Enabling Clause, as the Panel had not made any explicit "findings" regarding the consistency of the European drug preferences with paragraph 3(c). The appeal was thus confined to the question of whether the European system was consistent with paragraph 2(a) and with its footnote 3 requiring "non-discriminatory" preferences. On the latter issue, the Appellate Body found that the ordinary meaning of the term "non-discriminatory" was not sufficiently clear to permit it to choose between the competing views of discrimination put forth by India and the European Communities on that basis.[25] Both parties agreed that "discrimination" entailed disparate treatment of those "similarly situated," but disagreed on what it meant to be "similarly situated" – and an appeal to the ordinary meaning of the term "discrimination" did not resolve such a disagreement.

[23] Panel Rep. ¶7.161. [24] Panel Rep. ¶7.236. [25] AB Rep. ¶¶151–52.

The Appellate Body then turned to paragraph 3(c) of the Enabling Clause to provide further context for the interpretation of the non-discrimination obligation, and accepted the European argument that the absence of the word "all" before "developing countries" implied that the text imposed no obligation to treat *all* developing countries alike.[26] Further, both parties apparently conceded that the development needs of various countries could differ. Accordingly, the Appellate Body was "of the view that, by requiring developed countries to 'respond positively' to the 'needs of developing countries,' which are varied and not homogeneous, paragraph 3(c) indicate[d] that a GSP scheme may be 'non-discriminatory' even if 'identical' tariff treatment is not accorded to 'all' GSP beneficiaries."[27] It thus reversed the Panel's finding to the contrary. Likewise, the Appellate Body reversed the Panel's finding that the reference to "developing countries" in paragraph 2(a) was to *all* developing countries.[28] It held that preference-granting countries are permitted to treat beneficiaries differently when such differences "respond positively" to varying "development, financial, and trade needs."

The non-discrimination requirement was not without bite in the view of the Appellate Body, however, because it did require "that identical tariff treatment must be available to all GSP beneficiaries with the 'development, financial [or] trade need' to which the differential treatment [was] intended to respond."[29] Because there was no specific finding by the Panel regarding the consistency of the European drug-related preferences with paragraph 3(c), the Appellate Body was prepared to accept *arguendo* that drug trafficking related to a "development need." Even so, the preferences would still fail the non-discrimination test unless "the European Communities prove[d], at a minimum, that the preferences granted under the Drug Arrangements [were] available to all GSP beneficiaries that [were] similarly affected by the drug problem."[30]

The Appellate Body then held that the European Communities failed to carry the burden of proof on this issue. It emphasized that the drug-related preferences were available only to a "closed list" of 12 countries. The regulation creating the preferences did not set out any criteria for the selection of the countries, and it did not provide any

[26] AB Rep. ¶159. [27] AB Rep. ¶165. [28] AB Rep. ¶¶175–76. [29] AB Rep. ¶180.
[30] Id.

mechanism for adding or deleting countries as their circumstances changed. Under these conditions, Europe failed to demonstrate that its preferences were non-discriminatory.

Along the way, the Appellate Body contrasted the labor and environmental incentive arrangements in the European GSP scheme. Unlike the situation with the drug-related preferences, the regulation creating the labor and environmental incentives provided "detailed provisions setting out the procedure and substantive criteria that apply to a request ... to become a beneficiary under either of those special incentive arrangements."[31] The Appellate Body thus hinted that those aspects of the European scheme might pass the non-discrimination test if challenged, but did not speak to the concurrent issue of whether the labor and environmental incentives responded to legitimate "development, financial, and trade needs."

3 Legal commentary

3.1 An assessment of the WTO outcome

As with most hard cases, it is difficult to say which side was "right" on a purely legal basis. The case is hard because, as both the Panel and the Appellate Body acknowledged, the text of the Enabling Clause is ambiguous. Even assuming that footnote 3 was intended to create a binding non-discrimination obligation, as the parties to the case assumed, the absence of any definition for the concept opens the door to a wide range of interpretations. Any student of civil rights law, constitutional law, or even GATT Arts. I and III is well aware of the fact that "discrimination" is an extremely elastic notion. The phrase "developing countries" in paragraphs 2(a) and 3(c) is equally difficult to pin down. It is surely true, as the Appellate Body noted, that the drafters could have said "all developing countries," but did not. Yet, it is equally true that the drafters might have said "particular" or "selected" developing countries, or used some other phrasing to signify the acceptability of differential treatment, but did not. As always, inferences about the intentions of the drafters from phrasings that they did *not* employ are questionable at best.

[31] AB Rep. ¶182.

In the face of such ambiguity, the Panel relied primarily on historical context and the UNCTAD negotiations to give footnote 3 some definitive content. The 1971 waiver referenced in footnote 3 indeed contemplates "mutually acceptable" preferences, and the Agreed Conclusions from the UNCTAD negotiations may well have been a good indicator of what was "mutually acceptable." The Panel was also correct to note that a major impetus for the UNCTAD negotiations was to back away from the historical patchwork of discriminatory preferences already in place in favor of a *generalized* system of preferences. From these facts, the Panel inferred that any discrimination had to be limited to what was expressly contemplated by the Agreed Conclusions.

The Panel's approach resonates somewhat with an economic perspective on the GSP system that we develop in the next section, and which may help to clarify the object and purpose of the Enabling Clause as an aid to interpretation. An economic understanding of the MFN obligation suggests that it arises to avert certain negative externalities that would otherwise arise relating to bilateral opportunism and to erosion of the value of trade concessions. The situation prior to the UNCTAD negotiations was one in which the problems addressed by the MFN obligation had resurfaced because of a patchwork of discriminatory preferences in the trade policies of developed nations, often dating from the colonial era. The UNCTAD negotiations may be viewed as an effort to bring the attendant negative externalities under greater discipline, and the Agreed Conclusions may be seen as the embodiment of a negotiated arrangement with the following central characteristics: the developed nations agreed that they would tolerate the negative consequences for themselves associated with preferences for developing nations, at least within the agreed parameters. But they also committed themselves to ameliorate the negative consequences of discriminatory preferences for developing nations by moving toward the "generalized, non-reciprocal, and non-discriminatory preferences" contemplated by the 1971 waiver.

This understanding of the economic rationale for the UNCTAD negotiations lends further support to the conclusion of the Panel. If developed nations are allowed to engage in whatever degree of discrimination they wish without legal constraint, an essential purpose of the UNCTAD negotiations is clearly jeopardized. And even if nations are only allowed to afford differential treatment according to their assessment of the individual "development, financial, and trade needs" of beneficiary countries, the danger still arises that they will use such authority to justify discriminatory policies that benefit countries in favor rather than for any legitimate purpose. For these reasons, it is entirely plausible that negotiators would want to limit discrimination to fairly narrow considerations, such as status as a least-developed nation, and to forbid it otherwise.

An important counterargument must be acknowledged, however. The parties to the UNCTAD negotiations were aware of the potential political impediments to the implementation of GSP, and might well have thought that compromise on various margins, in ways not fully anticipated during the negotiations, would be mutually preferable to political impasse and the *status quo ante.* A 1968 Organization for Economic Cooperation and Development (OECD) report, for example, embraced the principle that "preferences should be granted to any country, territory or area claiming developing status (principle of self-election), but preference-giving countries might decline to grant such treatment to a particular country on *compelling grounds*" (emphasis added).[32] The scope of the term "compelling grounds" was not made clear. We cannot rule out the possibility that donor countries may have been unwilling to give much of consequence had they imagined that a tight prohibition on discrimination and reciprocity would apply going forward, and developing countries may well have been willing to take what they could get. This proposition is very much in the spirit of the argument put forward elsewhere by Robert Howse (2003), who contends that the language of footnote 3 was never intended to create a binding legal obligation.

It is also noteworthy that major GSP schemes put in place after UNCTAD II from the outset contained exemptions and restrictions that were not specifically contemplated in the Agreed Conclusions. The long list of factors that foreclose beneficiary status under US law, for example, has remained the same in large part since the Trade Act of 1974.[33] These early practices of donor countries were firmly in place at the time of the negotiations that resulted in the Enabling Clause.[34]

[32] See UNCTAD (1981, p. 21).

[33] The various restrictions and limitations on the early European scheme are described at some length in Borrmann et al. (1981).

[34] To be sure, some of the restrictions came under early criticism from commentators as a departure from the principles of non-discrimination and non-reciprocity. See, e.g. UNCTAD (1981, p. 39).

Had it been the intention of the Tokyo Round negotiators to outlaw the sort of conditionality that had emerged, for example, in the US scheme devised by the Trade Act of 1974, they might well have done so more forcefully than by a somewhat oblique reference in footnote 3 to the system contemplated by the also somewhat oblique 1971 waiver.

From this latter perspective, the Appellate Body might be seen to have the better of the argument. It is certainly difficult to quarrel with its conclusion that Europe's interpretation of the phrase "developing countries" in paragraphs 2(a) and 3(c) of the Enabling Clause is a linguistically plausible one, and for the reasons noted above it is not entirely clear that the non-discrimination obligation in footnote 3 rules out any differential treatment not expressly contemplated by the Agreed Conclusions. One might even wonder whether the Appellate Body went too far in suggesting that donor countries must prove that any differential treatment is justified by reference to differences in "development, financial and trade needs." The supporters of the 1971 waiver could have anticipated that GSP schemes would contain a wide range of other conditions and restrictions to make them politically saleable in the donor countries.

In short, we concur with both the Appellate Body and the Panel in their finding that the language of the Enabling Clause is ambiguous, and is insufficient on its own to resolve the dispute. It is thus appropriate to resort to other aids to interpretation in accordance with the Vienna Convention, including the "context" of the treaty language and its "object and purpose." There can be little doubt that a central "object and purpose" of the UNCTAD negotiations was to reduce discrimination in trade preferences subject to some enumerated exceptions, and that both the 1971 waiver and the Enabling Clause may be said to incorporate this goal by reference. The approach of the Panel surely does the most to promote this objective. But we must also bear in mind that GSP benefits are a "gift" of sorts, and that donors may well have been unwilling to confer them if constrained by tight non-discrimination (and other) requirements. Developing nations may well have been aware that various forms of conditionality would be the *quid pro quo*, and the 1979 Enabling Clause could easily have done much more to condemn it in clear language if that was the intention of its drafters. Perhaps unfortunately, therefore, an appeal to the "object and purpose" of the Enabling Clause is also less than conclusive.

One virtue of the Panel's approach, to be sure, is that it provides reasonably clear guidance for the future as to what is permissible and what is not. Except for the differential treatment expressly anticipated by the Agreed Conclusions, no discrimination is permissible. The approach advocated by Howse also admits of easy judicial administration, as he would find no binding legal obligation at all in footnote 3. The approach of the Appellate Body, by contrast, steering a middle course of sorts, leaves fundamental and potentially thorny questions unanswered, as the next section will indicate.

3.2 Implications of the Appellate Body decision for other aspects of existing GSP schemes

The Appellate Body ruling establishes two important principles: (1) footnote 3 of the Enabling Clause is a binding legal obligation, requiring "generalized, non-reciprocal, and non-discriminatory preferences;" and (2) donor countries may nevertheless afford differential treatment to beneficiary nations if it is based on differences in their "development, financial, and trade needs." These principles raise a wide array of issues to which the Appellate Body has not yet spoken.

Most obviously, what counts as a development, financial, or trade need? The Appellate Body did not rule on the question whether drug trafficking creates a "development need," finding it unnecessary to address matters on which the Panel made no finding. Yet, it seems clear that the drug-related preferences were enacted for the benefit of Europe, to reward cooperation in its efforts to reduce traffic in drugs toward Europe, rather than to assist the beneficiaries in addressing any perceived "development need" of their own. Many of the other criteria for beneficiary status found in modern GSP schemes, such as failure to aid in efforts to combat international terrorism, failure to enforce arbitral awards, or participation in a cartel such as the Organization of Petroleum Exporting Countries (OPEC), seem still farther removed from any "needs" of the beneficiary country. Perhaps incentive arrangements pertaining to labor rights and environmental protection can fit more comfortably into the rubric of "needs," but its scope remains completely open at this stage.

One also imagines that some constraint must exist on the *magnitude* of the differential treatment that is permissible to address heterogeneous development, financial, and trade needs. Even if drug trafficking qualifies as a "need," for example, could a donor country deny preferences altogether to nations that do not have a serious drug-trafficking problem while extending substantial preferences to those that do? If the differential treatment must be justified by different "needs," it would seem to follow that it cannot exceed the amount required to address any need adequately. But how would one quantify that amount or otherwise place a principled limit on it?

A related question is: do donor countries have unfettered discretion to select the "needs" that they will address through differential treatment and to ignore others? Europe limits its environmental incentives in its GSP scheme to the protection of tropical forests, for example, but suppose a nation with no tropical forest can make the case that its exceptional air pollution problem poses a greater obstacle to its development than any obstacles posed by the possible loss of tropical forest elsewhere? Would a failure to afford differential treatment to assist it in addressing its air pollution problem then amount to "discrimination?"

The puzzle as to what constitutes impermissible discrimination is only part of the bigger picture. The word "generalized" in footnote 3 refers not only to the universe of beneficiary nations, but also to the scope of product coverage. The GSP system envisioned by the UNCTAD negotiators would provide broad coverage for manufactured and semi-manufactured items, limited only by quantitative ceilings or safeguard measures to address concerns about import surges. Can the complete exclusion of enumerated import-sensitive manufactured products, as in the US statute as one example, be squared with the obligation to provide "generalized" preferences?

The obligation to afford "non-reciprocal" preferences also potentially imperils much of the conditionality in modern GSP schemes. Some of those conditions, such as the US requirement that beneficiaries provide support for efforts to combat terrorism and respect arbitral awards in favor of US nationals, require reciprocity essentially on their face. Others can surely be characterized as requiring reciprocity, such as the special incentives on labor and environmental matters in the European scheme. If footnote 3 truly prohibits "reciprocity," it seemingly poses an enormous threat to the elements of conditionality that have been present in various GSP schemes since their inception, and that may be essential to their perpetuation as political matter.[35]

In short, the Appellate Body decision puts in question many prominent features of the US, European, and other GSP schemes, features that in some cases have been part of those schemes from the outset. It invites future challenges by countries that suffer trade diversion because of discrimination or reciprocity, even perhaps by developed nations. Donor countries will have the burden to prove their compliance with the Enabling Clause since it has now been ruled to be an "exception" to GATT Art. I. That burden may prove a difficult one to carry.

If successful challenges to GSP schemes multiply going forward, it is entirely possible that donor countries will choose to forego GSP arrangements altogether. Nothing requires donor countries to maintain schemes that are no longer palatable politically, and some (including the US and European schemes) are structured to expire on their own unless the political will to renew them is present. A key question going forward, then, may be whether additional challenges will be brought as time goes on, or whether instead the interested nations will conclude that it is not in their mutual interest to rock the boat.

4 Economic analysis

The legal commentary in Section 2 suggests several questions about GSP schemes and their place in the multilateral trading system. Do these schemes further the development goals for which they were designed? What effect do the schemes have on the economic welfare of countries that are not granted preferential treatment? And why might the contracting parties wish to regulate the extent of differential treatment and the conditions attached by donors when, after all, the GSP schemes are "gifts" from the developed countries to their less developed trading partners?

[35] We note in passing another limitation on reciprocity contained in the Enabling Clause. Paragraph 5 provides, in pertinent part, that "developing contracting parties shall therefore not seek, neither shall developing contracting parties be required to make, concessions that are inconsistent with the latter's development, financial, and trade needs." Although this obligation arises in the context of "trade negotiations," GSP conditionality might be viewed as setting up a "negotiation" of sorts, and paragraph 5 would then limit the "concessions" demanded to matters not inconsistent with development, financial, and trade needs.

4.1 *Economic effects of tariff preferences*

We begin by describing the economic effects of tariff preferences both in the country or countries that receive the special treatment and in other trading partners of the preference-granting country. Suppose first that preferences are granted to a "small country" or to a group of countries that collectively are small. In the parlance of trade theory, a small country is one that cannot affect the world prices of the goods that it trades, because its imports and exports are insignificant relative to the size of world markets. When exporters in such a country face a given world price of p^* and an MFN *ad valorem* tariff rate of t_{MFN} they must sell their output for $p^*/(1 + t_{MFN})$ to be competitive in the foreign market. This price prevails as well in the home market of the exporting country, because producers will not sell at home for less than what they can earn on world markets, nor will they be able to sell for more given that they choose to export at that price in a competitive equilibrium. Figure 1 shows the production and consumption levels in the exporting country prior to the time it is granted tariff preferences.

The preferences excuse the exporters in the small country from the generally applicable tariff. These exporters are too small to affect the

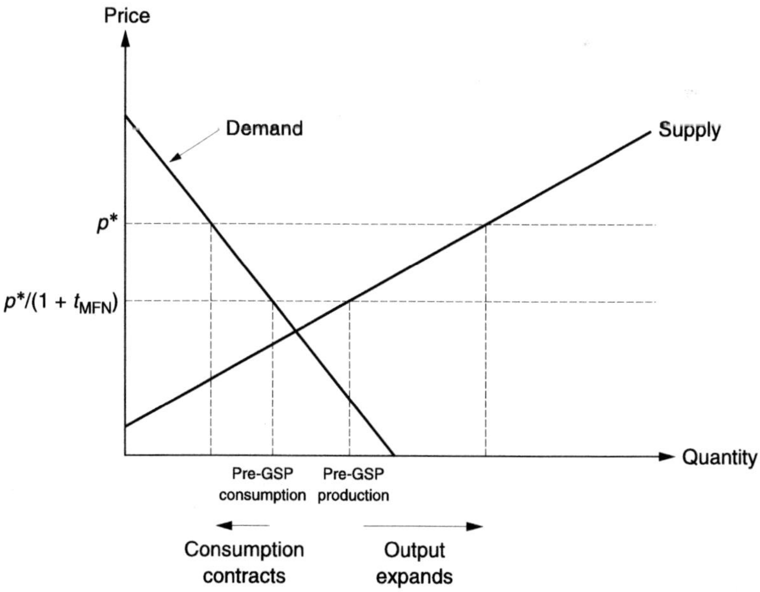

Figure 1

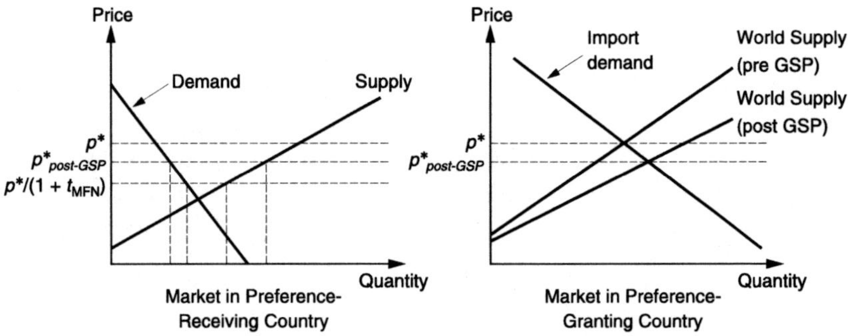

Figure 2

internal price in the preference-granting country, which remains at p^*. So, the exporters now can charge this higher amount and remain competitive in the foreign market. The figure shows that output expands as a result of the higher sales price, and that consumption in the exporting country contracts. For both reasons, exports grow.

The tariff preferences provide a "terms of trade" benefit to the exporting country. Producers gain, both because their original sales fetch a higher price, and because they expand output to the point where marginal cost equals p^*. Some of the gain to producers comes at the expense of domestic consumers, who lose surplus because they face a higher domestic price.[36] But the country enjoys a net gain in welfare equal to the trapezoidal area between the supply and the demand curves and bounded by p^* and $p^*/(1+t_{\mathrm{MFN}})$. Note that the price for exporters in countries that do not receive the preferential treatment remains at $p^*/(1+t_{\mathrm{MFN}})$. Thus, all growth in trade due to the GSP reflects *trade creation*; the other (small) countries that export to the preference-granting country suffer no harm in this case.

Now suppose that preferences are granted to a large country or to a group of countries that collectively is large. This situation is depicted

[36] Our analysis is predicated on the assumption that the prevailing tariff in the country that receives preferential treatment is greater than the MFN tariff in the country that grants the preferences. This assumption is reasonable in most cases, as average rates of protection are much higher in developing countries than in developed countries. If the assumption is violated, the preference-receiving country would export *all* of its industry output at price p^*, while domestic consumers would be served by imports from third-countries, where the prevailing price is $p^*/(1+t_{\mathrm{MFN}})$ and so the tariff-inclusive import price would be less than p^*. In the event, the terms of trade gain for the preference-receiving country is even larger than that described here, but it remains true that the preferences generate no negative externalities for third countries.

in Figure 2. As before, the granting of preferences will tend to raise the internal price in the preference-receiving country, as shown on the left-hand panel. But now the impact of the export growth on the world price cannot be ignored. The right-hand panel shows that total world supply to the donor country has expanded, which means that the market clearing price falls from p^* to $p^*_{\text{post-GSP}}$. The preference-receiving country still enjoys a terms-of-trade gain, but not as great as before.[37] Welfare rises by the (smaller) area bounded by the demand and supply curves and by the price lines $p^*/(1+t_{\text{MFN}})$ and $p^*_{\text{post-GSP}}$.

In this case, the export growth in the preference-receiving country reflects both trade creation and trade diversion. The trade creation is reflected in the fact that the GSP reduces the internal price in the preference-granting country, so its consumption expands and its home production contracts. The reduction in its home production is (more than) made up by its imports from the preference-receiving country. But the fall in the world price produces a terms-of-trade-loss for other countries that export to the preference-granting country. These countries see their exports displaced in part by goods from the preference-receiving country. They also earn less from what they do sell, and their welfare falls. In this case, the GSP imposes a negative externality on the exporting countries that do not qualify for the preferential treatment.[38] It is this negative externality that might explain why a country like India would object to the European GSP scheme.[39]

4.2 *Does GSP promote "development?"*

The Preamble to the 1971 Waiver, which provided the initial authority for tariff preferences that would otherwise violate GATT Art. I,

[37] The computational results presented by Brown (1987, 1989) show terms of trade gains from US and European GSP schemes for most beneficiary countries.

[38] Limão (2005) identifies another (political) economic externality that may result from tariff preferences. He points out that if the developed countries see their GSP schemes as a means to elicit cooperation from developing countries on non-trade issues, then the existence of these schemes may impede multilateral trade liberalization. The developed countries might regard their MFN tariff cuts as eroding the preferences afforded by their GSP schemes and thus limiting their ability to induce cooperation from their trading partners. Limão provides evidence that US tariff reductions in the Uruguay Round were smaller for goods imported on preferential terms than for similar goods that were not imported from favored partners.

[39] We also duly note the fact that the drug-related preferences in the European scheme extended to Pakistan and not to India, a situation that India may have found objectionable for political reasons.

states "... that a principle aim of the Contracting Parties is promotion of the trade and export earnings of developing countries for the furtherance of their economic development." To what extent can tariff preference schemes promote trade and export earnings for the furtherance of economic development? We address this question in the light of our brief analysis of the economic effects of tariff preference schemes.

As our analysis has shown, the granting of tariff preferences does serve to promote trade volume and export earnings in the preference-receiving countries. The magnitude of this effect for existing GSP schemes is a matter of some debate, but a consensus view might be that the revenue gains have been modest but not trivial.[40] Surely the gains could be larger but for the many product exclusions that the preference-granting countries have introduced to minimize pain to their own import-competing industries. But whatever their precise magnitude, the terms-of-trade gains provide a form of "development aid" inasmuch as they boost incomes for owners of export concerns and quite possibly for factors of production such as unskilled labor that are used intensively in export sectors in the developing countries. In this sense, the GSP schemes can be seen as serving their putative purpose.

Arguably, however, the contracting parties had more in mind. UNCTAD Resolution 21(ii) also made reference to a desire to promote industrialization and economic growth. To the extent that tariff preferences raise producer prices in the developing countries, they do encourage greater output of the eligible goods than would take place in their absence. However, production of those goods entails an opportunity cost, and it is hardly clear that GSP arrangements encourage the expansion of the industries that will do the most to promote economic growth over the long haul. That might prove to be the case if, for example, the export activities encouraged by the GSP schemes are "infant industries" subject to positive learning externalities. Given the many product exclusions and limitations in the existing GSP schemes, however, it would be a fortunate coincidence if the products that are eligible happened also to be the ones that generate learning spillovers. Likewise, given the way that donor nations exclude import-sensitive items from tariff preferences and otherwise "graduate" successful

[40] Sapir and Lundberg (1984), Karsenty and Laird (1986), and MacPhee and Oguledo (1991) all find modest gains in export volume and export earnings for beneficiaries of the GSP schemes. They find, however, that these gains are highly concentrated in a few, higher-income developing countries. Brown (1987, 1989) draws similar conclusions from a computable general equilibrium model.

industries and countries, one wonders whether the industries that offer the best opportunities for "growth" to developing countries are not precisely the ones in which preferences will never be offered, or where they will be withdrawn once signs of industrial success appear. Certainly, there have been no empirical studies to suggest that GSP schemes have promoted "growth" beyond simply conferring some rents on selected industries as described above.

Moreover, the benefits of tariff preferences are diminished in practice by compliance costs.[41] The available evidence suggests that many goods imported from developing countries that appear to be eligible for preferences do not receive them. UNCTAD (1981) concluded, for example, that the "utilization rate" for various GSP schemes – the ratio of imports actually receiving preferential treatment to the total imports that are eligible under each scheme – was under 50% for the US and European programs and barely over 50% for Japan. One reason given for the low ratios, though not the only reason, was the "difficulties which arise in complying with the rules of origin and other requirements of the schemes."[42] UNCTAD (1999) notes a further decline in utilization rates for some of the schemes, owing partly to an "erosion of preferences which in some cases are too low to compensate for the cost of compliance." Even in the cases in which preferences are obtained, compliance costs reduce their value.

The benefits from tariff preferences will be further diminished (or even become negative) if they lead to overinvestment in the sectors that are eligible for preferential treatment. After all, the very nature of a preference is to encourage the expansion of output to a level that would not be economical in the absence of the preference. The possibility that preferences may then distort investment decisions, rather than encouraging investment where long-term growth opportunities are present, has been noted elsewhere.[43] One reason to be concerned about such overinvestment is that preferences have often proven to be temporary, as product coverage and rules about conditionality and graduation have changed over time. See UNCTAD (1999). If the

[41] Keck and Low (2004) make a similar point in the course of their broader review of special and differential treatment, and mention several other considerations that we also note as limiting the benefits of GSP to developing countries.

[42] For a survey of the various approaches to the rules of origin in GSP schemes, see Chapter 6 in Murray (1977).

[43] See, for example, Finger and Winters (1998), who write that "preferences. . .permit – perhaps encourage – producers to have costs above those in nonpreferred countries."

private sector invests on the expectation that the preferences will be long-lasting, then there may be severe resource misallocation once the preferences are removed. Of course, such a misallocation of resources should not be a problem – at least for the country that is granted preferential treatment – unless the investors misjudge the likely duration of the GSP schemes, the likelihood of changes in their rules and product coverage, or the likelihood that the MFN tariff will fall (in short, an absence of "rational expectations"). But misjudgment is a real threat given all of the moving parts and the fact that the GSP programs are modified quite regularly.

Finally, there is some evidence in recent research that the benefits to developing countries from GSP schemes may be limited for another reason. Özden and Reinhardt (2003) argue that preferential tariff treatment may retard trade liberalization in beneficiary countries. This might be so because GSP preferences can reduce the incentive that export industries in developing countries have to lobby for trade liberalization at home as a means to garner market access abroad. Import liberalization by developing countries will also shift resources from import-competing to exporting sectors in those countries and may hasten the withdrawal of the preferences as their export sectors bump up against "competitive need" and graduation provisions under the GSP schemes. Export interests in developing countries may harbor mixed feelings about trade liberalization at home for this reason as well. Özden and Reinhardt examine empirically the effect that GSP removal (as through "graduation") has had on former beneficiaries' trade policies and find that countries that lose their eligibility for GSP subsequently undertake greater liberalization than those that retain their eligibility. Some studies suggest, furthermore, that developing countries with more liberal trade policies achieve higher rates of growth and development than countries that are more protectionist.[44] If Özden and Reinhardt are correct in their empirics, therefore, we have yet another reason to worry that the effects of GSP on growth and development may be less favorable than one might hope.

To summarize, there are no good estimates of the aggregate benefits that developing countries derive from the GSP schemes.

[44] See, for example, Dollar (1992), Sachs and Warner (1995), Edwards (1993), and Frankel and Romer (1999). These studies are not without their critics, however, and some like Rodriguez and Rodrik (2001) and Hallak and Levinsohn (2004) have questioned whether there really is evidence of a positive relationship between openness to trade and growth.

Economic theory predicts an improvement in the terms of trade on eligible products, which may be smaller than the preference margin if the developing countries collectively are large in the markets for their exports and so depress world prices as they expand their exports. Benefits beyond the pure terms-of-trade gain are possible if the export industries happen to be ones that generate positive learning spill-overs, but there is no evidence to suggest that products included in existing GSP schemes are more worthy of encouragement than others. Compliance costs associated with rules of origin and the like surely cut into the potential beneficial effects of GSP as well, and exclusions of products deemed "sensitive" in the donor countries have done so to an even greater extent. Finally, GSP schemes may have encouraged overinvestment in sectors that will prove only temporarily eligible and may have retarded the process of trade liberalization in the eligible countries. For all these reasons, the benefits generated by tariff preference schemes, while perhaps positive, are likely to be reasonably small.

4.3 Differential treatment and conditionality in tariff preference schemes

Whatever economic analysis has to say about the likely benefits of trade preferences in general, the members of the WTO evidently believe that tariff preference schemes do generate benefits for the favored countries and that these benefits are sufficient to justify a departure from the MFN principle. The question raised by India's challenge to the European drug-related preferences is not whether the gains generated by GSP justify the distortions that it creates, but rather what sort of discrimination within GSP schemes ought to be tolerated.

One might wonder why the members of the WTO would choose to regulate GSP at all. After all, such schemes represent unilateral "concessions" made by the developed countries to further the "development, financial, and trade" needs of a group of developing countries. Shouldn't a donor have the right to set the terms of his gift and specify the beneficiaries? Don't the developing countries have the choice whether to meet the conditions or not?

To address these questions, it is necessary to make some assumptions about the objectives of the WTO Agreement. Like Bagwell and Staiger (1999, 2002) and Grossman and Mavroidis (2003), we believe that the purpose of trade agreements is to limit the negative international externalities that countries create when they set their trade and industrial policies. An externality can arise when a welfare-maximizing government sets a positive tariff to improve its national terms of trade. But one need not accept that governments maximize national economic welfare as conventionally defined to conclude that agreements are meant to solve problems of international externalities. Sovereign governments can and do routinely undertake policy actions that do not promote aggregate national welfare. But their trading partners have no reason to interfere in these policy choices unless they suffer some harm as a result. Similarly, when two (or more) countries strike a bilateral (or plurilateral) agreement, non-parties to the agreement have no interest in it as long as the agreement does not adversely affect their interests. But policy choices, including decisions about trade policy, often do have external consequences. Without some sort of multilateral agreement encompassing all of the affected parties, countries will set their policies and conclude agreements without regard for the harm done to others, leading to an equilibrium from which a Pareto improvement is possible with the aid of multilateral rules. The law of the WTO can be understood as a mechanism to ensure that international externalities are taken into account.

If the objective of international agreements is to limit negative externalities, we can see why the WTO Members might wish to regulate GSP. As we have discussed, when a country affords preferential treatment to a group of countries that collectively are large in the market for some good, the effect is to lower the world price of that good and to generate a terms-of-trade loss for other countries that export the same or a similar good. A GSP scheme that targets certain countries for special treatment can bring harm to others that are not so favored. And a scheme that offers preferential treatment only when specified conditions are met can reduce welfare for those that choose not to fulfill the conditions.

The arguments for limiting differential treatment in the GSP schemes parallel those that have been made by economists and legal scholars to justify the MFN rule in GATT Art. I. Schwartz and Sykes (1997) argue that the MFN rule addresses a potential problem of concession erosion. Suppose country B receives a concession from country A in the course of a trade negotiation, and that country B is not entitled to MFN treatment from country A. Then, the value of the concession could be undermined by a subsequent agreement between country A and country C that provides the latter with even better terms than were granted to country B. Anticipating this possibility, country B would offer less for the concession from country A, and less trade liberalization would result. Thus, the MFN rule helps preserve the incentives for trade liberalization through international negotiation.

Bagwell and Staiger (2002, 2004) point to the related concept of *bilateral opportunism*. Suppose countries A and B import a common good from country C and export another good to that country. Suppose further that the three countries have reached an initial agreement that is jointly efficient, in the sense that no change in tariffs can increase the welfare of one government without reducing the welfare of another.[45] Then, in the absence of MFN, the governments of country A and C can always find another deal that benefits themselves at the expense of country B. As Bagwell and Staiger show, these countries can reduce the tariffs they apply to one another's goods in such a way that their multilateral (or weighted average) terms of trade do not deteriorate; the terms of trade loss each suffers from lowering a tariff is at least offset by the terms of trade gain each enjoys from improved access to the other's market. But the reduction of country C's tariff on imports from A induces trade diversion from competing country B and so harms that country. And the reduction of country A's tariff on imports from C expands world demand for C's export good, which spells a further loss for country B. Evidently, in the absence of MFN, countries A and C may be tempted to strike a deal that benefits each of them at the expense of the excluded country B.

Bagwell and Staiger go on to show that an MFN rule makes it more difficult for a pair of countries to engage in bilateral opportunism. With non-discrimination, country C must offer the same concessions to country B as it offers to country A. Thus, it cannot offer to "pay for" a tariff reduction by country A with a policy change of its own that benefits country A by diverting imports to it that would otherwise come from country B. Indeed, when the MFN rule together is combined

[45] Welfare here may be national economic welfare, if the governments are benevolent welfare maximizers, or more generally political welfare that includes other objectives besides just conventional economic welfare.

with strict adherence to the principle of "reciprocity," the scope for bilateral opportunism behavior is eliminated entirely.[46]

Similar problems of concession erosion and bilateral opportunism can arise in a trade regime that admits differential treatment in GSP. Suppose developed country A makes a concession to developing country B in the course of a trade negotiation. If country A subsequently offers reduced tariffs to developing country C, but not to country B, this can erode the value of the earlier concession to country B. As a consequence, country B may value the original concession less highly and so will have less incentive to open its own markets. As for bilateral opportunism, suppose that developed country A considers developing country B to be its friend and ally. By providing preferential access to its markets, country A generates economic gains for its ally while furthering its own political ends. Now if country A can do so selectively (by excluding "sensitive products") and discriminatorily (by making developing country C ineligible), then country A can ensure that there are few political costs at home, and that most of the gains to country B come at the expense of other countries, especially countries whose exports are similar to those of country B, such as developing country C.

Bagwell and Staiger (2002) have argued that the provisions of international trade agreements are intended to diminish or eliminate the scope for negative international externalities, and that agreements ought to be designed with this goal in mind. This perspective, with which we concur, points to a strict interpretation of footnote 3 of the Enabling Clause as a binding obligation for developed countries to treat all developing countries similarly in the GSP schemes, except for the permissible special treatment of the least-developed countries. However, we recognize that such an interpretation might well have a chilling effect on the willingness of developed countries to offer GSP benefits, which after all are unilateral concessions and not negotiated as part of any trade agreement. The political realist must ask whether eliminating the

[46] Bagwell and Staiger define reciprocity in GATT as the principle that changes in trade policy should leave world prices unchanged, or else those who effect the changes in world prices must compensate those who are harmed by it. The MFN rule ensures that each country faces a common terms of trade (relative price of imports compared to exports) and not a different terms of trade with each partner. Thus, strict adherence to principles of MFN and reciprocity would imply that any bilateral deal between countries A and C does not change the relative prices faced by each country, and, as such, does not cause any harm to that country.

scope for negative externalities is worth the cost of fewer "donated" GSP schemes. Once this trade-off is recognized, it becomes difficult to say how much differential treatment should be tolerated and under what circumstances. Economic analysis can highlight the trade-off, but only empirical and political analysis can determine the magnitude of likely negative externalities on the one hand, and the likely political response to stricter regulation of GSP on the other.

One other issue warrants brief mention. The externalities associated with trade policy are not the only externalities from global interaction. Pollution that damages the global commons or that simply crosses borders affords another class of examples, as do the costs and benefits that arise because of interdependent utilities across nations. (Indeed, GSP itself might be seen to result from an altruistic concern for the less fortunate.) One might argue that the negative externalities associated with discriminatory GSP schemes should be tolerated if discrimination nevertheless aids in addressing these other sorts of externality problems but there is an obvious difficulty with this line of argument. If preferential treatment is used to address alleged negative externalities, who among the WTO Member states should decide what constitutes a negative externality and how large its magnitude is? We see no principled way to discipline a process in which each nation decides for itself what "externalities" to address through discrimination or reciprocity. And absent any discipline, the danger of a return to the pre-UNCTAD days of widespread discrimination is apparent. If discrimination and reciprocity are to be permitted, therefore, we question whether they can be justified convincingly by a need to address other "externality" problems. Instead, the justification likely lies in the need to make GSP politically saleable in the donor countries, bringing us full circle to the set of trade-offs identified above.

References

Bagwell, K. and Staiger, R. W. (1999). An Economic Theory of GATT, *American Economic Review* **89**, 215–248.

Bagwell, K. and Staiger, R. W. (2002). *The Economics of The World Trading System*, Cambridge, MA and London: The MIT Press.

Bagwell, K. and Staiger, R. W. (2004). Multilateral Trade Negotiations, Bilateral Opportunism and the Rules of GATT, *Journal of International Economics* **63**, 1–29.

Borrmann, A., Borrmann, C. and Steger, M. (1981). *The EC's Generalized System of Preferences*, The Hague: Martinus Nijhof Publishers.

Brown, D. K. (1987). General Equilibrium Effects of the US Generalized System of Preferences, *Southern Economic Journal* **54**, 27–47.

Brown, D. K. (1989). Trade and Welfare Effects of the European Schemes of the Generalized System of Preferences, *Economic Development and Cultural Change* **37**, 757–776.

Dollar, D. (1992). Outward-Oriented Developing Economies Really Do Grow More Rapidly: Evidence from 95 LDC's, 1976–85, *Economic Development and Cultural Change* **40**, 523–544.

Edwards, S. (1993). Openness, Trade Liberalization, ad Growth in Developing Countries, *Journal of Economic Literature* **31**, 1358–1393.

Finger, J. M. and Winters, L. A. (1998). What Can the WTO Do for Developing Countries? In A.O. Krueger, ed., *The WTO as an International Organization*, Chicago: The University of Chicago Press, pp. 365–392.

Frankel, J. A. and Romer, D. (1999). Does Trade Cause Growth, *American Economic Review* **89**, 379–399.

Grossman, G. M. and Mavroidis, P. C. (2003). United States – Imposition of Countervailing Duties on Certain Hot-Rolled Lead and Bismuth Carbon Steel Products Originating in the United Kingdom: Here Today, Gone Tomorrow? Privatization and the Injury Caused by Non-Recurring Subsidies. In H. Horn and P.C. Mavroidis, eds., *The WTO Case Law of 2001*, Cambridge: Cambridge University Press, pp. 170–200.

Hallak, J. C. and Levinsohn, J. A. (2004). Fooling Ourselves: Evaluating the Globalization and Growth Debate, *NBER Working Paper No. 10244*, Cambridge, MA.

Howse, R. (2003). India's WTO Challenge to Drug Enforcement Conditions in the European Community Generalized System of Preferences: A Little Known Case with Major Repercussions for "Political" Conditionality in US Trade Policy, *Chicago Journal of International Law* **4**, 385–405.

Karsenty, G. and Laird, S. (1986). The Generalized System of Preferences: A Quantitative Assessment of the Direct Trade Effects and of Policy Options, *UNCTAD Discussion Paper 18*, UNCTAD, Geneva.

Keck, A. and Low, P. (2004). Special and Differential Treatment in the WTO: Why, When and How?, *WTO Staff Working Paper ERSD-2004-03*.

Limão, N. (2005). Preferential Trade Agreements as Stumbling Blocks for Multilateral Trade Liberalization: Evidence for the US, *Centre for Economic Policy Research Discussion Paper No. 4884*, London UK.

MacPhee, C. R. and Oguledo, V. I. (1991). The Trade Effects of the US Generalized System of Preferences, *Atlantic Economic Journal* **19**, 19–26.

Murray, T. (1977). *Trade Preferences for Developing Countries*, New York: John Wiley and Sons.

OECD Secretary General, (1983). *The Generalized System of Preferences: Review of the First Decade*, Paris: Organization of Economic Cooperation and Development.

Özden, Ç. and Reinhardt, E. (2003). The Perversity of Preferences: GSP and Developing Country Trade Policies, 1976–2000, *World Bank Working Paper 2955*, The World Bank.

Rodríguez, F. and Rodrik, D. (2001). Trade Policy and Economic Growth: A Skeptic's Guide to Cross-National Evidence, *NBER Macroeconomic Annual* **15**, 261–324.

Sachs, J. D. and Warner, A. M. (1995). Economic Reform and the Process of Global Integration, *Brookings Papers on Economic Activity* **1**, 1–95.

Sapir, A. and Lundberg, L. (1984). The US Generalized System of Preferences and its Impacts. In R. E. Baldwin and A. O. Krueger, eds., *The Structure and Evolution of Recent US Trade Policy*, Chicago: The University of Chicago Press, pp. 195–231.

Schwartz, W. F. and Sykes, A. O. (1997). The Economics of the Most Favored Nation Clause. In J. S. Bhandani and A. O. Sykes, eds., *Economic Dimensions of International Law: Comparative and Empirical Perspectives*, Cambridge: Cambridge University Press, pp. 34–79.

UNCTAD (1981). *Operation and Effects of the Generalized System of Preferences, Fifth Review*, New York, United Nations Conference on Trade and Development.

UNCTAD (1999). *Quantifying the Benefits Obtained by Developing Countries from the Generalized System of Preferences*, New York, United Nations Conference on Trade and Development.

10

United States – Anti-Dumping Act of 1916 (Original Complaint by the European Communities) – Recourse to Arbitration by the United States under 22.6 of the DSU, WT/DS136/ARB, 24 February 2004: A Legal and Economic Analysis

ROBERT HOWSE
University of Michigan Law School
ROBERT W. STAIGER*
University of Wisconsin

1 Introduction

This arbitration on the level of countermeasures, pursuant to the Dispute Settlement Understanding (DSU) 22.6, originates from findings against the United States with respect to a provision of the 1916 Anti-Dumping Act, which permits a private cause of action for treble damages against an alleged dumping importer or producer where the dumping meets certain criteria including, notably, a predatory intention. An unusual feature of this case is that, apparently, the provision in question has never been used, at least against the European Community (EC), the complainant. In any case, the provision in question was found to be in violation of the WTO Anti-Dumping Agreement, both because it would impose measures on dumping other than and in addition to anti-dumping duties, and because in so doing, the procedural requirements of the Anti-Dumping Agreement would not be followed.

* We thank participants at ALI meetings where we presented this paper for helpful comments, particularly Alan Sykes, Frieder Roessler, and Gary Horlick.

2 Legal issues

Article 22.4 of the WTO DSU provides that, where a Member suspends concessions in response to the failure of the losing party to implement a dispute settlement ruling where that Member was the complaining party, "The level of suspension of concessions or other obligations authorized by the DSB shall be equivalent to the level of the nullification or impairment." The *United States – Anti-Dumping Act of 1916* Arbitration addresses the meaning of equivalence between the violation of international law and the countermeasures that respond to the violation. It has generally been assumed that nullification or impairment refers to the trade impact on the winning Member of the violation, not the competitive relationship as such; thus, countermeasures are limited to the value of the trade foregone as a consequence of the continuing violation. (This assumption will be reexamined from an economic perspective later in this chapter.) In the *1916* Arbitration, the EC proposed countermeasures in the form of a "mirror" suspension, in relation to the United States, of the very obligation with which the United States continued to be in non-compliance. Thus, the availability under the US statute of a private right of action for treble damages against a foreign firm engaged in certain kinds of dumping behavior had been held to be contrary to the Anti-Dumping Agreement in a number of respects; the EC proposed, as a countermeasure, to amend its own legislation to make available to European companies a similar right of action for treble damages against US firms.

The arbitrator was required to decide whether such legal equivalence meets the requirements of Art. 22.4, regardless of a possible actual asymmetrical *trade* or *economic* impact. The arbitrator held, based largely on previous arbitration rulings, that the expression "level" in Art. 22.4 implied a quantitative limit on the trade or economic effects of the suspension of concessions or obligations; while a Member may take countermeasures in a non-quantitative form, suspending an obligation rather than a concession such as a tariff binding, nevertheless the economic or trade effect of the original violation creates a fundamental limit on such action. Holding that a fundamental objective of countermeasures under DSU Art. 22 was to induce compliance, and that punitive purposes were excluded, the arbitrator found that it could not endorse the proposed countermeasures of the EC, unless it had evidence that the trade or economic effect on the United States would not exceed the trade or economic effect on the EC of the continuing original violation.

This ruling is the opposite extreme of the ruling in the Foreign Sales Corporation (FSC) Arbitration (albeit based on the special rule for countermeasures in the SCM Agreement); just as in the FSC Arbitration (see Howse and Neven, 2004)[1] where the arbitrator largely dispensed with proportionality as a limit on countermeasures, and viewed considerations of actual trade or economic effect as dispensable, in the *1916* arbitration, the arbitrator appears to have taken a view of equivalence that is narrower than that warranted by the text of DSU 22.4 and the general international law jurisprudence on countermeasures.

First of all, with respect to the text of 22.4, the arbitrator focused on the word "level" without also considering its immediate context – the notion of "equivalence." The word equivalence implies proportionality between two things that are not entirely commensurate or reducible in value to a common metric. If 22.4 involved measuring and comparing the dollar value of the original violation in trade and economic terms with the dollar value of the proposed countermeasure in those terms, then the drafters would more plausibly have used the expression "equal" rather than "equivalent." One does not normally ask whether two quantities are equivalent to one another, but whether they are equal, less, or greater than the one or the other. Determining whether two things are equivalent, by contrast, may involve asking whether they are similar in value, even if they cannot (without arbitrariness) be measured quantitatively in a common metric.[2]

Second, as Cannizzaro notes, "normative countermeasures," where equivalence or proportionality is achieved by suspending a symmetrical obligation, have often been recognized as consistent with the principles of state responsibility. In the *Air Service Agreement* case, the United States engaged in a symmetrical breach of an aviation treaty in response to France's initial breach of the same obligations towards the United States under the treaty: the United States claimed that, despite France's argument that the losses to France entailed by this response exceeded

[1] Howse, Robert and Neven, Damien, 2004. "United States – Tax treatment for 'Foreign Sales Corporations' Recourse to Arbitration by the United States under Article 22.6 of the DSU and Article 4.11 of the SCM Agreement (WT/DS106/ARB): A comment," in Horn and Mavroidis (eds.) *The WTO Case Law of 2002*, The American Law Institute Reporters' Studies, Cambridge University Press, 2004.

[2] This is a complex issue conceptually: on the relationship between "egalite" and "equivalence" in economic justice, see A. Kojeve, *Outline of a Phenomenology of Right*, tr. Frost and Howse (2000).

those suffered by the United States from the initial breach, "the services were equivalent in law and hence proportional, . . ."[3]

In the *Air Service Agreement* case, the arbitral tribunal ultimately decided that normative equivalence could be based upon the importance in principle of the provision breached to both parties, i.e. its legal importance, but the tribunal also said that quantitative equivalence might be relevant as well depending on the circumstances. This is Cannizzaro's position, too. From this perspective, the Panel in the *1916 Arbitration* was not wrong to insist that the quantitative economic effect of the breach in relation to the countermeasures had to be considered as relevant to equivalence; rather, the Panel erred in suggesting that the economic effect of the breach must always be regarded as a limit on countermeasures, *regardless* of normative considerations, including the gravity of the breach. Again, this is the mirror image of the mistake of the FSC arbitrator, which threw out the window any consideration of the proportionality of the countermeasures to the economic effect of the original breach on the defendant.

The WTO obligation breached in the *1916* case was a particularly good candidate for a focus on normative equivalence, since the actual trade or economic effects of the private action for treble damages were so speculative; a US court had never in the past actually made such an award against an EC company, and, on the other hand, relatively few anti-dumping actions in the EC had been brought against US imports, making any economic or trade effects of the countermeasures quite speculative.

A further error of the arbitral Panel in its ruling was to confuse the issue of the limits on countermeasures with the issue of whether the purpose of countermeasures was to reestablish the pre-breach equilibrium between the parties, to achieve compliance, or to punish. The Panel was correct to reject "punitive" countermeasures as consistent with the DSU, and was also correct to identify the achievement of compliance as a fundamental objective of countermeasures (see Howse and Neven, 2004: the ILC Articles clearly establish that the achievement of compliance is the sole legitimate purpose of countermeasures (Art. 49.1), and the language of the DSU supports this understanding of countermeasures and state responsibility). The arbitrator was *not* correct, however, in suggesting that the rejection of *punishment*

[3] E. Cannizzaro, "The Role of Proportionality in the Law of International Countermeasures," EJIL (2001) 889–916, pp. 902–903.

as a purpose of countermeasures implied that normative considerations could not, in appropriate cases, result in countermeasures based on a *normative* equivalence, which might exceed, to some extent, the economic costs of breach. Thus, although the ILC Articles recognize achieving compliance as the goal of countermeasures, the understanding of proportionality in the Articles refers to the injury suffered by the retaliating state, *taking account of the gravity of the wrong and the rights in question.* It is thus clear that there is no necessary tension between the purpose of countermeasures as compliance (in contradistinction to punishment or "corrective justice") and the consideration of normative factors in determining the meaning of proportional or "equivalent" countermeasures; it is not *exclusively* economic harm that is to be taken into account in the evaluation of whether countermeasures are equivalent, even if it would be inappropriate to throw out the window considerations of the extent of economic harm in favor of normative considerations, as did the arbitral panel in *FSC.*

3 Economic issues

We identify and evaluate two key economic questions that arise in the Arbitrators' Report on the US Anti-Dumping Act of 1916. First, when one government introduces a measure that nullifies or impairs benefits under the Agreement for another GATT/WTO member, how is the level of nullification or impairment to be defined? And second, once defined, how should the level of nullification or impairment be measured? We consider each question in turn.

3.1 How is the level of nullification or impairment to be defined?

A first fundamental issue confronted by the Arbitrators in *US Anti-Dumping Act of 1916* is how to define the level of nullification or impairment. Within the GATT/WTO, a market access commitment is understood to mean a commitment to maintain "conditions of competition" between domestic producers and foreign exporters. Nullification or impairment then occurs when a government introduces a measure that alters the conditions of competition between domestic producers and foreign exporters from those that could have been reasonably expected based on an earlier negotiation.[4]

[4] See, for example, Analytical Index: Guide to GATT Law and Practice, Volume 2, WTO, 1995, pp. 657–658.

Based on the definition of nullification or impairment given above, a natural definition of the *level* of nullification or impairment might be the *magnitude* by which the new measure altered the conditions of competition from those that could have been reasonably expected at the time of the earlier negotiation. If the new measure is, for example, the introduction of a new tariff, then according to this definition, the level of nullification or impairment is simply the magnitude of the new tariff, expressed perhaps in specific form or perhaps in ad valorem form: the new tariff alters the conditions of competition between domestic producers and foreign exporters by raising the cost of foreign exporters in delivering their product to the domestic market. However, the Arbitrators clearly reject this view (p. 18, 5.30). Instead, they adopt the view that the level of the nullification or impairment is the "trade or economic effect" of the US Anti-Dumping Act of 1916 on the EU (p. 16, 5.23). This reduces to the following rule, quoted by the Arbitrators from the Arbitrators' Report in EC-Hormones: "We must estimate trade foregone due to the ..." measure in question (p. 16, 5.24).[5]

The "trade effects" approach adopted by the Arbitrators on this first fundamental issue raises a couple of central questions from an economic perspective. The first central question is, accepting for the moment that the trade effect is the appropriate focus, how is the "trade foregone" to be defined? Is this to be defined as the trade volume foregone at the *original exporter price*, or instead as the *equilibrium* trade volume foregone? These two magnitudes can be very different. For example, in response to a new tariff, exporters might reduce their prices to stabilize volumes, so that the equilibrium trade volume might change very little; but the trade volume at the original exporter price could still drop significantly. Figure 1 illustrates the point. With the foreign

[5] The Arbitrators emphasize (pp. 16-17, 5.24–5.28) that their trade-effects approach follows in line with the general approach adopted in earlier arbitrations. However, given the nature and application of the US Anti-Dumping Act of 1916, any possible trade effects would have had to take the form of a "chilling" or deterrent effect, and the Arbitrators considered but ultimately rejected the quantification of such effects as too speculative. Consequently, most of the Arbitrators' discussion with regard to the level of nullification or impairment caused by the 1916 Act focuses on direct monetary payments made by European companies to the United States as a result of final legal judgements or settlements under the 1916 Act. We focus our evaluation on the general economic rationale for the trade effects approach, and for simplicity we ignore in our discussion the additional means of nullification or impairment that arose more specifically in the context of the 1916 Act (e.g. final legal judgments against foreign firms).

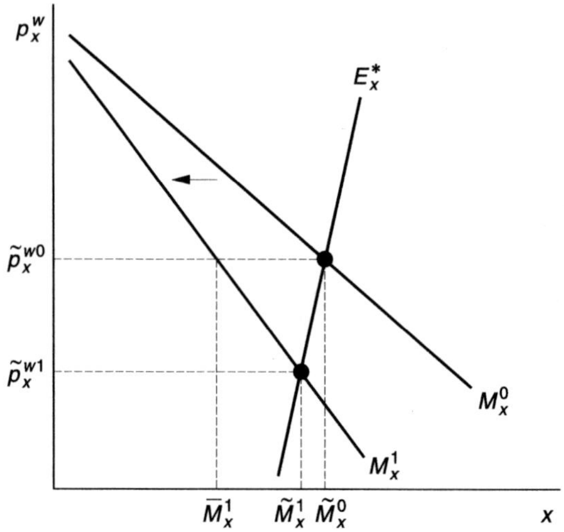

Figure 1

exporter ("world") price of good x, p_x^w, measured on the vertical axis, and the quantity of good x measured on the horizontal axis, Figure 1 depicts an initial domestic import demand curve labeled M_x^0 and the foreign export supply curve labeled E_x^*. At the initial equilibrium (where the foreign export supply curve and the initial domestic import demand curve intersect), the (market clearing) exporter price is $\tilde{p}_x^{w0}$, and foreign exporters supply to the domestic country exactly the volume of good x that the domestic country wishes to import, $\tilde{M}_x^0$. If the domestic country now imposes a new tariff on imports of good x, the domestic import demand curve shifts left to the curve labeled M_x^1. At the original exporter price $\tilde{p}_x^{w0}$, the import demand of the domestic country is now the volume $\bar{M}_x^1$. Hence, the trade volume foregone at the original exporter price due to the new tariff is given by $[\tilde{M}_x^0 - \bar{M}_x^1]$. On the other hand, according to the foreign export supply curve E_x^*, foreign exporters are willing to reduce their prices to stabilize volumes, and so the equilibrium (market clearing) import demand for the domestic country (determined in Figure 1 where the foreign export supply curve and the new domestic import demand curve intersect) is now the volume $\tilde{M}_x^1$. Hence, the equilibrium trade volume foregone due to the new tariff is given by $[\tilde{M}_x^0 - \tilde{M}_x^1]$.

In the situation depicted in Figure 1, should it be concluded that very little nullification or impairment has occurred as a result of the new domestic tariff, or rather that significant nullification or impairment has occurred? If the level of nullification or impairment is defined by the trade effect, the answer clearly would depend on which of these definitions of "trade effect," (i.e. the equilibrium trade effect $[\tilde{M}_x^0 - \tilde{M}_x^1]$ depicted in Figure 1 or the trade effect at original exporter prices $[\tilde{M}_x^0 - \bar{M}_x^1]$ depicted in Figure 1) is used.

The second central question raised by the trade-effects approach adopted by the Arbitrators is, why focus on the trade effect anyway? Once a departure is made from defining the level of nullification or impairment by the magnitude of changes in the "conditions of competition" (as in the magnitude of a new tariff), why not go all the way to the "welfare effect" on the complaining government? After all, the same trade effect could have vastly different welfare effects on a government, depending for example on the political pressure it faces or the adjustment costs shouldered by its firms and workers as a result of the changes in trade volume.

Hence, the trade-effects approach adopted by the Arbitrators raises two central questions: why focus on the trade effect?, and, how is the "trade foregone" to be defined? To begin to provide answers to these two questions, we first need to answer a prior question: What purpose is served in the WTO by the withdrawal of equivalent concessions? The Arbitrators' Report considers this, and observes that the United States and the EU suggest that the authorized withdrawal of equivalent concessions can serve several useful purposes (p. 12, 5.3), including the restoration of the balance of benefits under the Agreement, and as a means to induce compliance. The Arbitrators observe that, whatever the complete list of purposes of withdrawals of equivalent concessions in the WTO may be, "... a fundamental objective of the suspension of obligations is to induce compliance." (p. 13, 5.7). But the Arbitrators also suggest that the WTO rules dictate that the suspension of obligations cannot be punitive, and they indicate that the insurance that the suspension of obligations is not punitive is precisely that the withdrawal is "equivalent" (p. 13, 5.8).

According to the Arbitrators' interpretation (p. 13, 5.8), then, the role served by the definition of "equivalent level of nullification or impairment" is to *ensure against punitive withdrawals.* Armed with the Arbitrators' interpretation of the purpose served in the WTO by the withdrawal of equivalent concessions, we may now pose the question: why focus on the trade effect? The logic of the Arbitrators' interpretation seems to suggest that one would need ultimately to quantify the *welfare* impact of the change in conditions of competition on each government in assessing the level of nullification or impairment associated with the measure in question and determining whether a proposed withdrawal of concessions was or was not punitive. This logic suggests that a three-step analysis might therefore have been appropriate as a way to operationalize the Arbitrators' interpretation. To assess the level of nullification or impairment caused by the measure introduced by the defendant, one would focus on the trade impact of the defendant's measure and the welfare impact of this trade effect for the complainant. The three steps might run as follows:

Step 1: Measure the change in the conditions of competition brought about by the measure in question.
Step 2: Estimate the trade volume impact that is caused by the change in the conditions of competition. There is a question (as raised above) of whether this should be the equilibrium trade volume impact, or something else, but we will put this question aside for the moment.
Step 3: Factor in how the complaining government's welfare is affected by these trade volume changes. This will require knowledge of political pressures/dislocation costs suffered by the complaining government for any given change in trade flows.

In principle, this three-step analysis would provide an estimate of the welfare loss for the complaining government. And then, to ensure that the response is not punitive, the complaining government would be authorized to retaliate in such a way as to reduce the welfare of the defendant government by up to but not more than this amount. This would require a similar three-step analysis, but focusing instead on the trade impact of the complainant's proposed retaliatory measure and the welfare impact of this trade effect for the defendant government. Importantly, as Step 3 makes clear, by this logic it is not enough to quantify the trade effects alone – evidence on the relevant political pressures and dislocation costs must also be brought to bear in assessing the level of nullification or impairment.

But further reflection suggests that there are also alternative ways to operationalize the Arbitrators' interpretation, depending on what, exactly, is meant by "punitive." Does punitive retaliation mean imparting greater welfare loss on the defendant than was suffered by the complainant as a result of the measure in question? This first meaning of punitive is implicit in the three-step methodology described just above, and it embodies a retaliation rule that resembles "... an eye for an eye, a tooth for a tooth." Or does punitive retaliation instead mean imparting greater welfare damage on the defendant than the welfare increase that the defendant enjoyed from the introduction of the measure in question? Under this second meaning of punitive, the retaliation rule would be designed to return the defendant to its original welfare level that prevailed before the introduction of the measure in question: here, assessing the punitive nature of a retaliatory measure is all about quantifying the welfare impacts of various measures on the defendant, and there is no need to quantify the welfare impact of any measure on the complainant. One would still need to calculate trade effects associated with various measures at some level. And one would still need to know about the political/dislocation costs suffered by the defendant government from trade effects in different industries (i.e. the industry where the original measure was introduced, and the industry where the complainant's retaliatory measures will be applied). But the calculations would be quite different under this second meaning of punitive than under the first.

The Arbitrators do not discuss the complications raised just above, which are associated with the ambiguity over the precise meaning of "punitive," and simply assert that a retaliatory measure will not be punitive as long as it has no greater "trade or economic effect" on the defendant than the defendant's original action had on the complainant (p. 16, 5.23). How should this assertion be interpreted?

We now suggest that, while the Arbitrators do not provide any further rationale for their assertion, it is possible to interpret the trade-effects approach as approximating a system of remedies that provides for "expectation damages" and facilitates a form of *efficient breach.* According to this interpretation, at a broad level, concessions negotiated within the GATT/WTO can ultimately be viewed as protected by an overarching "liability rule" – with the magnitude of the "liability" specified according to the trade-effects approach – under which a government may then escape from its commitments without the need to secure the permission of any adversely affected trading partner. In a wide variety of settings (e.g. Arts. XIX, XXIII, XXVIII), this in turn provides governments with a way to adjust the bargain when settlement negotiations fail. The broad interpretation we have just described has been developed in various forms by Sykes (2000), Schwartz and Sykes (2002), and Lawrence (2003) from a legal perspective, and Schwartz and Sykes also describe a possible political interpretation of expectation damages.[6] Our discussion below complements these earlier writings, by developing an economic interpretation of this point.

To motivate this economic interpretation, let us return to our earlier discussion of the definition of "punitive," and consider its relation to compliance. As the Arbitrators record, the EU observes that "One could very well imagine that the best means to induce compliance would be to provide for punitive sanctions. However, the DSU does not allow for this possibility." (p. 16, note 49). But why does the DSU disallow this possibility? A possible interpretation is that the DSU is designed to induce compliance, but not at "any cost," i.e. not in all circumstances. Under what circumstances, then, is compliance to be induced? Perhaps only when it is "efficient" for the defendant country to comply. How do we know when this will be so? One possibility is to adopt the following interpretation of punitive: "A measure is *punitive* if it imposes a cost on the defendant that is so high that the defendant would comply even if it were not internationally efficient for the defendant to comply." If such an interpretation could be made operational, then authorizing "non-punitive" retaliatory sanctions would ensure that compliance was induced only when it was efficient from an international perspective to do so. The key question is, How could such an interpretation be made operational?

To describe how, and to ultimately relate this interpretation back to the trade-effects approach to remedies embraced by the Arbitrators, we begin by observing that there is a third definition of "punitive" that we have not yet considered. According to this definition, punitive retaliation occurs when the claimant punishes the defendant so severely that the *claimant* ultimately enjoys higher welfare than if the defendant had not introduced the measure in question to begin with. Under this

[6] See Sykes, Alan O., "The Remedy for Breach of Obligations Under the WTO Dispute Settlement Understanding: Damages or Specific Performance?" in Marco Bronckers and Reinhard Quick (eds.) *New Directions in International Economic Law*, Kluwer Law International (The Hague), 2000; Schwartz, Warren F. and Alan O. Sykes, "The Economic Structure of Renegotiation and Dispute Resolution in the World Trade Organization," *Journal of Legal Studies* **31**, 2002; and Lawrence, Robert Z., *Crimes & Punishments? – Retaliation Under the WTO*, Institute for International Economics (Washington, DC) 2003. Sykes (2000) and Schwartz and Sykes (2002) also offer a number of arguments for why the WTO might favor a liability-rule approach over the natural alternative of a "property-rule" approach, which would allow a government to escape from its commitments only after securing the permission of adversely affected trading partners. We refer the reader to those papers for further discussion of these and related issues.

third definition of punitive, the retaliation rule would be designed to return the claimant to its original welfare level that prevailed before the introduction by the defendant of the measure in question. At first glance, this third definition of punitive might sound strange, in that it builds from the view that the claimant actually enjoys the punishment. But of course, in the GATT/WTO, at some level this must be so: otherwise, since the GATT/WTO cannot coerce a claimant to punish (with a high tariff) if the claimant does not want to, the punishment would not be credible. So this third definition is not at all strange within the GATT/WTO context. And a little further reflection suggests that this third definition carries with it some appealing features from an economic perspective.

In particular, as long as the claimant remains below its best-response tariff, so that it would actually choose to raise its tariff to the full extent permitted by "non-punitive" retaliation under this third definition, the claimant is guaranteed to retain its original level of welfare (i.e. the claimant remains on its original "indifference curve") as a consequence of (i) the introduction by the defendant of the measure in question, and (ii) the permitted retaliation by the claimant.

Suppose, then, that the domestic government understands the consequences of introducing a new measure that would nullify or impair the benefits that its foreign trading partner enjoys under the agreement (i.e. it understands the level of retaliation that this measure will induce). In choosing whether or not to introduce the measure in question – and if so, at what level – the domestic government will naturally make a choice that allows it to achieve its highest level of welfare. But as the permissible retaliation by the foreign government keeps the foreign government on its original indifference curve, the domestic government's choice of whether to introduce the measure – and if so, at what level – amounts to making a choice that maximizes the domestic government's welfare while preserving the level of the foreign government's welfare. This, of course, describes a choice which is *internationally efficient.* Hence, under this third definition of "punitive," we would have a system of remedies that provides for "expectation damages" and facilitates efficient breach.

Figure 2 illustrates the essential point in a hypothetical two-country two-good world. We denote by τ the level of import protection levied by the domestic government on imports of good x from the foreign country, and we plot τ on the vertical axis of Figure 2. Similarly, we denote by τ^* the level of import protection levied by the foreign

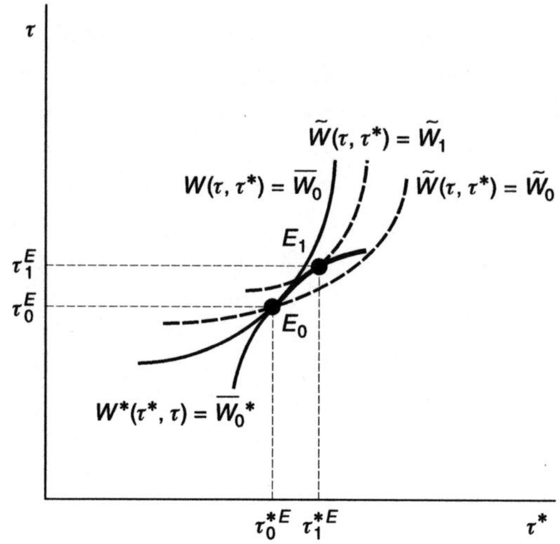

Figure 2

government on imports of good y from the domestic country, and we plot τ^* on the horizontal axis of Figure 2. We represent the welfare of the home government by the objective function $W(\tau, \tau^*)$ and the welfare of the foreign government by the objective function $W^*(\tau^*, \tau)$ For purposes of illustration, we suppose that the two governments have agreed to bind their tariffs at an internationally efficient pair of tariffs, denoted by (τ_0^E, τ_0^{*E}) and represented in Figure 2 by the point labeled E_0.

Two features of the efficient tariff pair (τ_0^E, τ_0^{*E}). are reflected at point E_0 in Figure 2. First, the indifference curves of the two governments, labeled as $W(\tau, \tau^*) = \bar{W}_0$ for the domestic government and as $W^*(\tau^*, \tau) = \bar{W}_0^*$ for the foreign government, are tangent to each other at the efficient point E_0. This is the defining feature of efficiency, because it indicates that there does not exist an alteration of the two tariffs which could make one government better off without hurting the other government. And second, the indifference curves are upward-sloping through the efficient point E_0, reflecting the natural feature that, at the efficient tariff pair (τ_0^E, τ_0^{*E}), each government would enjoy a welfare improvement if it were allowed to raise its own tariff unilaterally, while each government would suffer a welfare loss if the other government were allowed to raise its tariff unilaterally.

Now suppose that the domestic government experiences a "preference shock" – which might, for example, take the form of an increased sensitivity to political pressures from its import-competing industry x – and that this shock leads the domestic government to place heightened value on the ability to raise its own tariff unilaterally. In Figure 2, this is represented by a shift in the domestic government's indifference curve through the point E_0, to the *flatter* domestic indifference curve through E_0 represented by the dashed curve labeled $\tilde{W}(\tau, \tau^*) = \tilde{W}_0$ The indifference curve of the domestic government is now flatter through the point E_0, because the domestic government would now accept a greater increase in the foreign tariff τ^* (a movement along the horizontal axis in Figure 2) in exchange for the ability to raise τ by a given amount (a movement along the vertical axis in Figure 2), owing to the heightened value it places on the ability to raise its own tariff.

A first point to notice in Figure 2 is that, as a consequence of the preference shock experienced by the domestic government, the point E_0 no longer represents an efficient pair of tariffs. This is reflected in the fact that the foreign government's indifference curve $W^*(\tau^*, \tau) = \bar{W}_0^*$ and the domestic government's indifference curve $\tilde{W}(\tau, \tau^*) = \tilde{W}_0$ are not tangent at E_0.

The second point to notice in Figure 2 concerns the effect of a retaliatory rule, based on the third definition of punitive discussed above, on the domestic government's choice of whether, in light of its preference shock, to introduce a new measure in the form of a tariff which is higher than the bound rate τ_0 – and if so, at what level to raise its tariff. Recall from our earlier discussion of this retaliatory rule that, as long as the foreign government remains below its best-response tariff, so that it actually raises its tariff to the full extent permitted by "non-punitive" retaliation under this definition, the foreign government is guaranteed to retain its original level of welfare (i.e. the foreign government remains on its original indifference curve) as a result of (i) the introduction by the domestic government of the new measure, and (ii) the permitted retaliation by the foreign government.

Under this retaliatory rule, then, if the domestic government raises its tariff above the bound rate τ_0, the permissible retaliation by the foreign government keeps the foreign government on its original indifference curve. In terms of Figure 2, this means that the foreign retaliatory response under this rule that is triggered by a tariff choice of the domestic government above the bound rate τ_0 is described by the bold portion of the foreign government's indifference curve $W^*(\tau^*, \tau) = \bar{W}_0^*$

above and to the right of the point E_0. But understanding the retaliatory consequences of its tariff choice under this rule, the domestic government is then led to choose the tariff τ_1^E in Figure 2, thereby triggering the retaliatory response τ_1^{*E} by the foreign government permitted under this rule, and achieving its highest possible welfare level in light of this retaliatory rule, i.e. its highest possible welfare level along the foreign government indifference curve $W^*(\tau^*,\tau) = \bar{W}_0^*$. Under this retaliatory rule, then, the chosen act of "non-performance" (non-compliance) by the domestic government and authorized retaliatory response by the foreign government together result in the new efficient point E_1, where a domestic government indifference curve labeled $\tilde{W}(\tau, \tau^*) = \tilde{W}_1$ is tangent to the foreign government indifference curve $W^*(\tau^*, \tau) = \bar{W}_0^*$. This is the essence of efficient breach.

By means of Figure 2, we have illustrated how this third definition of "punitive" could give rise to a system of remedies that provides for "expectation damages" and facilitates a form of efficient breach. Of course, this particular retaliatory rule would be virtually impossible to implement, because doing so would require knowing the indifference curve of the complaining government and setting up the retaliatory rule to correspond to this indifference curve. Knowing government preferences with such precision is of course impractical. But even if this information were somehow made available and the retaliatory rule described in Figure 2 could be implemented, we now suggest that its use would be problematic within the WTO contracting environment. As we next describe, the problem with this retaliatory rule is that the "efficient breach" that it would facilitate between any two contracting parties would have systemic *spillover* effects on other contracts between other contracting parties within the WTO system, leading indirectly to breach in these contracts as well. Hence, a retaliatory rule akin to that described in Figure 2 could introduce a kind of *multilateral instability* into the WTO contracting environment.

To understand the point, let us suppose that the situation depicted in Figure 2 occurs in a wider multilateral setting. In particular, let us suppose for purposes of exposition that the WTO membership consists of four countries, two domestic countries that export good y in exchange for imports of good x, and two foreign countries that export good x in exchange for imports of good y. Let us now refer to the domestic and foreign country depicted in Figure 2 as domestic country 1 and foreign country *1, and let us assume further that each is the

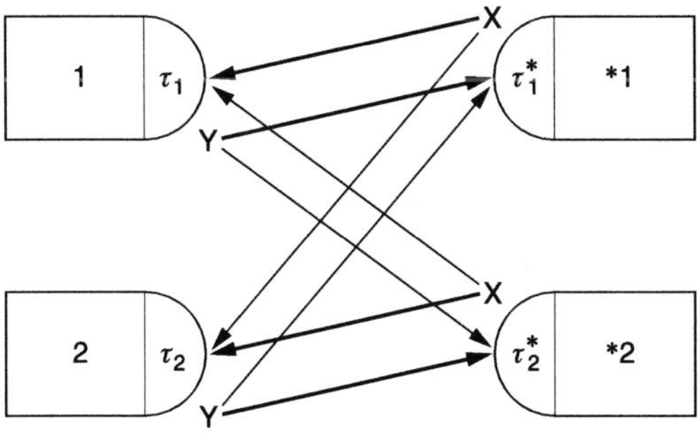

Figure 3

principal supplier of the other's import good. We then refer to the remaining two countries as domestic country 2 and foreign country *2, and similarly assume that each of these countries is the principal supplier of the other's import good. Finally, let us assume that each pair of principal supplying countries has negotiated a bilateral market access agreement that binds their respective MFN tariffs $((\tau_1, \tau_1^*), (\tau_2, \tau_2^*))$ at an internationally efficient level. Figure 3 illustrates the initial situation, with bold arrows indicating principal suppliers of a good and light arrows indicating lesser suppliers of a good.

Now suppose that, as in Figure 2, the domestic government 1 experiences a preference shock. And as in Figure 2, suppose that the system of remedies that provides "expectation damages" and allows for efficient breach is in place, and that under this system of remedies, the domestic government 1 breaches and the foreign government *1 retaliates so as to move from the point E_0 to the point E_1 in Figure 2. The key question is, Does the preference shock experienced by the domestic government 1 – and the breach and retaliation choices of domestic government 1 and foreign government *1 that this preference shock triggers – lead either the domestic government 2 or the foreign government *2 to choose to breach their contract also in light of the permissible retaliatory consequences of that breach? Generally, the answer to this question will be "Yes," and in this way a retaliatory rule akin to that described in Figure 2 would introduce multilateral instability into the WTO contracting environment.

Intuitively, the international efficiency of the bilateral tariff bindings negotiated between principal suppliers depends in general on *all* the tariffs in the system, and so when the tariffs of domestic government

1 and foreign government *1, (τ_1, τ_1^*), are allowed to change – as in the breach and retaliation contemplated in Figure 2 – the tariff bindings originally negotiated by domestic government 2 and foreign government *2, (τ_2, τ_2^*), are generally no longer efficient, implying an opportunity for efficient breach of their bilateral contract as well. Hence, under this system of remedies, the implications of one breached WTO contract would in general be propagated throughout the WTO system and could in principle lead to a growing spiral of breaches.[7]

In light of the multilateral instability problem described just above, it might be tempting to conclude that the nature of WTO contracts makes provisions for breach unattractive, and that therefore remedies within the WTO should be designed to prevent breach (i.e. should be punitive). We next observe, however, that there is exactly *one* retaliation rule that could accommodate breach and yet in principle is not susceptible to the multilateral instability problem described above: this retaliation rule can be interpreted as akin to the trade-effects approach embraced by the Arbitrators.

Intuitively, the point is simple. Referring back to Figure 3, the spillover onto domestic country 2 and foreign country *2 that is generated by the breach and retaliation of domestic country 1 and foreign country *1 occurs as a result of the altered "third-country" trade flows between (i) domestic country 1 and foreign country *2 and between (ii) foreign country *1 and domestic country 2, and the implications of these altered trade flows for the market-clearing prices experienced by domestic country 2 and foreign country *2. Hence, if a retaliation rule could be designed in such a way as to prevent the

[7] In principle, it might be possible that the resulting network of bilateral breaches could ultimately come to rest at a new internationally efficient point. But as a practical matter, the potential for instability seems real, and so we view these multilateral spillovers as a crucial fault associated with the remedies described in Figure 2. We also note that, by assuming that the tangency condition depicted in Figure 2 for the two-country case applies as well to an efficient point in our four-country example, we are implicitly assuming that the particular efficient MFN tariffs under consideration are "politically optimal" tariffs (see Bagwell, Kyle and Robert W. Staiger, "An Economic Theory of GATT, " *American Economic Review*, March 1999; and Bagwell, Kyle and Robert W. Staiger, The Economics of The World Trading System, MIT Press, 2002). More generally, as shown in Bagwell, Kyle and Robert W. Staiger, "Multilateral Trade Negotiations, Bilateral Opportunism and the Rules of GATT/WTO," *Journal of International Economics*, December 2005, efficient MFN tariffs in a multi-country setting do not imply a tangency such as that depicted in Figure 2, but these (non-politically-optimal) efficient points suffer from a related kind of instability even in the absence of preference shocks.

alteration of third-country trade flows when one country breaches and a second retaliates in accordance with the rule, then breach under such a retaliation rule would not induce spillovers to third countries, and so would not create reasons for further breach of other WTO contracts. But we now observe that if retaliation is calibrated so that the breaching country's reduction in imports – when measured at original exporter prices – is *matched in volume* by the reduction in exports it experiences as a result of retaliation by its principal supplying country – also measured at original exporter prices – then there is no reason for trade flows with third countries to change, and hence no reason for the market-clearing prices experienced by third countries to change.[8] In this general way, it may be seen that the trade-effects approach embraced by the Arbitrators has the attractive feature that it in principle *contains* breaches to the bilateral contracts directly involved (provided that foregone trade is measured at original exporter prices).

We have thus argued that an advantage of the trade-effects approach over *all* other approaches to the design of remedies that would permit breach is that the trade-effects approach provides a multilaterally stable remedy. A final question, though, is whether there are circumstances in which permitting breach under such a rule would be better than disallowing breach completely. After all, under the trade-effects approach, Figure 2 no longer applies, because Figure 2 illustrated the benefits of a different breach rule (and one that we subsequently argued would be multilaterally unstable). We now suggest that the trade-effects

[8] This point is related to the seminal observations of Kemp, Murray and Henry Wan Jr., "An Elementary Proposition Concerning the Formation of Customs Unions," *Journal of International Economics* 6, 1976. The essential observation underlying the present discussion, that reciprocal tariff changes in the presence of MFN leave third countries unaffected, is shown in Bagwell and Staiger (2005). We also note that we have couched our arguments in broad terms, so that we may interpret essential features of the trade-effects approach as that approach is applied in a wide variety of settings (e.g. Arts. XIX, XXIII, and XXVIII). However, our multilateral stability arguments are made under the assumption that both the initial breach and the retaliation are non-discriminatory, and hence conform to MFN. This assumption fits well in the context of Arts. XIX and XXVIII. But discriminatory measures are often at the heart of Art. XXIII disputes, and Art. XXIII provides explicitly for discriminatory retaliation, so this assumption will often be violated in the context of Art. XXIII, weakening our arguments for the multilateral stability of the trade-effects remedy in this context. While a deeper exploration of the stability properties of the trade effects approach in a discriminatory setting would be interesting and worthwhile, we simply observe here that the economic appeal of the trade-effects approach will be strongest in settings where deviations from MFN are relatively minor.

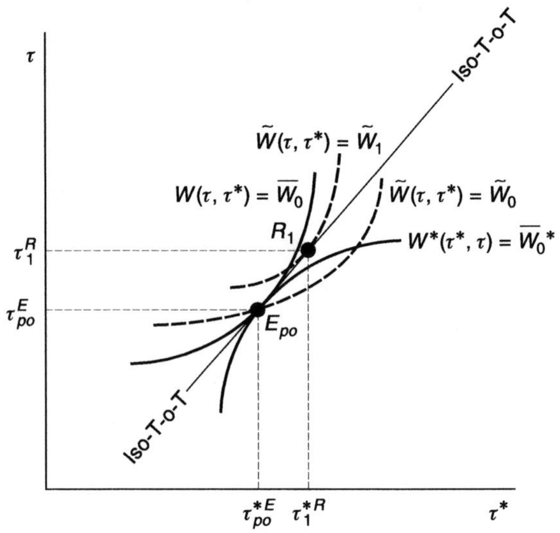

Figure 4

approach, in addition to generating a multilaterally stable remedy, provides a *local approximation* to the retaliatory rule illustrated in Figure 2 as long as governments begin from the efficient *politically optimal* tariffs.[9] Hence, if initial negotiations have carried governments sufficiently close to the efficient politically optimal tariffs and provided that shocks to the status quo are sufficiently small, permitting breach in the presence of remedies designed along the lines of the trade-effects approach must be preferred to disallowing breach completely (say, with strongly punitive remedies).

Figure 4 illustrates the main points, returning again for simplicity to a two-country world. Again we depict the domestic tariff τ on the vertical axis and the foreign tariff τ^* on the horizontal axis. But now the efficient point from which the two governments are assumed to begin is the politically optimal point, labeled E_{po}. As at the point E_0 in Figure 2 at the efficient point E_{po} in Figure 4, the indifference curves of the two governments are tangent. But at the politically optimal efficient point E_{po}, the government indifference curves are also tangent to the locus of domestic and foreign tariff combinations that preserve the terms of trade between the two governments (see Bagwell and Staiger, 1999).

[9] See Bagwell and Staiger (1999, 2002), for a development of the notion of politically optimal tariffs.

In Figure 4, this locus is labeled *iso-T-o-T*, and, as depicted, it must share the slope of the (domestic and foreign) government indifference curves at the efficient politically optimal point E_{po}.

The essential point from Figure 4 is that the *iso-T-o-T* locus, then, provides a local approximation to the indifference curves of *each* government around the politically optimal efficient point. So a retaliatory rule that traced out the *iso-T-o-T* locus would provide a local approximation to the retaliatory rule illustrated in Figure 2. This is illustrated in Figure 4, which depicts the point R_1 to which the two governments would move after a domestic preference shock as described above, if the domestic government faced the retaliatory rule described by the *iso-T-o-T* locus. As can be seen from Figure 4, for a sufficiently small preference shock, point R_1 can be brought arbitrarily close to an efficient point. Our final observation is then that the retaliation rule embraced by the Arbitrators *describes* an *iso-T-o-T* locus (provided that the trade effects are calculated at the original exporter prices). That is, the retaliation rule embraced by the Arbitrators is a *reciprocity* rule, under which domestic and foreign tariffs are altered in such a way as to bring about the same trade volume changes in each (domestic and foreign) market. But as shown by Bagwell and Staiger (1999), such reciprocal changes in tariffs *preserve the terms of trade.*

As a summary, we may return now to the two central questions raised by the trade-effects approach adopted by the Arbitrators: why focus on the trade effect? and, how is the "trade foregone" to be defined? We have provided a possible answer to the first question which suggests that the Arbitrators' focus on trade effects has merit from an economic perspective: the trade-effects approach to remedies can be interpreted as approximating a multilaterally stable system of remedies that provides for "expectation damages" and facilitates a form of efficient breach. And within the context of our answer to the first question, the answer to the second question is now clear: to gauge the reciprocal retaliatory responses that would preserve the terms of trade between the defendant and the claimant, the trade effects should be defined and compared at the original (i.e. pre-tariff-change) exporter prices.[10] That is, what should be quantified is the magnitude of the reduction in export volume that would be caused by the new measure at the original exporter prices.

[10] See Winters, L. Alan, "Regionalism and the Rest of the World: The Irrelevance of the Kemp–Wan Theorem," *Oxford Economic Papers*, 1997, for a discussion of the distinction between fixed equilibrium trade volumes and a fixed terms of trade.

In standard economic terms, this, in turn, is equivalent to quantifying the inward shift of the import demand curve at the original exporter price. From the perspective of the WTO, this can be interpreted as a market-access-based definition, because it quantifies the extent to which the alteration of the conditions of competition would have led to diminished export volume at the original exporter prices.[11]

3.2 How should the level of nullification or impairment be measured?

Having developed an economic interpretation for the Arbitrators' approach to defining the level of nullification or impairment, we now turn to our second question, and consider how the level of nullification or impairment should be measured. Under the interpretation developed in the previous section, the level of nullification or impairment should be measured by foregone trade flows (and any direct economic impacts not captured by the foregone trade flows, e.g. legal judgments paid by exporting firms to the importing government).

As for measuring foregone trade flows, according to our interpretation in the previous section, the appropriate measure is a "market access" measure, i.e. a measure of the extent to which the alteration of the conditions of competition would have led to diminished export volume at the original exporter prices. This, in turn, is equivalent to measuring the inward-shift of the import demand curve at the original exporter price.

There is also a question of whether to include any "chilling effect" in measuring the foregone trade flows (p. 24, 5.64). The Arbitrators conclude that attempts to quantify such effects would be too speculative (p. 25, 5.69), at least for the present case. Although, in general, such effects may well be important, and indeed the existence of effects analogous to these have been empirically documented in the context of US anti-dumping law (see, e.g. Staiger and Wolak, 1994 and Krupp and Pollard, 1996), the Arbitrators' position on this nevertheless seems reasonable, for at least two reasons.[12] First, the 1916 Act applies

[11] For further discussion of the links between standard economic arguments and the GATT/WTO concept of market access, see Bagwell and Staiger (2002).

[12] See Staiger, Robert W. and Frank A. Wolak, "Measuring Industry-Specific Protection: Antidumping in the United States," *Brookings Papers on Economic Activity: Microeconomics*, 1994, pp. 51–118; and Krupp, Corinne M. and Patricia S. Pollard, "Market Responses to Antidumping Laws: Some Evidence from the US Chemical Industry," Canadian Journal of Economics 29(1), February 1996, pp. 199–227.

only where predatory intent can be established, and available evidence suggests that only in rare instances of dumping could a claim of predatory intent have been credibly made.[13] Hence, given the rare circumstances in which the 1916 Act could be applied, it is unlikely that the mere existence of the Act could have a significant chilling effect on trade flows. And second, given the inherent uncertainties associated with any efforts to quantify chilling effects (as opposed to the effects of applied measures), it seems prudent to exclude consideration of chilling effects from efforts to quantify the *level* of nullification or impairment, though perhaps consideration of chilling effects could be the basis for a finding of the *existence* of nullification or impairment.

4 Conclusion: "Efficient Breach" and the law of the WTO

Our economic analysis shows how one can make sense of the arbitral Panel's decision to limit countermeasures to an amount thought to represent the economic cost of the continuing breach to the plaintiff WTO Member, and the Panel's corresponding rejection of the possibility of normative equivalence (albeit, in the Panel's case, based on a confused notion of punitiveness). Further, there may be good policy reasons to adopt an approach to compliance with WTO obligations based on the notion of "efficient breach." On this approach, it makes no sense to consider compliance as a superior outcome, if the breaching country can continue to breach while paying the full economic cost of its behavior.

The first set of legal issues, however, concerns whether in fact this approach is consistent with the law of the DSU as it is written. John Jackson has made a powerful case to the contrary.[14] Jackson points to a number of provisions in the DSU, including 3.7, which states, "The first objective of the dispute settlement mechanism is usually to secure the withdrawal of the measures concerned ...," provisions that provide for the withdrawal of the measure as the normal recommendation of the Dispute Settlement Body (DSB) and that provide that

[13] See, for example, Shin, Hyun Ja, "Possible Instances of Predatory Pricing in Recent Antidumping Cases," in Robert Z. Lawrence (ed.), *Brookings Trade Forum*, 1998, pp. 81–98.

[14] J. H. Jackson, "The WTO Dispute Settlement Understanding–Misunderstanding on the Nature of Legal Obligation," 91 American Journal of International Law 60 (1997).

compensation and suspension of concessions are not preferred "to full implementations of a recommendation [to withdraw the offending measure]." (DSU 22.1) Moreover, Jackson argues that both the continuing surveillance of implementation that is required by DSU 22.8, and the statement of "no obligation to withdraw the measure" (DSU 26:1(b)) in non-violation (nullification or impairment) findings, are further evidence of the continuing nature of the legal obligation under the DSU to withdraw the measure regardless of the existence of countermeasures for failure to do so.

Sykes counters Jackson as follows: "If the objective of the system is 'usually' to secure withdrawal of the offending measure (Art. 3.7), it is impliedly not always the objective. This passage seemingly leaves doors open to other options. The fact that the Panels and the AB must recommend withdrawal of the offending measure (Art. 19:1) says nothing about the existence of an obligation to follow a recommendation, in preference to paying damages as an alternative... And if compensation and retaliatory measures are not 'preferred' (Art. 22:1), neither does the text expressly say that they are legal or that a Member who elects compensation or retaliation is in violation of the rules."[15] Sykes goes on to note that the obligation of surveillance of implementation is consistent with a "damages" approach, since one would want to make sure that continuing damages and their level are consistent with the continuing non-implementation. As for the fact that there is no duty to withdraw the measure in the case of *non*-violation nullification and impairment, Sykes argues that this does not necessarily imply there *is* such a duty in the case of violation; it could simply be an instruction to the dispute settlement organs that they can dispense with a *recommendation* of withdrawal of the measure.

Sykes' analysis does show that the text of the DSU is ambiguous on the nature of legal obligation. However, the text of the DSU should not be read in isolation. It must be read in light of any other rules of international law applicable between the parties, and these include the customary international law of state responsibility. There are

[15] A. O. Sykes, "The Remedy for Breach of Obligations under the WTO Dispute Settlement Understanding: Damages or Specific Performance?" in M. Bronckers and R. Quick, eds., *New Directions in International Economic Law: Essays in Honour of John H. Jackson* (The Hague: Kluwer, 2000), pp. 347–357.

unquestionable aspects of the WTO dispute settlement system that reflect a "contracting out" of the law of state responsibility, now codified in the ILC articles – for example, the unavailability of reparations in dispute settlement to compensate the plaintiff for retrospective harm. But given there is ambiguity in the DSU on the nature of legal obligation, it would be appropriate to resort to the interpretation that is consistent with the customary international law of state responsibility, and that is clearly Jackson's interpretation. *Pacta sunt servanda* is fundamental to that law: countermeasures (as opposed to retrospective compensatory damages) are aimed at securing compliance, and they are not a substitute for it. Contracting out of custom should be clear and unambiguous.

There is perhaps one avenue of response to this objection that is open to Sykes: he could argue that the rules of state responsibility are beside the point, since the nature of the *primary* obligations in the WTO treaties is that they are obligations to compensate those harmed when the state in question does not act in conformity with the provision in question. This view of the primary obligations in the WTO treaties, however, seems directly contradicted by the explicit general statement of the nature of WTO obligation, contained in XVI:1 of the *WTO Agreement*: "Each Member shall ensure the conformity of its laws, regulations and administrative procedures with its obligations as provided in the annexed Agreements."

Moreover, when the drafters of the WTO treaties wished to express an obligation in terms of a duty to compensate for a given course of conduct, they knew how to do so. Likewise, if for example, one considers provisions on expropriation in investment provisions of trade agreements or in BITs, the drafters generally make clear where expropriation is per se illegal on the one hand, and where it is legal, conditional on compensation, on the other.

In sum, reading the provisions of the DSU in light of the customary international law of state responsibility, Jackson's view of the nature of the compliance obligation in the WTO is the stronger one. Nor are primary obligations under the WTO treaties in almost all cases obligations to compensate for engaging in the course of conduct addressed by the obligations. Yet these observations about *lex lata* in no way close the issue of whether as a matter of policy Sykes is right about "efficient breach" being a preferable approach to compliance. Our own economic analysis in this paper is consistent with Sykes' preferred policy direction. In addition, Esserman and Howse (2003) and

Howse and Nicolaidis (2003)[16] have argued that there may be cases that try the political legitimacy of the dispute settlement system, because the existing norms are too general or too controversial, or simply not written well enough to enable a legitimate outcome, where the finding of violation is acceptable (if obviously undesirable) to the loser. In these situations it might be desirable to have a mechanism where in effect, in relation to the findings of the dispute settlement organs, a losing party's obligations are actually waived in return for the payment of appropriate compensation to the winner (and here damages might well be a better form of "payment" than countermeasures). As conceived by Esserman and Howse, however, such a solution should still require consent of the winning party, which ought not be forced to give up its right to demand implementation.

A wholesale move away from *pacta sunt servanda* to "efficient breach" as the default approach to compliance in the WTO system would need to be based on a consideration of important systemic factors to:[17]

1) There are many different kinds of WTO obligations. Are some of these of a "public goods" nature, where the cost of non-compliance cannot be fully internalized by "payments" of the individual party or parties who are continuing to violate? (MFN, arguably, as well as transparency obligations).
2) Apart from the FSC arbitration, where (under the specialized rules of the SCM Agreement) an arbitral panel suggested that a party could demand countermeasures that represented economic harm to *all* WTO Members from a continuing violation (not just the complainant), the general approach is that countermeasures are awarded corresponding to the prospective economic harm to the winning party. In calculating a quantum for efficient breach, should one take into account only the economic cost to the complainant countries and ignore those to other countries who are not parties to the proceedings? Under the current rules of state responsibility,

[16] Susan Esserman and Robert Howse 2004, "The WTO on trial," *Foreign Affairs*, **82**(1), 130–140. Robert Howse and Kalypso Nicolaidis, (2003), "Enhancing WTO legitimacy constitutionalization or global subsidiarity?" *Governance*, **16**(1), 73–94.

[17] We have benefited from the illuminating discussion of related and similar considerations in John H. Jackson, "Status of WTO Dispute Settlement Reports: Obligations to Comply or Option to 'Buy Out'?" *American Journal of International Law*, January 2004, 109–125.

while it is improper to assess countermeasures against the losing party based on the harm to all WTO Members, nevertheless injured non-parties can still free ride as it were on the winning party's compliance efforts, since under the current rules, there remains an underlying obligation to bring oneself into conformity. The systemic implications of a losing Member buying itself out of its duty to comply with a payment based on harm to the complaining state(s) alone need to be carefully considered.

3) Are there equity issues raised by the fact that different WTO Members will have vastly different capacities to buy themselves out of obligations? What if the value to the breaching state is high but nevertheless it cannot afford to pay the cost that it is incurring on the victim state?

11

Japan – Measures Affecting the Importation of Apples (AB-2003-4): One Bad Apple? (DS245/AB/R): A Comment

DAMIEN J. NEVEN
Graduate Institute of International Studies, Geneva

JOSEPH H.H. WEILER
Jean Monnet Center for International Economic Law & Justice, New York University School of Law

1 Introduction

This chapter reviews the decision by the Appellate Body (AB) regarding measures affecting the importation of apples in Japan. Section 2 of the chapter presents some background facts. Section 3 considers the Sanitary and Phytosanitary (SPS) agreement and emphasizes the fact that it imposes a discipline on risk-reducing measures even in the absence of discrimination or protectionism. Section 4 discusses how the evaluation of risk-reducing measures can be undertaken in the context of the SPS agreement. Our discussion focuses on two issues: the scope of the mandate given to the adjudicators and the standard of review that they should apply. We emphasize the difficulty of the task faced by the adjudicators, namely to distinguish between determining the level of risk that a country will find optimal to support (which cannot be challenged) and determining whether risk-reducing measures are necessary to achieve the chosen level of risk. We further observe that the common methodology used by Panels, namely to evaluate the existence of risk in the absence of risk-reducing measures, has limited applicability. We also discuss how this approach can be abused, leading the adjudicators to slip from an evaluation of whether the measures are necessary to achieve a given level of risk to an implicit challenge of the level of risk itself (which should remain the preserve of the Members). Regarding the standard of review, we argue that a lower standard should be applied to measures that do not threaten fundamental principles like nondiscrimination. Section 5 considers the approach and the findings of the Panel and the AB in light of this discussion. Section 6 discusses the consistency requirement imposed by the SPS agreement regarding risk-reducing measures in different circumstances and argues that it can be a very effective tool to prevent abusive standards, without compromising the autonomy of the States in setting the optimal level of risk that they wish to bear. This section also discusses some of the implications of applying different standards of review to cases that involve discrimination or protectionism and those that do not. Section 7 briefly considers how the Panel and the AB handled methods of risk assessment, and highlights the fact that Japan was held to a very high standard of review. Section 8 discusses the approach of the Panel and the AB toward the precaution principle. We consider the precautionary principle in the context of the SPS agreement and argue that the agreement fits naturally with the distinction between risk and ambiguity and in this perspective allows for one type of rationale behind the precautionary principle (while seemingly excluding others). We also observe that there is at least one issue in which scientific evidence was ambiguous in the case. Accordingly, the Panel's and the AB's unwillingness to apply the precautionary principle in this case can be questioned.

2 The dispute's factual matrix

The disease targeted by Japan's phytosanitary measure in this dispute[1] is called "fire blight," often referred to by the scientific name for its bacterium, *Erwinia amylovora* or *E. amylovora.* The AB in its decision offers a useful summation of the case, which we employ here. Fruits infected by fire blight exude bacterial ooze, which is transmitted primarily through wind and/or rain and by insects or birds to open flowers on the same or new host plants. The bacteria *E. amylovora* multiply externally on the stigmas of these open flowers and enter the plant through various openings. In addition to the apple fruit, hosts of fire blight include pears, quince, and loquats, as well as several garden plants. Scientific evidence establishes, as the Panel found, that the

[1] We are relying on the synoptic presentation of the facts by the AB itself in WT/DS245/AB/R of 26 November 2003.

risk of introduction and spread of fire blight varies considerably according to the host plant.

The uncontested history of fire blight reveals significant transoceanic dissemination in the 200-plus years since its discovery. *E. amylovora*, first reported in the New York State in the United States in 1793, is believed to be native to North America. By the early 1900s, fire blight had been reported in Canada from Ontario to British Columbia, in Northern Mexico, and in the United States from the East Coast to California and the Pacific Northwest. Fire blight was reported in New Zealand in 1919, in Great Britain in 1957, and in Egypt in 1964. The disease has spread across much of Europe, to varying degrees, depending on the country, and also through the Mediterranean region. In 1997, Australia reported the presence of fire blight, but eradication efforts were successful and no further outbreaks have been reported. With respect to the incidence of fire blight in Japan, the parties disputed before the Panel whether fire blight had ever entered Japan; but the United States assumed, for purposes of this dispute, that Japan was, as it claimed, free of fire blight and fire blight bacteria. It might be added that Japan wished to remain free of the blight. It should also be noted that Japan's claim that the precise pathway of the pathogen across the Pacific was unknown, was neither contested before nor found to be wrong by the Panel or the AB. It is probably correct that the transoceanic pathway is still unknown. Nonetheless, that claim was, apparently, assumed to be irrelevant.

According to the United States, Japan instituted nine measures to preclude contamination:

(a) The prohibition of imported apples from US states other than apples produced in designated areas in the states of Oregon or Washington;
(b) the prohibition of imported apples from orchards in which any fire blight is detected on plants or in which host plants of fire blight (other than apple trees) are found, whether or not infected;
(c) the prohibition of imported apples from any orchard (whether or not it is free of fire blight) should fire blight be detected within a 500-meter buffer zone surrounding such orchard;
(d) the requirement that export orchards be inspected three times yearly (at blossom, fruitlet, and harvest stages) for the presence of fire blight for purposes of applying the abovementioned prohibitions;

(e) a post-harvest surface treatment of apples for export with chlorine;
(f) production requirements, such as chlorine treatment of containers for harvesting and chlorine treatment of the packing facility;
(g) post-harvest separation of apples for export to Japan from fruits destined to other markets;
(h) certification by the US plant protection officials that fruits are free of fire blight and have been treated post-harvest with chlorine; and
(i) confirmation by Japanese officials of the US officials' certification and inspection by Japanese officials of disinfection and packaging facilities.

The United States claimed that the only products exported from the United States to Japan were "Mature, Symptomless" apples that presented no risk of pathogenic transmission, and that therefore, in relation to this product, the measures in question violated the SPS, notably Arts. 2(2) and 5(1).

The Panel consolidated all Japanese measures into one, but accepted that, although officially only mature, symptomless apples were exported, other immature, symptomatic apples had to be presumed to be part of the trade through fraud and error, and that consequently, the Japanese measures would have to be assessed in relation to both groups.

3 SPS – objectives and rationale

This case is not considered doctrinally path-breaking or economically problematic. In it, the AB seemed to consolidate and refine, rather than revise, its previous SPS jurisprudence. It is thus a good case to understand the run-of-the-mill SPS physiognomy. Notable in this case is the fact that, yet again, even such a technologically sophisticated country as Japan was unable to comply with the requirement of risk assessment.

The SPS measures existed, of course, before the adoption of the SPS Agreement. Naturally they would be subject to the traditional GATT disciplines notably Arts, III and XX.[2] In some respects, the

[2] Article XI would, of course, also apply to SPS measures; but as is well known, the combination of the grandfathering provisions of the GATT and the Ad Note to Art. III, meant that most SPS type measures would normally be reviewed in the context of Art. III.

interpretative community of the GATT/WTO – governments, adjudicators, lawyers, and economists, etc. – is "hard-wired" to the underlying objective and rationale of Art. III: separating those State measures that are genuinely instituted to protect against risk to human, animals, and plants from those that, by design or otherwise, are there to protect domestic production and cannot be justified in full or in part on legitimate SPS grounds.

At the heart of the SPS Agreement, and one of the principal sources of the difficulties inherent in its interpretation and application, is its apparent addition to the traditional "discrimination" or "protectionism" rationale of GATT disciplines (which SPS still maintains[3]) of a second "unjustified obstacle" rationale that goes beyond Art. XI measures. The principal locus of the new "obstacle" rationale is to be found in Art. 2(2) SPS and those provisions that flow from it, notably Art. 5.

> Members shall ensure that any sanitary or phytosanitary measure is applied only to the extent necessary to protect human, animal or plant life or health, is based on scientific principles and is not maintained without sufficient scientific evidence, except as provided for in paragraph 7 or Article 5.

As stated above, the consequence of Art. 2(2) is that Members may have in place or institute an SPS measure that has neither the object nor the effect of favoring domestic products – indeed, there might not even be a domestic product to compete with the import in question – and yet have such a measure challenged and found incompatible with SPS discipline because, for example, it places an undue burden on producers in the exporting State. If a State cannot show that its phytosanitary measures are really necessary for safety and health, as defined by science, those measures simply cannot stand. Further, the State's established procedures for risk assessment must now themselves comply with a WTO discipline.

In its field of application, SPS represents a dramatic shift, similar (though not identical) to that occurring in the EC in 1974 with the European Court of Justice's clarification in the *Dassonville* case that the prohibition of measures having an effect equivalent to quantitative restrictions applied to nondiscriminatory measures. The rationale for

[3] Art. 2(3) SPS.

the broad shift in *Dassonville* and the more limited but similar shift in the SPS agreement is the realization that, in the area of regulatory measures designed to protect against risk, there apparently exist many instances of "inappropriate" State measures that unnecessarily create obstacles to trade without serving the rationale of health or safety, and that these measures may exist without protectionist intent or effect. Note that even under the pre-SPS GATT regime, it was quite common to find State measures failing the test of proportionality and least-restrictive-measure, i.e. they were found to be excessive for their declared purpose. But they were always found to be so in the context of a complaint alleging discrimination and protectionism and as part of the proof of such alleged discrimination and protectionism. Under SPS, a complaint may be brought, as in *Apples* or in *Hormones*, without the need to allege or prove any degree of protectionism or discrimination.

One can wonder about the type of circumstances in which this discipline may apply. First, in the absence of a protectionist motive, the States may have an incentive to apply more stringent standards to imported products than to domestic products. This circumstance arises because the cost of meeting the standards raises the producers' marginal cost, but the cost increase is typically not fully passed on to consumers (except in extreme cases of perfect competition). Profits also fall. A State will not take foreign profits into account when designing health standards, but it will consider domestic profits. Hence, standards applicable to product categories that are imported will be more stringent (more costly at the margin for a given health benefit) than standards applicable to domestic product categories. Standards applicable to product categories that are both imported and produced domestically will fall in between. Overall, States thus have an incentive to impose higher standards when the cost of meeting the standard is partly borne by foreigners. By imposing some consistency in standards across different product categories (Art. 5.5), the SPS agreement will prevent the States from doing this. Second, the impression is given that the States might burden themselves unnecessarily by adopting excessive or "inappropriate" measures because of deficient methodologies of risk assessment, perhaps because of their limited ability to conduct appropriate risk assessment.

In this essay we want to focus on a particular dimension of the SPS Agreement, namely its application in the context where neither discrimination nor protectionism is the center of the inquiry.[4] Our underlying thesis is that the implication of the shift from a "discrimination" type of inquiry to an "obstacle" type of inquiry has not been fully worked out by Panels and the AB.

4 On the evaluation of risk and risk-reducing measures

Members are entitled to adopt appropriate SPS measures that reduce risk. But when may a Panel determine that an SPS measure is "inappropriate"? In order to clarify the task of the adjudicators, it is useful to consider a situation involving "risk" as one in which several outcomes could arise in the future. To simplify exposition, we can focus on two outcomes: a bad outcome (*B*) and a good outcome (*G*). Let us also assume that the likelihood that each outcome will

[4] The following is the preamble to the SPS, which articulates its principal objectives:

Reaffirming that no Member should be prevented from adopting or enforcing measures necessary to protect human, animal or plant life or health, subject to the requirement that these measures are not applied in a manner which would constitute a means of arbitrary or unjustifiable discrimination between Members where the same conditions prevail or a disguised restriction on international trade;

Desiring to improve the human health, animal health and phytosanitary situation in all Members;

Noting that sanitary and phytosanitary measures are often applied on the basis of bilateral agreements or protocols;

Desiring the establishment of a multilateral framework of rules and disciplines to guide the development, adoption and enforcement of sanitary and phytosanitary measures in order to minimize their negative effects on trade;

Recognizing the important contribution that international standards, guidelines and recommendations can make in this regard;

Desiring to further the use of harmonized sanitary and phytosanitary measures between Members, on the basis of international standards, guidelines and recommendations developed by the relevant international organizations, including the Codex Alimentarius Commission, the International Office of Epizootics, and the relevant international and regional organizations operating within the framework of the International Plant Protection Convention, without requiring Members to change their appropriate level of protection of human, animal or plant life or health;

Recognizing that developing country Members may encounter special difficulties in complying with the sanitary or phytosanitary measures of importing Members, and as a consequence in access to markets, and also in the formulation and application of sanitary or phytosanitary measures in their own territories, and desiring to assist them in their endeavours in this regard;

Desiring therefore to elaborate rules for the application of the provisions of GATT 1994 which relate to the use of sanitary or phytosanitary measures, in particular the provisions of Art. XX(b).

prevail can be assessed in terms of probabilities, so that *B* arises with a probability *p* and *G* arises with a probability $(1-p)$. In some circumstances, it may be difficult to formulate these probabilities, for instance, when there are competing theories regarding the development of a disease. We will discuss below (in Section 8) how decisions should be made in those circumstances, which involve some "ambiguity," and how the SPS agreement treats such ambiguity. For the time being, we assume that probabilities can be estimated.

It is also useful to distinguish between the level of risk that will prevail in the absence of any risk-reducing measures and the level of risk that a State will consider desirable. This can be formulated in terms of probabilities; let *p* be the probability that a bad outcome will arise in the absence of any risk-reducing measures. The level of risk that a State will want to enforce (will consider as optimal) can be denoted p^*.

In this context there arise two questions, which feature prominently in the case. First, what is the mandate of the Panel? Second, what standard of review should the Panels adopt?

4.1 *The mandate of the adjudicator*

What is the mandate of the Panel? Is the Panel meant to question the level of risk that the State wishes to enforce (i.e. p^*)? Or is it simply meant to question the measure that has been adopted in order to achieve this level of risk? The AB has consistently insisted that Members retain the autonomy to set their own level of acceptable risk, which may differ from one Member to another (see, for instance, *Australian Salmon*[5] and *Hormones*). Article 4(1) is premised on this primordial understanding:

> Members shall accept the sanitary or phytosanitary measures of other Members as equivalent, even if these measures differ from their own or from those used by other Members trading in the same product, if the exporting Member objectively demonstrates to the importing Member that its measures achieve the importing Member's appropriate level of sanitary or phytosanitary protection.

Obviously, Art. 4(1) contemplates a situation where the levels of SPS protection may differ.

[5] See, e.g. AB in *Australian Salmon*, paragraph 125.

Hence, it appears that the mandate of the Panel is limited to the evaluation of whether the disputed measures are necessary in order to achieve the desired level of risk, and, in particular, whether these measures are supported by scientific evidence.

Before discussing how the Panel and the AB approached this mandate, a few remarks on the level of risk absent any measure (p), the optimal (desired) level of risk (p^*), and risk-reducing measures (which reduce the probability from p to p^*) may be useful.

(i) It is clear that the level of risk absent any measure (p) will differ among various countries. This is so simply because of differences in local conditions, so that some countries will be less exposed to risk than others (for instance, because of different climatic or geographical conditions). Plants and animals belonging to the same family, as well as humans, may also differ in their susceptibility to certain risk factors in different jurisdictions. It is known, for example, that certain ethnicities are more susceptible to particular diseases than are others.

One also expects that the risk-reducing measures necessary to achieve a given level of desired risk (p^*) will differ among countries for the same reasons. Indeed, Art. 2(2) does not, in and of itself, demand or necessarily result in the harmonization of phytosanitary measures across countries. For example, measures pertaining to the type of packaging or treatment of foods necessary to ensure those foods' sanitary condition when put into the stream of commerce might be perfectly safe for a cold climate and yet unsafe for a warm climate, thus requiring different phytosanitary regimes. Of course, the evaluation of risk in the absence of measures, as well as the measures that are in place to reach the desired level of risk, could be subject to dispute, without disputing the standard of safety that the State wishes to afford for its population. For instance, what may be contested and will be in dispute is the extent to which the measure a State adopts to ensure that standard of safety is necessary to achieve that standard, given objective conditions affecting the control of the risk in the importing country. It is assumed that both the importing State and the exporting State have a shared understanding of acceptable risk. It is also not disputed, as might be the case, that the exporting country's phytosanitary regime covering the exports is appropriate for the conditions in the exporting country.[6] What is claimed is that there are objective circumstances that pertain in the importing country but not in the exporting country, which render unsafe in the importing country a product considered safe in the exporting country.

(ii) One can also expect that the desired (optimal) level of risk that States will choose to support will differ. The optimal level of risk will result from a tradeoff between the benefits of reducing risks and the cost of risk-reducing measures. The willingness to pay for risk-reducing measures will be determined by preferences, in particular the degree of risk aversion, and resources (the budget constraints that governments face). These factors will likely differ from country to country. For instance, one expects that States under stringent budget constraints will be less willing to pay for a reduction of risk. Some societies have a greater awareness of, and sensitivity to, ecological concerns than other societies. One notices these differences in such mundane policies as roadside billboard advertising, waste-disposal regimes, etc. Sometimes one observes such different sensibilities even in matters of health and safety. Policies towards airbags, seatbelts, and smoking differ from society to society, indicating a complex set of different values reflective of and constitutive of societal identity. One can imagine similar differences in phytosanitary regulation areas. Certain medicines are banned in some countries and not in others. Certain medicines require a doctor's prescription and a trained-pharmacist dispensing service in some countries, but are sold over the counter in other countries.

Local conditions will also affect the cost of risk-reducing measures. Overall, one can thus expect some variance among States in the optimal level of risk that they will choose to support.

(iii) As States can freely choose their optimal level of risk, nothing would seem to prevent a State from selecting, in principle, a level of zero risk (in the language of the AB itself), i.e. $p^* = 0$. However, one should not attach too much attention to this possibility, for at least two reasons. First, as mentioned above, the SPS agreement imposes a consistency requirement on measures in different circumstances. Since the implementation of zero risk

[6] There could, of course, be SPS disputes where the importing country challenges the sufficiency of the measure even for the exporting country, or challenges the manner in which the regime in the exporting country is administered.

would entail a very great cost, which would have to be borne in a variety of different circumstances, it is likely to be prohibitively costly. Second, and more importantly, the notion of a "zero risk" level is an abstraction. It is really a limit case that may not matter very much in practice. Whatever the protective measure in place, it is likely that there will always be a strictly positive probability that a bad outcome will prevail. From this perspective, referring to a "de minimis" notion of risk may be better than employing a notion of zero risk. A "de minimis" risk can be seen as a risk that belongs to a small interval close to zero. The upper bound of this interval could be defined as a level of risk so small that it cannot be measurably affected by risk-reducing measures.

(iv) The task of the adjudicators is delicate; they will be confronted with risk-reducing measures that are challenged. But they need to distinguish between the level of risk that the States have chosen (which cannot be challenged) – which is presumably ensured by the risk-reducing measures under review – and the necessity of the measures to achieve this level of risk.

Facts are often untidy. Consider the following situations. Imagine two different regimes, under which the same medicine might be permitted for over-the-counter sale in one of the countries, but must be dispensed by an authorized pharmacist in the other. This latter measure is being challenged. The adjudicator will need to distinguish between the following hypotheses: first, this may be an instance of differences in preferences that lead to different optimal risks. If so, the measure should be considered SPS-compliant. Second, it may very well be that the States have the same optimal level of risk but that different risk-reducing measures are necessary to achieve that level of risk in the two countries (for instance, because the general public is less well-educated in the latter). In this instance, the measure should also be considered SPS-compliant. Third, it may very well be that the States have the same optimal level of risk and that the risk-reducing measures have the same effectiveness in the two countries. In this instance, the stricter measure is not necessary and should not be considered SPS-compliant.

(v) To ascertain the SPS compliance of contested phytosanitary measures requires an examination of whether the *measures* themselves are necessary to ensure health and are based on, and maintained with due regard to, scientific principles and evidence. If the

> measures themselves are based on scientific evidence and satisfy all other requirements of the SPS discipline, the only question will be whether they were applied correctly to any given import. But SPS measures are almost invariably contested in the context of a specific dispute where, as stated above, specific products found safe and healthful in one jurisdiction are excluded from another on the basis of a competing set of phytosanitary measures. *De facto*, what the Panels typically end up doing, at least in part – and *Apples* is a good example of this – is to examine whether or not, on the basis of the evidence before them, the products in question are "safe." That is, in this case, whether or not the actual apples exported to Japan posed a risk.

This approach may be appropriate if considered as a sufficient condition to find that a measure is not SPS-compliant. Indeed, if it is found that the level of risk, in the absence of any risk-reducing measure, is "zero" or falls within a "de minimis" interval, then, a fortiori, risk-reducing measures are not necessary. Any such measure can be deemed non-SPS-compliant.[7]

However, this approach can easily descend into a challenge to the level of risk that the State considers optimal. If we are correct in saying that, in applying Art. 2 and its derivatives, the adjudicators end up evaluating the risk-reducing measures' compatibility with the SPS by trying to assess whether or not the evidence adduced supports the conclusion that the products in question are safe or unsafe, then it can readily be seen how easy it could be to substitute, as the critical test of safety and consequently of SPS compliance, the risk sensibility of the adjudicator or of the expert witness for that of the importing State.

Sometimes this result is due to a subconscious rejection of the full implications of the regulatory autonomy granted to the States to set the level of optimal risk. This unwillingness or subconscious rejection is sustained, in part, by a certain ambivalence in the SPS toward the notion of real, full autonomy: note, for example, how Art. 4 speaks of the

[7] It could also be argued that evaluating whether there is credible scientific evidence to demonstrate a health risk from the apples, the beef, or the salmon in question is the only method of establishing whether in fact and in law the phytosanitary regulations in question are themselves necessary for protection of health, based on scientific principle, and, especially, supported (i.e. applied as in the contested case at hand) by sufficient scientific evidence.

"*appropriate* level of sanitary or phytosanitary protection" (emphasis added). Could this not be read as an invitation for the WTO adjudicator to find that the *level* of protection itself (rather than the measure put in place to ensure that level) is inappropriate?

Moreover, the vocabulary and, at times, the structure of scientific risk assessment is often such that the distinction between the objective prediction of probability and the value placed on such a prediction is confused. The expert witness will be asked, or the scientific evidence will be perused, to determine the degree of risk that the pathogen will find its way into Japanese commerce, and the answer might be that the risk is "negligible." Strictly speaking, the scientific evidence should restrict itself as much as possible to the quantification of probability of an occurrence. But typically, experts will be invited to assess the "risk" – an evaluation that might involve a combination of both the scientific probability of an occurrence and a political determination of acceptable danger. The lexical expression "negligible risk" might thus constitute no more than a term for a very low probability, which must then be evaluated in the context of the polity that is assessing the risk. But the term might also fold into it that very value judgment: so small, so negligible, that it is not worth bothering about. That combined judgment is always part of a context that affects the value-judgment element. To an expert from the wildflower-rich country of Switzerland, the risk of contamination of a particular species of flora is 1:10,000,000 and hence "negligible," and not worth bothering about. If that species were, however, the only species of its kind in some other country, or if it were of considerable economic or cultural significance, the very same probability of 1:10,000,000 might not seem negligible at all.

Hence, the adjudicators – Panel and AB – might end up pronouncing on the reasonableness of the standard of protection of the importing State, rather than on the extent to which science supports the conclusion that the products might compromise that standard. Whereas the adjudicator may appropriately question the good faith of the asserted standard, and whereas the SPS itself stipulates certain conditions for consistency of risk within regulatory areas, ultimately the question of determining the actual degree of risk aversion is meant to be left to the State.

This potential slippage between issues is also important to the extent that it affects certain perceptions and positions of both the adjudicators and the parties. As regards the adjudicators, even though it is the AB's decision at issue, the relationship between AB and Panel in cases such as this is critical, since the findings as to whether the measures in question are based on scientific principles and are supported by sufficient scientific evidence are matters of fact to be established by the Panel, they should be overturned only with difficulty, and they are the basis on which the AB makes its own findings and issues its Report.

4.2 The standard of review

The second issue concerns the standard of review that Panels should adopt while examining SPS measures. In *Hormones*, the European Communities drew a distinction between a "*de novo*" approach and the unhappily termed "deference" approach.

> In the view of the European Communities, the principal alternative approaches to the problem of formulating the "proper standard of review" so far as Panels are concerned are two-fold. The first is designated as "*de novo* review." This standard of review would allow a Panel complete freedom to come to a different view than the competent authority of the Member whose act or determination is being reviewed. A Panel would have to "verify whether the determination by the national authority was "correct" both factually and procedurally." The second is described as "deference." Under a "deference" standard, a Panel, in the submission of the European Communities, should not seek to redo the investigation conducted by the national authority but instead examine whether the "procedure" required by the relevant WTO rules had been followed.[8]

We do not believe that "deference" is a particularly useful term, nor do we believe that the alternative to a *de novo* review is simply a review of procedural propriety. Far more helpful are the distinctions drawn in many national administrative- and constitutional-law systems, where the review turns to the strictness of the scrutiny to be applied to a measure. Typically, in judicial review of an administrative action, the adjudicator does not seek to put himself or herself in the position of the administrative authority (*de novo* review) but does more than simply review procedural proprietary. The adjudicator will apply some test of reasonableness. An adjudicator will overturn a measure only if it was unreasonable (or even egregiously unreasonable) for an administrative authority to decide as it has. By contrast, if the measure

[8] *Hormones*, AB paragraph 111.

in question threatened a fundamental value, such as a basic, protected constitutional right, a much stricter scrutiny would be applied, seeking a compelling reason to adopt the measure in question. The details differ in different jurisdictions, but these kinds of underlying distinctions are commonly found.

In *Hormones*, the AB gave a singularly unhelpful response to the European Community's contention, by stipulating a nebulous standard based on Art. 11 of the DSU, which requires the Panels to base their findings on an "objective assessment of the facts," whatever that may mean. The AB simply avoided the serious issue underlying the EC submission. This response might have served in the context of a predominantly discrimination-oriented regime ex GATT. But it cannot serve in the differentiated WTO, which has, side by side, discrimination- and obstacle-based disciplines. Article 11 is a catchall phrase that would apply to all disputes and thus does not address what in our minds is the real question. The prohibition against discrimination and protectionism is arguably the most fundamental principle underlying WTO trade disciplines. As such, when a State measure is discriminatory and protectionist, one might argue that it should receive very strict scrutiny with a high burden of justification on the State that promulgates such a measure. By contrast, a nondiscriminatory SPS measure, one might argue, is more akin to an administrative act, and as such should be subject to a lower burden of justification. The failure of the AB to deal seriously with this issue in *Hormones* did not make it go away, as will be seen from our analysis of some of the central issues in the case.

Particular concerns also arise when slippage occurs, namely when the adjudicator, by evaluating the level of risk absent any measure, ends up challenging the optimal risk chosen by the State (as discussed above).

Once the inquiry turns to the degree to which there is or is not scientific evidence to impugn the safety of a product (as an indirect method of evaluating SPS compliance of the State measure that would exclude the product as unsafe), it is very easy to substitute one's own judgment for that of the administrative agency of the importing State. "If," the Panel implicitly reasons, "it has not been proven to *our* satisfaction that there is sufficient scientific evidence to establish a real danger, then *ipso jure* the State measure is not SPS-compliant."

The SPS, like the WTO and GATT more generally, is not altogether helpful on the standard of review to be exercised in such cases. Must it allow the State in question a margin of error? Should not the question be whether a reasonable government, in promulgating a certain sanitary standard, reasonably come to the conclusion that measure X is necessary to ensure sanitary and phytosanitary protection? This standard of review would mean that only unreasonable (rather than wrong) measures would be struck down. By focusing on the product's safety as a means for determining the measure's compliance with the SPS, there is a risk of upsetting the apple cart, and of WTO Panels putting themselves in the business of government, rather than in the business of reviewing governance. The Panels end up applying a test that, in most countries, administrative tribunals in similar situations would consciously seek to avoid.

5 Risk assessment in *Apples*

In *Apples*, the Panel appears to have followed the very methodology outlined above. Its inquiry into the compatibility of the phytosanitary measures put in place by Japan became at its core an assessment of the risk posed to Japan by apples imported from the United States. In relation to each alleged risk, the Panel weighed the scientific evidence presented by the parties as interpreted and augmented by the consulted experts. Once the level of risk was established, it was used as a yardstick to measure the compliance of the phytosanitary instruments with the SPS.[9]

Sometimes the Panel's factual conclusions were categorical:

> We therefore conclude ... that there is not sufficient scientific evidence to conclude that mature, symptomless apples would harbour endophytic populations of bacteria.[10]

On other occasions they were more nuanced:

> We conclude ... that, with respect to mature, symptomless apple fruit, the risk that the transmission pathway be completed is "negligible." Nevertheless, the experts consulted by the Panel, while firmly considering that the transmission by mature apple fruit is unlikely, suggested ... that apples from severely blighted orchards ... not be exported.[11]

One notes here the more qualified terms – "negligible" and "unlikely." One also notes how the "experts," and through them the Panel,

[9] Sections 8.177 et seq. of Panel Report. [10] Section 8.128 of Panel Report.
[11] Section 8.152 of Panel Report.

end up engaging in the business of government, rather than review of reasonableness of governance by government.

> We therefore conclude that errors of handling or illegal actions are risks that may be, in principle, legitimately considered by Japan. These risks have been acknowledged by the experts, even though they consider them to be "small" or "debatable."[12]

There would thus be a small risk that apples containing the fire blight might enter the stream of commerce in Japan despite all precautions. However, on the all-important issue of the existence of a transmission vector from such apples to Japanese fruit, the Panel concluded that:

> "... the experts considered the completion of the pathway to be unlikely."[13]

Of course, one should note, "unlikely" does not mean "impossible." And the dispositive paragraph states as follows:

> We therefore conclude ... that it has not been established with sufficient scientific evidence that the last stage of the pathway (i.e., transmission of the fire blight to a host plant) would likely be completed.[14]

Ultimately, Japan's claim fails on these findings. Since the risks are minimal, the measures put in place by Japan can easily be found to have no rational relationship to the available scientific evidence.[15] In effect, the Panel did not hold that there was no risk; it held that the risk was so small that it did not justify the measures.

One could interpret the Panel's finding as suggesting that the risk belonged to a "de minimis" interval. In this perspective, the Panel's approach and its conclusion that the measure cannot be SPS-compliant would be appropriate.

However, one could certainly question whether the Panel established that the risk fell within a "de minimis" interval. In particular, it is odd that the Panel made a finding that apples from orchards with fire blight should be excluded, even though there was no scientific basis for this.

It is also striking that the Panel never wondered about the optimal level of risk that Japan wanted to enforce. If it had indeed established

[12] Section 8.161 of Panel Report.
[13] Section 8.166 of Panel Report.
[14] Section 8.168 of Panel Report.
[15] Section 8.198 of Panel Report.

that the level of risk absent any measure was within a "de minimis" interval, it would not matter. However, it would seem that it is the Panel's duty always to inform itself of the optimal level of risk that the State has chosen. This seems essential in order to avoid confusing the level of risk that the measure implies with the question of whether the measure was necessary to achieve this chosen level of risk.

Once in the hands of the AB, given the factual nature of the findings, there is not much the AB is willing or able to do. Thus, in Recital 163 of the AB Report we find:

> As we see it, the Panel examined the evidence adduced by the parties and considered the opinions of the experts. It concluded as a matter of fact that it is not likely that apple fruit would serve as a pathway for the entry, establishment or spread of fire blight in Japan.[16] The Panel then contrasted the extent of the risk and the nature of the elements composing the measure, and concluded that the measure was "clearly disproportionate to the risk identified on the basis of the scientific evidence available."[17] For the Panel, such "clear disproportion" implies that a "rational or objective relationship" does not exist between the measure and the relevant scientific evidence, and, therefore, the Panel concluded that the measure is maintained "without sufficient scientific evidence" within the meaning of Article 2.2 of the *SPS Agreement.* We note that the "clear disproportion" to which the Panel refers, relates to the application in this case of the requirement of a "rational or objective relationship between an SPS measure and the scientific evidence."

Further, what is not discussed in the case is the application of a standard of review and, in particular, whether as a means for testing SPS compliance one should adopt the approach discussed above: first you check whether, procedurally and substantively, the sanitary and phytosanitary rule was based on science and supported by sufficient scientific evidence. You conduct this review in the manner in which, for example, the French Constitutional Council reviews *ex ante* legislation and not in the American "case and controversy" manner. Then, if necessary, you review, in administrative-law fashion, whether a reasonable state authority applying the rules, which have already been found to be in and of themselves SPS-compliant, could reasonably have reached the result in the specific case. Japan argued, artlessly, that insufficient deference was given to its "approach" to scientific evidence,

[16] Panel Report, para. 8.176. [17] Ibid., para. 8.198.

a contention summarily rejected. Again, implicitly, the AB endorsed the Panel's methodology, which focused on the evaluation of risk, with all the potential slippage that this methodology entails.

What is never addressed in the legal give-and-take is the weight to be given to the experts' assessment of small risk, likely and unlikely risk, and negligible risk; and, more generally, what the upper bound of the "de minimis" interval could be. There seems to be consensus that there is *some* risk. What weight to be given to this amount of risk is a matter that, one would have thought, should be contextualized. In the assessment of Panel, one has the impression that, despite the existence of some risk, a uniform regulatory rule would be applicable to all.

6 Consistency and discrimination

If one is to retain the current orthodoxy according to which, even under the SPS, the Members enjoy autonomy to set their own levels of acceptable risk, it is not, strictly speaking, the task of the Panels and the AB to review that national policy decision. So long as the Members adhere to the various disciplines of the SPS, notably that they engage in an appropriate process of risk assessment and management and that their determination of the risk and the measures to combat it are based on scientific evidence, the review should stop there. The Panel can review the measures for proportionality and hold incompatible with the SPS those provisions that are "more trade-restrictive than required to achieve their appropriate level of sanitary or phytosanitary protection."[18] But what the "appropriate level" of protection is, remains, according to the doctrine developed by the AB in *Hormones* and *Australian Salmon*, a matter for each Member.

The Panels and the AB may, however, as part of their inherent jurisdiction, review the good faith of these determinations by a State. This is a very delicate task – it is never easy for an international tribunal of any kind to base its decision and motivate its decision on the ground of bad faith – that usually amounts to a finding that it simply does not believe the State party in question. It would seem to us that two interconnected devices may render this task somewhat easier.

In the first place, Members in SPS cases should be prodded by the Panels to articulate the level of risk against which the measures

[18] SPS Article 5(6).

in question are designed. In fact, it is difficult to understand how a Member can engage in the kind of risk assessment required by Art. 5 SPS without such an articulation. An inability to articulate the level of risk, even if not in precise quantitative terms, may have significant probative value in indicating that the required risk assessment ex Art. 5 was deficient. In addition, it would be the only way for the Panel to do what falls to it, which is to review whether the measures adopted are indeed scientifically grounded and necessary to ensure or mitigate against the risk level so articulated. In this regard, we respectfully disagree with the ruling of the AB in *Hormones*, in which it held that:

> [t]o the extent that the Panel purported to require a risk assessment to establish a minimum magnitude of risk, we must note that imposition of such a quantitative requirement finds no basis in the *SPS Agreement*[19]

The AB may not find an explicit basis in the Agreement, but without some indication of the magnitude of risk aimed at, both Panel and AB risk descending into intuitive approximations.

Members might, of course, put the cart before the horse: examine the measures they have in place and construct from them, retroactively, the level of risk that supposedly informed the choice of the measure in question. This is where the second "bad faith" device may be employed. It is permissible to check the autonomous determination of the level of risk against the requirement of consistency in Art. 5(5) SPS.

> With the objective of achieving consistency in the application of the concept of appropriate level of sanitary or phytosanitary protection against risks to human life or health, or to animal and plant life or health, each Member shall avoid arbitrary or unjustifiable distinctions in the levels it considers to be appropriate in different situations, if such distinctions result in discrimination or a disguised restriction on international trade. Members shall cooperate in the Committee, in accordance with paragraphs 1, 2 and 3 of Article 12, to develop guidelines to further the practical implementation of this provision. In developing the guidelines, the Committee shall take into account all relevant factors, including the exceptional character of human health risks to which people voluntarily expose themselves.

In *Hormones*, the Panel gave a rather narrow definition to the meaning of "different situations," construing the terms to apply to risks

[19] Hormones, AB 186.

resulting from the "same substance" and creating the "same adverse health effects."[20] This would be of limited utility in this dispute, since it is the very absence of fire blight in Japan that informed its measure. Article 5.5 could, however, be read to apply to situations in, for example, a similar sector (in this case safety of plant life,) assuming that all other things are more or less equal. If, for example, as in this case, it were found that Japan insisted on a very low tolerance to risk in relation to fire blight, but in other comparable situations was willing to tolerate far higher levels of risk to the health of plant life, one might be justified in drawing the conclusion, absent a convincing justification from Japan, that its measure was a disguised restriction on trade and hence non-SPS-compliant. The Panel specifically stated in *Hormones* that its ruling there should not be seen as either defining or "further limiting" the meaning of the term "different situation" in Art. 5.5. And the AB confirmed a broader approach:

> Clearly, comparison of *several* levels of sanitary protection deemed appropriate by a Member is necessary if a Panel's inquiry under Article 5.5 is to proceed at all. The situations exhibiting differing levels of protection cannot, of course, be compared unless they are comparable, that is, unless they present some common element or elements sufficient to render them comparable. If the situations proposed to be examined are *totally* different from one another, they would not be rationally comparable and the differences in levels of protection cannot be examined for arbitrariness.[21]

It is to be noted, however, that one cannot apply the consistency clause in the manner suggested above in an overly rigid or mechanical manner. One cannot impugn a set level of risk simply and only because one finds that the State is not consistent in related fields. If this were so, State measures affecting imported products would always have to be pitched at the very lowest standard tolerated in the importing State, militating against, for example, a progressive raising of standards. Article 5.5 should not be construed as a mechanism that would force harmonization to the bottom. But the language of the provision – each Member shall avoid arbitrary and unjustifiable distinctions – could be comfortably used to reject abusive standards without compromising the regulatory autonomy of the State under orthodox understanding. If the State could not explain the maintenance

[20] *Hormones*, Panel 8.176. [21] *Hormones*, AB 217.

of such distinctions, there would be a means of finding them incompatible with SPS without expressly impugning the good faith of the State. We would like to emphasize that the consistency requirement should not necessarily be seen as a device aimed at uncovering crypto-protectionism. Unjustifiable distinctions can eradicate not only the purposively abusive SPS measure but also the unthinking, careless measures that are detrimental to trade without a real social justification. It is important to note that, according to Art. 5.5, arbitrary or unjustified distinctions are impugned not only if they result in discrimination but also if they result in a disguised restriction on trade. In the context of SPS, a disguised restriction on trade need not be in the context of a protectionist scheme.

The principal innovation of SPS was the introduction of a legal discipline that was not rooted in protectionism. A State measure may be found to be SPS-noncompliant even if, as in *Apples*, there is no finding of protectionism and discrimination. As noted by the AB in *Hormones*, a State measure may be found to be GATT-compliant (i.e. not in violation of, for example, Arts. III and XI) and yet still be noncompliant with SPS. At the same time, a measure that is discriminatory or protectionist is, *ipso jure*, also in violation of the SPS. We have argued in this essay that measures which are putatively discriminatory and protectionist merit stricter scrutiny by the adjudicators, and the burden of justification on the State employing them should, necessarily, be higher than in a situation where the disputed measures are not alleged to be discriminatory or protectionist.

If this is so, this would, in the context of SPS, produce a certain legal paradox, the implications of which can only be sorted out as the jurisprudence develops. Imagine two states applying an SPS measure identical to the one we find in *Apples*. In State A, there is very little production of the product in question and, let us stipulate, the economics of the market are such that protectionism is neither the object nor the effect of the measure in question. In State B there is, by contrast, significant production of the product in question, and the effect of the SPS measure in question is to afford protection and raise suspicion as to the aim of the measure. It would seem that the measure in State B would, and perhaps should, receive stricter scrutiny. Assume further that the measure is "truly" compliant. The result could be that, since State A had a lower burden of justification, its SPS measure would be found not to violate the Agreement, whereas State B, with the higher burden of justification, might find its measure impugned. Hence, the same measure would be SPS-compliant in one country but not in the other. This may be a source of concern in the following sense: State B's measure appears more suspect because of the protective effect. But at the same time, precisely because State B has significant production of the product in question, the consequences of contamination could be much more devastating than in State A, yet State B, with the higher level of risk, ends up with the higher burden of justification and the greater risk of having its measure impugned.[22] This anomaly may be used as an argument against a thesis that would differentiate the burden of justification based on the factors of protectionism and discrimination. But that, in turn, militates against a principle of judicial review, found in most jurisdictions, according to which a public measure that violates a fundamental norm should receive a higher level of scrutiny.

7 Risk assessment

Whilst acknowledging that the Japanese risk-assessment exercise studied several possible hosts of fire blight, including the apple fruit, the Panel then found that the risk assessment was not "sufficiently specific" because the conclusion of the assessment did not purport to relate exclusively to the introduction of the disease through apple fruit, but rather more generally, apparently, through any susceptible host/vector. As the AB explained, the Panel also "found the discussion of possible pathways to have 'intertwined' the risk of entry through apple fruit with that of other possible vectors, including vectors considered more likely to be potential sources of contamination than apple fruit," and hence more damaging. Finally, although the assessment noted the *possibility* of entry, establishment, or spread of fire blight through this vector, it did not properly evaluate the *probability* of the occurrence of such events. The result was to invalidate the risk assessment conducted by Japan.

For Japan, the issue was one of methodology in which Members should enjoy discretion provided that the risk could be established. The AB solidly upheld the Panel and insisted, following its ruling in *Hormones*, that the assessment would have to follow the potential

[22] Of course, because of more damaging consequences, country B may wish to select a lower level of optimal risk. Assuming, however, that both countries have selected a "de minimis" risk, the anomaly will remain.

specific pathogens of the disease, and that these would have to be assessed in relation to the contemplated SPS measure in question.

We do not propose to critique in this piece this reasoning of the AB, except to note that the pattern which now emerges from several SPS cases suggests that, absent an international standard that a State might follow, it will be rather difficult for all countries, and notably developing countries, to conduct the kind of risk assessment that would satisfy the stringent methodological requirements stipulated by the AB.

The legal issue concerned here also goes to the standard of review, which likewise is more assumed than discussed. On the one hand, the AB seems to suggest that there is plenty of leeway for alternative methodologies. Thus, in Recital 204 we read:

> Contrary to Japan's submission, however, the Panel's reading of *EC – Hormones* does not suggest that there is an obligation to follow any particular methodology for conducting a risk assessment. In other words, even though, in a given context, a risk assessment must consider a specific agent or pathway through which contamination might occur, Members are not precluded from organizing their risk assessments along the lines of the disease or pest at issue, or of the commodity to be imported. Thus, Members are free to consider in their risk analysis multiple agents in relation to one disease, provided that the risk assessment attributes a likelihood of entry, establishment or spread of the disease to each agent specifically. Members are also free to follow the other "methodology" identified by Japan and focus on a particular commodity, subject to the same proviso.

This passage suggests a reasonableness standard rather than a categorical one. But this seems to be negated by the categorical manner in which Japan is to follow the *Australia Salmon* test of 5.1.[23] We do not want to suggest here that the AB was necessarily wrong from a legal point of view. But it does tip the scales considerably against poorer and less

[23] . . .a risk assessment within the meaning of Art. 5.1 must:

(1) *identify* the diseases whose entry, establishment or spread a Member wants to prevent within its territory, as well as the potential biological and economic consequences associated with the entry, establishment or spread of these diseases;
(2) *evaluate the likelihood* of entry, establishment or spread of these diseases, as well as the associated potential biological and economic consequences; and
(3) evaluate the likelihood of entry, establishment or spread of these diseases *according to the SPS measures which might be applied.* (original italics) (Recital 121 *Australia Salmon*).

scientifically equipped and sophisticated Members. The powerful Members seem to get at least two, if not three, bites at this apple. First, they will have much greater clout when negotiating international standards, which then will be *de facto* imposed on less powerful Members. Second, it will be difficult for less powerful Members to match the powerful Members' scientific apparatus when their regimes come into conflict. And finally, the powerful Members will, of course, have more resources to attempt to extricate themselves from an uncomfortable international standard.

8 The precautionary principle

We have assumed so far that probabilities can be attached to future events. This assumption arises when the mechanisms through which, for instance, a disease can spread are well understood and when the circumstances affecting the spread of the disease can be observed. Hence, the likelihood of each possible outcome can be estimated with confidence. By contrast, a disease may be poorly understood, and there may be competing theories regarding its development, with no evidence to support one or the other. Accordingly, there may be several probability distributions over possible events, depending on which theory is used.[24] As indicated above, there is no scientific explanation behind the spread of the fire blight across the ocean, so this may be such an instance.

Before discussing how the SPS agreement considers such cases and discussing the approach of the Panel, some insight from decision theory on how to proceed under these two sets of circumstances may be useful. In other words, should the uncertainty surrounding the evaluation of probabilities affect decisions?

8.1 Risk and ambiguity

The work of Von Neumann and Morgenstern (1944) has shown that when an objective probability distribution can be defined over a set of outcomes, preferences will be linear in probabilities, at least as long as they respect the "independence axiom." That is also to

[24] Taking it for granted that there is no likelihood that can be attached to possible probability distribution. If it were the case, they could be aggregated to yield one distribution.

say that decisions can be formulated as the result of the maximization of expected utility.

Savage (1956) considered a situation where the decision-maker cannot rely on objective probability distribution. He considered a set of possible events and analyzed the choices that an individual would make over alternative gambles that yield different payoffs in these events. He assumed that the individual would always be able to make a choice. He further assumed that the choice between two gambles would not be affected by a modification of the payoffs that accrue when both gambles yield the same payoff (the independence axiom again). For instance, assume that there are two events, H and L, which are not exhaustive, so that Non H and Non L can also arise. The first gamble yields a payoff of 1 if H occurs and 0 if L occurs. The second gamble yields 0 if H occurs and 1 if L occurs. Both gambles give a payoff of "*d*" if neither H nor L occurs. The independence axiom says that a change in "*d*" should not change the choice between the two gambles. Savage showed that from the observation of choices made under these assumptions,[25] one could generate a relationship between events that is nothing but a subjective probability relationship (such that events could be ordered as more or less probable).

This finding has an important consequence: it says that when no underlying probability distribution is available, preferences will be linear in subjective probabilities. Decisions can be formulated as the maximization of subjective expected utility. This also implies that, faced with alternative probability distribution over a set of events, a decision-maker should pick one and behave as if the resulting probabilities were certain.

To illustrate, consider the following experiment, by Ellsberg (1961). There are two urns, each with 100 balls, which can be either red or black. In Urn 1, the proportion is unknown. For Urn 2, it is known that there are 50 red and 50 black balls. An agent is asked to choose between the following bets: bet red, in which case he gets a prize if a red ball is extracted and zero otherwise; or bet black, in which case he gets a prize if a black ball is extracted and zero otherwise. Consider, first, possible bets over Urn 2. Agents will naturally be indifferent as to betting red or black. Asked the same question of Urn 1, agents will typically provide the same answer. This can be seen as a situation

[25] And a couple of additional technical assumptions.

where there are 101 possible theories about the allocation of balls in the Urn. Agents form the subjective assessment that, in the absence of any information to distinguish among the theories, they are all equally likely, and hence attach a subjective probability of 0.5 that a red (or black) ball will be extracted from Urn 1.

In this framework, there is thus nothing special about scientific uncertainty. Precaution is just like protection: optimal risk-reduction efforts can be obtained from a standard cost-benefit analysis (see Gollier, 2001, for a discussion), using subjective probabilities.

Some suspicion about the validity of the framework, however, arises if agents in the example above are asked an additional question, namely whether they prefer to bet red for Urn 1 or bet red for Urn 2. It turns out that most agents prefer to bet red for Urn 2, rather than bet red for Urn 1. This implies that red from Urn 2 is perceived as more likely than red from Urn 1. But if an agent also prefers to bet black for Urn 2 rather than black for Urn 1, non-red from Urn 2 would appear more probable than non-red from Urn 1. This is inconsistent with the notion that the choice of agents reveals probabilities. That is also to say that choices cannot be compared according to their expected utility. As shown by Ellsberg (1961), the problem arises because the axiom of independence is violated.

This experiment indicates that some agents may be ready to pay more for reducing a risk that is more uncertain. Alternative models of decision have also been developed that do not rely on the axiom of independence. For instance, Henry and Henry (2003) describe a model[26] in which agents face different probability distributions over a set of events. Uncertainty is thus described in terms of a family of distributions. In their framework, choices cannot be compared in terms of expected utility (independence is not assumed) but can be compared in terms of a weighted average of the maximum and the minimum of expected utility that obtains across the possible probability distributions. This allows for a representation of preferences in terms of an attitude to risk (the usual risk aversion as depicted by the shape of the utility function) and an attitude toward the uncertainty with respect to the true probability distribution, which is referred to as the degree of aversion toward ambiguity. The latter is represented

[26] Originally developed by Ghirardato et al. (2002).

by the weights that are given respectively to the maximum and the minimum of expected utility.[27]

Finally, it is worth noting that the decisions that agents take in this framework can also be seen as displaying some "precaution." The aversion of the agents to ambiguity leads them to take some actions in which they give some weight to worst theories.

8.2 *Risk, ambiguity, and precaution in the SPS agreement*

As discussed above, the AB confirmed that Japan's phytosanitary measures were maintained "without sufficient scientific evidence" and hence the measures were not in conformity with Art. 2.2 of the SPS agreement. At the same time, the AB ruled that the phytosanitary measures imposed by Japan were "not imposed in respect of a situation where relevant scientific evidence [was] insufficient," so that temporary measures could not be justified under Art. 5.7. The AB noted in particular that the Panel had come across an important amount of relevant evidence and that "a large quantity of high quality scientific evidence ... had been produced over the years and ... that the experts had expressed increasing confidence in this evidence." Altogether, the AB thus seems to have considered (i) that there is reliable scientific evidence on the risks involved in the spread of the disease at stake, and (ii) that the evidence confirmed that the risk of having the disease spread through imported apples was small.

Importantly, the AB also reiterated the Panel's observation that Art. 5.7 "was designed to be invoked in situations where little, or no, reliable evidence was available on the subject matter at issue."

It is striking that the structure of the SPS agreement, as well as the interpretation of the agreement given by the AB (and Panel), fit with the distinction between risk and ambiguity. It appears in particular that Art. 5.7 can be used when ambiguity is strong.

The "sufficiency of scientific evidence" in Art. 2.2. and the "(in)sufficiency of relevant scientific evidence" in Art. 5.6 thus also appear to refer to different concepts. The use of similar terms could be confusing, and these concepts could be spelled out more clearly. The structure of the test as to whether a measure would be allowed

[27] For instance, the max-min criteria proposed by Gilboa and Schneider (1989) (such that individuals should behave as if the true theory is the one that yields the lowest expected utility) can be shown to display a strong aversion to ambiguity (see Henry, 2002).

could also be clarified: following the terms of the discussion above, a restrictive measure could be allowed if uncertainty could not be confidently characterized in terms of a probability distribution. If uncertainty could be confidently characterized in terms of probability distribution, a restrictive measure might still be allowed if it significantly reduced the occurrence of an event that, according to this probability distribution, is sufficiently likely and sufficiently damaging. Hence, it would appear that any test of whether a measure could be lawful should start with Art. 5.7 (and not Art. 2.2) and question the ambiguity of scientific evidence. A precise evaluation of the measure at stake (under Art. 2.2) would be conducted only if it were concluded that scientific evidence was sufficiently "unambiguous."

The question of how ambiguity should be measured in practice in cases where consensus cannot be detected is, however, difficult. It would presumably involve a measure of the subset of possible events for which probabilities are (dis-)similar under the range of possible distributions put forward by experts.

The previous discussion indicates that Art. 5.7 of the SPS agreement can be seen as the expression of a precautionary principle. However, it reflects a particular motive for precaution, namely the presence of ambiguity. Yet, as discussed by Gollier (2001), there are other possible justifications for precautionary actions, and those are not explicitly mentioned in this provision.[28]

These other justifications arise in particular from the dynamic nature of scientific uncertainty. When future risks depend on past consumption (as in the case of climate change), the question arises whether preventive efforts should be undertaken today or tomorrow. On the face of it, the expectation that knowledge will improve over time, and hence that actions will be more efficient in the future, would appear to caution against premature actions. This is the argument that is often advanced to justify the US refusal to sign the Kyoto protocol. It is what Gollier refers to as the "learn, then act" principle. However, if knowledge is improved through the observation of the risks themselves, matters may be different. In those circumstances, the observation of damages today should lead to more preventive actions.

[28] Gollier (2001) uses the subjective expected-utility framework. However, the dynamic effects that he investigates would appear to apply in other frameworks, at least at the level of general principles.

Second, it may be that postponing preventive actions will also increase future risks; in those circumstances, the prospect of being poorer in the future may lead to a reduction in the amount of pollution today.

Third, the extent to which current decisions change flexibility in the future may also be a concern. Some risks may be subject to irreversibilities, and the lack of preventive measures may reduce the options in the future. In other words, there may be an option value in undertaking preventive action, which in principle can be estimated using real option theory.

Hence, the question arises whether the SPS agreement should not reflect those particular circumstances when precautionary actions are particularly appropriate, namely when future risks are increased, flexibility is impaired, and learning proceeds by observation of current trends.

8.3 Precaution in Japan – Apples ?

As discussed above, the Panel and the AB ruled that the phytosanitary measures imposed by Japan were "not imposed in respect of a situation where relevant scientific evidence is insufficient," so that temporary measures could not be justified under Art. 5(7). Still, the absence of scientific explanation behind the spread of fire blight across the ocean may be an instance of ambiguity.

Apples is thus a good illustration of the rather constricted nature of Art. 5(7) as an expression of a broader and more capacious notion of precaution. For example, there is, on the one hand, considerable scientific evidence on the mechanisms that explain the potential transmission mechanisms of fire blight. On the other hand, there is no accepted, consensus account that actually tracks and explains how fire blight traveled across the oceans to reach Australia or certain Asian countries. A capacious notion of precaution might suggest that, pending the discovery of the actual transoceanic pathway, a State may be entitled to invoke Art. 5(7).

This raises a question of framing. If you frame the question as to the "macro" pathway in its historical context, one would be driven to the conclusion that there was no scientific evidence. If, by contrast, you frame the question as to the specific mechanisms that explain how the pathogen might migrate from a blighted apple to a healthy one, there is evidence. It is not clear why, in this case, the second framework is more appropriate than the first one. Once again, we come back to the all-important issue of the standard of review. Had the Panel taken the view that its task was not to establish the risk posed by imported apples, but to establish the reasonableness of the Japanese measure and the circumstances of its application to the specific imports from the United States, it would also have asked itself whether it was reasonable for the Japanese government to look, in the context of 5(7), at the first rather than the second framework, as articulated above. Because the Panel slipped into the business of risk assessment itself, rather than assessment of risk assessment, it could come to its conclusion, which the AB uncritically followed.

References

Ellsberg, D. (1961). Risk, Ambiguity and the Savage Axioms, *Quarterly Journal of Economics* **75**(5), 643–669.

Ghirardato, P., Maccheroni, F. and Marinacci, M. (2002). Ambiguity from the differential viewpoint, Working Paper No. 17/2002 ICER.

Gilboa, I. and Schmeidler, D. (1989). Max-min expected utility with non unique priors, *Journal of Mathematical Economics* **18**, 141–153.

Gollier, C. (2001). Should We Beware of the Precautionary Principle?, *Economic Policy* **33**, 301–328.

Henry, M. (2002). Generalized entropy measures of ambiguity and their measurement, mimeo, Columbia University.

Henry, C. and Henry, M. (2003). Etat de la connaissance scientifique et mobilisation du principe de precaution, *Revue Economique* **54**, 1277–1289.

Savage, L.J. (1956). *The Foundation of Statistics* Wiley, New York.

Von Neumann, J. and Morgenstern, O. (1944). *Theory of Games and Economic Behavior*, Princeton University Press, Princeton.

INDEX

Note: Cases are indexed under short forms (official abbreviations); Agreements are indexed under abbreviations (e.g. SCM for Subsidies and Countervailing Measures Agreement).